FLEXIBLE WORKFLOWS

Dissertations in Artificial Intelligence

Artificial Intelligence (AI) is one of the fastest growing research areas in computer science with a strong impact on various fields of science, industry, and society. This series publishes excellent doctoral dissertations in all sub-fields of AI, ranging from foundational work on AI methods and theories to application-oriented theses.

Editor-in-Chief:
Professor Dr. Ralph Bergmann
Department of Business Information Systems II, University of Trier,
54286 Trier, Germany

Volume 354

Previously published in this series:

Vol. 353 Leonid Berov, From Narratology to Computational Story Composition and Back – An Exploratory Study in Generative Modeling
Vol. 352 Kai Sauerwald, Semantics of Belief Change Operators for Intelligent Agents: Iteration, Postulates, and Realizability
Vol. 351 Peter Bourgonje, Shallow Discourse Parsing for German
Vol. 350 Steven Kutsch, Knowledge Representation and Inductive Reasoning using Conditional Logic and Sets of Ranking Functions
Vol. 349 Markus Schwinn, Ontologie-basierte Informationsextraktion zum Aufbau einer Wissensbasis für dokumentgetriebene Workflows
Vol. 348 Pascal Welke, Efficient Frequent Subtree Mining Beyond Forests
Vol. 347 Johannes Hellrich, Word Embeddings: Reliability & Semantic Change
Vol. 346 Mark Wernsdorfer, Symbol Grounding as the Generation of Mental Representations
Vol. 345 Alexander Steen, Extensional Paramodulation for Higher-Order Logic and its Effective Implementation Leo-III
Vol. 344 Jan Ole Berndt, Self-Organizing Multiagent Negotiations – Cooperation and Competition of Concurrently Acting Agents with Limited Knowledge
Vol. 343 Emmanuelle-Anna Dietz Saldanha, From Logic Programming to Human Reasoning: How to be Artificially Human
Vol. 342 Marc Finthammer, Concepts and Algorithms for Computing Maximum Entropy Distributions for Knowledge Bases with Relational Probabilistic Conditionals
Vol. 341 Jasper van de Ven, Supporting Communication in Spatially Distributed Groups – Privacy as a Service for Ambient Intelligence
Vol. 340 Nina Dethlefs, Hierarchical Joint Learning for Natural Language Generation
Vol. 339 Jens Haupert, DOMeMan: Repräsentation, Verwaltung und Nutzung von digitalen Objektgedächtnissen
Vol. 338 Mari Carmen Suárez-Figueroa, NeOn Methodology for Building Ontology Networks: Specification, Scheduling and Reuse
Vol. 337 Nicola Pirlo, Zur Robustheit eines modellgestützten Verfolgungsansatzes in Videos von Straßenverkehrszenen
Vol. 336 Matthias Thimm, Probabilistic Reasoning with Incomplete and Inconsistent Beliefs
Vol. 335 René Schumann, Engineering Coordination – A Methodology for the Coordination of Planning Systems
Vol. 334 Marvin R.G. Schiller, Granularity Analysis for Tutoring Mathematical Proofs
Vol. 333 Marc Wagner, A Change-Oriented Architecture for Mathematical Authoring Assistance

ISSN 0941-5769 (print)
ISSN 2666-2175 (online)

Flexible Workflows
A Constraint- and Case-Based Approach

Lisa Grumbach
German Research Center for Artificial Intelligence, Branch Trier, Germany

IOS Press

AKA

© 2023 Akademische Verlagsgesellschaft AKA GmbH, Berlin

All rights reserved. No part of this book may be reproduced, stored in a retrieval system, or transmitted, in any form or by any means, without prior written permission from the publisher.

ISBN 978-3-89838-770-5 (AKA, print)
ISBN 978-1-64368-396-6 (IOS Press, print)
ISBN 978-1-64368-397-3 (IOS Press, online)
doi: 10.3233/DAI354

Bibliographic information available from the Katalog der Deutschen Nationalbibliothek (German National Library Catalogue) at https://www.dnb.de

Dissertation, approved by Trier University, Germany
Date of the defense: 27 February 2023
Supervisors: Prof. Dr. Ralph Bergmann, Prof. Dr. Norbert Kuhn

ORCID page of the author: https://orcid.org/0000-0002-2247-8270

Publisher
Akademische Verlagsgesellschaft AKA GmbH, Berlin

Represented by Co-Publisher IOS Press
IOS Press BV
Nieuwe Hemweg 6B
1013 BG Amsterdam
The Netherlands
Tel: +31 20 688 3355
Fax: +31 20 687 0019
email: order@iospress.nl

LEGAL NOTICE
The publisher is not responsible for the use which might be made of the following information.

Acknowledgements

First of all, I would like to thank both my supervisors *Prof. Dr. Ralph Bergmann* and *Prof. Dr. Norbert Kuhn* for giving me the opportunity of starting a PhD after my studies.

I am very grateful to have had *Ralph* as first supervisor always providing me very valuable and constructive feedback that made it rather easy to improve my work. Moreover, I really appreciate his thought-provoking impulses and spontaneous ideas that lead me in the right direction. Discussions were always solution-oriented and very helpful. Thank you for your great supervision and mentoring.

I would like to thank my second supervisor, *Norbert*, for his uncomplicated support. He brought several new perspectives to my research and provided some unfamiliar and out-of-the-box thinking. This helped me a lot to see the bigger picture. Though I was not able to realize all ideas, several relevant research perspectives resulted from these discussions.

Furthermore, a special thanks goes to my student researchers *Thomas Pulber*, *Michael Museler*, *Erik Schake*, and *Peter Schramm*, who substantially supported me with setting up and implementing diverse functionalities and features of the prototype. Several bachelor and master theses also made an important contribution to my work. This includes *Lukas Malburg*, *Hai Ngoc Cu*, *Alexander Bartz*, *Sebastian Seer*, and *Erik Schake*. All of the collaboration and discussions were worthwhile.

I would like to thank all my colleagues for the pleasant working atmosphere and the uncomplicated and helpful collegial interaction, even though the upcoming home office regularity in the last three years have reduced our point of contact to a minimum. This especially holds for *Eric Rietzke*, *Markus Schwinn*, and *Gilbert Müller* for sharing a part of our PhD journeys, and for the core ProCAKE team - *Christian*

Zeyen, *Lukas Malburg*, *Maximilian Hoffmann* - who provided great teamwork and support. Besides, I would like to thank *Silke Kruft*, *Axel Kalenborn*, *Saadet Bozaci*, and *Daniel Kuhn* for the daily walks during lunch break with off-topic talks, which I really enjoyed.

Moreover, I would like to thank my friends *Britta Herres* and *Lena Sembach*, who gave their best to refresh and expand my theoretical and mathematical knowledge. I am very grateful for the support of my sister *Janine*, who gave me deep insights into the regarded domain of deficiency management in construction with her architectural expertise and gave me feedback about the respective modelled workflows. I would like to thank *Julia Gierens* and *Roman Grewenig* for their thorough proofreading, which helped me to improve the understandability and to detect some mistakes.

And last but not least I would like to thank my *family* - my *mom*, my *dad*, my sisters *Janine* and *Sarah*, my nephews *Kiyan* and *Nino*, my niece *Emily*, and *Roman* in particular - as they contributed to my success in various ways. On the one hand they always believed in me and encouraged me to continue, on the other hand they took care of pleasant distractions and never asked too often about the status of my work. Having such support in the back really motivated me.

Lisa Grumbach
Trier, December 2022

Abstract

Traditional workflow management systems support process participants in fulfilling business tasks through guidance along a predefined workflow model. Flexibility has gained a lot of attention in recent decades through a shift from mass production to customization. Various approaches to workflow flexibility exist that either require extensive knowledge acquisition and modelling effort or an active intervention during execution and re-modelling of deviating behaviour. The pursuit of flexibility by deviation is to compensate both of these disadvantages through allowing alternative unforeseen execution paths at run time without demanding the process participant to adapt the workflow model. However, the implementation of this approach has been little researched so far.

This work proposes a novel approach to flexibility by deviation. The approach aims at supporting process participants during the execution of a workflow through suggesting work items based on predefined strategies or experiential knowledge even in case of deviations. The developed concepts combine two renowned methods from the field of artificial intelligence - constraint satisfaction problem solving with process-oriented case-based reasoning. This mainly consists of a constraint-based workflow engine in combination with a case-based deviation management. The declarative representation of workflows through constraints allows for implicit flexibility and a simple possibility to restore consistency in case of deviations. Furthermore, the combined model, integrating procedural with declarative structures through a transformation function, increases the capabilities for flexibility. For an adequate handling of deviations the methodology of case-based reasoning fits perfectly, through its approach that similar problems have similar solutions. Thus, previous made experiences are transferred to currently regarded problems, under the assumption that a similar deviation has been handled successfully in the past.

Necessary foundations from the field of workflow management with a focus on flexibility are presented first. As formal foundation, a constraint-based workflow model was developed that allows for a declarative specification of foremost sequential dependencies of tasks. Procedural and declarative models can be combined in the approach, as a transformation function was specified that converts procedural workflow models to declarative constraints. One main component of the approach is the constraint-based workflow engine that utilizes this declarative model as input for a constraint solving algorithm. This algorithm computes the worklist, which is proposed to the process participant during workflow execution. With predefined deviation handling strategies that determine how the constraint model is modified in order to restore consistency, the support is continuous even in case of deviations.

The second major component of the proposed approach constitutes the case-based deviation management, which aims at improving the support of process participants on the basis of experiential knowledge. For the retrieve phase, a sophisticated similarity measure was developed that integrates specific characteristics of deviating workflows and combines several sequence similarity measures. Two alternative methods for the reuse phase were developed, a null adaptation and a generative adaptation. The null adaptation simply proposes tasks from the most similar workflow as work items, whereas the generative adaptation modifies the constraint-based workflow model based on the most similar workflow in order to re-enable the constraint-based workflow engine to suggest work items.

The experimental evaluation of the approach consisted of a simulation of several types of process participants in the exemplary domain of deficiency management in construction. The results showed high utility values and a promising potential for an investigation of the transfer on other domains and the applicability in practice, which is part of future work. Concluding, the contributions are summarized and research perspectives are pointed out.

Contents

Chapter 1. Introduction   **1**
    1.1   Motivation   1
    1.2   Research Aims   4
    1.3   Methodology   7
    1.4   Research Projects   10
    1.5   Outline   11

Chapter 2. Foundations on Flexible Workflow Management   **13**
    2.1   Process Aware Information Systems   13
    2.2   Business Process Management   15
    2.3   Workflow Management   21
    2.4   Workflow Flexibility   34
    2.5   Related Work   49

Chapter 3. Domain & Potentials   **55**
    3.1   Deficiency Management in Construction   55
    3.2   Potentials of a Flexible Workflow Approach   59
    3.3   Main Concept   67

Chapter 4. Prerequisites   **69**
    4.1   Graphs   69
    4.2   Block-Oriented Workflows   70
    4.3   Execution Paths and Operators   74
    4.4   Execution Semantics of Workflow Blocks   76

Chapter 5. Constraint-Based Workflow Engine   **79**
    5.1   Concept of the Workflow Engine   80
    5.2   Workflow Model   82
    5.3   Foundations on Constraint Satisfaction Problems   86
    5.4   Workflow Engine   88

5.5	Deviation Handling	109
5.6	Related Work	116

Chapter 6. Case-Based Deviation Management   **121**
6.1	Foundations on Case-Based Reasoning	122
6.2	Foundations on Time-Series Similarity Measures	133
6.3	Case-Based Approach to Deviation Management	145
6.4	Retrieving Similar Workflows	150
6.5	Reuse for Deriving Work Items	163
6.6	Related Work	182

Chapter 7. Prototype   **187**
7.1	Flexible Workflow Approach	187
7.2	Architecture	190
7.3	Prototypical Implementation	192

Chapter 8. Evaluation   **213**
8.1	Contributions	214
8.2	Research Question RQ0	215
8.3	Evaluation Criteria	216
8.4	Hypotheses	220
8.5	Setup	222
8.6	Simulation Results	231
8.7	Conclusion of Evaluation	246

Chapter 9. Conclusion   **249**
9.1	Summary	249
9.2	Research Perspectives	253

Appendix A. Proof of Trace Equivalence   **259**

Appendix B. List of Variables   **277**

Appendix C. Curriculum Vitae   **283**

Bibliography   285

Index   317

List of Figures

2.1	Business Process Life Cycle	17
2.2	Build Time vs. Run Time	19
2.3	Detailed Business Process Life Cycle	20
2.4	Workflow Reference Model - Components & Interfaces	25
2.5	Workflow Classification with regard to Business Value and Frequency	27
2.6	Workflow Classification with regard to Task Complexity and Task Structure	28
2.7	Possible Workflow State Space	32
2.8	Prevalent Way of Workflow Management	34
2.9	Notions of Change	37
2.10	Classification of Change	39
2.11	Taxonomy of Flexibility	40
2.12	Examples of Flexibility Types	44
2.13	Flexibility Type Spectrum with regard to Flexibility Configuration and Process Model Completeness	45
2.14	Flexibility Type Spectrum with regard to Flexibility Configuration and Degree of Impact	46
2.15	Flexibility Type Spectrum with regard to Flexibility Configuration and User Experience	47
2.16	Trade-Off between Flexibility and Support due to the Extent of Pre-Definition	48
3.1	Simple Ideal Workflow Model for Deficiency Management in Construction	57
3.2	Extended Workflow Model for Deficiency Management in Construction, Part 1	60
3.3	Extended Workflow Model for Deficiency Management in Construction, Part 2	61

3.4	Extended Workflow Model for Deficiency Management in Construction, Part 3	62
3.5	Extended Workflow Model for Deficiency Management in Construction, Part 4	63
3.6	Business Process Life Cycle with Flexible Workflow Engine	68
4.1	Example of a Workflow Graph	71
4.2	Single Task Block	72
4.3	Sequence Block	73
4.4	Parallel and Exclusive Control-Flow Block	74
4.5	Single-Branch Exclusive Block	74
5.1	Flexible Workflow Approach with a Constraint-Based Workflow Engine	80
5.2	Workflow Model for the Flexible Workflow Approach	83
5.3	Constraint Satisfaction Problem Solving	87
5.4	Workflow Model and Instance for the Flexible Workflow Approach	89
5.5	Constraint Satisfaction Problem for Computing Work Items	90
5.6	De Facto Workflow with Next Position	94
5.7	Workflow Model and Instance for the Flexible Workflow Approach	96
5.8	Xor and Loop Construct Including Additional Information	98
5.9	Example of a Workflow Graph Decomposed into Workflow Blocks	102
5.10	Loop Control-Flow Block	106
5.11	Exemplary Workflow Block with a Loop	108
5.12	Exemplary Sequential Workflow with Deviation	113
5.13	Possible Strategies for Handling Sequential Deviations	114
5.14	Exemplary Workflow with Exclusive Pattern and Deviation	114
5.15	Possible Strategies for Handling Deviations in Exclusive Patterns	115
6.1	CBR Cycle	124
6.2	Reuse Principle	125
6.3	CBR Knowledge Containers	126
6.4	Exemplary Block-Oriented Semantic Workflow Graph	131

LIST OF FIGURES

6.5	Exemplary Similarity Assessment with Dynamic Time Warping (DTW)	136
6.6	Exemplary Similarity Assessment with the Smith-Waterman-Algorithm (SWA)	138
6.7	Case-Based Approach for Handling Deviations	147
6.8	Exemplary Pre-Processing	155
6.9	Exemplary De Jure Workflow with Query and Case	171
7.1	Flexible Workflow System for Handling Deviations	189
7.2	Architecture of the Prototypical Implementation of a Flexible Workflow System for Handling Deviations	191
7.3	System Classes of the CAKE Data Model	195
7.4	Extension of the System Classes of the CAKE Data Model with *NESTGraph* elements	196
7.5	Start Page of the Web Application - GUI with a List of Workflow Models and Instances	198
7.6	Editor View for Modelling De Jure Workflows	199
7.7	Editor View for Modelling De Jure Workflows with Constraint Tab	200
7.8	Execution View with Worklist and De Jure Workflow	200
7.9	Monitoring View with Information about the Workflow Instance	201
7.10	Class Diagram of the Declarative Formula for Transformation Process	203
8.1	De Facto Workflow Spectrum related to Fig. 2.7	223
8.2	Setup of Simulation Experiments	225
8.3	Experiential Evaluation for the Experienced Process Participant	228
8.4	Experiential Evaluation for the Inexperienced Process Participant	229
8.5	Experiential Evaluation for the Non-Conforming Process Participant	230
8.6	Number of Tasks for Each Replay	232
8.7	Maximum Computation Time for Each Replay	233
8.8	Maximum Computation Time for Each Replay Zoomed in on 0 - 1.000 ms	233
8.9	Maximum Computation Time for Each Replay for All Different Modes of the Workflow Engine	234

8.10 Maximum Computation Time for Each Replay for Different Modes of the Workflow Engine Zoomed in on 0 - 1.200 ms 235
8.11 Average Computation Time for Each Replay for Different Modes of the Workflow Engine 236
8.12 Average Computation Time for Each Replay for Different Modes of the Workflow Engine Zoomed in on 0 - 300 ms 237
8.13 Average and Maximum Computation Time for Different Sizes of the Case Base for Both Null Adaptation Variants 238
8.14 Total Number of Deviations for Each Replay for the Experienced Process Participant 239
8.15 Total Number of Deviations for Each Replay for Different Modes of the Workflow Engine for the Experienced Process Participant 239
8.16 Utility for the Experienced Process Participant for Each Replay for Different Modes of the Workflow Engine 240
8.17 Average Utility for the Experienced Process Participant for Different Case-Based Modes of the Workflow Engine and Different Sizes of the Case Base 241
8.18 Edit Distance in Relation to Number of Executed Tasks for the Inexperienced Process Participant for Each Replay 242
8.19 Utility for the Inexperienced Process Participant of Each Replay and Different Modes of the Workflow Engine 243
8.20 Average Utility for the Inexperienced Process Participant for Different Case-Based Modes of the Workflow Engine and Different Sizes of the Case Base 244
8.21 Improvement of the Edit Distance and Number of Executed Tasks for the Non-Conforming Process Participant for Each Replay 245
8.22 Utility for the Non-Conforming Process Participant for Each Replay for Different Modes of the Workflow Engine 246
8.23 Average Utility for the Non-Conforming Process Participant for Different Case-Based Modes of the Workflow Engine and Different Sizes of the Case Base 247

List of Tables

5.1 Exemplary Use of the Variable s_{end} in CSP_W 92
5.2 Exemplary Computation of Work Items according to Algorithm 5.1, 1st and 2nd Iteration 105
5.3 Mapping Loop Pattern to Logical Formula with Possible Second Iteration ($addConstraints()$) 109

List of Definitions

Definition 2.1 (Process-Aware Information System)   14
Definition 2.2 (Business Process)   16
Definition 2.3 (Business Process Management)   16
Definition 2.4 (Business Process Model and Instance)   18
Definition 2.5 (Business Process Management System)   21
Definition 2.6 (Workflow)   23
Definition 2.7 (Workflow Management System)   23
Definition 2.8 (Workflow Engine)   26

Definition 4.1 (Directed Graph)   69
Definition 4.2 (Subgraph)   69
Definition 4.3 (Degree, In-Degree, Out-Degree)   70
Definition 4.4 (Workflow)   70
Definition 4.5 (Workflow Block)   71
Definition 4.6 (Single Task Block)   72
Definition 4.7 (Sequence Block)   72
Definition 4.8 (Exclusive or Parallel Control-Flow Block)   73
Definition 4.9 (Single-Branch Exclusive Control-Flow Block)   73
Definition 4.10 (Block-Oriented Workflow)   74
Definition 4.11 (Execution Path, Execution Path Set)   75
Definition 4.12 (Sequential Execution Paths)   75
Definition 4.13 (Sequential Combination of Execution Path Sets)   75
Definition 4.14 (Parallel Execution Paths)   75
Definition 4.15 (Parallel Combination of Execution Path Sets)   76
Definition 4.16 (Execution Path Set of Workflows)   76
Definition 4.17 (First and Last Element of an Execution Path)   76
Definition 4.18 (Execution Path Set of a Single Task Block)   77
Definition 4.19 (Execution Path Set of a Sequence Block)   77

Definition 4.20 (Execution Path Set of an Exclusive Control-Flow Block) 77
Definition 4.21 (Execution Path Set of a Parallel Control-Flow Block) 77
Definition 4.22 (Execution Path Set of a Single-Branch Exclusive Control-Flow Block) 78

Definition 5.1 (Constraint Satisfaction Problem) 87
Definition 5.2 (Solution) 88
Definition 5.3 (Prevention of the Execution of a Block) 99
Definition 5.4 (Declarative Formula for a Task Node) 100
Definition 5.5 (Declarative Formula for a Sequence Block) 100
Definition 5.6 (Declarative Formula for an Exclusive Control-Flow Block) 101
Definition 5.7 (Declarative Formula for a Parallel Control-Flow Block) 101
Definition 5.8 (Declarative Formula for a Single-Branch Exclusive Block) 101
Definition 5.9 (Loop Control-Flow Block) 106

Definition 6.1 (NESTGraph) 130

Definition A.1 (Adapted $CSP_B{}^*$) 260

List of Acronyms

AI Artificial Intelligence

API Application Programming Interface

BP Business Process

BPEL Business Process Execution Language

BPM Business Process Management

BPMN Business Process Model and Notation

BPMS Business Process Management System

CAKE Collaborative Agile Knowledge Engine

CBR Case-Based Reasoning

CRM Customer Relationship Management

CSP Constraint Satisfaction Problem

DCR Dynamic Condition Response

DTW Dynamic Time Warping

ECA Event-Condition-Action

EPC Event-Driven Process Chain

ERP Enterprise Resource Planning

GUI Graphical User Interface

JSON JavaScript Object Notation

KfW Kreditanstalt für Wiederaufbau

LTL Linear Temporal Logic

MUC Minimal Unsatisfiable Core

NWA Needleman-Wunsch-Algorithm

PAIS Process-Aware Information System

POCBR Process-Oriented Case-Based Reasoning

ProCAKE Process-Oriented Case-Based Knowledge Engine

RDF Resource Description Framework

REST Representational State Transfer

SME Small and Medium-Sized Enterprise

SWA Smith-Waterman-Algorithm

SWRL Semantic Web Rule Language

TBR Trace-Based Reasoning

UML Unified Modeling Language

WfM Workflow Management

WfMC Workflow Management Coalition

WfMS Workflow Management System

XML Extensible Markup Language

YAWL Yet Another Workflow Language

ZEW Leibniz Centre for European Economic Research

Chapter 1

Introduction

The introductory chapter of this thesis outlines the key topic of the presented work. This includes a motivational statement and a description of the issues that are tackled by this work in Section 1.1. Subsequently in Section 1.2, the resulting research questions in conjunction with the aims that are to be achieved are elaborated. Section 1.3 describes the applied design science methodology and single steps that were performed to create useful artifacts. The main contributions that emerged during this work are summarized in this context as well. In Section 1.4, two research projects are presented briefly, as the developed artifacts primarily were part of these. The outline of the remaining chapters of this thesis and their content is concisely depicted in the concluding Section 1.5.

1.1. Motivation

Small and Medium-Sized Enterprises (SMEs), i.e. companies with no more than 250 employees, are the mainstays of the European economy. They constitute 99 % of all businesses in the European Union [45] covering two thirds of total employment from 2013 to 2019 [6].

Currently, the digital revolution is ongoing, but in contrast to large companies, SMEs appear to be lagging behind. The Leibniz Centre for European Economic Research (ZEW) concludes in a survey from the year 2016 [156] that digitalization in the mid-sized sector still has major potential and until now progresses with rather slow pace. According to this study, only one fifth of SMEs have begun digital networking of products and services, mostly because of a lack of competencies. Two years later in 2018, several investigations confirm the trend of the ongoing digital revolution. A survey from the Kreditanstalt für Wiederaufbau (KfW) [78] states that the number of realized digitalization projects is increasing over the last few years, though larger companies tend to carry out such undertakings almost twice as often (<5 vs. >50 employees). Additionally, SMEs with more than 50 employees invest 24 times the amount for digitalization than that of smaller enterprises, which indicates an outpacing of the smallest companies [78].

Digitalization substantially contributes to a fast, full, and transparent order processing and hence, execution of operational processes as a basis for good customer relations. For this purpose, the design of currently applied information systems plays a significant role. Process-Aware Information Systems (PAISs) [42] address the management and integration of business documents, data, and processes through digital support and are substantial to accomplish digitalization. The main incentive of using such systems is to increase efficacy as well as efficiency of operational processes. Another benefit of PAISs is the possibility of supervision and control of all running and completed transactions, allowing traceability [146, p. 4] and transparency. Traditional PAISs perfectly fit the needs of large companies, but are scarcely applicable for SMEs.

Large companies differ from SMEs in several characteristics. Their business processes and documents are usually standardized due to a huge amount of homogeneity. Their workforce is much bigger and consequently, more capacity for manifold expert knowledge is available. Furthermore, due to these increased opportunities, especially considering financial scope, large companies are ahead in the progress of digitalization. The use of information systems, like e.g. PAISs, is prevalent. Although SMEs share the same objectives that PAISs could fulfil, such systems are not established, as there are various reasons for the unsuitability of traditional PAISs for SMEs.

In contrast to large companies, SMEs have to deal with a highly dynamic business environment. The amount of business transactions of SMEs is substantially smaller and processes are less standardized, but rather weakly structured [177]. Additionally, compared to large companies, the number of served customers is much smaller and their relationship is much closer. Generally, an optimal satisfaction of customers' needs, which are constantly changing, constitutes a key

1.1. MOTIVATION

success factor in the future [36, 127]. One of the most important criteria for profitability is therefore fulfilling individual needs. Due to this, the conducted workflows may vary significantly from case to case. They are characterized by specific surrounding conditions, special incidents, or even coincidences due to customers' needs or changing circumstances. Thus, a higher degree of flexibility might be a competitive advantage [85, 127, 157] as ideally a faster and customized processing of business cases is achieved.

Traditional PAISs rarely support this desired flexibility but rather control workflow execution by means of traditional engines [31, 83, 183, 199]. They prescribe the course of action without any possibility to deviate [30] [205, p. 310], as it is assumed that workflows can be modelled to a great extent prior to execution [31]. However, in reality all upcoming situations and evolving circumstances can neither be modelled nor be anticipated [64, 110]. Such systems are thus rapidly considered to be a burden as they restrict users in their workflow and users tend to become frustrated [205, p. 311]. This in turn results either in so-called workarounds, where in the worst case users bypass the system [159, 183], or in a suboptimal workflow execution [31]. The error rate might increase [183] [205, p. 311] and transparency as well as traceability is neglected [31]. Hence, the advantages of digitalization and introducing an information system, especially efficiency, are thwarted [83].

Another important characteristic of SMEs refers to the available expertise and corresponding knowledge transfer. Employees are quite versatile and tend to work as generalists rather than specialists [177]. Established processes and knowledge about how things are done are implicit, not stored digitally and tacit knowledge is often only shared orally. Employees execute processes like best practices on the basis of informal rules and procedures. Experts mostly pursue workflows due to their experiential knowledge and even deviate without affecting the outcome especially without losing control or missing the objective, but rather optimizing the process [21, 29]. Apart from that, inexperienced employees need to rely on support from colleagues concerning the aspect of knowledge transfer. A solution for this issue would be an effortful modelling of expert knowledge, resulting in a large effort for knowledge acquisition and leading to a high demand of several resources for maintenance, which is not feasible for SMEs and indicates a further impediment.

This implies another obstacle for SMEs which is the lack of various resources such as financial or personnel for realizing the adoption of an information system. The required overhead concerning employee capacities for workflow modelling, control, and maintenance, which is significant, is not manageable. Furthermore, no expert knowledge is existent concerning process management or even no explicit business processes are obvious. A further challenge poses the employee resistance to accept new technologies, as the operating employees rarely get in touch with technical systems, especially in certain sectors, like the craft sector.

This work investigates how to create an easy-to-maintain flexible workflow system that meets these requirements of SMEs. For this purpose, supporting operators in fulfilling their tasks successfully even in case of unforeseen deviations, especially without the need for a huge effort, constitutes the key challenge. To address this issue several partial aims are pursued and research questions need to be answered that are elucidated in the next section.

1.2. Research Aims

The main objective of this work is to develop a novel approach for a flexible workflow management that particularly meets specific requirements of SMEs. Here, the previously indicated requirements are considered in particular. This includes *flexibility* for a customized processing of business cases, *knowledge transfer* for explicitly storing tacit knowledge, and a *low effort* to deploy the workflow approach in order to preserve resources. Therefore, a more efficient supervision of customized business processes and enhanced assistance possibilities is pursued. Several flexible workflow approaches exist that either require complete knowledge about all possible workflow executions at build time or demand a remodelling at run time. Realizing flexibility in such a manner is inappropriate for SMEs. Flexibility in the context of SMEs should mainly imply the ability to deviate from the prescribed course of action due to unexpected circumstances during run time without required actions for manually adapting the process instance. The approach *flexibility by deviation* [166] exactly matches these desired characteristics. Hence, the main objective of this work is to adopt and implement this concept in such a way that it is suitable for SMEs concerning the previously mentioned requirements. This

1.2. RESEARCH AIMS

results in the following key research question, which is investigated in this work:

RQ0: *How can flexibility by deviation be implemented to support specific requirements of SMEs, such as flexibility, knowledge transfer and low effort?*

To answer this question, several partial aims need to be addressed. For the approach *flexibility by deviation*, the foremost prerequisite is to tolerate deviations during workflow execution that have not been intended by the designed ideal process model. In common workflow systems, either the possibility to deviate is not provided or deviations lead to exceptional states, which need to be handled. Thus, the process flow is disrupted and not supported continuously. This in turn leads to a decreased user acceptance and a tendency to circumvent the system [21], such that the actual process flow can neither be controlled nor retraced. Therefore the workflow model should serve as a guideline that assists rather than restricts. This requires a formal workflow model that allows for deviations during execution without leading to exceptional states or deadlocks. For this purpose, the following question needs to be addressed.

RQ1.1: *How can a formal workflow model be designed in such a way that deviations can be allowed?*

Additionally, another important aspect concerning adequate workflow representation for SMEs needs to be considered. Workflow modelling is usually based on procedural paradigms, e.g. the most commonly used Business Process Model and Notation (BPMN) [193]. With such a language, processes can be expressed in an intuitive way, but are rigid considering their execution [46, 138]. For the use of specific workflow modelling languages that are more flexible, i.e. declarative approaches, expert knowledge is required, which presupposes further resources that SMEs cannot afford. Therefore, the designed workflow approach should not require knowledge about a formal language, but rather a low user effort to achieve flexibility. Standard procedurally defined workflow models should serve as basis for the approach, but nevertheless the specification of simple constraints, which are additionally considered, should be possible. Consequently, a further question arises.

RQ1.2: *How can established procedural models be transformed to be used by the designed workflow approach and how can these models be enhanced with additionally specified constraints?*

As the resulting workflow model is able to allow deviations, consequently these deviations need to be considered for further workflow control. Hence, the crucial point is to facilitate a successful workflow termination in case of a deviation by suggesting appropriate work items. To manage upcoming deviations, various existing approaches apply previously specified rules, which require a cumbersome modelling of expert knowledge [4, 22, 29, 40, 53, 124, 201]. This results in a large effort for knowledge acquisition and leads to high costs for maintenance.

Strategies need to be determined that decide automatically how to continue with the workflow. Thus, it will be investigated how predefined strategies can be formulated domain-independently. Therefore, another research question needs to be addressed.

RQ1.3: *How can a successful completion of a deviating workflow be achieved in a controlled and automated manner?*

Moreover to improve this support in undesired or unpredictable situations, it is explored how decisions can additionally base on domain-specific knowledge with a minimum necessary effort for knowledge acquisition. In real life, if unexpected situations occur, experienced users might be aware of how to cope with the situation, while inexperienced users need to rely on their support. Hence, one issue that will be investigated relates to incorporating previous experiences in the decision process, such that experiential data is used to enhance the workflow control. The aim is to derive decision-relevant knowledge from historical data, e.g. terminated processes that have been traced. It is assumed that through this, the workflow system is able to help experienced but likewise inexperienced users. As another expected benefit, knowledge transfer would be guaranteed and the preservation or even establishment of so-called best practices would be assured. This leads to two issues. First, the following question needs to be addressed.

RQ2.1: *How can one or several similar and reusable terminated processes be identified in order to derive and propose work items to resolve the deviating situation?*

To this end, an adequate similarity measure needs to be defined. Since these similar processes might not be applicable in a straightforward way, an adaptation method needs to be designed. As a result, these previous experiences can be exploited for adjusting to the current situation appropriately.

RQ2.2: *How can the currently regarded process be adapted through identifying and transferring valuable process execution characteristics from the most similar retrieved processes in order to generate an adapted process that can offer support until termination?*

The main intention of the pursued workflow approach is to find an optimal balance between control and flexibility, to provide both guidance as well as low restriction and to offer support and likewise foster user acceptance. Traceability should not be neglected and adaptability should be increased.

The overall approach intends to lead to a continuous process improvement [197], as the ideal process can be learned through analysing all occurring executions and thus, optimization potentials can be exploited. Ultimately, an intelligent learning workflow engine should be created.

Artificial Intelligence (AI) [155] is a key technology for various support strategies in Business Process Management (BPM) [205], as it allows for automated decision making and thus, facilitates the users work. To create artifacts that address the previously presented research aims, renowned AI methods, namely Constraint Satisfaction Problem (CSP) solving [153] as well as Case-Based Reasoning (CBR) [1, 149], are applied as key technology for handling unforeseen occurring deviations, automated decision making, and controlling worklist suggestions.

1.3. Methodology

This research work was carried out according to the methodology of *design science* in information systems [69, 130]. Design science "supports a pragmatic research paradigm that calls for the creation of innovative artifacts to solve real-world problems"[68, p. 9]. The goal of design-science research is to gain insights into objectives of information systems and to seek for, develop, and evaluate adequate solutions to accomplish a certain purpose. Design science "addresses important unsolved problems in unique or innovative ways or solved problems in more effective or efficient ways" [69, p. 81]. This problem-solving paradigm aims at designing novel and innovative artifacts for the application in information technology through rigorous and practice-relevant research [69].

Utility and rigor are the two most important characteristics, which are to be considered during a design-science research work. The utility of a developed artifact, as essentially pursued benefit, needs to be assessed and particularly improved through a "build-and-evaluate-loop"[69, p. 78] in order to achieve effectiveness and efficiency. Rigor refers to the chosen research methodologies and used theoretical foundations. According to Österle et al. [130] there are four main steps: analysis, design, evaluation, and diffusion. In the analysis phase, the research gap and issue are identified while considering actual business needs. Afterwards, artifacts are to be designed through rigorously applying recognized methodologies and theoretical foundations, which can result in a construct, a model, a method, or an instantiation. These created artifacts are subsequently evaluated concerning their quality, efficacy, and most importantly utility. These scientific findings and results should be published to achieve a knowledge diffusion. The described steps should be repeated iteratively to improve the created artifacts.

The main objective of this work is the development of a novel concept for flexibility by deviation. In the analysis phase, requirements of SMEs for a useful workflow support have been identified based on related literature as well as face-to-face meetings with project partners. Accordingly, several desired characteristics of the pursued approach have been derived.

In order to allow for a deviant workflow execution to evade prescribed workflow models, a constraint-based workflow engine is designed, which is the first artifact of this work. Therefore the proven technique of constraint solving was transferred to serve the purpose of a workflow engine. As formal basis, a constraint-based workflow representation is defined. A transformation function for block-oriented workflows into constraints is developed, which is evaluated in a proof. A constraint satisfaction problem algorithm which builds upon the previously mentioned constraint net, represents an artifact of the type model. This CSP in turn constitutes the basis of the constraint-based

1.3. METHODOLOGY

workflow engine. This workflow engine is responsible for computing the work items in a specific and possibly exceptional state of a running workflow based on several strategies that restore consistency. Its prototypical implementation represents an instantiation artifact that was evaluated concerning runtime and compared to similar approaches.

So far, the suggestions of how to continue with a running workflow instance in case of a deviation are not based on sound knowledge but rather arbitrary applied strategies in order to restore a consistent constraint net. Therefore, the approach is evolved in a further step, which involves experiential knowledge to improve the utility. A concept for a case-based deviation management that extends the constraint-based workflow engine is developed. This approach exploits the established methodology of case-based reasoning. This comprises several artifacts. A similarity measure for comparing sequential execution traces as well as two different adaptation mechanism to reuse one or several retrieved similar cases as solution are proposed. Based on both of these adaptation approaches, the worklist suggestions build on former experiences and entail customized and ideally optimized workflow termination.

In summary, the main goal of the presented approach is to provide work items to the process participant even in case of deviations. These work items can be calculated either through the constraint-based workflow engine, or one of two adaptation methods that based on the sequence similarity measure, which are a null adaptation variant and a generative constraint-based adaptation of the workflow instance. These three different approaches are evaluated and compared concerning their utility for process participants. A technical experiment in combination with an illustrative scenario is performed. To this end, a synthetic data set of workflow traces is created on the basis of the investigated use case scenario *deficiency management in construction*. This data set is divided into a training set and a test data set, which is used as case base, that serves as data basis for the algorithms, while performing a ten-fold cross validation. For each query, the workflow execution is simulated by means of the application of the workflow engine. In order to evaluate the utility for all common kinds of process participants, distinct realistic user types are defined, each applying a different strategy of how to continue with the workflow after a deviation. Ultimately, the results of this experiment give indications for possible improvements and further evolutions, in order to start a new iteration of the build-and-evaluate-loop as follow-up of this thesis.

1.4. Research Projects

Substantial contributions to the presented work result from the authors' participation in two research projects. Both will be presented in the following in more detail.

1.4.1. SEMAFLEX

SEMAFLEX[1] was a research project aiming for a semantic integration of flexible workflow and document management [59]. This project was a joint research work from Trier University and Trier University of Applied Sciences. The main goal of this project was to support SMEs in managing flexible processes by semantically integrating workflow and knowledge-based document management. With application partners from a construction company, we investigated the process of deficiency management, as it is a highly flexible but also a supervised process. Methods of document classification and information extraction were applied to upcoming documents. These were subsequently mapped to parts of the workflow. As a result, executed tasks could be traced automatically. This logged workflow can contain deviations, which were handled by an intelligent flexible workflow engine in order to continue and terminate the workflow successfully. This workflow engine builds the foundation of this thesis.

1.4.2. SEMANAS

SEMANAS[2] was a research project with the aim of a semantic support for grant application processes [60] and was carried out at the Trier University of Applied Sciences. The main objective was to achieve flexibility in data-centric and knowledge-intensive processes through the semantic integration of process and document knowledge. Through

---

[1]SEMAFLEX was funded by Stiftung Rheinland-Pfalz für Innovation, grant no. 1158, German: "Integriertes semantisches Management von Prozessen und Geschäftsdokumenten zur Unterstützung flexibler Geschäftsabläufe im Mittelstand"

[2]SEMANAS was funded by Federal Ministry of Education and Research (BMBF), grant no. 13FH013IX6, German: "Semantisch unterstütztes Antragsassistenzsystem"

the use of an ontology for knowledge collection, the derivation of context-relevant new knowledge based on inference mechanisms and through this, process support is enabled. As a use case scenario, the application for subsidy procedures in the agriculture sector was regarded. In this context, the flexible workflow engine was enhanced and refined through a case-based deviation management.

1.5. Outline

The remaining chapters of this thesis describe the necessary foundations, the developed concepts, and the results of the evaluation. Chapter 2 deals with the main topic, which reflects the subject of this work. Workflow management with a focus on flexibility is elucidated and relevant characteristics are sketched. Furthermore, related approaches that address flexible workflow management in a similar manner are discussed in this chapter.

Chapter 3 introduces the domain *deficiency management in construction*, which is regarded as use case in this work. On this basis the potentials and necessities of a flexible workflow approach are emphasized. The main goals and a general concept for workflow flexibility by deviation for SMEs are exemplified with the presented use case. Subsequently in Chapter 4, formal notations for workflows and all essential dependencies are defined as basis for the concept.

In Chapter 5, the constraint-based workflow engine is explained in detail. Initially, the necessary foundations are introduced. This comprises not only the constraint satisfaction problem in general, but also the specific definition of the applied constraint model. The workflow engine as such is depicted by the constraint solving algorithm for computing work items as well as supporting methods such as handling loops, detecting deviations or restoring consistency. To conclude this chapter, related work concerning constraint-based approaches for workflow flexibility is sketched.

Chapter 6 illustrates the approach for a case-based deviation management that enhances the constraint-based workflow engine with regard to a holistic workflow solution. This chapter starts with an introduction to case-based reasoning and time-series similarity measures as basis for the approach. Subsequently, deviation management is sketched in the context of the CBR cycle to provide a brief insight into the realization of each phase. As a main necessity for the retrieval phase, the designed similarity measure, which is based on time series, is described in detail. Furthermore, the reuse phase, in which one of two different adaptation algorithms is applied, either a null adaptation or a generative adaptation based on constraints, is illustrated. Concluding this chapter, related approaches concerning case-based management of deviations will be discussed.

The prototypical implementation of this flexible workflow approach is presented in Chapter 7. This includes an overview of the overall concept, a characterization of the proposed architecture and a detailed description of the single implemented components.

The following Chapter 8 revolves around the evaluation. First, the contributions of this thesis are summed up and research question RQ0 is addressed. Subsequently, the regarded evaluation criteria and assessed hypotheses are stated. The experimental setup is outlined including a description of the data generation. Results from the conducted evaluation of the proposed flexible workflow approach are shown, analysed, and finally discussed critically.

The thesis concludes with the final Chapter 9, which comprises a summary of the contributions, a discussion of the achieved aims, but also entailed drawbacks, and an outlook on potential improvements as well as promising future fields of research.

Chapter 2

Foundations on Flexible Workflow Management

Before presenting the pursued concept for a flexible workflow approach, relevant foundations are introduced. This chapter primarily focusses on workflow management with necessary prerequisites and in particular workflow flexibility. Foundations that concern the adopted methods and technologies of the presented concept are introduced in subsequent chapters, more specifically CSPs in Section 5.3 and CBR as well as time-series similarity measures in Section 6.1, respectively Section 6.2.

In this chapter, starting from the most general, namely process-aware information systems in Section 2.1, more specific systems are introduced, continuing with business process management and finally going into detail about workflow management. In Section 2.2 business processes as such are characterised and the business process lifecycle is described from different perspectives. The section concludes by sketching the differences of business processes and workflows. Subsequently, Section 2.3 comprises relevant aspects of workflow management such as workflow classification and modelling paradigms. Workflow terminology foremost in the context of flexibility and its different types are elucidated in-depth in Section 2.4. The chapter concludes with related work concerning flexible workflow approaches and a discussion about their different concepts and shortcomings in Section 2.5.

2.1. Process Aware Information Systems

The latest general paradigm shift in the modern working world refers to the conversion from the industrial society to the information society.

This transformation process was strongly influenced by the movement of business re-engineering and is based on the computerisation of economy and society [129, p. 14]. Potentials due to novel business solutions are exploited that change whole economic sectors [129, p. 9]. Through this computerisation, processes, leadership, products, interorganizational coordination, and markets were changed [129, p. 11]. The business re-engineering movement began in the early 1990s and reconsidered the common practice used up to then.

In the 1970s to 1990s, information systems were strongly focussed on the sole management of data, particularly saving and enabling access to information [42, p. XIII]. The used approaches were foremost data-driven. In a company, it was common to employ several standalone information systems for the separate management of diverse information, e.g. Enterprise Resource Planning (ERP) systems or Customer Relationship Management (CRM) systems. This resulted in several disadvantages and inefficiencies. The "logic of business processes was spread across multiple software applications and manual procedures"[42, p. 5]. Work had to be coordinated manually and some data needed to be stored redundantly, which easily lead to inconsistencies or even errors [42, p. 4]. In some cases the employees were not aware of any explicit process, but the workflows implicitly resulted from intuitively dealing with tasks and through interaction with colleagues and systems [42, p. 7]. Hammer and Champy were the pioneers that first proposed to integrate business processes and information technology [146, p. V] and recognized the arising potential. Processes were seen as novel model for organising businesses through linking business strategy with information systems and are thus able to provide new entrepreneurial solutions [129].

Process-orientation in information systems continuously increased and consequently, PAISs evolved.

Definition 2.1 (Process-Aware Information System). *A process-aware information system (PAIS) is "a software system that manages and executes operational processes involving people, applications, and/or information sources on the basis of process models." [42, p. 7]*

The use of a PAIS allows for the integrated management of various resources such as activities, employees, data, and services in order to achieve added value [146, p. V]. On the other hand it enables the "splitting of monolithic applications into smaller components and services, which can then be orchestrated by PAIS." [146, p. 4] Thus, this entails a separation of concerns, which implies several benefits. Process logic and application code are segregated and can therefore be adapted individually without affecting the other one [42, p. 7][146, p. 4]. Nevertheless, standardized interfaces ensure a smooth communication and the integrity of data through the integration of these single components. Frequent procedures may be mapped to explicit models, create a common understanding of the work for all people involved in the process, and decrease misunderstandings [42, p. 7]. The processes mapped to a formal model can additionally be enacted in an automated manner and, as a result, provide further benefits. This includes increased efficiency through, among other aspects, allocation and optimization of resources, such as information or services [42, p. 7]. Furthermore, through the depiction of the actually happening process in the system, the management department can get insights into the status of the work that is done at any time and in a rather uncomplicated way. Thus, monitoring and verification purposes are enabled [42].

PAIS can have different forms and focuses. They vary from groupware, which simply supports the communication between several participants, to business process management systems, which completely control the course of actions. In this work, the partial aspect of business process management is regarded and therefore will be explained in more detail in the following section.

2.2. Business Process Management

The foremost goal of each company is to achieve profit in order to guarantee its existence and foster competitiveness. Each company produces some kind of value in their daily work. This includes material goods and marketed products such as cars or food, as well as immaterial services, e.g. consulting or health care. To create each of these, several activities need to be performed by different employees, usually in a coordinated way. Additionally, there are various other necessary organizational procedures to organize and coordinate work structures, e.g. travel expense claims or employee recruitment, which are relevant for added value to a lower extent. But nevertheless, several tasks need to be synchronized for a smooth operating. All these can be put into process form. "Business processes are the key instrument of organizing these activities"[205, p. 4].

2.2.1. Business Processes

Manifold definitions of business processes with various distinct focuses exist, which will be shortly presented in the following.

One business process consists of one to many activities [205, p. 83]. One activity is seen as a unit of work. The goal of the business process can either be a physical product or a service [150, p. 23]. Another integral part are relevant data objects that are processed during enactment as input or output of activities [7]. Hammer describes a process as "end-to-end work across an enterprise that creates customer value."[63, p. 4] Thereby the necessary cross-sectoral work to achieve added value is emphasized. The scheduling of activities, which is denoted as control-flow, is defined through the order of the connected activities and controlling structures [7][129, p. 62]. Scheer and Jost emphasize the content-related and temporal dependencies of activities [76]. Österle adds that the execution of a process is represented by a sequence of activities that are supported through information technology [129, p. 63]. A definition that includes all previously mentioned aspects, which are concisely summarized, and that is used throughout this thesis is as follows.

Definition 2.2 (Business Process). *A Business Process (BP) consists of a set of activities that are performed in coordination in an organizational and technical environment. These activities jointly realize a business goal. Each business process is enacted by a single organization, but it may interact with business processes performed by other organizations. [205, p. 5]*

To handle business processes and all aspects that need to be considered, business process management (BPM) is established. BPM supports companies on the operational level, to achieve strategic goals, through the use of information systems. "Business process management is a customer-centered approach to organizational management."[63, p. 6] BPM is not only responsible for coordinating work, but also entailing aspects like analysis and monitoring. Essentially, its potential is to improve productivity and therefore efficiency as well as reducing costs [182].

2.2. BUSINESS PROCESS MANAGEMENT

Definition 2.3 (Business Process Management). *Business process management (BPM) includes concepts, methods, and techniques to support the design, administration, configuration, enactment, and analysis of business processes. [205, p. 5]*

2.2.2. Business Process Life Cycle

Each business process undergoes a life cycle that typically consists of four phases (see Fig. 2.1), where each phase has some output that is processed in the next step (see side notes). First, in the *design and analysis* phase, the business goal to be achieved is defined in an informal specification. This model is further transferred to a first process model in a formal language as well as refined in several iterations. Therefore, the formal model can be analysed and simulated in order to validate and verify the designed process concerning syntactic and semantic correctness. Furthermore, the actually created process can be checked against the desired behaviour and possibly be adjusted or improved before deployment. The result of this step in the business process life cycle is a *process model*.

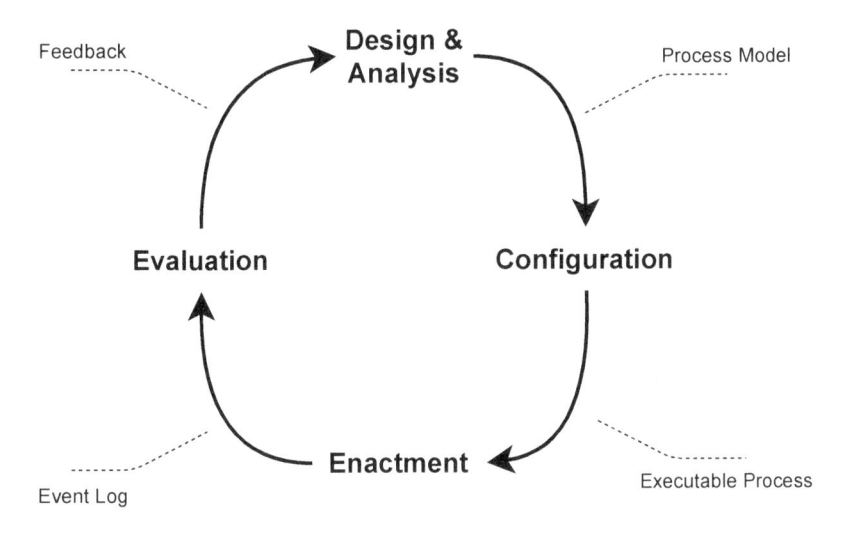

Figure 2.1. Business Process Life Cycle adopted from Weske [205, p. 12] and based on Di Ciccio et al. [25]

The next phase comprises the *configuration*. The designed business process is implemented, to be executable by a software system. The previously designed formal model is enhanced with required technical specifications. Moreover, the software system needs to be configured in order to be able to handle the process enactment appropriately. This includes the integration of necessary services, the provision of suitable interfaces for the process participants, and the management of data transactions [205, p. 13]. Once the implementation is completed, the execution of the business process can be tested. The outcome of this phase is an *executable process*.

The *enactment* of the business process represents the third phase of the business process life cycle. Here, process models are transposed to process instances at run time, representing one single concrete business case. The software system controls the process execution, by initiating activity enactments and providing resources according to the process model. Furthermore during this phase, the current status of the process can be monitored through various statistics or visualisation techniques. After enacting a business process, an *event log* arises that records what actually happened.

In the last phase, *evaluation*, collected data about the process, such as event logs, can be analysed, e.g. through applying process mining techniques. The results are used for improvements, optimization, or a complete redesign of the process. Subsequently, the cycle starts all over integrating the generated *feedback*.

2.2.3. Build vs. Run Time

In traditional business process management there is a strict differentiation between build time and run time (see Fig. 2.2). At build time, processes are designed and specified as formal models. These process models can further be configured and verified at build time [146, p. 31]. If a process activation is triggered, such a process model is instantiated and hence, transposed to run time but without connection to the original process model. A process engine creates a process instance on the basis of this process model, executes and manages it [146, p. 33]. This approach ideally fits to static control structures [205, p. 310]. Dynamic adaptations are not supported, as they imply modifications of the process model, which affect the process instance during run time [205, p. 310].

Therefore, business processes are distinguished into model and instance.

2.2. BUSINESS PROCESS MANAGEMENT

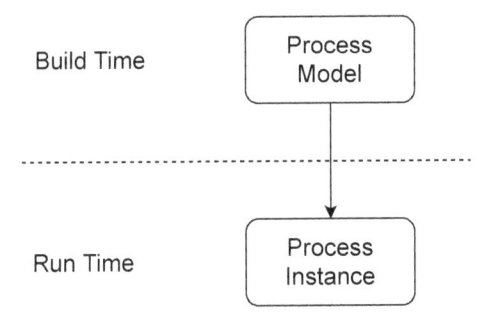

Figure 2.2. Build Time vs. Run Time

Definition 2.4 (Business Process Model and Instance). *A business process model consists of a set of activity models and execution constraints between them. A business process instance represents a concrete case in the operational business of a company, consisting of activity instances. Each business process model acts as a blueprint for a set of business process instances, and each activity model acts as a blueprint for a set of activity instances.[205, p. 7]*

A process model thus tries to represent all different possible valid ways of handling a certain issue [182]. Several distinct process instances can stem from this one model, which each reflect the state of execution for a single process instance. Alternatively, process models are denoted as type or schema, but throughout this work the notion *process model* is used.

In Fig. 2.1 the phases of BPM are shown in an abstracted way. On the basis of build and run time, and the distinction between process model and instance, the process life cycle is refined. Fig. 2.3 rather focuses on the user and data perspectives, showing involved persons and illustrating the handling of processes. Still, this is a simplified visualisation, but nevertheless represents the essential aspects.

First, a model that represents a certain process to achieve some business goal is designed by a process engineer at build time (see (1)). Each model can be instantiated at run time, resulting in the creation of a process instance (see (2)). Based on this instance, activities, which are enabled for execution, can now be suggested to the process participants (see (3)). The process participant processes any of these work items, by choosing one task, completing it, and thus, triggering an update of the instance (see (4)). At run time, process instances are not completed, but in progress. This data is denoted as *pre mortem data* [182]. All terminated instances are stored as event logs that record "all relevant events occurring during the execution of a process instance" [146, p. 35] (see (5)). These event logs, called *post mortem data* [182], enable the process engineer to monitor and analyse the process performance (see (6)), potentially resulting in improvements through adaptations of the process model, which is called evolutionary change [146, p. 41] (see (7)). At build time, off line process mining techniques for analysis can be applied [182].

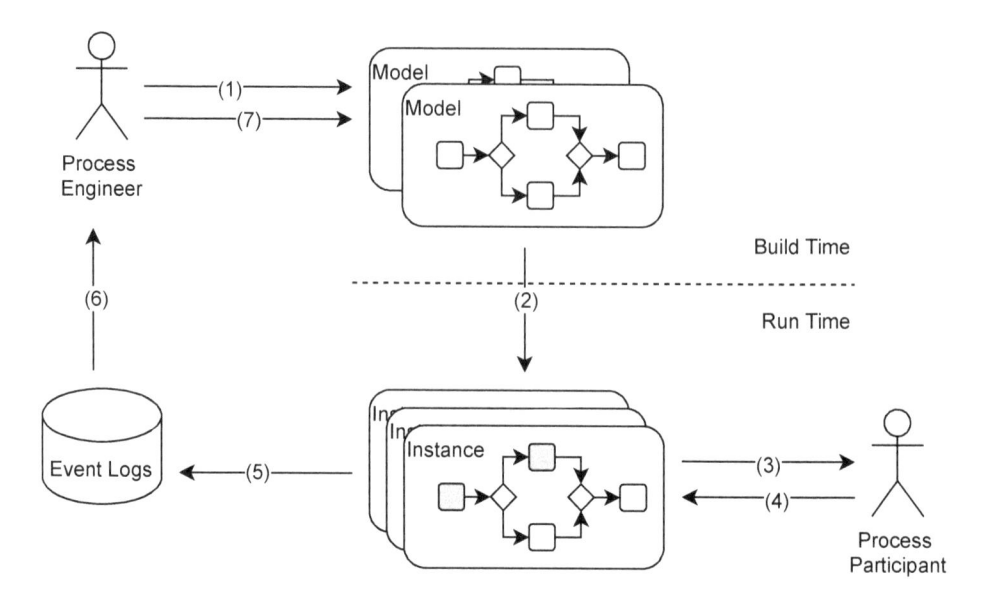

Figure 2.3. Detailed Business Process Life Cycle based on Reichert and Weber [146, p. 41]

In this process life cycle, no flexibility is possible. The instances rigidly follow one model. If an evolutionary change is made, a new independent model evolves. To indicate that deviations might occur between designed model and actual instance, van der Aalst explicitly differentiates between *de jure* and *de facto* model [181]. The de jure model describes the ideal handling of the issue, hence what process participants are prescribed to do [182]. In contrast, the de facto model reflects the reality, thus, how the process is actually handled [182]. In this approach, as deviations from the de jure model are allowed explicitly, process instances are referred to as de facto workflows, which represent the traced process instances independent from the process model.

Cugola further differentiates process instances by introducing the terms *observed* and *actual process* [28]. The observed process corresponds to the traced sequence of tasks, whereas the actual process also includes tasks, that were executed by the process participant but without notice and control of the system, thus, bypassing it. Though, the actual process maps the reality exactly, unfortunately the system is not aware about activities that happen outside the system. Consequently, the de facto workflow as observed process is used as data basis. More details about the actual workflow approach are explained in Chapter 3.

2.2.4. Business Process Management System

Information systems are the main digital support for managing and embedding business processes in the organizations' environment. To achieve set business goals, employees need to interact and work with systems. Business processes are established for this coordination and to facilitate this synergy. The efficacy and efficiency mainly depends on this interplay of these resources [205, p. 4]. Information systems specialized for business processes are called business process management systems and are defined as follows.

Definition 2.5 (Business Process Management System). *A Business Process Management System (BPMS) is a generic software system that is driven by explicit process representations to coordinate the enactment of business processes.[205, p. 6]*

"BPMS are created to narrow the gap between business goals and their realization by means of information technology."[205, p. 112]

While business process management and workflow management is sometime considered the same and these notions are used in a similar context, in this thesis a slight difference is exposed, as also stated in some other work. The notions process and workflow are used in this thesis according to the made definitions.

2.3. Workflow Management

A business process represents the real world course of actions, while a workflow takes place in an automated manner through the use of an information system [150, p. 28]. Workflow Management (WfM) is settled on the operational level of the company [48, p. 3]. Business process management rather takes the economic perspective of a process, specifying how to reach defined strategies at the organizational level, and workflow management refines these processes by enhancing them with concrete specifications about automating the execution, coordination of activities at the operational level [205, p. 111], and adequate disposition as well as distribution of resources. Not all kinds of business processes can be handled reasonably by WfM. A main characteristic is the possibility of partial automatization capabilities and a certain regular frequency of occurrence of the process.

2.3.1. Benefits of Workflow Management

The use of WfM promises several advantages to enterprises. The utmost goal is to create a high-performance process [63, p. 7] resulting in various benefits. The foremost impact is an improvement of process handling, including, among other aspects, shorter throughput times, increased productivity, higher transparency, quality assurance, and ultimately better customer service [150, p. 32]. From an economic perspective this yields lower costs, reduced assets, faster speeds and greater accuracy [63]. Ultimately, the overall enterprise performance is improved [63].

The goals of WfM are manifold and some advantageous aspects are inherent. Through a higher transparency of the current workflow status, an increased customer satisfaction can be achieved, as the processing of its request is obvious [48, p. 48] [63, p. 7]. The same holds for the companies' management or other responsible employees, who can inform themselves whenever required [48, p. 49]. As process participants are more guided and supported through the provision of necessary resources as data or services, an improved quality and reduction of errors is expected [48, p. 48].

The coordination of the work or part of the work is simplified and partly done in an automated manner. This includes parallelization of activities, dynamic allocation of available resources and thus, avoidance of standby and downtime, which leads to a shortening and consequently to an optimization of throughput times [48, p. 49]. This in turn results in a reduction of costs. Workflow management systems represent a middleware for the integration of various hard- and software components to simplify the interaction [48, p. 49] and to guarantee data integrity.

Due to monitoring capabilities, the actual state can be compared to the target state continuously, which allows for an assurance of performance quality [48, p. 48]. An impact for the employees of the company is a unification of graphical user interfaces and therefore better usability [48, p. 49]. Another objective is adaptability to organisational or external changes [48, p. 49]. However, the ultimate goal of workflow management is the automation of process control [48, p. 49].

2.3.2. Workflows

The most important distinction criteria between business processes and workflows is the automation, which is emphasized in the following definition.

Definition 2.6 (Workflow). *A workflow is "the automation of a business process, in whole or part, during which documents, information or tasks are passed from one participant to another for action, according to a set of procedural rules."[210]*

Alonso et al. [7] describe a workflow as "a representation of the business process in a machine readable format." This aspect is also emphasized by Weske [205, p. 306], who mentions the additional information about technical aspects to make a business process automatically executable. This indicates the use of an information system for workflow control. As described in Subsect. 2.2.3, build and run time can be transferred to workflows. Workflow models are specified at build time and instantiated to workflow instances transposing to run time.

Analogous to BPMS and slightly more specifically, workflow management systems are defined as follows.

Definition 2.7 (Workflow Management System). *A Workflow Management System (WfMS) is "a system that defines, creates and manages the execution of workflows through the use of software, running on one or more workflow engines, which is able to interpret the process definition, interact with workflow participants and, where required, invoke the use of IT tools and applications." [210]*

Thus, a WfMS represents the operational environment for workflow management, including design, execution and monitoring of workflows

[64]. In addition, the WfMS is responsible for ensuring the correct enactment and distribution of resources [48, p. 228]. Wainer et al. find an appropriate formulation, by designating the WfMS as a "dispatcher" when workflows are executed [196]. Which components are typically part of a WfMS is described by the workflow reference model.

2.3.3. Workflow Reference Model

Due to various distinct developments of WfMSs during their emergence and the necessary integration and collaboration of several components, the demand for a standardization arose [150, p. 161]. For this reason, the Workflow Management Coalition (WfMC) was founded in 1993. One of their main contributions was the workflow reference model [209]. It represents a generic architecture for WfMS with the intention of establishing standardized components and interfaces (see Fig. 2.4) [209]. It is constructed modularly to offer and simplify interchangeability as well as compatibility with various software or hardware constructs. There are six main components and five interfaces with different responsibilities. For communication between the different components, a *workflow API and interchange formats* (see Fig. 2.4) are supplied such that transmission of data is standardized.

The centerpiece is the *workflow enactment service* (see Fig. 2.4), which is responsible for the assignment of resources such as persons, applications or services [150, p. 142]. The necessary interaction between process participant and the system is coordinated by this module [150, p. 142]. The service is build upon one to several *workflow engines*. These workflow engines are responsible for controlling workflow execution at run time [48, p. 231]. First, workflows are instantiated and initialized based upon their models that are interpreted. The workflow engine is in charge of synchronizing and computing the status of workflow instances due to the information from external triggers.

To create a process model that may be instantiated, *process definition tools* (see Fig. 2.4) are used. Here, the workflow including its structure and detailed task specifications need to be defined based on a certain workflow modelling language, which is decoupled and therefore independent from the execution context. These tools additionally allow for an analysis of process models, e.g. simulation or verification of syntax. The process models can be imported by the workflow API to be executable.

2.3. WORKFLOW MANAGEMENT

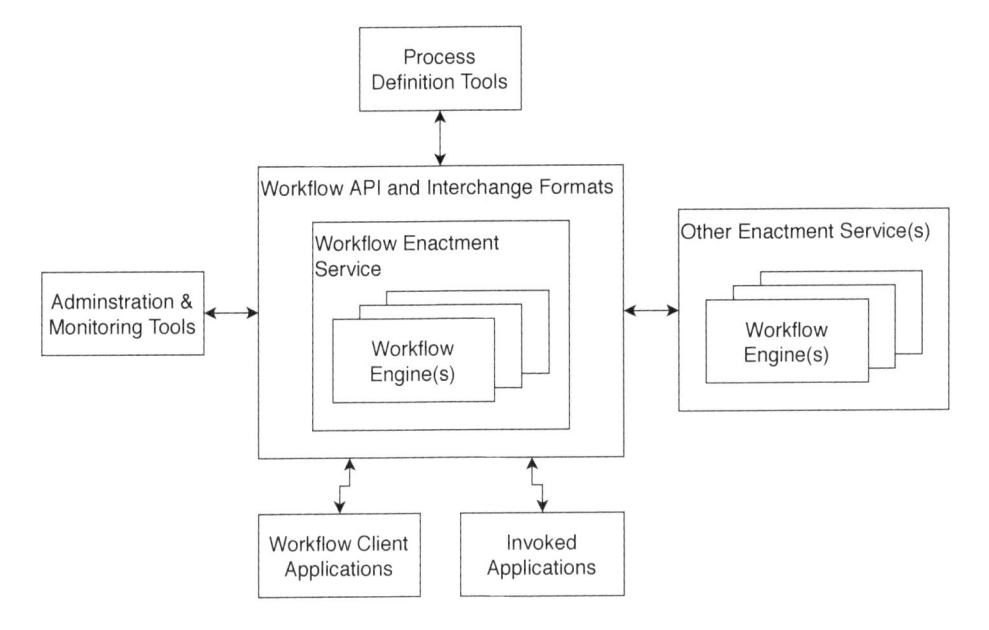

Figure 2.4. Workflow Reference Model - Components & Interfaces based on the Workflow Management Coalition [209]

The operator uses the WfMS through different *workflow client applications* (see Fig. 2.4). The most popular one is the so called *worklist*, which contains the pending tasks that are executable. The worklist of one process participant contains *work items* that represent tasks that are executable and for which the specific process participant is qualified for [146, p. 37]. One work item can be part of several worklists. If one work item is chosen for execution by a process participant and thus, allocated, all other worklists containing the same item are updated by removing the concrete item [146, p. 38]. Furthermore, necessary services that are involved in the task enactment are provided as client application [146, p. 38]. The process participant receives notifications about a status change of the workflow through these client applications. The workflow enactment service provides the necessary data or even services through the interface that connects both modules. In the opposite direction, status updates are sent that are processed by the workflow engine. This includes terminated tasks, modified or created data objects.

Besides, other applications may be invoked by the workflow engine, in case tasks comprise automated services (see *invoked applications* in Fig. 2.4). The workflow enactment service also may cooperate with *other independent workflow enactment services*, comprising several workflow engines. This comes into play, when several processes are interwoven across the corresponding WfMSs and interoperability, i.e. exchange of data, needs to be achieved [48, p. 232].

Finally, workflow progress can be monitored, analysed, and supervised through *administration and monitoring tools* (see Fig. 2.4), accessing information from the workflow enactment service through another interface. Thus, various tools are conceivable. For instance, optimization potentials can be discovered or error detection can be used for a future prevention of the former mentioned. Additionally, this interface can be used to handle unexpected issues, set parameters, or allocate resources [182].

The issue that is regarded in this work concerns the handling of upcoming deviations, but yet a continuous support for workflow execution. The objective is to compute adequate work items considering the current situation. Thus, the component *workflow engine* plays the most important role for this work.

Definition 2.8 (Workflow Engine). *A workflow engine is a software service or "engine" that provides the run time execution environment for a workflow instance."[209]*

The workflow engine is responsible for interpreting the workflow model, which includes instantiating a corresponding workflow instance and computing work items. The work items, which form the worklist, are distributed to responsible employees by a separate component, the worklist handler, which is part of a client application [209].

2.3.4. Workflow Classification

Workflows can be classified into several categories. There are a few different distinctions depending on the considered characteristics. An early classification by Hammer distinguished three process types: *core*, *support*, and *governing* processes [63, p. 11]. The core processes are responsible for creating the actual value for the customers and are thus essential for business [63, p. 11]. They are also named *primary* processes [187, p. 9]. Support processes, additionally denoted as *enabling* or *secondary* [187, p. 10], represent internal auxiliary procedures, e.g. personnel matters as recruitment or travel expense claims [63, p. 11]. *Governing*, or *managerial* [187, p. 10], processes include all management issues, like strategic planning [63, p. 11].

2.3. WORKFLOW MANAGEMENT

This classification has evolved considering different aspects and is transferred to workflows. Four distinct types have been established: *production, administrative, collaborative,* and *ad hoc workflows*. Depending on the characteristics of the workflow, the suitability of support through traditional WfMSs and the necessary functionalities and focusses vary.

These workflow types can be classified depending on the frequency of execution, i.e. whether the same workflows occur very often or are rather unique, and on their business value or objective, i.e. whether the outcome of the workflow contributes to the added value of the business or is more of a supportive procedure. For this comparison see Fig. 2.5.

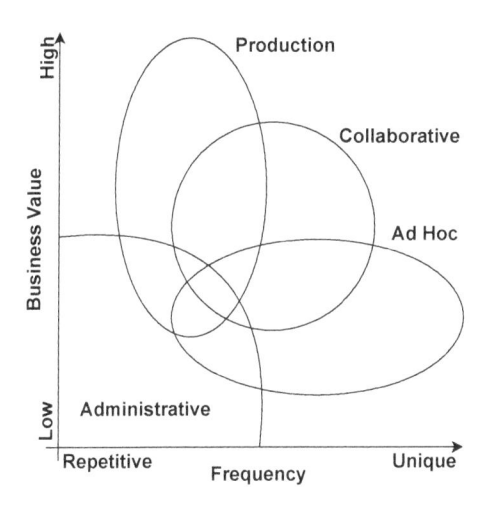

Figure 2.5. Workflow Classification with regard to Business Value and Frequency based on Alonso et al. [7]

Another main differentiation relates to the predictability or degree of structuring that is possible at build time, in contrast to the complexity of tasks and the workflow itself (see Fig. 2.6) [42, p. 14].

A detailed description of the four workflow types is given in the following:

- *Production workflows* represent the core processes of a company that are directly related to the business goal [7], i.e. building a house for a construction company. These workflows are highly repetitive and predictable. Therefore the course of action is completely structurable with no degree of freedom for the operator

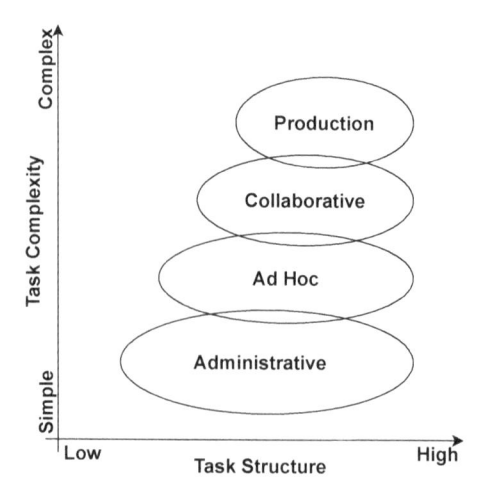

Figure 2.6. Workflow Classification with regard to Task Complexity and Task Structure based on Alonso et al. [7]

[48, p. 43]. Dumas et al. underline as important characteristic of production workflows the "more or less complex but highly stable task coordination rules"[42, p. 14].

- *Administrative workflows* are repetitive as well as predictable and consist of simple task coordination rules that are known by participants [7]. Usually these workflows are standardized and occur very frequently. The most common example for these workflows are bureaucratic processes, such as travel expense claims.

- *Collaborative workflows*, as indicated by the notion, require coordination with a high number of participants. They represent iterative tasks until an agreement is found, which is not always a simple forward progress but rather several iterations [7] and therefore can hardly be structured.

- *Ad hoc workflows* are not predefined and in some cases limited to data provision. Usually each workflow is unique [7], as the activities cannot be structured in advance [48, p. 43]. The coordination is done by participants instead of system support.

Some classifications only take one dimension into account. For instance, van der Aalst [182] sorts workflows according to their possible

2.3. WORKFLOW MANAGEMENT

amount of prespecification and model-conformity. *Unframed* workflows are not explicitly specified as a process model [182]. *Ad hoc framed* implies a model that is only used once for instantiation before it is adapted or abandoned [182]. *Loosely framed* workflows are defined in a process model, but deviations are permitted [182]. *Tightly framed* workflows follow the traditional idea of WfM, as a model is defined that is strictly adhered to [182].

A similar distinction is made on the basis of structurability, through the terms *ad hoc, semi-structured* and *structured*. Ad hoc describes the same as in the above taxonomy, notably a low repetition rate and a high complexity [71]. Structured is comparable to the previously defined tightly-framed and semi-structured is somewhere in-between with a high frequency and a pre-determined structure, but also possible deviations [71]. Processes that can hardly be predefined are associated with knowledge-intensive processes [146, p. 44]. They essentially require expert knowledge of the process participants for task handling, decision making and process control [25].

2.3.5. Workflow Modelling

Workflow modelling is the prerequisite for a workflow execution as general conditions are determined. Therefore several perspectives with varying purposes have to be regarded. Moreover the used language with the respective paradigm is an essential factor for the expressive power and available functionality. Both aspects are presented in detail subsequently.

2.3.5.1. Perspectives

For a holistic contemplation of a process, different perspectives have to be considered. Each of them is modelled individually to reduce complexity and guarantee a separation of concerns. The basic modelling perspectives were manifested in business engineering [129, p. 30] and are represented in the ARIS model [164]. This includes three aspects: function, organization and data. Meanwhile, six fundamental perspectives are established that refine these previously mentioned three aspects through adding behaviour, operation and time.

- *Function:* The function perspective encompasses the specification of single process components, from atomic to complex activities or subprocesses [146, p. 21f]. These represent units of work at different aggregation levels [205, p. 77] and can be defined informally or formally, e.g. syntactically or semantically [205, p. 78].

- *Behaviour:* The behaviour perspective deals with the relation between these previously defined process components. This concerns the order of activities or other constraints like preliminary conditions, called control-flow [146, p. 22-25]. Therefore, van der Aalst uses the term control-flow perspective and describes it as the "backbone of a process model."[182]

- *Information:* The information perspective, denoted as *data* perspective in the ARIS model, adds data objects to the activity perspectives. Input and output relations are specified, describing the data-flow [146, p. 25f]. This includes data dependencies as well as decision-relevant data [205, p. 78].

- *Organization:* The organization perspective comprises competencies, responsibilities and permissions due to the organizational structure of the business. It covers roles of individuals or whole departments concerning the hierarchy, authority and substitution in case of absence or hindrance [146, p. 26f].

- *Operation:* The operation perspective allows for an incorporation of tool or system support. Services that are linked to activities can be specified in this context [146, p. 27ff].

- *Time:* The time perspective includes temporal constraints such as durations or deadlines of activities and actions to be taken in case of exceedance like escalation stages or notifications [146, p. 29][182]. Moreover, temporal restrictions can also refer to resources or process participants, such as availability times or working hours [42, p. 25]

These perspectives are potentially complemented with additional relevant ones depending on the use case and business context. Dumas et al. [42] mention in particular business rules that represent organizational policies and compliance demands independent from specific processes [42, p. 25f], as well as exception handling with recovery measures or mechanisms, which is not included in a traditional workflow model [42, p. 26].

2.3.5.2. Paradigms

"A process modelling language provides concepts for representing processes." [46]. It "provides appropriate syntax and semantics to precisely specify business process requirements, in order to support automated process verification, validation, simulation and process automation." [94] There are three different abstraction levels for varying purposes when creating a process model.

The levels range from a conceptual view to a formal or an execution description [182]. Formal models base on mathematical theory and are necessary for a precise definition. They form the basis for an automated processing. Conceptual models are a means of simplifying the modelling process to a meta level, abstracting from formal details. Conceptual languages adopt workflow patterns that were defined to describe key functionalities language-independent [186]. Thus, a common ground is established for understandability and comparability of different languages. Conceptual models are used by process stakeholders for a first specification. The description on the execution level is in a machine-readable format, which can be executed automatically and is used by the workflow engine.

A differentiation is additionally made between modelling paradigms, where the two extremes of paradigms are procedural, also denoted as imperative, and declarative [46]. Procedural modelling is also called "inside-to-outside approach" [182]. When using this paradigm, it is explicitly described which activities are to be executed in which order and under which circumstances. Procedurally modelled workflows explicitly specify the allowed behaviour, and in consequence all possible allowed execution paths represented as sequential information [46]. Here, the control flow of tasks as well as the related flow of data items is modelled, which results in a high complexity and a huge modelling effort. However, an advantage of those models is the explicit mapping of procedural execution paths and thus, an intuitive understanding is simplified even for non-professionals. Various languages have been established, ranging from Petri nets [148] over Unified Modeling Language (UML) [44], and Event-Driven Process Chains (EPCs) [77] to the most commonly used BPMN [193] or the execution language Business Process Execution Language (BPEL) [9]. These languages are in most cases graph-based [94], as their formal basis is graph theory, using Petri nets [148].

With declarative process modelling, paraphrased as "outside-to-inside approach" [182], however, forbidden behaviour and states of the workflow are defined. Thus, circumstantial information is specified [46]. This paradigm ideally fits to modelling loosely structured processes. When adding a constraint, the valid state space usually is restricted. In contrast to graph-based approaches, declarative languages are denoted as rule-based, formally basing on formal logic. An established method is called Event-Condition-Action (ECA) rules [94]. ConDec [136, 137] is a constraint-based declarative workflow modelling language that is used by the prototypical workflow system DECLARE [135, 184, 207]. It is based on Linear Temporal Logic (LTL) as formal foundation.

Procedural workflows explicitly describe valid procedures, while it is almost impossible to cover all alternatives. Therefore, procedural models lack a subset of accepted execution orders in most cases. In contrast, declarative constructs describe specific undesired states, leading to the acceptance of every other state [134], and thus, implicitly providing flexibility concerning workflow execution. Declarative models may be much more simple but still flexible. A drawback of this approach is the lack of explicitly specified procedural executions. Therefore no obvious task suggestions can be made in any state of the workflow. Furthermore, minimizing complexity, keeping track and preserving maintainability becomes more difficult with increasing size of the model, i.e. the amount of constraints [62, 111].

Concerning flexibility, procedural and declarative languages differ significantly. This is illustrated in Fig. 2.7.

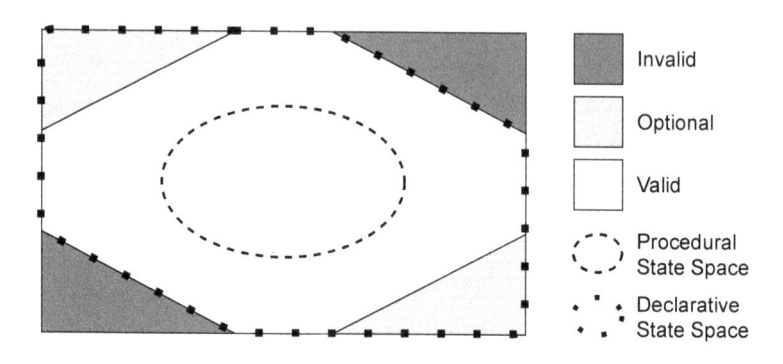

Figure 2.7. Possible Workflow State Space based on Pešić [134]

The rectangle represents the whole state space of one workflow. The grey coloured areas indicate invalid states, while dark grey outlines strictly forbidden behaviour and light grey shows undesired but potentially permissible states. With a procedural language only a subset of possibly valid states is defined in a model (see oval with dashed frame in Fig. 2.7), as all execution paths need to be specified explicitly. Every possible behaviour cannot be anticipated and knowledge about a workflow is rarely complete. In case a new valid execution path arises, it must be integrated explicitly into the model, to stretch the accepted state space. In contrast, declarative models define the invalid states through obligatory constraints and possibly ones that optionally should be adhered to (see grey coloured triangles in Fig. 2.7). The allowed state space comprises every state except the invalid ones (see shape with dotted frame in Fig. 2.7). The implicit flexibility that is offered through declarative workflow modelling needs to be restricted by adding constraints.

Besides these two presented contrasting paradigms, there exists a variety of other approaches that partially are a mixture of both, but also some that have a completely different focus. Object-oriented or artifact-centric approaches are some examples [182]. Moreover, a refinement of declarative approaches is possible as well, e.g. in constraint-based, rule-based or case handling [109], depending on the applied modelling technique.

2.3.6. Limitations of Traditional Workflow Management Systems

Traditional WfMSs, with foremost procedural modelling languages, have one main drawback, which is the unability to deal with flexibility. The long-time prevalent way of workflow management was as sketched in Fig. 2.8.

A certain business process was envisioned by a company, in particular by process stakeholders, as an ideal procedure to achieve some specific goal. This implicit knowledge of the composition of activities is then cast into a process model, the de jure process. This de jure process is used by operators to fulfil a task. Enacting this process results in one or generally several process instances, the de facto processes. Usually there is no feedback transfer about occurred inconsistencies between de jure and de facto process, but the de jure process is simply left as is and never adjusted. Due to several and diverse reasons, the de facto process does not comply with the envisioned business process most of the time, but more or less severe discrepancies exist. "Every

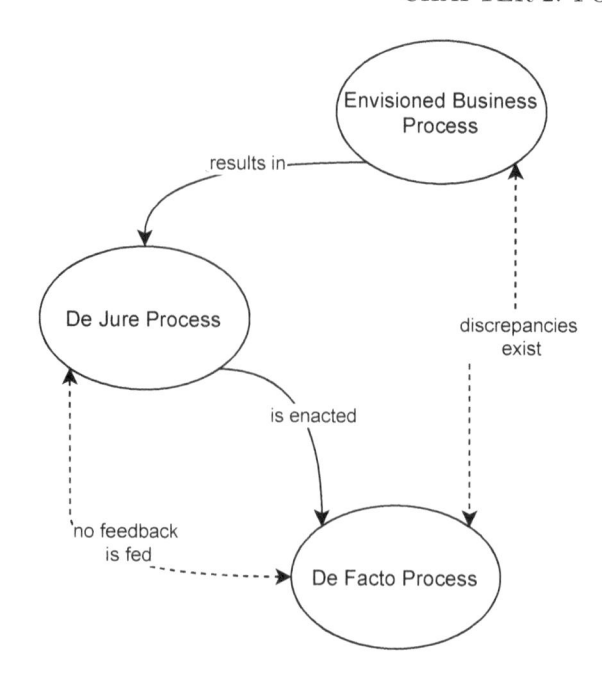

Figure 2.8. Prevalent Way of Workflow Management based on Han et al.[64]

good process eventually becomes a bad process." [63, p. 12] This shift can have manifold reasons, e.g. varying customer needs, evolving technologies or simply competition [63, p. 12]. A continuously changing business environment [205, p. 4] or unexpected incidents are some more issues that need to be tackled, but also increasing market demands [109] require flexibility.

Furthermore, traditional WfMSs focus on support for repetitive and predictable processes [146, p. 43] and are sometimes rather limited to certain sections like banking or insurance [42, p. 9].

There are several possible regulations to improve this situation that can all be summarized under the term flexibility. Flexibility "allows reducing the gap between process models [...] and what is happening in the real world" [109]. Before introducing techniques for achieving workflow flexibility, the notion as such and a necessary dissociation to relating terminology is presented in the following.

2.4. Workflow Flexibility

Workflow flexibility has gained much attention in recent research and the need for integration in PAISs and its importance is stated frequently [65, 147]. Flexible approaches concerning workflow management have been focused in research for more than a decade [166] and are investigated and applied in various branches, e.g. healthcare [103]. Flexibility techniques and their impacts are manifold. In summary, flexibility deals with adaptability, variability, and evolution [146, p. 43]. The essence of flexibility is to decide about the adequate amount and choice of untouched versus adaptable process parts [182].

2.4.1. Terminology

In the context of workflow flexibility, there are various notions that are used frequently. The terminology is often applied inconsistently in research literature. Therefore, there are several definitions of these frequently used notions with slight differences such that only a vague common understanding is established. To establish the used vocabulary and their interpreted definitions in this thesis, notions are clarified in this section and put into relation, grounded in various references.

2.4.1.1. Dynamism

The property *dynamic* is paraphrased as "something is true at a given time, but false some time later"[7]. This can be related to the business environment in which a process is executed and where a flexible reaction is necessary for success. *Dynamic change* is narrowed down to "handling old cases in a new workflow process definition"[183], where the problem that comes with evolutionary changes is referred to (see Subsection 2.4.2)).

2.4.1.2. Evolution

Workflow *evolution* concerns the "ability of the process implemented in a PAIS to change when the corresponding business process evolves." [146, p. 47] Thus, a new workflow model emerges that creates variability.

2.4.1.3. Variability

Every change in a process model results either in a new *version* or in a new *variant* of this definition. A new version will be established after a transition period such that at a certain point in time all process instances will be transacted according to this new version, thus, the process model evolved. However, a new process variant exists simultaneously to the original process model and the instances will build upon either of them, as long as they are valid. Which variant is executed is sometimes not known prior to instantiation, as the values of decisive parameters are initially unclear [146, p. 45]. Variants are based on the same core process but some parts vary depending on certain conditions, but nevertheless can be specified [146, p. 45]. Variants emerge due to reuse and subsequent refinement of processes [146, p. 89].

2.4.1.4. Adaptability

Adaptability "represents the ability of a PAIS to adapt the process and its structure [...] to emerging events." [146, p. 46] These events can be exceptions or special situations and they can either be anticipated or unexpected [146, p. 46]. Adaptation is one method to create a flexible workflow management.

2.4.1.5. Looseness

Looseness describes that only the objective of a process is determined, but the procedure to get there is not known or rather unpredictable [146, p. 46].

2.4.1.6. Flexibility

Flexibility "describes the ability of a process to change"[141]. Mejri et al. [109] and van der Aalst [182] add that both foreseen as well as unforeseen changes that are caused by the business environment should be handled. Burkhardt and Loos [20] describe handling flexibility issues as a simplifying process, but without adding complexity. Thus, flexibility is a rather abstract notion and needs to be categorized more clearly.

2.4.2. Classification of Change

The notion *flexibility* can refer to several aspects of business processes. Flexibility can affect various characteristics and have different impacts. A classification of criteria that can be subject to those changes according to Regev et al. [141] is shown in Fig. 2.9.

2.4. WORKFLOW FLEXIBILITY

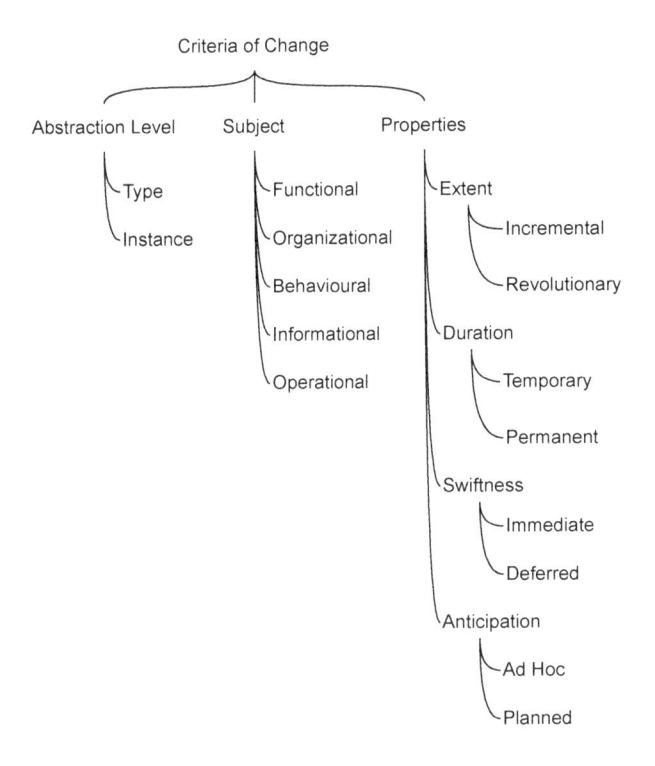

```
                        Criteria of Change
         ┌──────────────────┼──────────────────┐
   Abstraction Level     Subject           Properties
         │                 │                    │
         ├─ Type           ├─ Functional        ├─ Extent
         │                 │                    │      ├─ Incremental
         └─ Instance       ├─ Organizational    │      └─ Revolutionary
                           │                    │
                           ├─ Behavioural       ├─ Duration
                           │                    │      ├─ Temporary
                           ├─ Informational     │      └─ Permanent
                           │                    │
                           └─ Operational       ├─ Swiftness
                                                │      ├─ Immediate
                                                │      └─ Deferred
                                                │
                                                └─ Anticipation
                                                       ├─ Ad Hoc
                                                       └─ Planned
```

Figure 2.9. Notions of Change by Regev et al. [141]

A main criteria is the abstraction level of change. On the one hand, changes can be made to process models. This affects all future as well as possibly running process instances. The need for such changes, denoted as *process type* or *schema evolution* [199] is typically caused by a redefinition of intentions such as the process goal or business strategy [141]. On the other hand, changes can be applied directly on the instance level to single instantiated processes. This so-called *instance evolution* becomes necessary due to unusual or exceptional situations [141]. Soffer [173] distinguishes flexibility according to this criteria as well. She denotes schema evolution as *long-term flexibility* and instance evolution as *short-term flexibility* [173].

Another important aspect is the perspective in which the change takes place. Five subjects are differentiated by Regev et al. [141] that refer to a subset of the modelling perspectives introduced in Subsection 2.3.5.1. The *functional* perspective relates to the overall goal of the process, whereas *operational* changes apply to parts of the process, mostly single activities as well as their characteristics and specifications. *Behavioural* considers the interrelations and dependencies between activities such as preconditions. The *informational* perspective additionally takes the information flow into account. Participants and their roles are captured by the *organizational* perspective.

A third dimension of classification refers to the properties of changes. A process can be changed *incrementally*, which means the old process is transformed into a new one, or *revolutionary*, which means the old process is completely exchanged by a new one. Changes can be *temporary* or *permanent*, see *duration*. They can be deployed *immediately* or in a *deferred* way, see *swiftness*. This depends on the abstraction level. For running process instances a decision has to be made, whether the made changes are transferred or only impact newly created instances. Changes can also be distinguished considering the question of anticipation, i.e. whether the changes are *planned* or *ad hoc*.

Van der Aalst and Jablonski [183] set up a slightly different classification of change considering six disparate criteria, which are partly interrelated (see Fig. 2.10). The first distinction is made based upon the reason of change. Changes might have external triggers, such as shifts in the *business, legal* or *technological* context. Whereas reasons that come from the inside might result from *logical design errors* or *technical problems* within the information system. Another dimension is the effect a change has, which can be just *momentary*, affecting single processes, or *evolutionary*, which impacts all future processes. This is comparable to the temporary or permanent duration of change in Fig. 2.9. Change can affect different perspectives, which are relevant in process management (cf. Subsect. 2.3.5.1). The *process* perspective concerns the process itself and modifications of the tasks and their relations. Changed roles or resources that are responsible for certain tasks related to the *organization* perspective. Every change that involves control data belongs to the *information* perspective. The *operational* perspective includes modifications on operations themselves and the *integration* perspective is responsible for linking all other four perspectives together. Thus, changes in this perspective reflect altered relations of single perspectives.

The implication of changes can be manifold. They can trigger the *extension, reduction, replacement*, or *re-linking* of some parts of the process. Furthermore, the point in time of changes is differentiated. Changes can either be applied at *entry time*, thus before instantiation

2.4. WORKFLOW FLEXIBILITY

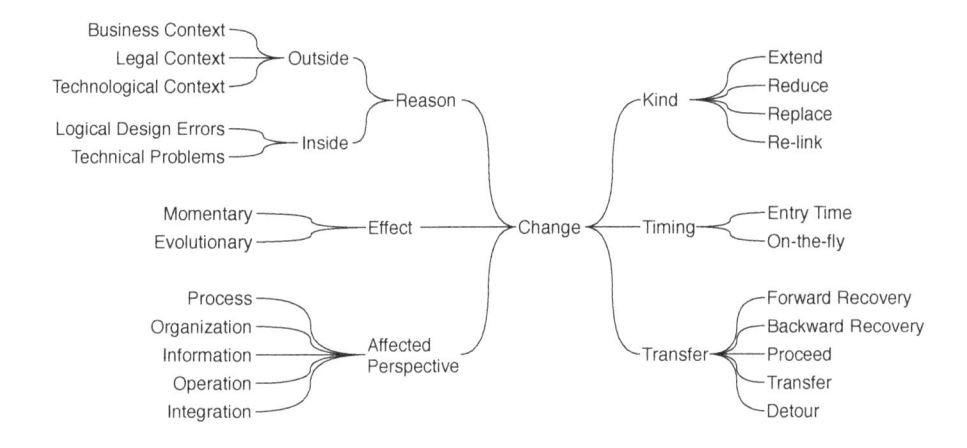

Figure 2.10. Classification of Change based on van der Aalst and Jablonski [183]

or *on-the-fly* at any time during execution. The sixth characteristic of change refers to the handling of changes in a process model and their transfer to ongoing and future instances. *Forward recovery* describes the abortion of running instances followed by an offline handling and termination. *Backward recovery* is similar, as running instances are interrupted, but corrective measures are taken that reset the process and enable a restart. *Proceed* implies no special action that is taken, but ongoing processes are terminated according their version of a process model and all future instances are started taken the new version into account. *Transfer* is a more complex strategy, as the changes are also transferred to running instances. With a *detour* only the changed instance is affected, while every other process instance is left untouched.

For Rosemann and Recker [152] flexibility not only consists of the type of change but also of the trigger or the reason for the necessary flexibility. They speak about those two parts as the "extrinsic trigger for change" and the "intrinsic process adaptation" [152]. Kumar and Narasipuram [86] divide flexibility into three different parts as well. They describe the previously mentioned extrinsic trigger for change as the "stimulus that generates requirements for flexibility" and the intrinsic process adaptation as "strategies or tactics employed to achieve flexibility". Additionally they see the flexibility itself as a third part [86]. These three perspectives should build upon each other to achieve the adequate flexibility.

This in-depth description of characteristics of change showed that flexibility can have manifold forms. Various aspects need to be regarded in order to choose the right focus and an adequate specific manifestation for the considered domain and use case. The next section introduces flexibility types and their characteristics.

2.4.3. Taxonomy of Flexibility

A taxonomy of flexibility is shown in Fig. 2.11 with different labels for concepts and methods. Heinl et al. [65] differentiate mainly between two different concepts of workflow flexibility, derived from the definition of *flexible* in a dictionary: *Flexibility by Selection* and *Flexibility by Adaption*. Both approaches differ in the manner of how flexibility is achieved.

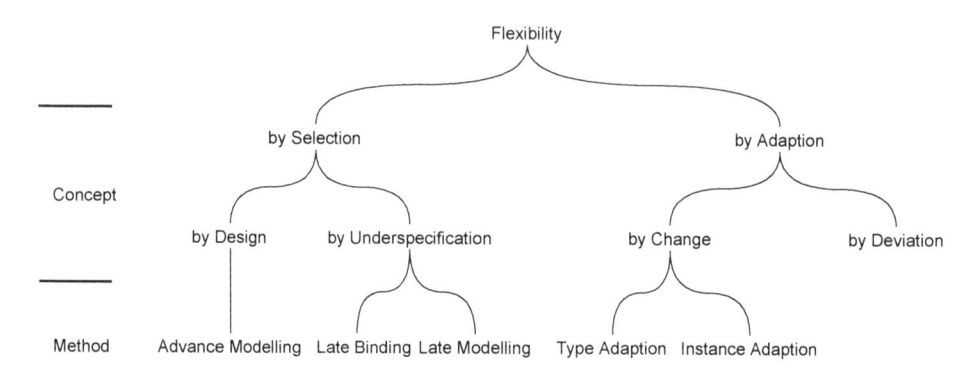

Figure 2.11. Taxonomy of Flexibility by Heinl et al. [65] and Schonenberg et al. [166] based on Pešić [134]

Flexibility by Selection is paraphrased as "end user flexibility" [65] and comprises every alternative execution path that is within the scope of the defined process model. "A user should have the freedom to choose between different execution paths if necessary." [65] This type of flexibility describes the ability to generate different process instances at run time, if those were integrated at build time in the process model. It refers to the expressive power of the used modelling language in such a way that workflow evolution is not necessary for handling situations [127]. This entails the main drawback that only anticipated scenarios can be mapped and thus, supported. Every other situation will lead to an exception and cannot be handled. Van der Aalst and Jablonski [183] denote this as *Flexibility by Configuration*. They argue that the best to do is to prevent changes and for this

2.4. WORKFLOW FLEXIBILITY

purpose offer a modelling language that is adequate to map the desired flexible characteristics for process execution. Other notions used in the same context are *pre-designed flexibility* [86] or *a priori flexibility* [74, 127].

Flexibility by Selection can be offered through *advanced* or *late modelling*. Advanced modelling describes the predefinition of all possible alternative execution paths before run time, whereas through late modelling some parts of the process model can be left undefined as black-box. In both types of flexibility by selection, the possible amount of flexibility clearly depends on the scope of the workflow modelling language.

Flexibility by Adaption comes into play when flexibility by selection cannot be applied, but the circumstances require workflows, either the model or instance, to be adapted. "It must be possible to change the workflow management application during runtime."[65] This strategy is used to handle necessary changes successfully [183]. An alternative expression is *just-in-time responsive flexibility* [86] or *a posteriori flexibility* [74, 127].

Here, *type adaption* is distinguished from *instance adaption*. Type adaption impacts every future instance, whereas instance adaption can differ in the extent of where changes are integrated. This comes down to some of the instances, all running instances that have not encountered the changes, yet or solely all future instances. The authors omit so-called ad-hoc modelling in their classification scheme, as this possibility is not feasible according to their opinion [65].

A more common classification of process flexibility is presented by Schonenberg et al. [166]. They distinguish four main principles. For an overview of all presented concepts see Fig. 2.11.

2.4.3.1. Flexibility by Design

Flexibility by design describes the incorporation of all possible alternative execution paths at build time in the process model. Therefore all execution paths need to be known prior to execution. At run time the process participant can choose from several alternative activities at some points of time in the process. As a result, workflow models tend to become very complex and even confusing. Furthermore, integrating required compliant process fragments into these models may result in so-called *process pollution* [169]. But still, unpredictable situations or frequently changing circumstances cannot be supported. This flexibility corresponds to the method of advance modelling of the concept flexibility by selection and is rather limited. The implementation possibilities depend on the modelling paradigm. A simple example in an imperative language is the choice construct, where at one step the process participant can choose between different ways to continue such that at minimum two distinct workflow instances are possible considering the order of activities. The term *flexibility by definition* is used synonymously [182].

2.4.3.2. Flexibility by Underspecification

When certain parts of the execution of a process are unknown at build time, *flexibility by underspecification* fits perfectly. The process model is left incomplete with placeholders for these parts, but nevertheless can be started and instantiated. During run time, when encountering such an undefined part, concrete activities that fill the blank need to be specified to be able to continue and ultimately complete the workflow. Thus, the choice of activities and their execution order is deferred. Two types of underspecification are distinguished: *late binding* and *late modelling*. Late binding requires a predefined set of possible fragments to choose from, which are specified at build time, where the flexibility simply comes into play through selection. Through late modelling the process participants can freely specify the process part from scratch or reuse previously defined process parts. A main drawback of this kind of flexibility is that either a set of possible placeholder fills need to be obvious at build time or modelling expertise is required at run time from the process participants. Besides, no structural changes are supported.

2.4.3.3. Flexibility by Change

With *flexibility by change* the process participant is able to change the process model at run time according to his specific needs. This type of flexibility is reflected by the previously introduced flexibility by adaption. Flexibility by change can be implemented in various ways depending on the situation and its requirements. It needs to be determined if changes are made on model or instance level and if they affect only certain chosen instances or all future ones. In some cases process instances need to be migrated, depending on the progress compared to the position of changes. The main drawback of this approach is that process participants need to intervene manually

2.4. WORKFLOW FLEXIBILITY

and take charge of adjustments by themselves and therefore require process modelling expertise. The user acceptance in practice is thus rather low. Another important aspect is the compliance, which needs to be checked after changes were made. This compliance check might be more easy to automate at run time, as at this point in time more specific information is apparent that can be consulted for validation [157].

2.4.3.4. Flexibility by Deviation

Flexibility by deviation describes the possibility of not pursuing proposed execution paths during run time but rather deviating from the prescribed process model without modifying it. This type of flexibility is rather largely unresearched and only a few approaches with concrete implementations are available. Therefore no prevailing methods exist. One system that partially adopts this approach is FLOWer [188], which allows the process participant to insert tasks at run time. These tasks handle the enactment of other tasks of the currently executed workflow, like skip, undo or redo. However, this is very restrictive and the process participant has to intervene manually.

2.4.3.5. Example

To illustrate the different flexibility types, a simple example and its variants are shown in Fig. 2.12. Here the desired workflow instance contains an activity d that is not contained in the model, but should replace activity b (see line 1). Each necessary change is marked in yellow. With flexibility by design, this desired execution path is integrated at build time in the model, by enhancing the model with an alternative routing possibility to activity b. Flexibility by change would allow for an adaptation of the model at run time, such that the desired instance is valid. In the example in Fig. 2.12 activity b is substituted by d. Another possible remodelling could result in the model from flexibility by design, which is not listed for the sake of simplicity. Through flexibility by underspecification, an adaptation is necessary at build time, in such a way that activity b is replaced by a placeholder, either left completely unknown (see upper row in line 4) or keeping fragments from which the process participant can choose (see lower row in line 4, b or d) in case late binding is used as method. With flexibility by deviation the workflow model is completely left untouched. Nevertheless, the process participant is allowed to deviate at run time and can enact the desired workflow instance. This is enabled in various ways. Hence, no specific approach is shown in this example.

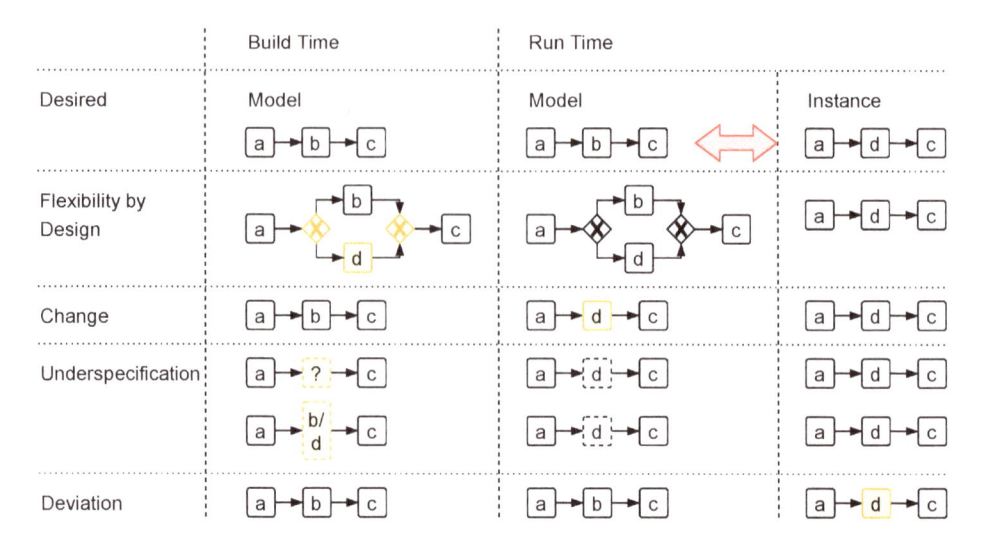

Figure 2.12. Examples of Flexibility Types

2.4.3.6. Alternative Notions

Besides this taxonomy of flexibility, there are various other classifications. One of them is worth mentioning, but is based on a different definition of flexibility itself and is therefore rather limited. According to Sadiq et al. [158] the term flexibility comprises only the possibility of an incomplete process model at build time, which is then complemented at run time due to specific needs. Flexibility is differentiated further into three different types of flexibility, namely *by definition*, *by granularity* and *by templates*. This definition is rather limited, as these three mentioned kinds of flexibility are contained in the previously specified *flexibility by design* and *by change* and rather describe specific methods for achieving changes. *Flexibility by definition* is equivalent to *flexibility by design*, as it encompasses the alternative execution paths that are included at build time in the process model. *Flexibility by granularity* describes the ability to include abstract parts in the process model that can be specified in detail at run time, which corresponds to *flexibility by underspecification*, more specifically late modelling or binding. *Flexibility by templates* means that several

2.4. WORKFLOW FLEXIBILITY

different simple templates are defined for one process model instead of trying to include all possible alternatives into one complex and unmanageable model, making it more easy to find the perfect fitting one. This type of flexibility relates to process variants.

This work will be build upon the classification by Schonenberg et al. [166], as it is up-to-date and the most reasonable and all-inclusive differentiation. To expose the unique features of the presented flexibility types, a comparison will be made in the next section.

2.4.4. Flexibility Type Comparison

When comparing the different flexibility types, some characteristics are different, whereas some are relatively similar. When relating the process model completeness with the point in time, when flexibility is achieved, i.e. build time in contrast to run time, the classification in Fig. 2.13 emerges. Flexibility by underspecification allows a partial

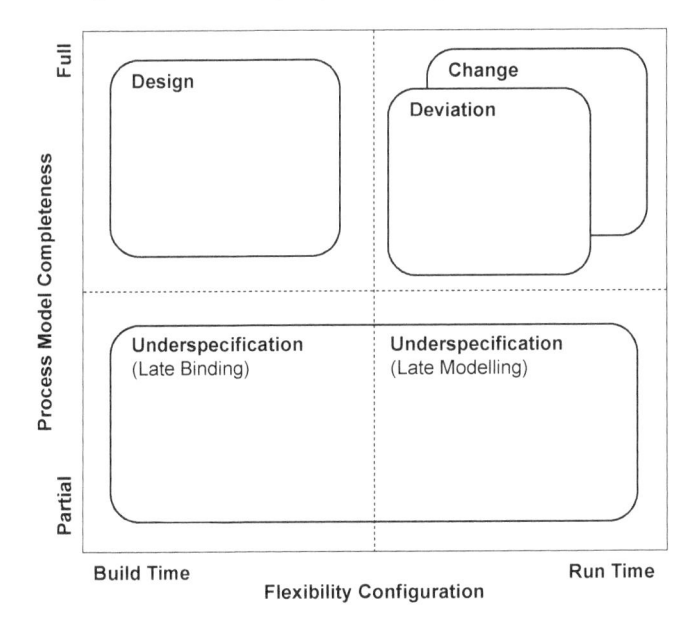

Figure 2.13. Flexibility Type Spectrum with regard to Flexibility Configuration and Process Model Completeness based on Schonenberg et al. [167]

process model and both integration of flexible constructs at build and run time. Flexibility by design builds upon a full process model and the possible amount of flexibility is determined at build time. Requiring a full process model, but still being able to allow flexibility at run time, holds for both flexibility by change as well as deviation. Thus, with this comparison, the unique feature of flexibility by deviation does not become clear.

Comparing the point in time when flexibility is achieved with the degree of impact, either influencing process model or process instance, all types overlap to some extent (see Fig. 2.14). Flexibility by underspecification can affect the process model at build time as well as at run time, whereas flexibility by design only influences the design of the process model at build time. Flexibility by change takes place exclusively at run time, but can have an effect on the process model as well as on the process instance. In contrast, through flexibility by deviation solely the process instance can be changed at run time.

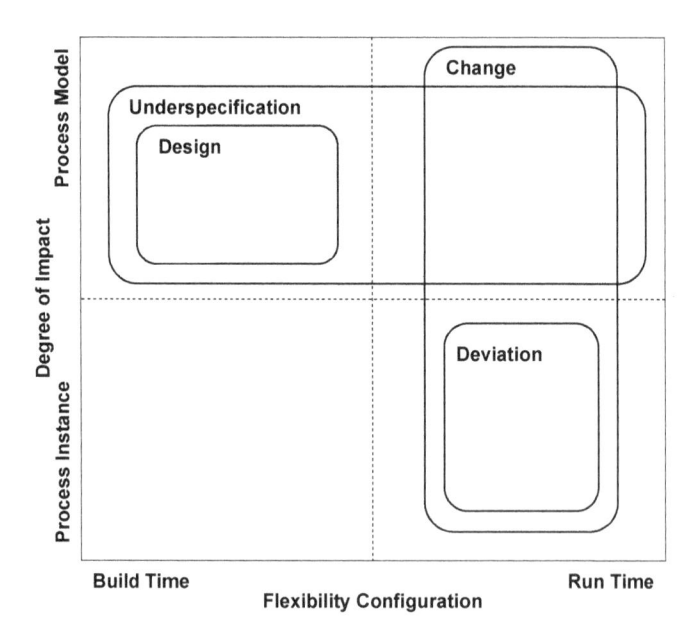

Figure 2.14. Flexibility Type Spectrum with regard to Flexibility Configuration and Degree of Impact based on van der Aalst [182]

To clarify the difference between flexibility by change and by deviation, a further differentiation concerning necessary user experience is made (see Fig. 2.15). Here, the main advantage of flexibility by deviation is emphasized, as it is the only type that allows flexibility at run time without the need of a high user experience or expertise.

Concluding, there are various types of workflow flexibility that differ concerning several aspects. The challenge is to find the flexibility

2.4. WORKFLOW FLEXIBILITY

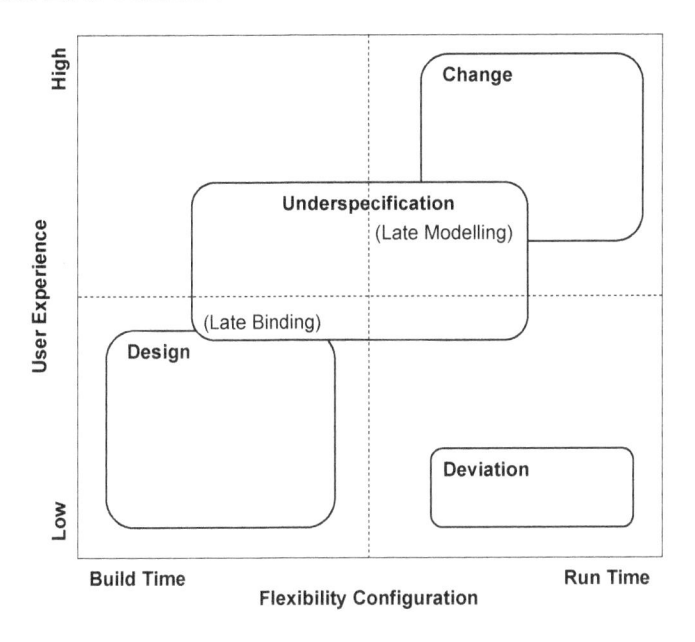

Figure 2.15. Flexibility Type Spectrum with regard to Flexibility Configuration and User Experience

type that is adequate for the specific considered requirements, which are sometimes even conflicting [109].

Flexibility by design, change and underspecification either require an entire awareness about all possible upcoming situations at build time in order to manually model all possible alternatives, or a remodelling of the workflow is necessary at run time. Both strategies are nearly impossible for SMEs. One reason is that unforeseen situations or unexpected circumstances can happen at any time. Moreover, remodelling a workflow requires certain expertise. This includes detailed knowledge about the process itself and the impacts that the changes can entail. Process participants are usually only aware of a specific part of the process that relates to the tasks they need to accomplish, but the remaining parts are like black boxes. Thus, undesirable side effects may occur due to this superficial knowledge and inexperience. Furthermore, process participants lack process modelling know-how in order to be able to remodel the workflow. With flexibility by deviation, the process participant is able to execute tasks that are not suggested as next activity, as the worklist is only seen as a guideline. An increased user acceptance is therefore assumed. Single instances may not fit to the process model. This however raises the problem of deciding how to continue with the deviating workflow to achieve a successful completion. To solve this problem a workflow engine that facilitates flexibility by deviation is presented in this work.

Moreover, when achieving flexibility for processes, it is inevitable to regard to which extent and what type of flexibility is necessary and appropriate for the specific use case [20]. In either direction, usability decreases, whereas too much flexibility additionally decreases support in most cases [50, 135]

2.4.5. Flexibility Trade-Off

When modelling workflows, it is generally important to find the ideal balance between control and flexibility depending on the domain in which the WfMS is applied. The benefit is significantly dependent on this trade-off. Flexibility and support seem to be two opposing properties of a WfM (see Fig. 2.16) [134, 167]. Here, support describes the extent to which the system is responsible for decision making and to which extent the user can decide independently [134]. Thus, support behaves proportionally to the extent of pre-definition. The more is predefined, the more the user is supported, but the less flexible behaviour is permitted. The challenge is to find the right balance between these two properties.

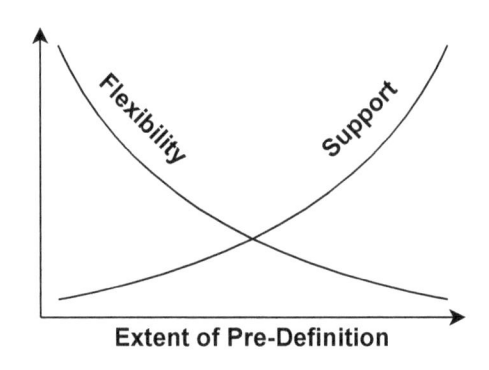

Figure 2.16. Trade-Off between Flexibility and Support due to the Extent of Pre-Definition based on Pešić [134]

This also affects the aspect of usability that decreases in either direction, starting from the most balanced point. Too much flexibility impedes the acceptance of a system due to a lack of guidance, whereas too much support might restrict and lead to a workaround and a bypassing of the system. Bider [19] argues similarly and uses the notion *rigidity*. He argues that rigidity also needs to be balanced with flexibility to achieve a high user acceptance [19]. As the perfect amount of rigidity cannot be accomplished from the beginning, flexibility needs to be enabled in the background. For an easy-to-use system, the user needs to be guided in a simple way. Thus, too much flexibility from the beginning on is also counterproductive for usability.

Another important point that indirectly relates to support is compliance. The more flexibility is allowed the more effort is necessary to validate compliance [157]. As resources are often scarce, a trade-off has to be made as well. A high flexibility but potentially no compliance needs to be weighed against rigid workflow behaviour that is compliant.

For creating an adequate flexible workflow management, all these aspects need to be considered and required characteristics and applied methods need to be assessed. The concept of the developed flexible workflow approach for the use case that is regarded in this thesis will be presented in Chapter 5.

2.5. Related Work

Workflow flexibility has been focused on in research for more than a decade now and thus many approaches exist. As the previous section has shown, there are various characteristics and aspects that can be investigated and concentrated on. But still some issues fall short, notably flexibility by deviation or, broadly speaking, the automated handling of unforeseen situations and exceptions. Nonetheless, there is potential for future research.

In the following, an overview of related approaches will be given.

Besides established modelling languages, like BPMN, rather novel declarative languages for handling flexibility issues emerge, i.e. flexibility by design, as they offer implicit flexibility to some extent.

Freeflow is a constraint-based language that is based on an extended state model of activities in order to separate the user view from the system view [41]. Due to these extended capabilities of specifying dependencies, a more flexible design of workflows is possible that results in flexibility at run time.

Tucupi is a workflow approach based on constraints that specify pre and post conditions [196]. Hence, the sequence of activities is dynamically build at run time during execution. Additionally, authorized users are able to adapt specific constraints at run time. Nevertheless, these constraints are very simple and neither repetition of activities nor temporal constraints except regarding order are possible.

Khomyakov and Bider [79] pursue a similar rule-based approach. They create the workflow through dynamic planning at run time after each executed activity. At build time, three different types of rules need to be specified, i.e. obligations, prohibitions and recommendations [79]

ESProNa (Engine for Semantic Process Navigation) is a workflow engine that builds upon a novel constraint-based modelling language [73]. The constraints can be specified for each of the process perspectives presented in Subsection 2.3.5.1 and can additionally be enhanced with semantic and relational knowledge on the basis of Resource Description Framework (RDF) data graphs. The workflow approach applies reasoning in combination with a planning component to automatically evaluate the process model concerning executability on the basis of the specified constraints.

Klingemann [84] proposes an approach that additionally allows for a modelling of non-structural goals. Modelling elements are enhanced by so called *flexible elements* (FE) that contain execution alternatives. The workflow engine optimizes the workflow model during run time, thereby balancing goals that are to be achieved. These can base on quality criteria, structural aspects as well as combined parameters.

A main disadvantage of these approaches is that they are based on knowledge that needs to be specified effortfully beforehand. Aside from that, it is unclear or rather unrealistic that the known information is sufficient to map all upcoming situations.

With flexibility by change, process participants are enabled to adapt the running instance due to altered conditions. Various approaches exist that apply different methods to supervise these adaptations in order to ensure valid and consistent results and to guarantee legitimacy. However, knowledge or rules need to be specified beforehand for this purpose, which additionally creates overhead.

ADEPT is an adaptive WfMS that mainly implements flexibility by change [144]. A graph-based modelling language is used that builds upon block structuring to ensure correctness by construction [142]. ADEPT$_{\text{flex}}$ as part of the WfMS includes a set of possible change operations, i.e. insert, omit or skip the order of activities

2.5. RELATED WORK

[143]. Modelled pre and post conditions for these operations allow for evaluating correctness and consistency, and thus, decide about denying or allowing the specific change [143]. Additionally ADEPT offers schema evolution with techniques for a safe propagation of changes to running instances [144]. Furthermore, it allows for specifying temporal constraints of tasks, like maximum duration or deadlines that are observed through temporal constraint networks [144].

In the ensuing project ADEPT2, the possible ad hoc change operations were further refined and extended [30, 145]. Furthermore, the modelling capabilities were enhanced, as additionally process fragments can be reused through plug & play [30]. The ADEPT platform has been further elaborated and subsequently transformed to a commercial product, which is already used by different industries, the AristaFlow BPM Suite [32].

KitCom is a prototypical implementation and extends the AristaFlow BPM Suite [81, 157]. It uses the FlexCom method to guarantee compliance and flexibility simultaneously. At build time, individual control processes concerning compliance measures are implemented with parameters that are connected to the procedural workflow model. During execution, if these conditions come into effect, the modelled control process is injected automatically into the workflow instance to meet the compliance requirements. Hence, this approach allows for automated dynamic change.

MOKASSIN is another flexible workflow approach that focusses on the distributed and collaborative execution [74]. They define so called control-flow dependencies to extend and relax the standard execution semantics. As formal basis, ECA rules are used, which describe the control-flow and the dependencies. Additionally, these ECA rules are used to support dynamic changes, but to a limited extent.

Vieira et al. pursue a similar rule-based approach but for handling a different obstacle, in particular dealing with incomplete and negative information [192]. As formal basis they use an ontology where semantic knowledge is stored, such as semantic rules or proximity properties. Two mechanisms that exploit this ontology are applied, on the one hand to compute presuppositions, and on the other hand for choosing and evaluating alternatives, for instance subworkflows, resources, or users [191].

WASA is a workflow approach that has been developed specifically for scientific applications that supports flexibility by change [194, 204].

The user can actively intervene in the execution process by skipping, stopping or repeating an activity [203]. Dynamic changes are allowed through including modelling activities in the workflow model at build time for such process parts that are unknown, which corresponds to flexibility by underspecification [203]. Furthermore during run time, the user is able to integrate these modelling activities at any time in the process, allowing him to adapt some parts at run time [203].

Wagner applies a different technique to yield flexible run time changes [195]. The approach *agentworkflow* is based on hierarchical nested subworkflows that can be substituted under consideration of different aspect. One agent is responsible for the flawless connection and (re-)configuration of the subworkflows and each of these subworkflows is controlled by another agent, formally basing on Petri nets.

Worklets are similar to agentworkflows, as they represent self-contained subworkflows that can be nested and dynamically connected at run time [3]. Worklets can be specified with Yet Another Workflow Language (YAWL) and a service evaluates at run time on the basis of contextual data, which worklets can substitute a task of the workflow instance.

With CF4BPMN, which is an extension for BPMN, controlled flexibility is enabled [107]. Possible changes are specified as constraints, defining roles with authorizations such that compliance is ensured. These possible changes are marked in BPMN models. The unique aspect of this approach is the graphical component of visualising possible parts of the process where the process participant is allowed to apply changes.

DECLARE is a constraint-based workflow approach using ConDec [137] as declarative modelling language [135, 184, 207]. The language is formally based on linear temporal logic formulae that are translated to automata. The approach is suitable for loosely structured processes and allows ad hoc changes at run time by adapting constraint models.

Approaches that implement flexibility by underspecification are a kind of mixture of flexibility by design and by change, as they on the one hand require flexible modelling aspects for placeholders and late binding capabilities at build time, but on the other hand modelling expertise is necessary at run time, at least to a certain extent.

The approach called *pockets of flexibility* perfectly fits to the type flexibility by underspecification [158]. The workflow is divided in the core process and the integrated pockets of flexibility. These

2.5. RELATED WORK

pockets represent placeholders that are concretised at run time. One pocket of flexibility consists of workflow fragments and a build activity that defines through declarative constraints how the pocket can be composed. Thus, procedural and declarative modelling constructs are combined in one model. Late modelling and late binding are both implemented through this approach.

WorkWare is a flow-based modelling language that allows unspecified parts [75]. The pursued concept intends an interactive decision making involving the process participants where necessary and thereby supporting emergent workflow behaviour.

Schmalen [165] proposes a reference model for adaptive WfM that allows ad hoc changes through late modelling. Through introducing the concept of breakpoints, parts of the workflow instance can be blocked during execution and thereby enabling structural modifications at run time, at least in the disabled subworkflow. Predefined adaptation rules ensure that consistency is preserved despite the made changes. In the work of Minor et al. [115], a concept is introduced that enhances the previously described approach as ad-hoc changes of ongoing workflows are supported by means of case-based reasoning. Therefore, new concepts for a workflow modelling language and a workflow enactment service are described and a similarity measure on the basis of a graph edit distance is specified to allow for a reuse of change experience.

YAWL is a novel modelling language, allowing a variety of workflow patterns [185]. Control-flow as well as other dependencies including all of the existing modelling perspectives (cf. Subsection 2.3.5.1) can be specified. The formal basis for the language are extended workflow nets. Worklets, as described before, can be used for dynamic changes during run time [2].

Case handling was developed as a new paradigm with focus on data and what can be done instead of how it can be done [188]. The overall workflow, denoted as case, is always regarded as a whole. Process participants are aware of every information available instead of concentrating on one work item. Tasks are activated on the basis of available information in contrast to terminated activities as precondition. Data can be added or modified at any time of the workflow independent from related tasks. Furthermore, the concept of roles and authorizations is expanded to executing, skipping and redoing activities. Thus, the approach allows controlled deviations on task and process level.

FLOWer is a system that applies the case handling paradigm and offers a modelling language to define several different relations between tasks and data [188]. The previously mentioned aspects are also implemented in FLOWer, most importantly the possibility to deviate flexibly at run time without losing control, which is limited to skip, redo, undo, and creating a new instance of a task.

PHILharmonicFlows is a workflow framework for the support of object-aware processes [23, 88]. The focus is on the data flow similar to the case handling paradigm. Process modelling is based on the specification of relations between tasks, data, functions, and users.

Concerning flexibility by deviation, no approaches exist that are able to cope without manually predefined knowledge or a necessary active interference of the process participant to achieve a deviation. Some approaches concerning exception handling exist that will be presented in Chapter 6.

Chapter 3
Domain & Potentials

This chapter gives an overview of the main concept, which allows for workflow flexibility by deviation, and its potentials in the regarded domain of deficiency management in construction. In the first Section 3.1, an exemplary typical, ideal but simple workflow for deficiency management in construction will be presented. On the basis of an extended workflow, which aims at mapping all possible occurring situations, the gap between ideal and factual state space is revealed. Due to this discrepancy, arising potentials and general necessities of a flexible approach that is adequate for SMEs are pointed out in the subsequent Section 3.2. Finally in Section 3.3, the pursued flexible workflow approach is sketched in comparison to the traditional process cycle.

3.1. Deficiency Management in Construction

As elucidated in the introduction of this thesis, SMEs are the target group of the designed approach. To emphasize the potential of a flexible workflow system for SMEs, one concrete real-world use case is presented in this section, which is also referred to as running example and used throughout the evaluation of the approach.

Deficiency management in construction has proven potential as use case for handling with a flexible PAIS [51]. In the research project SEMAFLEX, we cooperated with a construction company that gave us a first insight into the process. As they did not use any information system so far, there was no process model available. Therefore, we developed a simple ideal workflow model in consultation with the employees that represents the standard way of handling a deficiency in construction (see Fig. 3.1). The workflow is seen from the perspective of a construction management.

3.1.1. Simple Ideal Workflow Model for Deficiency Management in Construction

In the shown workflow in Fig. 3.1, tasks are represented as rectangles, whereas ovals indicate data nodes. Control-flow nodes (e.g. exclusive blocks marked with an "×") are shown as rhombuses. The solid lines represent the control-flow and dashed lines mark data-flow. Each data node represents a document, which consists of several data attributes that influence different other tasks. Some annotations are written next to control-flow edges, to add information about the decisions taken and their impact. These annotations refer to information that can be drawn from the documents in most cases.

The ordinary processing of a case concerning deficiency management starts with receiving a notice of defects. The subsequent activities correspond to checking preconditions for a possible repair on the basis of different data, e.g. the contract. This includes verifying the scope of work and warranty, as well as inspecting the reported defect. For this purpose, documents such as the approval or photos of the inspected defect are involved. After checking the competence, the scope of responsibility of the affected part of the building is investigated. Subsequently, the reported defect is either forwarded to the subcontractor who is responsible for the affected unit of work or the defect is processed further by the own company. If the latter applies, the cause and thus, the responsibility has to be identified. If the defect was caused by the company, the repair is planned, performed, and then either accepted or these steps are repeated until acceptance. In case the responsibility is on the subcontractors' side, the following step after notification is receiving the information about a terminated repair. The workflow finishes in both cases (own company or subcontractor repairing the defect) with a customer notification about the completed repair process and the corresponding corrected or declined defect, if no other exception caused a termination priorly.

This workflow describes the ideal scenario and processing of a workflow. Nevertheless, unusual situations happen and circumstances change continuously, whether due to varying customer requirements

3.1. DEFICIENCY MANAGEMENT IN CONSTRUCTION   57

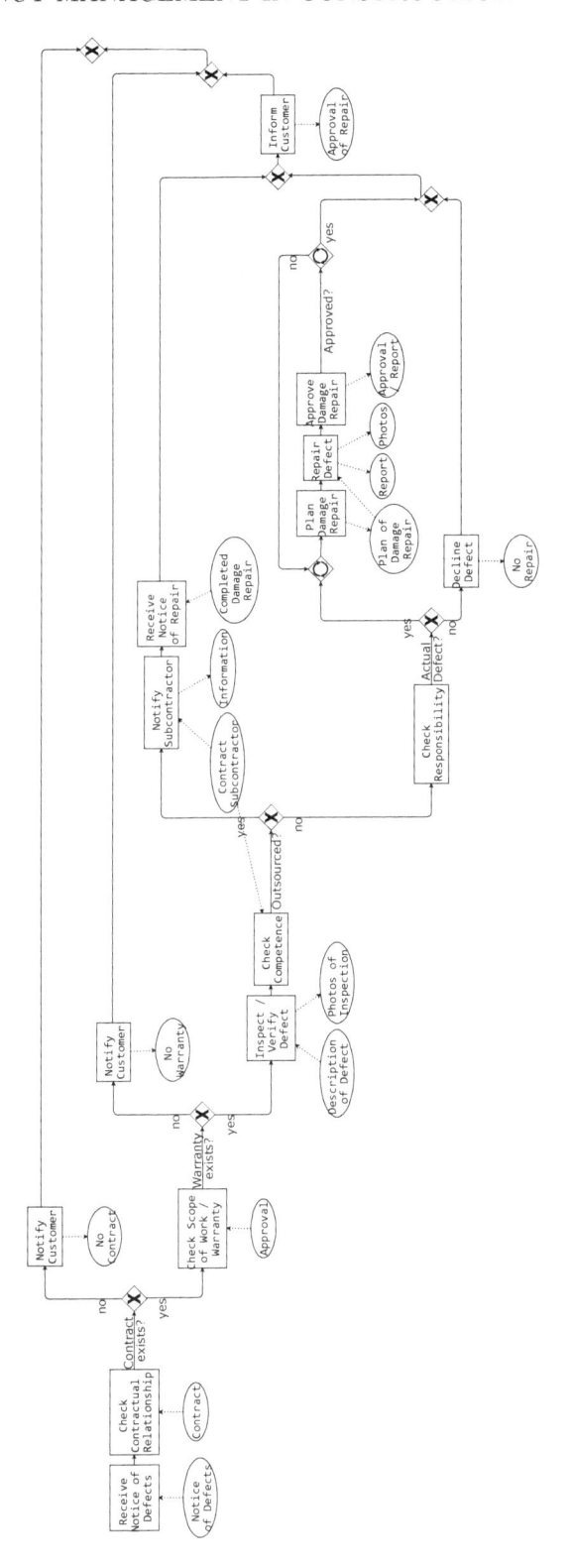

Figure 3.1. Simple Ideal Workflow Model for Deficiency Management in Construction

or modified legal restrictions and obligations. The range of possible deviations is rather complex. To map as many deviations as possible, obviously only foreseeable ones, we developed a second workflow model (cf. Fig. 3.2 - 3.5).

3.1.2. Extended Workflow Model for Deficiency Management in Construction

Based on the simple workflow model, we increased the degree of detail and tried to consider all possible alternative, realistic, and frequent scenarios. This lead to a very large and complex workflow model trying to capture the reality. This complex model resulted foremost from various discussions with an architect who frequently takes on the task of construction supervision and as a consequence is responsible for deficiency management.

The more complex and detailed workflow for deficiency management in construction allows more alternative executions paths that not only mix up the order of tasks but also contain newly introduced process parts. One main difference concerns the start of the workflow. In many cases the customer only sends an informal message that something was not build properly or that a defect appeared. Depending on the companies' guiding principles, a formal notice of defects, containing a deadline and urgency among other things, is subsequently requested, or the defect handling is based on the informal message. Afterwards, in contrast to the simple model, several checks can be made, but can also be omitted, e.g. in case of tacit awareness about the required decision knowledge. Furthermore, the tasks *Check Scope of Work* and *Check Warranty* can be executed in parallel.

Another differing aspect in some cases is the lack of a clear division or assignment of one unit of work regarding a possible subcontractor. An agreement with the involved subcontractor might be required before repairing the defect. Furthermore, two additional alternatives are integrated into the model, which mainly concern the billing of the repair. This results either in requesting an insurance for bearing the incurred costs or suggesting to pay a compensation to the customer, e.g. in case the defect is not severe.

In this detailed model some additional documents and data objects appear, but without impact on the control-flow. In most cases some alternative documents were added, which serve as input for some tasks, but with an optional character, as one of those documents is sufficient to obtain the required information. For instance, the contractual relationship can be checked on the basis of a *confirmation of order*, an *invoice*, an *offer*, the *contract* itself, or even a *verbal confirmation*.

These dependencies partially result from the point of time during the project, at which some of the documents do not exist yet. In some cases, tasks can be handled without explicit documents and decisions are made on the basis of other data. One example is the so-called *fictitious approval*, which is depicted as data object in Fig. 3.3, but it rather arises due to specific circumstance, for instance the occupancy of the building or the timeline. Some decisions prior to control-flow nodes are more sophisticated due to the influence of several or additional data attributes.

As can be seen from this detailed workflow model, the complexity increases rapidly when adding new alternatives, as there are various interdependencies, e.g. between data objects. Deviating from the prescribed path of the simple workflow model without deeper knowledge or predetermined strategies is challenging and raises questions about how to proceed. Nevertheless, as it is practically impossible to consider all possible upcoming situations, deviations need to be supported in an automated manner in order not to impede efficacy, efficiency, and ultimately flexibility.

3.2. Potentials of a Flexible Workflow Approach

The potentials of a flexible workflow approach are derived by analysing the current state of the art in SMEs. Furthermore, some examples are described that present actual use cases of a flexible approach. Based on this, requirements are listed.

3.2.1. State of the Art

The current way of handling deviations in the company with which we cooperated during the SEMAFLEX project is rather rudimentary and does not consider any of these desired aspects. It is assumed that a majority of SMEs, especially in certain industries like the craft sector, are comparable, particularly regarding the prevalence of digitalization and the use of information systems. So far, the reported deficiencies were registered and updated locally in a document with tabular form.

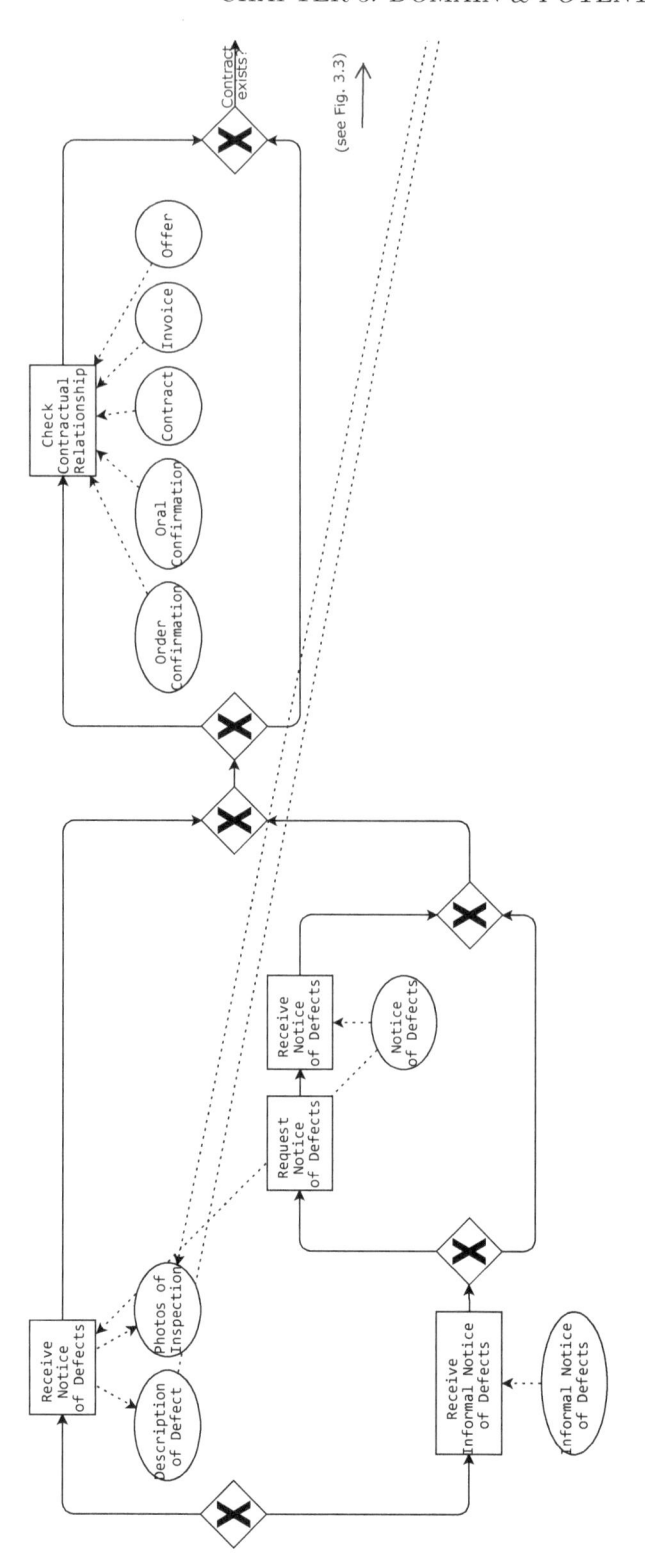

Figure 3.2. Extended Workflow Model for Deficiency Management in Construction, Part 1

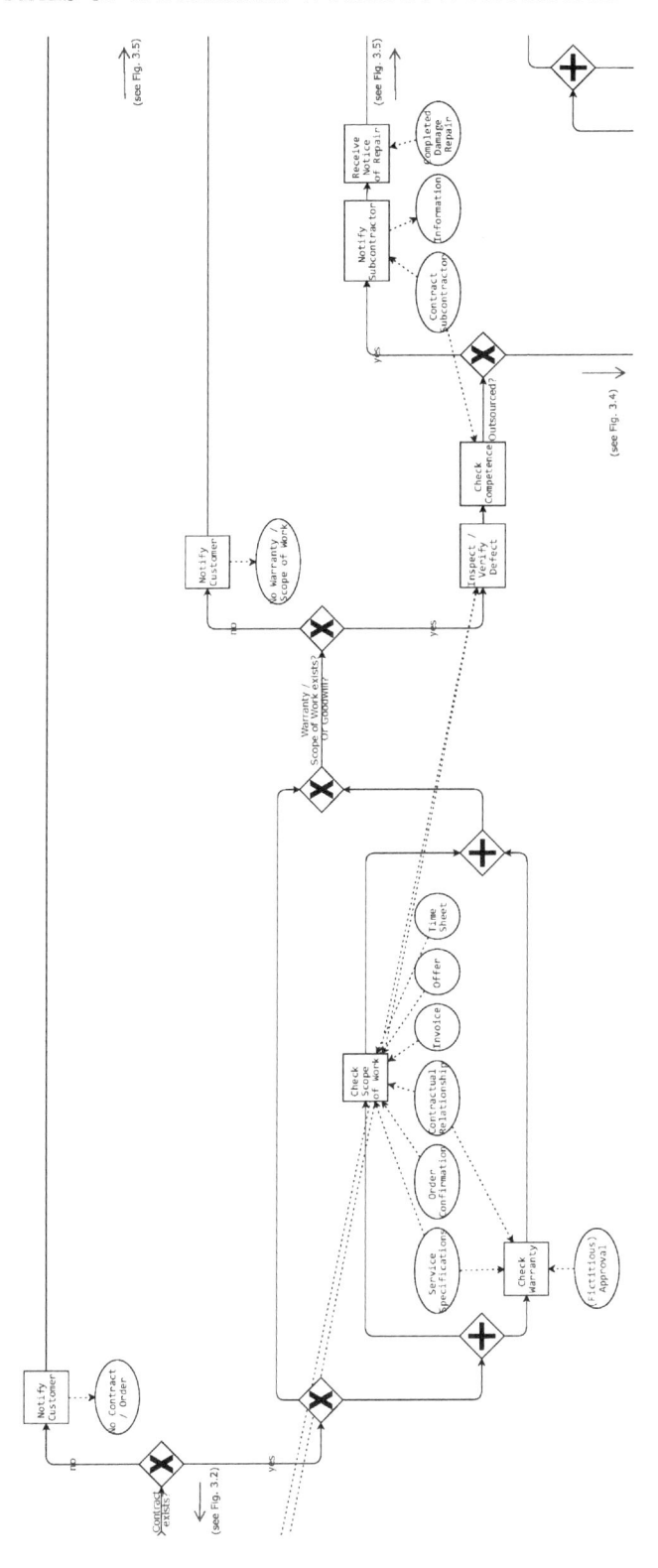

3.2. POTENTIALS OF A FLEXIBLE WORKFLOW APPROACH 61

Figure 3.3. Extended Workflow Model for Deficiency Management in Construction, Part 2

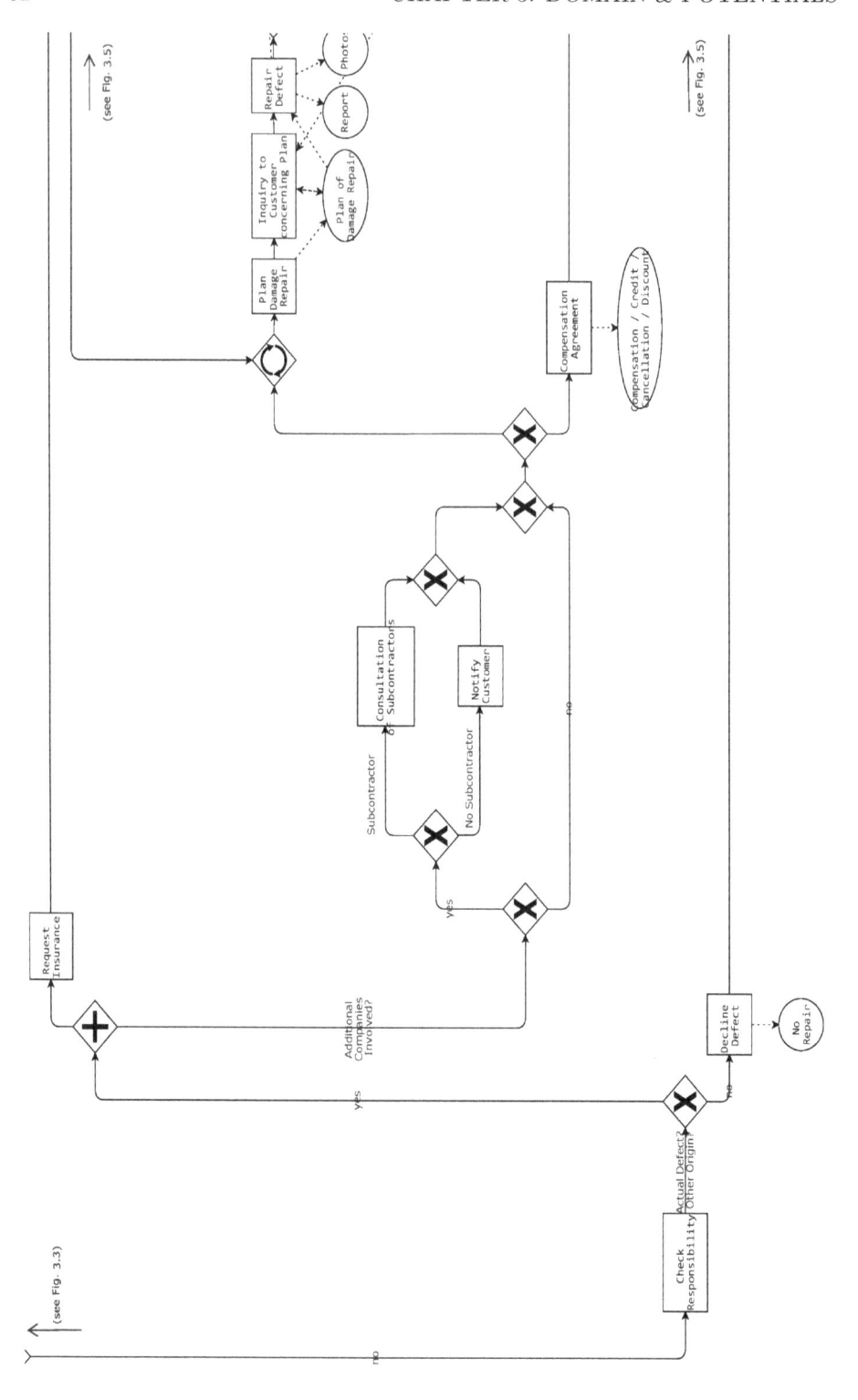

62   CHAPTER 3. DOMAIN & POTENTIALS

Figure 3.4. Extended Workflow Model for Deficiency Management in Construction, Part 3

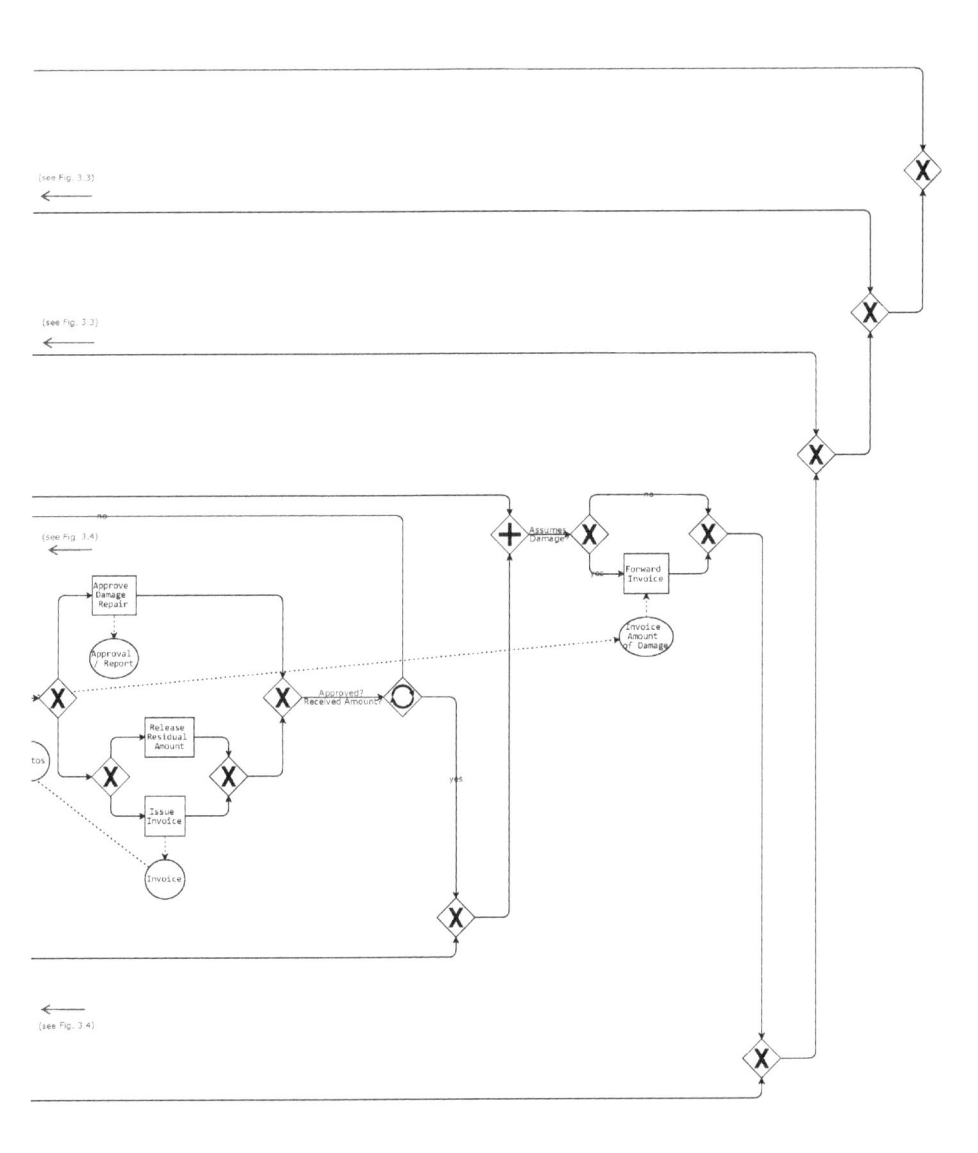

3.2. POTENTIALS OF A FLEXIBLE WORKFLOW APPROACH 63

Figure 3.5. Extended Workflow Model for Deficiency Management in Construction, Part 4

Updates that come from different sources, whether from the worker at the construction site or from a secretary in a bureau, are integrated in a cumbersome way. Obtaining some necessary information along the way is rather inconvenient and additionally requires a lot of communication.

Furthermore, the way of handling a deficiency is only available as tacit knowledge. Our interview with the construction company during the SEMAFLEX project showed that no explicit processes exist. The knowledge about how things are done and particularly how to solve problems is tacit and only known by experienced employees. Especially when exceptions or unusual situations occur, newly introduced employees are quickly overstrained and need to rely on support by long-term employees, which requires additional effort. Knowledge transfer, sharing, and reuse is so far done manually.

Thus, the introduction of a PAIS would yield several benefits. Nevertheless, standard PAISs with a traditional workflow integration raise some downsides. Above all, the lack of flexibility is the main drawback. In SMEs, the processes are not standardized, but rather individually adapted to customers needs. As employees tend to be more versatile and cover several competencies, unbureaucratic decisions and deviations are common. In case process participants undergo an unknown situation during the use of standard WfMS, they need to stick to the standard procedure or circumvent the system, which neglects flexibility and results in workarounds or suboptimal situations.

Another prerequisite for the use of a PAIS is the necessary knowledge and overhead concerning usage and maintenance. Both aspects need to be kept quite low in order to achieve an effective application and simultaneously a high acceptance, as SMEs rather have few personnel resources and no experience concerning workflow management and PAISs. Hence, a flexible workflow system adequate for SMEs should be easy to use and maintain.

3.2.2. Exemplary Use Cases

A typical use case where flexibility by deviation is beneficial is if a construction worker is on site and gets aware of a defect. S/he very likely implicitly knows about the scope of work and warranty without checking the contract additionally, and hence, avoiding the bureaucratic burden. Thus, s/he is able to directly inspect and verify

3.2. POTENTIALS OF A FLEXIBLE WORKFLOW APPROACH 65

the defect by taking some photos. With a flexible PAIS, that could run in an instance on his mobile phone, the employee is enabled to directly upload these photos and inform the system about the task execution. All previous tasks can be marked as skipped or implicitly executed depending on the context or set preferences. On the basis of an adapted workflow instance, new task suggestions can be computed. In this example, flexibility would lead to an increased efficiency and acceptance.

Thus, the system is no burden for the experienced process participant, as unlike in standard WfMSs not every step has to be executed explicitly from the beginning on. Actually enacted tasks are monitored and even if deviations occur, possible succeeding work items are computed and proposed, as in this example: *Check Competence*. Additionally, conclusions considering implicit semantic information can be drawn from the workflow model, taking preceding skipped activities into account. Here, the system would derive that a contract exists between customer and company and that the reported defect is in the scope of work and included in warranty.

Two different workflow models were shown in the previous section. Common practice is that a very simple workflow, which represents the ideal course of action, is modelled (cf. Subsect. 3.1.1), whereas in reality a variety of other situations can occur that do not match the implemented workflow (cf. Subsect. 3.1.2 and additional unpredictable execution paths). With the presented approach it should be possible to apply such a simplified ideal workflow model to the WfMS. Nevertheless during execution, deviations from this model are allowed. Still, the flexible WfMS should support the user on the basis of, e.g. previously made experiences or simply by restoring model consistency due to defined strategies.

For instance, when considering the start of the workflow, the possibility of receiving solely an informal message about a deficiency is not included in the simple workflow model. An inexperienced employee is not aware of how to handle such a situation. If an experienced operator encountered such circumstances before and decided to simply proceed with the workflow without requesting a formal notice of defects, this terminated workflow instance can be used for knowledge transfer. The vision is to reuse these previously executed tasks after the deviation as proposal in order to increase support and efficiency. In the example, *Check Contractual Relationship* would be suggested among other tasks. Thus, exceptions, deadlocks, and workarounds are prevented.

3.2.3. Requirements

In summary, the following requirements for a flexible workflow approach that supports SMEs in particular exemplified by the workflow of deficiency management in construction are derived:

RE1: Flexibility

- Allowed Deviations
- Continuous Support

RE2: Knowledge Transfer

- Preservation
- Sharing
- Reuse

RE3: Low Effort

- Usability
- Maintainability
- Experience

One main required aspect of the presented approach is flexibility. Deviations from the predefined workflow model should be allowed. However, continuous support during workflow execution should be guaranteed without leading to deadlocks or requiring workarounds. The second essential aspect addresses the basis for the success of such a continuous support that is to say knowledge transfer. Previously made experiences by process participants should not remain tacit, but necessarily be preserved somehow in order to share this knowledge and ultimately to reuse it for a profound decision making. An additional impact of this knowledge transfer is the possibility to identify and establish "best practices". The third substantial requirement that is important for a successful deployment in SMEs concerns a low effort to achieve the previously mentioned points, i.e. flexibility and knowledge transfer. No expert knowledge or past experiences should be required in order to be able to use and maintain the presented WfMS.

The recognized demands are consistent with the research by Gessinger and Bergmann [51] to a great extent. In this work three main requirements for systems to be adequate for deficiency management in construction are identified. Two of them are relevant for the presented work. The first one considers a support for process flexibility, which is the essential aspect that is tackled by this work. The third requirement regards the preservation and sharing of knowledge about best-practice processes, which is another substantial point of this work. Knowledge transfer is the technique that simplifies a controlled support of a flexible execution and thus, it is a necessary prerequisite and an improvement to the quality of support. Gessinger and Bergmann [51] emphasize that this knowledge sharing and reuse is essential to adequately deal with the continuously rising demand for decision support in processes.

To integrate the described flexibility, the standard workflow cycle needs to be modified, which is introduced in the following section.

3.3. Main Concept

The main drawback of the standard workflow cycle (cf. Fig. 2.3) is the lack of deviation possibilities. A main aspect that is allowed in the developed concept of this work is the ability to deviate. This means that the enacted task does not comply with the proposed elements in the worklist. This issue is represented in Fig. 3.6. Due to this occurred deviation, the flexible workflow engine is forced to interfere by adapting the workflow instance in order to re-enable worklist computations. A more detailed description of the functionality of the workflow engine and applied methods is given in the following chapters. Chapter 5 elucidates the constraint-based workflow engine, which is foremost responsible for offering flexibility. Furthermore, the constraint-based language is introduced, through which it is possible to automatically generate workflow models on the basis of procedurally modelled workflows. Hence, no deeper knowledge about a formal language is necessary and no additional effort has to be taken to allow deviations. The case-based deviation management, which is explained in Chapter 6, further refines the handling of deviations by integrating experiential knowledge into the process of computing work items.

The high topicality of the regarded issue in BPM research is also

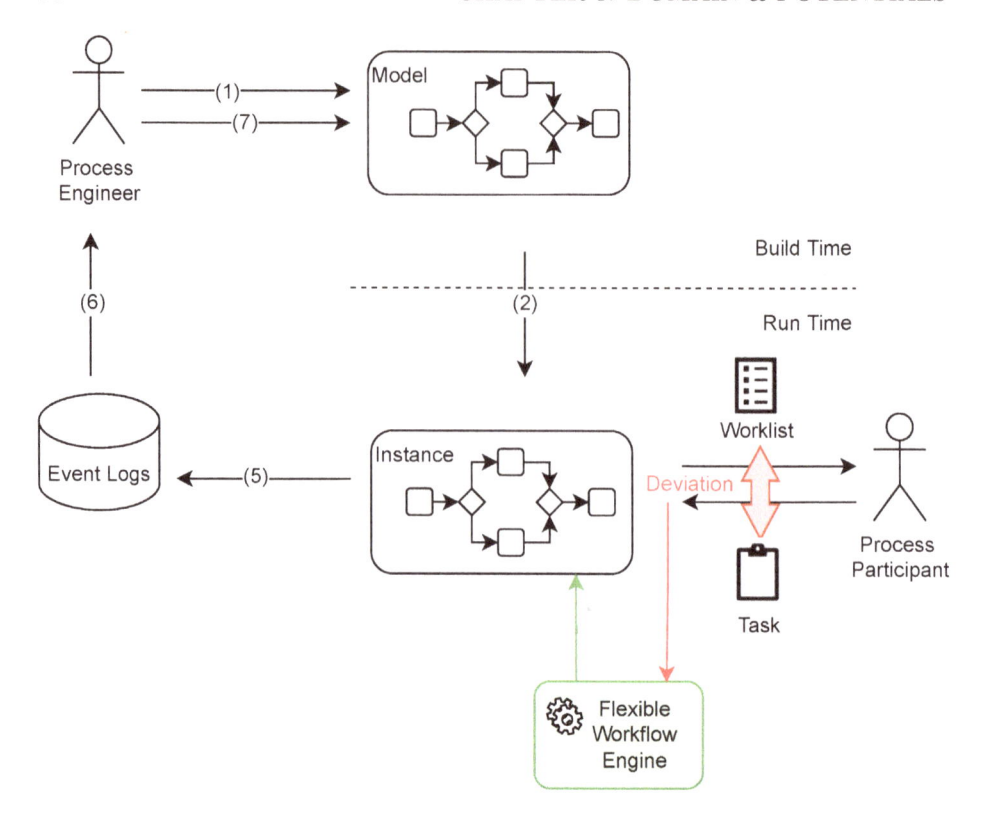

Figure 3.6. Business Process Life Cycle with Flexible Workflow Engine

reflected by a survey of van der Aalst [182]. He presented several core issues considered in BPM research [182]. In this work some of them are investigated and concepts are introduced that can be categorized into the presented classification by van der Aalst [182]. In the *auditing* field the activity *detect* is tackled by the constraint-based workflow engine that detects deviations from the process model by comparing the de facto instances to the de jure process model. In a subsequent step *promote* is regarded. To establish best practices, all terminated process instances can be mined to a new process model and parts can be transferred to the previous de jure workflow. Concerning *navigation* the activity *explore* is supported by this approach. Running instances are compared to terminated ones to initiate actions at run time, e.g. recommending deviating tasks. *Recommend* is only partly assisted, as there is no concrete optimization goal in the considered workflows, but only success. In this concern the most promising steps are chosen to be suggested to the process participant for execution.

Chapter 4

Prerequisites

This chapter addresses necessary prerequisites. For a formal specification of the developed approach, some basic definitions are crucial. Workflows are described as a special form of graphs, which are defined in Sect. 4.1. The approach is not applicable to all forms of workflows, but limited to block-oriented workflows. Therefore, this restriction to block-orientation is specified and exemplified with small instances in Sect. 4.2. Furthermore, to clarify the execution semantics, which are characterized in Sect. 4.4, execution paths and operators are defined preliminarily in Sect. 4.3.

4.1. Graphs

Workflows describe the way of how to reach one specific goal through the execution of several tasks. These tasks are connected in a specific direction and order. Directed graphs serve this purpose precisely and thus, are used as a formal basis for workflows. The subsequent definitions are made according to Cormen et al. [27].

Definition 4.1 (Directed Graph). *A directed graph G is a pair (N, E), where N is a finite set and E is a binary relation on N: $E \subseteq N \times N$. The set N is called the node set of G, and its elements are called nodes. The set E is called the edge set of G, and its elements are called edges.*

Graphs can further be decomposed into subgraphs, which only represent parts of the original graph.

Definition 4.2 (Subgraph). *Let $G = (N, E)$ be a graph, then $G' = (N', E')$ is a subgraph of G, iff it holds that $N' \subseteq N$ and $E' \subseteq E$.*

Further, as one important property of nodes, the *degree* with two specializations is introduced.

Definition 4.3 (Degree, In-Degree, Out-Degree). *In a directed graph, the out-degree of a node is the number of edges leaving it, out-degree(n) = $|(n, m)|$ with $n, m \in N$ and $(n, m) \in E$, and the in-degree of a node is the number of edges entering it, in-degree(n) = $|(m, n)|$ with $n, m \in N$ and $(m, n) \in E$. The degree of a node in a directed graph is its in-degree plus its out-degree.*

To specify the composition of nodes and edges, this property can be restricted through values that are valid.

4.2. Block-Oriented Workflows

A definition of block-oriented workflows is presented on the basis of a graph-based definition of workflows in general. Workflows are composed of tasks that interact with data objects. These tasks are connected, defining dependencies such as order. Control-flow nodes are responsible for splitting up one task sequence into two sequences or inversely joining two sequences into one. These control-flow nodes reflect a logical operation, such as "and" to express parallel tasks. Different edge types are used to connect these workflow elements. Data-flow edges indicate the input or output of a data object for a task. Control-flow edges specify the order among tasks or between a task and a control-flow node.

Definition 4.4 (Workflow). *A workflow is a directed graph $W = (N, E)$ where N is a set of nodes and $E \subseteq N \times N$ is a set of edges. Nodes $N = N^D \cup N^T \cup N^C$ can be data nodes N^D, task nodes N^T, or control-flow nodes N^C. In addition, $N^S = N^T \cup N^C$ is referred to as the set of sequence nodes, i.e., task nodes as well as control-flow nodes. Edges $E = E^C \cup E^D$ can be control-flow edges $E^C \subseteq N^S \times N^S$, which define the order of the sequence nodes, or data-flow edges $E^D \subseteq (N^D \times N^S) \cup (N^S \times N^D)$, which define how data is shared between the tasks.*

An example workflow graph is shown in Fig. 4.1. Task nodes $N^T = \{t_1, t_2, t_3, t_4\}$ are represented by rectangles and data nodes $N^D = \{d_1, d_2\}$ are depicted as ovals. Rhombuses indicate control-flow

4.2. BLOCK-ORIENTED WORKFLOWS

nodes $N^C = \{cs, cj\}$, in this case a parallel control-flow block ("+") with a split cs and a join node cj. Control-flow edges connect task and control-flow nodes. Dashed lines mark data-flow edges that represent input or output relationships.

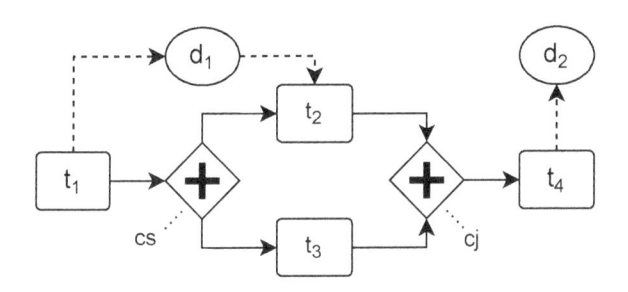

Figure 4.1. Example of a Workflow Graph

The exemplary workflow simultaneously fulfils every criteria of block-oriented workflows, which are introduced subsequently. The designed workflow engine is able to handle these specific kind of workflows. The paradigm of regular block structuring was introduced by Reichert [142] to guarantee model correctness by construction [80, 120]. This additionally enables an easily ensured consistency when adapting such workflows.

A block-oriented workflow is composed of single blocks that comprise various types. These blocks can in turn contain several blocks or be nested in one another. The most important property of these blocks is being well-formed due to a single definite starting and ending point.

The definition of block-oriented workflows that is made in this work only integrates some types of workflow blocks. In particular, such types are considered that conform to the most common and essential control-flow patterns that are part of prevalent workflow modelling languages [205, p. 126–130]. This is done in order to simplify the introduction of the approach and to reduce complexity. Furthermore, a study showed that business process modellers only use a fraction of languages like BPMN [216]. Thus, it is assumed that the used subset of patterns offers basic sufficient functionality. Further patterns, which are required in a specific domain, might be introduced in future work.

The main element of block-oriented workflows is a workflow block, which is defined as follows.

Definition 4.5 (Workflow Block). *Let $W = (N, E)$ be a workflow. A workflow subgraph $B = (N_B^S, E_B^C)$ is called workflow block, if it holds $N_B^S \subseteq N^S$ and $E_B^C = \{(n, n') | (n, n') \in E^C \wedge n, n' \in N_B^S\}$ and it has one of the forms, which are defined in Def. 4.6 - 4.9 together with the definition of their first and last element, $first(B) \in N_B^S$ and $last(B) \in N_B^S$.*

The simplest form of a workflow block comprises only one task node.

Definition 4.6 (Single Task Block). *A single task block consists of a single task node $B = B^t$. Then we define $N_B^S = \{t\}$ and $E_B^C = \emptyset$ with $first(B) = last(B) = \{t\}$*

Fig. 4.2 shows a single task block with task t.

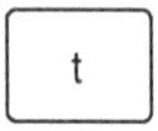

Figure 4.2. Single Task Block

To allow more than one task as a workflow block, two workflow blocks can be connected sequentially.

Definition 4.7 (Sequence Block). *A sequence block consists of a sequence of two workflow blocks $B = B^{(B_1, B_2)}$ with $B_1 = (N_{B_1}^S, E_{B_1}^C)$, $B_2 = (N_{B_2}^S, E_{B_2}^C)$ as workflow blocks of B and a control-flow edge $e = (last(B_1), first(B_2))$ and it holds $E_B^C = \{e\} \cup E_{B_1}^C \cup E_{B_2}^C$ and $N_B^S = N_{B_1}^S \cup N_{B_2}^S$. For the first and last elements of the block B we define $first(B) = first(B_1)$ and $last(B) = last(B_2)$.*

Fig. 4.3 shows an example of a sequence block, where blocks B_1 and B_2 (dashed rectangles) are concatenated sequentially, connected with a directed control-flow edge. This indicates that block B_1 has to be completed before block B_2 is enabled and can be started. B_1 and B_2 can in turn be any kind of workflow block according to Def. 4.6 - 4.9. The sequence block conforms with the sequence workflow pattern [205, p. 126–128].

Additionally to the sequential connection of two workflow blocks, control-flow nodes can be linked to workflow blocks, to serve different purposes and meanings.

4.2. BLOCK-ORIENTED WORKFLOWS

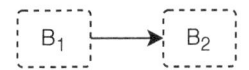

Figure 4.3. Sequence Block

Definition 4.8 (Exclusive or Parallel Control-Flow Block). *A control-flow block can be either an exclusive or a parallel block $B = B_{XOR}^{(B_1,B_2)}/B = B_{AND}^{(B_1,B_2)}$, with $B_1 = (N_{B_1}^S, E_{B_1}^C)$, $B_2 = (N_{B_2}^S, E_{B_2}^C)$ as workflow blocks of B. B contains an opening control-flow node $cs \in N_B^C$ (control-flow split) with an out-degree of two, two branches, which are outgoing from cs, each containing a workflow block (B_1 and B_2), whose control-flow lead to a matching closing control-flow node $cj \in N_B^C$ (control-flow join) with an in-degree of two. The control-flow nodes and block elements are connected through the following set of edges: $E_B^{C'} = \{(cs, first(B_1)), (cs, first(B_2)), (last(B_1), cj), (last(B_2), cj)\}$ and it holds $E_B^C = E_B^{C'} \cup E_{B_1}^C \cup E_{B_2}^C$ and $N_B^S = \{cs\} \cup \{cj\} \cup N_{B_1}^S \cup N_{B_2}^S$. First and last elements are the control-flow nodes: $first(B) = cs$ and $last(B) = cj$.*

Fig. 4.4 shows two exemplary control-flow blocks. Workflow blocks are represented as rectangles with dashed lines and control-flow nodes as rhombuses. Exclusive control-flow nodes are marked with an "×" and parallel control-flow nodes with a "+". The first control-flow node in each of the blocks indicates the control-flow split (named cs in Def. 4.8) and the last control-flow node indicates the control-flow join (named cj in Def. 4.8). This corresponds to the control flow patterns named *and split, and join, xor split* and *xor join* [205, p. 130f]. Here, the *and* patterns indicate that two concurrent branches are either opened up or merged again. In contrast, the two branches that follow an *xor split* are exclusive, such that one branch is chosen and the other one discarded. The *xor join* simply implies that the chosen branch is terminated, but in contrast to the *and* pattern no active synchronization of both branches takes place [205, p. 128f].

A special form of the exclusive control-flow block contains only one workflow block in one path, whereas the other path is left empty to indicate the conditional execution of the workflow block.

Definition 4.9 (Single-Branch Exclusive Control-Flow Block). *A single-branch exclusive control-flow block is an exclusive block $B = B_{XOR}^{B_1}$, where $B_1 = (N_{B_1}^S, E_{B_1}^C)$ is a workflow block of B, containing*

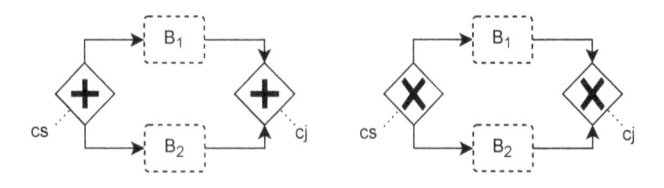

Figure 4.4. Parallel and Exclusive Control-Flow Block

an opening control-flow node $cs \in N_B^C$ with an out-degree of two, one branch with a workflow block (B_1), an empty branch and a matching closing control-flow node $cj \in N_B^C$ with an in-degree of two. The control-flow nodes and block elements are connected through the following set of edges: $E_B^{C'} = \{(cs, first(B_1)), (last(B_1), cj), (cs, cj)\}$ and it holds $E_B^C = E_B^{C'} \cup E_{B_1}^C$ and $N_B^S = N_{B_1}^S \cup \{cs\} \cup \{cj\}$. The first and last element are the control-flow nodes: $first(B) = cs$ and $last(B) = cj$.

Fig. 4.5 shows an exemplary single-branch exclusive block, where the control-flow split node has two outgoing edges, but only one of them leads to another workflow block, whereas the other one directly connects with the control-flow join node.

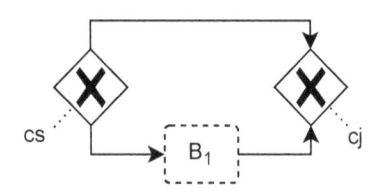

Figure 4.5. Single-Branch Exclusive Block

On the basis of these definitions for possible workflow blocks, the concept of block-oriented workflows can be specified accordingly.

Definition 4.10 (Block-Oriented Workflow). *A workflow $W = (N, E)$ is called block-oriented workflow, if it consists of a single workflow block.*

4.3. Execution Paths and Operators

For a definition of the execution semantics of block-oriented workflows, the general notion of execution paths and possible operators are introduced first.

4.3. EXECUTION PATHS AND OPERATORS

Definition 4.11 (Execution Path, Execution Path Set). *For a set of tasks N, an execution path $F_i = \langle f_1, ..., f_n \rangle$ is a sequence of tasks with $\{f_1, ..., f_n\} \subseteq N$. The function $pos(f_i)$ specifies the position of the element f_i in the sequence. $\mathcal{F} = \{F_1, ..., F_m\}$ is called execution path set, which contains several execution paths.*

For example, consider a set $N = \{a, b, c, d\}$, then $F_1 = \langle a, c, d \rangle$ is an execution path with $pos(c) = 2$.

In the following, we define operators on execution paths and execution path sets.

Definition 4.12 (Sequential Execution Paths). *Execution paths can be linked by the following operator: "$\circ$" combining both sets of activities sequentially in order as specified by the expression. Let $F_1 = \langle f_1, f_2, ..., f_n \rangle$ and $F_2 = \langle g_1, g_2, ..., g_m \rangle$ be execution paths and F_2 is appended to F_1, then the overall sequential execution path is defined as follows: $F_1 \circ F_2 := \langle f_1, f_2, ..., f_n, g_1, g_2, ..., g_m \rangle$.*

As an example, consider two execution paths $F_1 = \langle a, b, c \rangle$ and $F_2 = \langle d, e \rangle$. Then, $F_1 \circ F_2 = \langle a, b, c, d, e \rangle$.

Definition 4.13 (Sequential Combination of Execution Path Sets). *A sequential linking of execution path sets, indicated with the operator "$\odot$", describes all possible concatenations of single valid execution paths. Let $\mathcal{F}_1$ and $\mathcal{F}_2$ be execution path sets, then $\mathcal{F}_1 \odot \mathcal{F}_2 := \{F_1 \circ F_2 | F_1 \in \mathcal{F}_1 \wedge F_2 \in \mathcal{F}_2\}$.*

As an example, consider two execution path sets $\mathcal{F}_1 = \{\langle a, b, c \rangle, \langle m, n \rangle\}$ and $\mathcal{F}_2 = \{\langle d, e \rangle, \langle o, p, q \rangle\}$. Then, $\mathcal{F}_1 \odot \mathcal{F}_2 = \{\langle a, b, c, d, e \rangle, \langle m, n, d, e \rangle, \langle a, b, c, o, p, q \rangle, \langle m, n, o, p, q \rangle\}$.

Definition 4.14 (Parallel Execution Paths). *Let $F_1 = \langle f_1, f_2, ..., f_n \rangle$ and $F_2 = \langle g_1, g_2, ..., g_m \rangle$ be execution paths, then $F_1 \bowtie F_2$ is the execution path set consisting of all possible serializations of F1 and F2. This indicates the arbitrary merging of both paths into a single one, given that each sequential orders are adhered to. The operator is defined as follows: $F_1 \bowtie F_2 := \{\langle f_1 \rangle \circ rest_1 | rest_1 \in (\langle f_2, ..., f_n \rangle \bowtie F_2)\} \cup \{\langle g_1 \rangle \circ rest_2 | rest_2 \in (F_1 \bowtie \langle g_2, ..., g_m \rangle)\}$. It holds: $F_1 \bowtie F_2 = F_2 \bowtie F_1$.*

As an example, consider two execution paths $F_1 = \langle a, b \rangle$ and $F_2 = \langle c, d \rangle$. Then, $F_1 \bowtie F_2 = \{\langle a, b, c, d \rangle, \langle a, c, b, d \rangle, \langle a, c, d, b \rangle, \langle c, a, b, d \rangle, \langle c, a, d, b \rangle, \langle c, d, a, b \rangle\}$.

Definition 4.15 (Parallel Combination of Execution Path Sets). *Let $\mathcal{F}_1$ and $\mathcal{F}_2$ be execution path sets. Then, a parallel combination of single elements of both sets is denoted through the following symbol: $\mathcal{F}_1|\mathcal{F}_2 := \bigcup F_1 \bowtie F_2$ with $F_1 \in \mathcal{F}_1$ and $F_2 \in \mathcal{F}_2$. It holds: $\mathcal{F}_1|\mathcal{F}_2 = \mathcal{F}_2|\mathcal{F}_1$.*

As an example, consider two execution path sets $\mathcal{F}_1 = \{\langle a,b,c\rangle, \langle m,n\rangle\}$ and $\mathcal{F}_2 = \{\langle d,e\rangle, \langle o,p,q\rangle\}$. Then, $\mathcal{F}_1|\mathcal{F}_2 = \langle a,b,c\rangle \bowtie \langle d,e\rangle \cup \langle a,b,c\rangle \bowtie \langle o,p,q\rangle \cup \langle m,n\rangle \bowtie \langle d,e\rangle \cup \langle m,n\rangle \bowtie \langle o,p,q\rangle$.

4.4. Execution Semantics of Workflow Blocks

Execution semantics of workflow blocks express how the execution of workflow instances is handled. These execution semantics are specified on the basis of the previously described execution paths and operators.

Definition 4.16 (Execution Path Set of Workflows). *Let $W = (N, E)$ be a block-oriented workflow with sequence nodes $N^S = N^T \cup N^C$. Then, an execution path set $\mathcal{F}(W) = \{F_1(W), ..., F_m(W)\}$ is a set containing all possible valid execution paths of W, where each $F_i(W) = \langle f_1, ..., f_n\rangle$ with $\{f_1, ..., f_n\} \subseteq N^S$ describes one valid and complete execution path of W as a sequence of activities, which represents the execution of certain sequence nodes from N^S. For an execution path $F_i(W)$, every node that is not contained in $F_i(W)$ is not considered as executed to achieve this single valid execution of W.*

Every valid execution path starts with the first element and ends with the last element of the workflow block

Definition 4.17 (First and Last Element of an Execution Path). *Let B be a workflow block. For a valid execution path $F_i(B) = \langle g_1, ..., g_n\rangle$ we define $first(B) := g_1$ and $last(B) := g_n$.*

Let B be a workflow block of W. Then, valid execution paths $\mathcal{F}(B)$ for B are defined in Def. 4.18-4.22 depending on the type of B. No element can occur multiple times in an execution path, as repeated executions are not considered yet.

The execution path set of a single task block is rather simple, as it only contains one element.

4.4. EXECUTION SEMANTICS OF WORKFLOW BLOCKS

Definition 4.18 (Execution Path Set of a Single Task Block). *Let B be a single task node t according to Def. 4.6, then $\mathcal{F}(B) = \mathcal{F}(B^t) := \{\langle t \rangle\}$, which means task t has to be executed.*

For the execution of a sequence block, there exist various valid execution paths.

Definition 4.19 (Execution Path Set of a Sequence Block). *Let B be a sequence of two workflow blocks $B = B^{(B_1, B_2)}$ according to Def. 4.7. Then, $\mathcal{F}(B) = \mathcal{F}(B^{(B_1, B_2)}) := \mathcal{F}(B_1) \odot \mathcal{F}(B_2)$.*

This means that the execution of block B_1 has to terminate before block B_2 can be started. This implies the termination of every executed sequence element $s_1 \in N_{B_1}^S$ before activating any sequence element $s_2 \in N_{B_2}^S$. Let $F_i(B_1)$ be a valid execution path of block element B_1 and let $F_j(B_2)$ be a valid execution path of block element B_2, then both valid orders combined consecutively form an overall valid order.

Definition 4.20 (Execution Path Set of an Exclusive Control-Flow Block). *Let B be an exclusive control-flow block $B = B_{XOR}^{(B_1, B_2)}$ according to Def. 4.8. Then, $\mathcal{F}(B) = \mathcal{F}(B_{XOR}^{(B_1, B_2)}) := \{\langle cs \rangle\} \odot \mathcal{F}(B_1) \odot \{\langle cj \rangle\} \cup \{\langle cs \rangle\} \odot \mathcal{F}(B_2) \odot \{\langle cj \rangle\}$.*

This means that the executions of both blocks are mutually exclusive. This results in two sets of possible valid execution paths. Let $F_i(B_1)$ be a valid execution order of block element B_1 and let $F_j(B_2)$ be a valid execution order of block element B_2. Either B_1 is executed, preventing the enactment of any task of B_2, or B_2 is executed, which in turn prevents the enactment of any task of B_1.

Definition 4.21 (Execution Path Set of a Parallel Control-Flow Block). *Let B be a parallel control-flow block $B = B_{AND}^{(B_1, B_2)}$ according to Def. 4.8. Then, $\mathcal{F}(B) = \mathcal{F}(B_{AND}^{(B_1, B_2)}) := \{\langle cs \rangle\} \odot \mathcal{F}(B_1) | \mathcal{F}(B_2) \odot \{\langle cj \rangle\}$.*

This means that two block elements are executed concurrently. Both blocks have to be executed and terminated prior to the activation of possible following blocks and thus, prior to the activation of the control-flow join node cj. Temporal dependencies between single elements of the different blocks do not exist, but sequential orderings of both blocks themselves need to be adhered to.

Definition 4.22 (Execution Path Set of a Single-Branch Exclusive Control-Flow Block). *Let B be a single-branch exclusive control-flow block $B = B_{XOR}^{B_1}$. Then, $\mathcal{F}(B) = \mathcal{F}(B_{XOR}^{B_1}) := \{\langle cs, cj \rangle\} \cup \{\langle cs \rangle\} \odot \mathcal{F}(B_1) \odot \{\langle cj \rangle\}$.*

An exclusive control-flow block which comprises only one block element is synonymous to an option. Either block B_1 is executed or it is skipped. If the block element is executed, the workflow block needs to terminate before activating the control-flow join node cj. Otherwise, if B_1 is skipped, the control-flow split "cs" and join node "cj" denote the beginning and end of the control-flow block.

Chapter 5

Constraint-Based Workflow Engine

The constraint-based workflow engine, as one core element of this thesis, is described in this chapter. The concrete specification and composition of the CSP, which performs the task of the workflow engine, have been introduced in previous works [55, 56, 58]. These definitions and algorithms are adopted to a great extent, but with slight adjustments due to some refinements and advancements.

First in Section 5.1, the concept is briefly introduced. This includes an overview of generally provided features and possible or necessary interactions between process participants and the system. In Section 5.2 the workflow model that builds the formal foundation for the workflow engine and its applied algorithms is specified. The de jure workflow as well as the declarative constraints, which can be integrated, are described initially. As prerequisite for the constraint-based workflow engine, foundations on constraint satisfaction problems are introduced in Section 5.3. Subsequently in Section 5.4, several algorithms are explained. Based on constraint solving, the work items are computed. The CSP itself and its elements are specified in detail. The transformation function that allows procedurally modelled workflows to be processed by the workflow engine is explained subsequently. Another algorithm is responsible for an extension of the CSP, in case a loop construct is encountered or tasks are repeated unexpectedly. The following Section 5.5 depicts a simple method for deviation detection concerning the CSP. Typical scenarios are listed and strategies for restoring consistency are pointed out. The concluding Section 5.6 sketches related work considering flexible constraint-based workflow approaches.

5.1. Concept of the Workflow Engine

Considering the standard process cycle (see Fig. 2.3), this concept for a flexible workflow management integrates several additional components and processing steps in order to achieve an adequate handling of deviations. The novel elements are shown in Fig. 5.1 as refined version of Fig. 3.6.

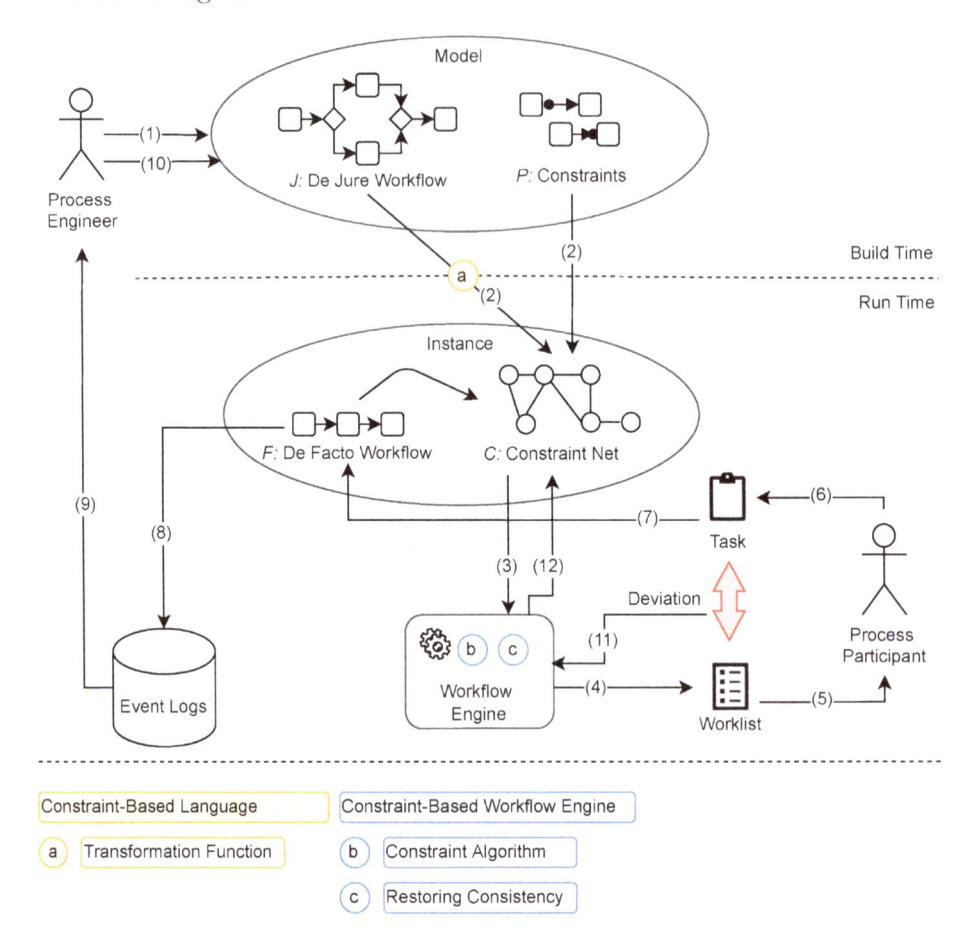

Figure 5.1. Flexible Workflow Approach with a Constraint-Based Workflow Engine

In comparison with the standard cycle from Fig. 2.3, the flexible workflow system builds upon a model and instance that both consist of two elements. Additionally to the de jure workflow, which can be modelled with a procedural language, declarative constraints can be specified. This model with all its elements is transposed to an instance

5.1. CONCEPT OF THE WORKFLOW ENGINE

when run time starts (see (2) in Fig. 5.1). The instance consists of the de facto workflow, which simply represents the executed and traced tasks in a sequential way, and a constraint net. The constraint net is essential for the workflow engine, as it is utilized as data input for the CSP algorithm. During instantiation, the de jure workflow J and the constraints P are translated into the constraint net C, which is enhanced on the basis of the de facto workflow during execution. Thus, one main element of the flexible approach is the transformation function that converts a procedural block-oriented workflow to a logical formula (see ⓐ in Fig. 5.1).

The procedure that includes the following steps (see (3) to (10) in Fig. 5.1) stays the same: computing a worklist, executing a task, enhancing the workflow instance resulting in an event log, which might trigger an evolution of the workflow model. The main difference of this flexible approach in contrast to the standard process cycle is that an occurred deviation results in additional steps. A deviation, which means that the executed task is not part of the worklist, activates the flexible workflow engine (see (11) in Fig. 5.1). In this case, the constraint algorithm is not able to produce a solution any more, as one or several constraints are violated. Consistency needs to be restored in the constraint net (see ⓒ in Fig. 5.1). Thereby the instantiated constraint net is adapted (see (12) in Fig. 5.1) in order to re-enable the workflow engine to compute work items (see ⓑ in Fig. 5.1). This allows the process cycle to start all over with the run time part at step (3).

The implementation of flexibility by deviation as presented in this thesis was embedded in the architecture of the SEMAFLEX [59] and the SEMANAS project [60]. An important characteristic of this approach is that the information about a task enactment (cf. (6) in Fig. 5.1) can result from various sources. This is either a user interaction, e.g. a manual selection of a task being performed, or due to upcoming documents, which are analysed automatically and mapped to a certain task, whose enactment is derived subsequently. The latter could be realized in future work through the integration and combination of methods for document classification and information extraction from Schwinn [170], as envisioned and prototypically implemented in SEMAFLEX and SEMANAS. In this work, it is simply assumed that a terminated task enactment is registered by the flexible workflow system, regardless of the source of this information.

These logged task enactments construct the actually conducted workflow as a sequence of activities that have been performed. While the workflow engine proposes tasks which should be done next, the process participant is not forced to follow these suggestions. In principle, the process participant is able to do what s/he wants and in which order s/he wants. S/he can either follow the tasks in the worklist, suggesting the standard course of action, or do something else. Through both, the actual workflow can then be recorded and identified. Progress in turn affects the workflow engine, including detected deviations.

For a suitable representation of the workflows regarding this viewpoint, a modelled workflow, *de jure workflow*, and an executed workflow, *de facto workflow*, are explicitly differentiated similar to van der Aalst [181]. In this work, the notion *de facto workflow* is used for an enacted instance, which stores the actually conducted transactions sequentially and might deviate from those instances that conform with the de jure workflow. If all de facto workflows are summarized to one workflow model, reflecting the actual behaviour of the workflow and not the desired one, this would represent the de facto model, as introduced by van der Aalst [181].

5.2. Workflow Model

For the workflow model, an approach is pursued that combines procedural and declarative paradigms. Thus, the workflow model consists of two elements, which are sketched in Fig. 5.2. The de jure workflow J, which represents the ideal way of handling the considered issue, is modelled with a procedural business process modelling language, e.g. BPMN. Additionally, declarative constraints P can be specified manually to represent particular requirements where special attention is necessary. Those constraints affect parts of the process, such as a subset of tasks, and are not necessarily included in the de jure workflow. They are implemented on the basis of the DECLARE language [184].

The presented workflow model and as a consequence the concept of the workflow engine as well focuses on the functional, behavioural and informational perspectives. This mainly relates to the task representation itself [3], the control-flow and data-flow of activities. Organizational,

---

[3]In Chapter 6, a data structure is presented that enables each task to be

5.2. WORKFLOW MODEL

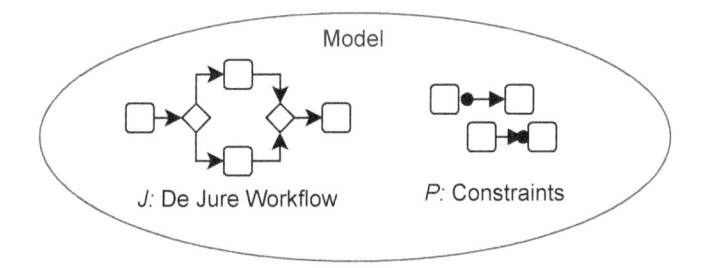

Figure 5.2. Workflow Model for the Flexible Workflow Approach

operational and time perspectives are not part of this research work.

5.2.1. De Jure Workflow

In the presented concept for a flexible workflow management, the de jure workflow is only of descriptive nature. It is utilized for specifying an initial simple model that contains the ideal order of tasks and known alternatives. The de jure workflow is not considered to map the entire state space of possible situations. Its purpose is foremost guidance in order to support rather than strictly prescribe. Thus, deviations are still allowed. This relates to the inner circle shown by a dashed line of the possible workflow state space presented in Fig. 2.7, which is denoted as procedural state space.

Procedural modelling is used for this de jure workflow, as it is more intuitive and comprehensible than declarative modelling [138]. Task sequences that every process participant is aware of can be modelled straightforwardly. Thus, the presumable lack of expertise in SMEs can be accommodated. The implemented constraint-based workflow engine is currently restricted to the handling of block-oriented workflows (cf. Def. 4.10), as they are well-formed and therefore, easier to handle. Consequently, J corresponds to a block-oriented workflow $J = (N_J, E_J)$ with nodes N_J and edges E_J.

An example for such a block-oriented de jure workflow is shown in Fig. 3.1, which represents the simple ideal workflow model for deficiency management in construction illustrated in a similar but simplified fashion compared to BPMN.

---

enhanced by semantic information.

5.2.2. Additional Constraints

The de jure workflow is used to control the suggested execution order of tasks, but this order is not regarded as mandatory and consequently can be violated. Hence, the de jure workflow is only considered as guidance, but deviations are tolerated. Nevertheless, some deviations are undesired or even critical and should never occur, especially when compliance or safety aspects are regarded. For this reason, additional constraints P can be modelled manually, to explicitly specify undesired or even invalid workflow states. This relates to the declarative state space depicted in Fig. 2.7. Consequently, the invalid state space can be reduced or even marginalised.

Following the presented concept of flexibility by deviation, those constraints might actually be violated by the user, as the workflow engine never prescribes an activity and thus, is not able to actively prevent violations. Nevertheless, the violation of constraints and therefore, the occurrence of specific undesired situations can be detected easily. Depending on the kind of constraint violation the workflow engine must react adequately. When a deviation is detected, the workflow engine must reason about the next task and propose it without entering an exceptional state. In future work this reparation step might be evolved in order to take more detailed information into account. This can involve a severity specification, a warning message or even a proposed corrective measure. But such a mechanism is outside of the scope of this work.

The most probable deviations include the five following ones: skip, undo, redo, create an additional instance, and invoke a task. For the modelling of constraints that countervail these types of deviations, declarative constructs are used. A main advantage of declarative models is that one constraint easily represents single relations of tasks. Constraints can be regarded separately but can be combined as well without the need of a connection. This implies another benefit of declarative workflow models that is exploited for the presented approach. Declarative constraints implicitly offer flexibility. This characteristic transferred to flexibility by deviation can be interpreted in the following way: If a deviation occurs, it is rather easy to omit the violated constraints and simply consider all remaining ones in order to restore a consistent state. A procedural model that encounters a deviation needs to be remodelled, which is a complex task, in order

5.2. WORKFLOW MODEL

to eliminate inconsistencies and as a result to be applicable for the workflow engine.

For the declarative constraints, which can be modelled additionally, five different constraint types of the DECLARE language [184] are utilized, which countervail possible deviations. For the definitions, two tasks t_1 and t_2 with $\{t_1, t_2\} \subseteq N_j^S$ and one number $x \in \mathbb{N}$ are necessary.

- Precedence(t_1, t_2): Task t_2 can only be executed after t_1.
- Response(t_1, t_2): Task t_1 requires the subsequent enactment of t_2.
- Existence(t_1): Task t_1 is mandatory.
- Not Co-Existence(t_1, t_2): Task t_1 and t_2 exclude each other.
- Absence(t_1, x): Task t_1 can only be executed x times.

The set of constraints P is part of the workflow model (see Fig. 5.2) and can contain any number of those constraints, which are additionally modelled.

Precedence and *Response* prevent undesirable skipping, concerning previous or subsequent tasks. These two constraints relate to the formulation of pre- and post-conditions. *Existence* contradicts the skipping and undoing of a task. Redoing and creating additional instances of a task are intercepted by the constraint *Absence*, as it restricts the number of executions. *Not Co-Existence* avoids invoking undesired task enactments, at least depending on the enactment of another task.

When such constraints are modelled additionally, it is ensured that they comply with the de jure workflow and do not contradict parts of this model. Otherwise the addition is rejected, as it would lead to an inconsistent model and further hinder the workflow engine.

An alternative way of handling such discrepancies is to integrate these constraints despite possible conflicts, but as optional. Through this voluntary nature, the workflow engine is still able to compute work items by ignoring or rather violating these constraints when finding a solution. Nevertheless, these constraints can be valuable knowledge for the case-based deviation management, which will be presented in Chapter 6. Consider an occurred deviation that violates some constraints. If those were previously contradicting the "optional" constraints and are then removed in order to restore consistency, these optional constraints might become relevant and could be reactivated for a profound control of the workflow execution. This abstract idea needs to be investigated in future work, as its elaboration is not part of this work.

With the proposed workflow model, research question **RQ1.1** (see Section 1.2) is addressed. The de jure workflow is seen as guideline and deviations are tolerated. It is complemented by constraints that can easily be omitted in case of non-compliance, such that no exceptional state will occur, but the workflow engine can proceed. How this continuous support will be achieved, is explained in subsequent chapters.

Preventing the user from deviating with this flexible workflow approach can only be achieved if the user manually chooses tasks from the worklist, as only tasks are proposed that lead to a valid workflow state. Deciding what can be executed next is easy for procedurally modelled workflows, if no deviations are possible. However, if a deviation occurs, one would not be able to suggest an appropriate further proceeding. Constraints suit this situation perfectly, as even if one is violated it might be retracted, and still valid suggestions can be computed on the basis of remaining constraints. To take advantage of the implicit flexibility that such a declarative approach offers, each construct of the de jure workflow, modelled imperatively, is automatically transformed into corresponding declarative expressions as prerequisite for the presented enactment approach.

In the next section, constraint satisfaction problems are introduced in general as foundation for the presented workflow engine.

5.3. Foundations on Constraint Satisfaction Problems

A Constraint Satisfaction Problem (CSP) is a powerful formulation in the wide field of AI that is used for problem representation and solving. It formally represents one particular issue that can be solved by finding a valid state under given restricting conditions and relations of some entities and their characteristics. The solving process is of combinatorial nature and additionally involves optimization criteria

5.3. FOUNDATIONS ON CONSTRAINT SATISFACTION PROBLEMS

in many cases. CSP solving has been researched for many years. This class of problem is applicable in various domains, e.g. logistics [151] or aircraft [179, 189], and is utilized by other problem solving paradigms such as planning and scheduling [153].

According to Russell and Norvig [154, p. 137] a CSP is defined as follows:

Definition 5.1 (Constraint Satisfaction Problem). *A constraint satisfaction problem $CSP = (X, D, C)$ consists of a set of decision variables $X = \{X_1, X_2, \ldots, X_n\}$, a set of constraints $C = \{C_1, C_2, \ldots, C_m\}$ and a set of domains $D = \{D_1, D_2, \ldots D_n\}$. Each decision variable has a domain D_i, which is a non-empty set of possible values for X_i. A constraint C_j is a relation over a subset of the variables $\{X_k, \ldots, X_l\} \subseteq X$, specifying the set of combination of allowed values.*

As shown schematically in Fig. 5.3, the problem which is to be solved is formally expressed by a set of variables that can be assigned values of its domain, whose validity is restricted by a set of constraints.

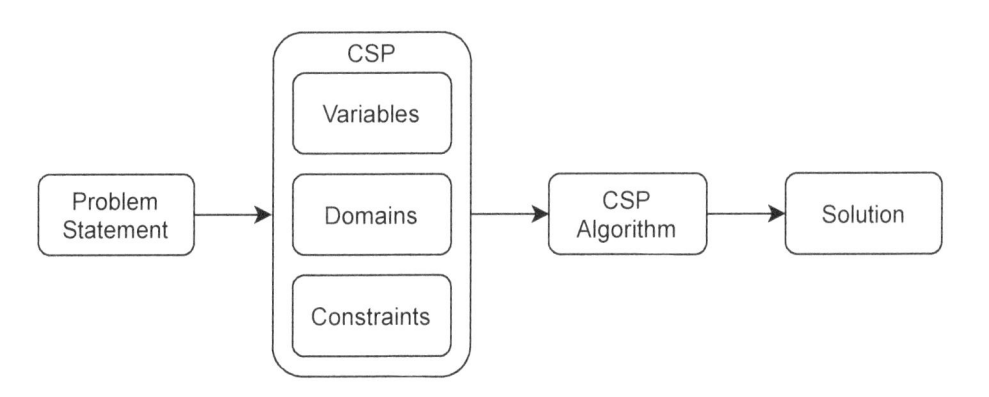

Figure 5.3. Constraint Satisfaction Problem Solving based on Squalli et al. [174]

The CSP itself is characterized by these three sets of variables, domains, and constraints, which all can have distinct forms. The variables and their domains can have different characteristics [154, p. 139]. *Discrete* variables can have *finite*, in the simplest form *boolean* variables with the domain $\{true, false\}$, or *infinite* domains. *Continuous* domains are common as well depending on the considered problem and its model.

Furthermore, constraints can be of different types [154, p. 140]. This concerns on the one hand the number of variables involved and on the other hand the obligation of fulfilment. *Unary* constraints only consider one single variable, *binary* ones relate two variables, whereas *higher order* constraints affect the value assignment of several or in the most extreme case all of the variables. If constraints are mandatory in such a way that a solution strictly needs to comply, they are denoted as *absolute*. In contrast, the term *preference* constraint indicates the desire of fulfilment, but no obligation exists. This property can simplify the choice between several solutions or allow for more possibilities that are accepted.

On this specification of a CSP, an algorithm is applied in order to compute a solution to the initially identified problem statement. A solution is defined as follows [154, p. 137]:

Definition 5.2 (Solution). *An assignment of values to some or all of the variables $V = (X_1 = a_1, \ldots, X_k = a_k)$ with $a_1 \in D_1, \ldots, a_k \in D_k$ is called state of the problem that is denoted as consistent, if it does not violate any constraint. If values are assigned to every variable, the assignment is named complete. A consistent and simultaneously complete assignment is called solution* sol. *For a variable X_i, the notation $[X_i]^{sol}$ stands for the value a_i assigned to X_i.*

In general, the class of CSPs, and thus, the algorithm for finding a solution, is NP-complete. To deal with the vast state space of a CSP, different algorithms can be applied. The technique of constraint propagation [87] is applied to explore and to simultaneously reduce the state space. For CSPs with discrete variables and finite domains, all types of search algorithms, for instance backtracking [87], can be used effectively in order to find a solution. As most of these methods are rather inefficient for large problems, certain heuristics need to be adopted to speed up the solving process.

A CSP serves as the core method for identifying valid task suggestions on the basis of the previously defined workflow model (cf. Sect. 5.2). This proposed workflow engine will be explained in the following section.

5.4. Workflow Engine

The workflow engine with the necessary input data is pictured in Fig. 5.4. When a workflow is started, a workflow instance is created. This

5.4. WORKFLOW ENGINE

includes the de facto workflow $F = (N_F, E_F)$, which tracks enacted tasks and is therefore continuously complemented during progress. This workflow is a special type of block-oriented workflow, as it only consists of sequential control-flow due to the successive tracking of enacted tasks.

Furthermore, the workflow instance contains a constraint net C that formally bases on logical formulae. C is fed by both the de facto workflow F and the combined workflow model, i.e. J and P. This constraint net is used as input for the workflow engine, whose functionality is implemented through a constraint satisfaction problem CSP_W and several algorithms exploiting this CSP.

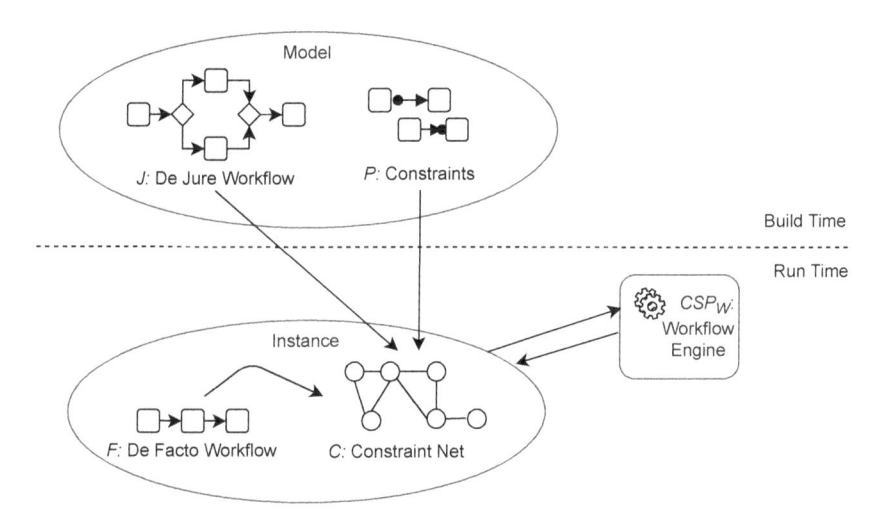

Figure 5.4. Workflow Model and Instance for the Flexible Workflow Approach

All elements shown in Fig. 5.4 are explained in detail in the following section. First, the constraint satisfaction problem in general is defined in Section 5.3. Subsequently in Subsection 5.4.1, a concrete CSP that is utilized to compute work items is presented. Furthermore, the composition of the used constraint net is specified. It essentially builds upon a transformation function, specified in Subsection 5.4.2, that is able to transform procedural block-oriented workflows into declarative constraints, which can be handled by the workflow engine. This declarative representation is proven to represent the same traces as procedural block-oriented workflows, elucidated in Appendix A. Concluding in Subsection 5.4.3, the strategy of handling loops and repeated executions of tasks is described.

5.4.1. Computing Work Items

In case of an unforeseen deviation during workflow execution, traditional workflow approaches often fail in offering continuous user support. Consequences are exceptional states or in the worst case dead ends. Flexible approaches try to improve this decreased or even lack of support. In the presented flexible workflow concept, CSP solving is exploited to avoid such undesirable situations. The concrete problem which is regarded as CSP is to compute work items based on the previously defined workflow model and instance (cf. Fig. 5.7). In case of an occurrence of a deviation, violated constraints need to be retracted in order to re-enable the workflow engine. But due to the declarative nature of the data model, this necessary change is rather simple.

In this section, the transfer of the CSP solving paradigm to the general task of the workflow engine, to be more precise the computation of all valid work items in a specific state of the workflow at one specific point in time, is introduced. How deviations are handled is described in the subsequent section 5.5.

5.4.1.1. Problem Description CSP_W

The issue of computing work items, thus, the responsibility of the constraint-based workflow engine, is defined as $CSP_W = (X, D, C)$. An abstract specification is given in Fig. 5.5.

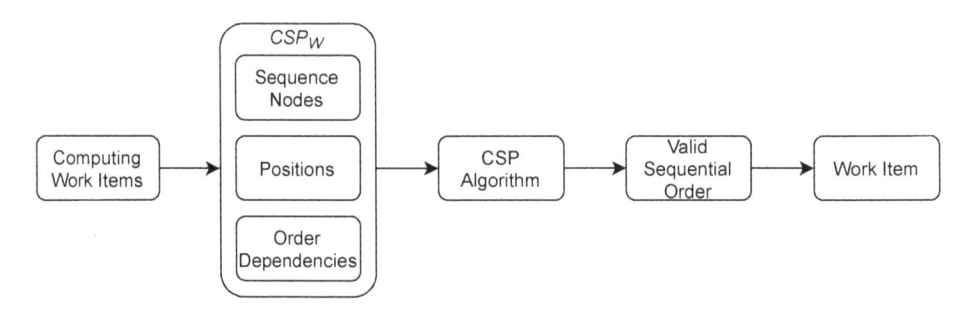

Figure 5.5. Constraint Satisfaction Problem for Computing Work Items

As mentioned previously, a main aspect of the pursued workflow approach is that tasks are traced sequentially one after another during execution, building the de facto workflow of the workflow instance. This characteristic is exploited for the CSP definition of the workflow

5.4. WORKFLOW ENGINE

engine CSP_W. The solution of CSP_W corresponds to one valid execution path $F_i(J)$ of the workflow J, which specifies one valid sequential order of tasks. From this execution path, a work item can be derived that is appropriate for the current status of the de facto workflow. For this purpose, sequence nodes are regarded as decision variables s, the domains contain values that represent the elements' positions $pos(f_j)$ in $F_i(J)$ and the constraints specify order dependencies. Each of these parts of the CSP are elucidated with a formal description in the following paragraphs.[4]

The input data for the algorithm comprises

1. the de facto workflow F, specifying a partially completed workflow,

2. the de jure workflow J, that represents the ideal course of events and

3. possibly additional constraints P.

5.4.1.2. Decision Variables

For the definition of the set of decision variables, the de jure workflow $J = (N_J, E_J)$ with $N_J^S = N_J^T \cup N_J^C$ is essential. Workflow tasks and control-flow nodes, summarized as sequence nodes N_J^S, are regarded as decision variables. For each sequence node $s_i \in N_J^S = \{s_1, \ldots, s_n\}$, a discrete variable with the same identifier s_i is created and added to S'.[5]

$$S' = \{s_i | s_i \in N_J^S\} \quad (5.1)$$

Subsequently, S' is supplemented with one single variable s_{end} to be able to determine whether the workflow has completed, such that[6]

$$S = S' \cup \{s_{end}\} \quad (5.2)$$

---

[4]In order to simplify the explanation of the algorithm only single executions of tasks are regarded until now. In Subsect. 5.4.3, CSP_W is extended to enable the handling of loop patterns and repeated task executions.

[5]The task nodes, previously denoted as $N_J^T = \{t_1, \ldots, t_n\}$, and control-flow nodes, so far indicated through cs for control-flow split and cj for control-flow join nodes, are summarized through unified identifiers s_i to simplify expressions, as no differentiation between the two types is necessary.

[6]The set of decision variables is preliminarily denoted as S to simplify the explanation of the construction of the CSP, but will be extended with some other variables in subsequent sections, in order to complement the set X.

This is necessary, as some constraint violation explicitly depends upon workflow completion. During CSP solving each variable is assigned a value reflecting the ordinal number of the task in the execution sequence and thus, each task is positioned sequentially related to all other tasks. On the basis of the variable s_{end}, the CSP is able to assert several aspects. Considering the solution of CSP_W, every task that is assigned a higher integer value than s_{end} is regarded as not enacted and derived from that, these tasks are not part of $F_i(J)$. Consequently, on the one hand, a mandatory enactment of a task can be mapped through forcing the assignment of a value to the task variable lower than to s_{end}. On the other hand, it can be assured that some tasks have not been conducted through allocating values higher than the value of s_{end}. Through these basic properties, more complex relations can be verified as well, for instance a required execution of a task after a certain one, relating to the DECLARE constraint *Response*, can be expressed through specifying the sequential order and depending on that a mandatory enactment of the second task.

A simple example of the significance of s_{end} is illustrated in Table 5.1. The exemplary workflow W contains four task nodes that are

Table 5.1. Exemplary Use of the Variable s_{end} in CSP_W

Workflow W	
Execution Paths	
$F_1(W)$	$\langle t_1, cs, t_2, cj, t_4 \rangle$
$F_2(W)$	$\langle t_1, cs, t_3, cj, t_4 \rangle$
Constraints	$\{t_1 < cs, cs < t_2, cs < t_3,$ $((t_2 < cj \wedge s_{end} < t_3) \vee$ $(t_3 < t_4 \wedge s_{end} < t_2)),$ $cj < t_4, t_4 < s_{end}\}$
Solutions	
$\text{sol}_1(W)$	$(t_1 = 1, cs = 2, t_2 = 3, cj = 4, t_4 = 5, s_{end} = 6, t_3 = 7)$
$\text{sol}_2(W)$	$(t_1 = 1, cs = 2, t_3 = 3, cj = 4, t_4 = 5, s_{end} = 6, t_2 = 7)$

partly nested in an exclusive control-flow block with two control-flow nodes. The characteristic of the exclusive control-flow block is mapped through the use of the variable s_{end}. During execution, one of the two tasks t_2 or t_3 needs to be excluded from enactment, which is reflected by the two possible valid execution paths $F_1(W)$ and $F_2(W)$ (see row 2 in Table 5.1). Therefore, special conditions need to be included in the constraint set besides the order relations. These particular prerequisites specify that the excluded task, either t_2 or t_3, is assigned a higher value than s_{end} (see second and third line in row "Constraints" in Table 5.1). For a better comprehension, the valid solutions sol$_1(W)$ and sol$_2(W)$ to the corresponding CSP_W that applies those constraints are shown in row 4 of Table 5.1. Here, it becomes obvious that the tasks with higher values than s_{end} are not part of the execution paths and thus do not contribute to a valid enactment of the workflow.

5.4.1.3. Domains

The assignment of values to variables represents a sequential order of all tasks. This not only includes already executed tasks, which are part of the de facto workflow, but also possible future executions of tasks until termination of the workflow. Thus, a valid order, determined by ascending integer values, of tasks is calculated. As it is only of interest which task can be executed next at a specific point in time, it is negligible if any other tasks might be or have been executed in parallel. Consequently, the domain for each decision variable s_i is finite and represented by a set of integer values with n as the number of sequence nodes extracted from the de jure workflow and an additional value included in each D_{s_i} for the variable s_{end}.

$$\{d_1, \ldots, d_n, d_{n+1}\} \subseteq D_{s_i} \subseteq \mathbb{N} \text{ with } |D_{s_i}| \geq n+1 \text{ and } n = |N_J^S| \quad (5.3)$$

In the simplest case, each domain is a series of integers starting from 1, adding one up until $n+1$, thus, $D_{s_i} = \{1, 2, ..., n, n+1\}$. Nevertheless, any other set of values with different offsets or minimum/maximum value are permissible as long as all values are distinct such that sequential relations can be expressed. Therefore, the domain sets need to contain at least $n+1$ numbers to ensure that only unique values are assigned. This variability of possible domain values is exploited to show the equivalence of execution semantics of block-oriented workflows and the designed case-based workflow engine and will be explained in more detail in the Appendix A.

5.4.1.4. Algorithm

To identify all tasks that might be enacted next, a *solution* to CSP_W is searched for. An algorithm is applied that utilizes CSP solving in order to compute the worklist. Therefore several CSPs with different configurations need to be solved.

In the example in Fig. 5.6, the de facto workflow F contains three tasks that were enacted so far. Each task that is a valid work item could be assigned to position 4, denoted as *current*. This aspect is exploited in the CSP algorithm. For each task that has not been executed so far, it is validated if an assignment of the current position would lead to a valid solution of the CSP. If so, it is a valid work item and can be added to this set. If no solution exists, the task is not valid at the currently regarded position in the de facto workflow.

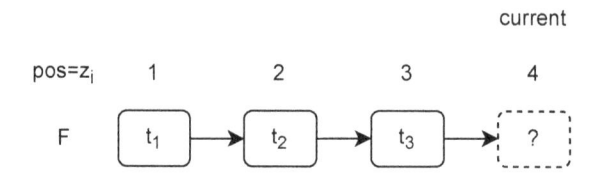

Figure 5.6. De Facto Workflow with Next Position

The CSP solving algorithm is applied during workflow execution at the initialization of each workflow and after each task enactment.

The algorithm, which is shown in Algo. 5.1, receives the previously defined $CSP_W = (X, D, C)$ and the current de facto workflow $F = (N_F, E_F)$ as input. As output, the variable *workItems* is introduced, which represents the set of tasks that can be enacted next without violating constraints.

Algorithm 5.1: computeWorkItems(CSP_W, F)

Input : $CSP_W = (X, D, C), F = (N_F, E_F)$
Output: *workItems*: Tasks that might be executed next
1   *workItems* $\leftarrow \emptyset$;
2   **foreach** $x \in S \setminus N_F^S$ **do**
3   *current* $\leftarrow D_x[|N_F^S| + 1]$;
4   **if** $solveCSP(X, D, C \cup \{x = current\}) \neq \emptyset$ **then**
5   *workItems* $\leftarrow$ *workItems* $\cup \{x\}$
6   **return** *workItems*;

For each task that has not been executed so far, a solution is searched. These tasks can be found easily, as they exist in the set of all sequence nodes S, but not in F, yet. In each iteration, one of these decision variables is chosen (x) and declared with a value. The value of this possible assignment to tasks, denoted here as *current*, is determined by the size of the de facto workflow F adding one (see line 3 in Algo. 5.1), which can also be expressed as the number of nodes, as this is the position that will be occupied in the execution path by the task that is executed next (cf. Fig. 5.6). The value in the domain at this position is assigned to *current*.

This assignment is added temporarily to the set of constraints (see line 4 in Algo. 5.1). Thus, it is checked if the specific task is a valid next task of the de facto workflow. As one solution of the CSP can only validate one task, a worklist with all valid work items can be generated through applying the CSP algorithm several times with different configurations. If every solution to CSP_W would be computed, this would result in redundant and unnecessary computations. To accelerate proceedings, only one solution for each of these configurations is necessary to determine the validity of the task being added to the worklist. It is only of interest if the task is valid at this exact position, whereas the rest of the solution is irrelevant.

If the CSP solving algorithm finds a solution, this task can be executed next and is therefore appended to *workItems* (see line 5 in Algo. 5.1). If no solution is found, the process participant must not execute the task as next step and thus, it is not proposed. The result, meaning the work items, are contained in the variable *workItems* when the algorithm terminates. In the following, all constraints that are used in CSP_W are introduced.

5.4.1.5. Constraints

The utilized constraint set is composed of different single sets. Figure 5.7 gives an overview of their origins. Additionally, these sets differ in the included types of constraints and their purposes.

Thus, C is defined as follows:

$$C = \{alldifferent(S)\} \cup C^M \cup C^A \cup C^I \qquad (5.4)$$

The x-variable constraint $alldifferent(S)$ ensures that each sequence node variable is assigned a distinct value and thus, the solution repre-

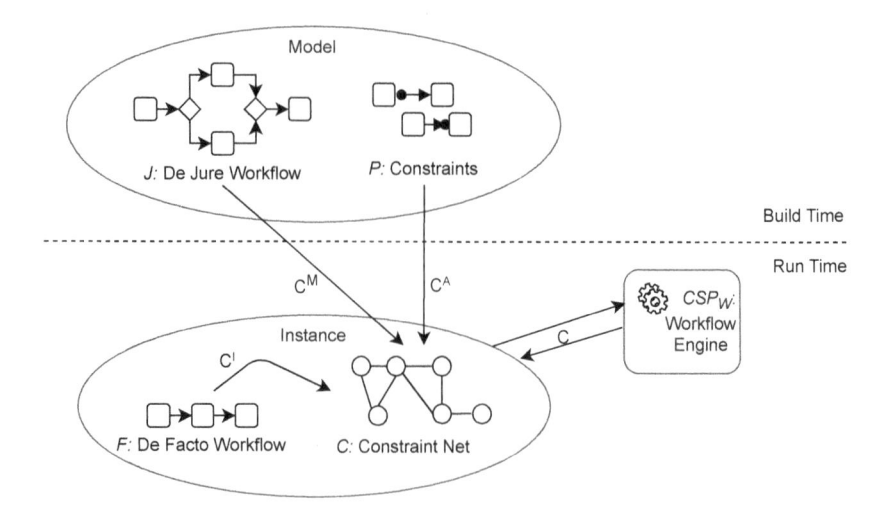

Figure 5.7. Workflow Model and Instance for the Flexible Workflow Approach

sents one unique sequential execution path, as a bijective mapping of domain values to decision variables is achieved.

The first set C^M represents the procedural workflow model itself, the de jure workflow J. C^A comprises the constraints that can be modelled directly in declarative form additionally to the de jure workflow P. C^I maps the de facto workflow F and its fixed order of already executed and tracked tasks. This set of constraints continuously evolves, as the de facto workflow is enhanced while logging the current execution state.

5.4.1.5.1. Model Constraints   Constraints that arise from the model can be split up into three different subsets.

$$C^M = Dec(J, s_{end}) \cup C^{DF} \cup C^{CF} \tag{5.5}$$

The first set $Dec(J, s_{end})$ is represented by a function that takes all sequential dependencies of task and control-flow nodes into account and is responsible for the correct order. The function is elaborated in Subsection 5.4.2.

5.4.1.5.2. Data-Flow-Dependent Constraints C^{DF} concerns sequential reliances that stem from data objects. Additional constraints are generated on the basis of data-flow dependencies, as they implicitly indicate task orders [205, p. 268]. Thus, if some data object d is

5.4. WORKFLOW ENGINE

output of task s_1 and input of task s_2, as in Fig. 4.1, s_1 necessarily precedes s_2, as otherwise the status of d would be inconsistent or falsified and hence, lead to an undesired state.[7] As assigned values are mapped to the position in the execution path and ascending values indicate a sequential order, the value of the preceding task should be lower than of the subsequent one. A binary constraint relating the two task variables with a less-than relation is created for this purpose.

$$C^{DF} = \{s_1 < s_2 | s_1, s_2 \in N_J^T : \exists d \in N_J^D : (s_1, d), (d, s_2) \in E_J^D\} \quad (5.6)$$

5.4.1.5.3. Control-Flow-Dependent Constraints Due to the construction of the CSP, it is possible to influence the control of the workflow on the basis of additional information that is represented by a control variable. The purpose of control-flow nodes is additionally transferred to constraints in order to further automate the support. On this basis, tasks are excluded from enactment proposals, if the control variable is allocated a certain value.

For these decisions, a set of control variables A is introduced.

$$A = \{a_1, ..., a_h\} \text{ with } h \in \mathbb{N} \quad (5.7)$$

These control variables are added to the set of decision variables as boolean variables.

$$X = S \cup A \quad (5.8)$$

Consequently, the domain for each of these control variables only consists of the values *true* and *false*.

$$D_a = \{true, false\} \text{ for all } a \in A \quad (5.9)$$

For each xor or loop construct (see Fig. 5.8), two constraints are included (see Equ. 5.10).

With a control variable a that represents a boolean decision variable and either takes *true* or *false* as value, it can be derived which path in the workflow should be followed. Concerning workflow control, the execution of the oppositional path is prevented, e.g. if the information of a is known to be *true*, task s_2 should not be enacted ($s_{end} < s_2$).

---

[7]It is assumed, that output data objects are foremost available for further access, when the producing task has terminated. This property is called "control flow follows data flow" [205, p.269].

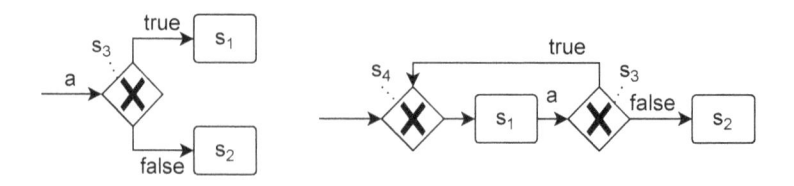

Figure 5.8. Xor and Loop Construct Including Additional Information

$$C^{CF} = \{(a = true) \Rightarrow (s_{end} < s_2) \wedge (a = false) \Rightarrow (s_{end} < s_1) | \\ a \in A \wedge s_1, s_2 \in N_J^T : \exists s_3, s_4 \in N_J^C : ((s_3, s_1), (s_3, s_2) \in E_J^C \vee \\ (s_3, s_4), (s_3, s_2), (s_4, s_1) \in E_J^C) \wedge \\ \textit{out-degree}(s_3) = 2 \wedge \textit{in-degree}(s_4) = 2\}$$
(5.10)

5.4.1.5.4. Additional Constraints The constraints that can be modelled manually in addition to the ones resulting from the de jure workflow, which were presented in Subsection 5.2.2, are transferred to logical formulae. Each type of constraint has a corresponding formal definition to be used in the CSP solving algorithm. Thus, the set C^A results from these translations. Depending on the type of constraint, some are transferred to several binary relations that are connected either disjunctively or conjunctively (see Equ. 5.12-5.14).

$$C^A = \{s_1 < s_2 \qquad\qquad | Precedence(s_1, s_2) \in P\}$$
(5.11)

$$\cup \{(s_{end} < s_1) \vee (s_1 < s_2 \wedge s_2 < s_{end}) \quad | Response(s_1, s_2) \in P\}$$
(5.12)

$$\cup \{s_1 < s_{end} \qquad\qquad | Existence(s_1) \in P\}$$ (5.13)
$$\cup \{(s_{end} < s_1) \vee (s_{end} < s_2) \quad | Not\ Co\text{-}Existence(s_1, s_2) \in P\}$$
(5.14)

As so far no repetitive execution of tasks is supported, the constraint *Absence*(s_1, x) is not defined yet, but it will be introduced in Subsection 5.4.3 in the context of loop handling.

5.4. WORKFLOW ENGINE

5.4.1.5.5. Instance Constraints
The third constraint set maps the current state of the de facto workflow. At a specific point in time during execution of the workflow, some tasks are already enacted. Their sequential execution position in the de facto workflow is determined and therefore the respective variables s_i have a fixed assignment of a constant value z_i. This is an immutable property of the CSP, as it represents the past. Thus, through these unary constraints, a partial solution for the CSP is described that cannot be modified.

$$C^I = \{s_i = z_i | s_i \in N_F^S \wedge pos(s_i) = z_i\} \quad (5.15)$$

5.4.2. Transforming Procedural Block-Oriented Workflows to Declarative Formulae

A prerequisite for the presented enactment approach is that each construct of the de jure workflow, modelled imperatively, is automatically transformed into corresponding declarative expressions by the function $Dec(B, s_{end})$. The resulting formula is integrated in the constraint set C of CSP_W and consequently can be handled by the proposed constraint-based workflow engine.

5.4.2.1. Auxiliary Function $not(B, s_{end})$

First, an auxiliary function is described, in order to simplify the definition of the actual transformation function. Input of this function is a workflow block B and it delivers constraints as logical formula, which are suitable for the CSP algorithm and represent the prevention of an execution of the respective block element. Therefore, an important characteristic of CSP_{WF} is utilized, namely, that every task assigned a higher value than s_{end} is considered not to be enacted.

Definition 5.3 (Prevention of the Execution of a Block). *To prevent the execution of a block, constraints are created according to the following function:*

$$not(B, s_{end}) = \begin{cases} \{s_{end} < t\} & \text{if } B = B^t \\ \{not(B_1, s_{end}), not(B_2, s_{end})\} & \text{if } B = B^{(B_1, B_2)} \\ \{s_{end} < cs, s_{end} < cj, not(B_1, s_{end}), & \text{if } B \in \{B_{XOR}^{(B_1, B_2)}, \\ not(B_2, s_{end})\} & B_{AND}^{(B_1, B_2)}\} \\ \{s_{end} < cs, s_{end} < cj, not(B_1, s_{end})\} & \text{if } B = B_{XOR}^{B_1} \end{cases}$$

If block B consists of an individual task node, one single constraint is sufficient to prevent the execution by assigning a higher value than s_{end} to the task variable itself. For a sequence of two workflow blocks, the function $not(B, s_{end})$ needs to be called recursively with both blocks and both recursively dissolved formulae need to hold. The strategy for control-flow blocks is similar. Additional to the recursive calls, a literal is created for each control-flow node. Through these, higher values are assigned to the variables of the control-flow split and join cs, cj compared to s_{end}. Those constraints are combined with recursively calling $not(B, s_{end})$ for the contained workflow blocks.

5.4.2.2. Transformation Function $Dec(B, s_{end})$

The following function creates a set of constraints, which restricts the sequential orders of the tasks, considering a block-oriented workflow. This constraint set can then be used as part of the overall constraint set for calculating the worklist (see Equation 5.5). For a more clear overview, the function for each of the workflow block types is specified separately.

Definition 5.4 (Declarative Formula for a Task Node). *Let B be a single task node t according to Def. 4.6, then*

$$Dec(B, s_{end}) = Dec(B^t, s_{end}) = \{t < s_{end}\}$$

If a workflow block consists of a single task node, it only needs to be ensured that this task is executed prior to termination of the workflow, thus, the task variable needs to be assigned a value lower than the value of the variable s_{end}.

Definition 5.5 (Declarative Formula for a Sequence Block). *Let B be a sequence of two workflow blocks $B = B^{(B_1, B_2)}$ according to Def. 4.7. Then,*

$$Dec(B, s_{end}) = Dec(B^{(B_1, B_2)}, s_{end}) =$$
$$\{last(B_1) < first(B_2), Dec(B_1, s_{end}), Dec(B_2, s_{end}),$$
$$last(B_2) < s_{end}\}$$

For a sequential block, both formulae that result from the recursive call need to be adhered to and the last element of the first block needs to occur prior to the first element of the second block.

5.4. WORKFLOW ENGINE

Definition 5.6 (Declarative Formula for an Exclusive Control-Flow Block). Let B be an exclusive control-flow block $B = B_{XOR}^{(B_1,B_2)}$ according to Def. 4.8. Then,

$Dec(B, s_{end}) = Dec(B_{XOR}^{(B_1,B_2)}, s_{end}) =$
$\{((cs < first(B_1) \wedge last(B_1) < cj \wedge Dec(B_1, s_{end}) \wedge not(B_2, s_{end})) \vee$
$(cs < first(B_2) \wedge last(B_2) < cj \wedge Dec(B_2, s_{end}) \wedge not(B_1, s_{end}))),$
$cj < s_{end}\}$

An exclusive workflow block allows for two different ways of execution. Either the first block is performed, which excludes the second block, ensured through the use of the function *not*, or vice versa. Sequential orders are guaranteed through arranging the values of the control-flow nodes compared to the first and last element of the executed workflow block. Furthermore, the formulae of the block that is executed need to be integrated recursively, through the use of e.g. $Dec(B_1, s_{end})$.

Definition 5.7 (Declarative Formula for a Parallel Control-Flow Block). Let B be a parallel control-flow block $B = B_{AND}^{(B_1,B_2)}$ according to Def. 4.8. Then,

$Dec(B, s_{end}) = Dec(B_{AND}^{(B_1,B_2)}, s_{end}) =$
$\{cs < first(B_1), last(B_1) < cj, Dec(B_1, s_{end}),$
$cs < first(B_2), last(B_2) < cj, Dec(B_2, s_{end}),$
$cj < s_{end}\}$

The formula for a parallel control-flow block is similar to the exclusive block. None of the blocks are excluded but both paths need to fulfil the correct order, as previously described for one of the blocks.

Definition 5.8 (Declarative Formula for a Single-Branch Exclusive Block). Let B be a single-branch exclusive block $B = B_{XOR}^{B_1}$ according to Def. 4.9. Then,

$Dec(B, s_{end}) = Dec(B_{XOR}^{(B_1)}, s_{end}) =$
$\{((cs < cj \wedge not(B_1, s_{end})) \vee$
$(cs < first(B_1) \wedge last(B_1) < cj \wedge Dec(B_1, s_{end}))),$
$cj < s_{end}\}$

The particularity of a single-branch exclusive block is that one possible option is not to execute the contained workflow block, thus the control-flow join node succeeds the split node directly. This entails that the execution of the workflow block is prevented, obtained through $not(B_1, s_{end})$. The other possibility and therefore disjunctively connected is represented by the execution of the workflow block within the control-flow blocks resulting in the same formula as described in the previous definitions.

This transformation function $Dec(B, s_{end})$[8], which is the basis for transforming a procedural model into a declarative formula, addresses research question **RQ1.2** (see Section 1.2). To this end, the result of the function is combined with the manually modelled constraints P, explained in Subsection 5.2.2, and used as input for the workflow engine.

5.4.2.3. Example

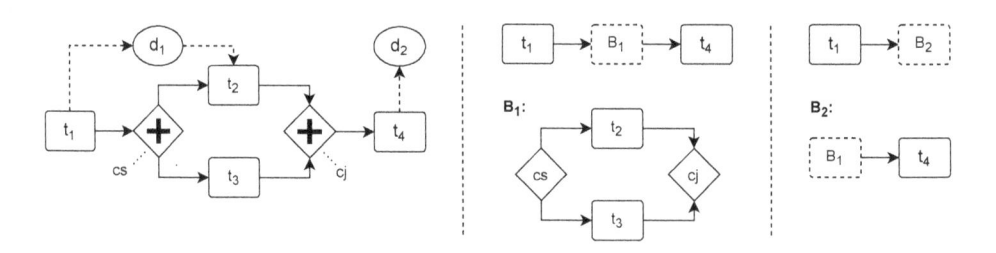

Figure 5.9. Example of a Workflow Graph Decomposed into Workflow Blocks

In order to illustrate the operating principle of the transformation function $Dec(B, s_{end})$, the simple workflow from Fig. 4.1 is used. In Fig. 5.9, the original workflow is abstracted step by step through workflow blocks, such that the recursive calls and decomposition are traceable.

The original workflow on the left side in Fig. 5.9 can be abstracted by enclosing all elements of the control-flow block to a workflow block B_1 (cf. middle part in Fig. 5.9). The last two blocks of this abstracted sequence can be enclosed to a block B_2 (see right part of Fig. 5.9).

The following listings specify the appropriate CSP description for

---

[8]A proof of trace equivalence for the declarative and procedural execution semantics is presented in detail in Appendix A.

5.4. WORKFLOW ENGINE

the exemplary workflow.

$$CSP_{WF} = (X, D, C) \tag{5.16}$$

The decision variables are composed of the sequence nodes S' and the additional variable s_{end}, but as no control variable is included in the control-flow structure no other variable is added.

$$S' = \{t_1, t_2, t_3, t_4, cs, cj\} \tag{5.17}$$
$$S = S' \cup \{s_{end}\} \tag{5.18}$$
$$X = S \tag{5.19}$$

The values of the domains are the same for each of the variables and contain seven different numbers. This can be for instance the following ones:

$$\forall t_i \in S : D_i(t_i) = \{1, 2, 3, 4, 5, 6, 7\} \tag{5.20}$$

The constraint set comprises three different sets, other than the *alldifferent* constraint. While there are no additional, manually modelled constraints, the instance constraint set is empty, as the workflow just started and thus, the de facto workflow has just been initialized without any tasks. The constituent parts of the constraint set that represents the model are three single sets. Control-flow structures with control variables are not present in the exemplary workflow and only one data-flow dependency results from data object d_1, which is output of task t_1 and input of task t_2.

$$C = \{alldifferent(t_1, t_2, t_3, t_4, cs, cj, t_{end})\} \cup C^M \cup C^A \cup C^I \tag{5.21}$$
$$C^A = \emptyset \tag{5.22}$$
$$C^I = \emptyset \tag{5.23}$$
$$C^M = Dec(J, s_{end}) \cup C^{DF} \cup C^{CF} \tag{5.24}$$
$$C^{DF} = \{t_1 < t_2\} \tag{5.25}$$
$$C^{CF} = \emptyset \tag{5.26}$$

A detailed dissolution of the transformation function $Dec(B, s_{end})$ is shown in the following. The first step is to resolve the sequence $B^{(t_1, B_2)}$

on the basis of Def. 4.7.

$$\begin{aligned}
Dec(J, s_{end}) &= Dec(B^{(t_1, B_2)}, s_{end}) \\
&= \{last(t_1) < first(B_2), Dec(B^{t_1}, s_{end}), Dec(B_2, s_{end}), \\
&\quad last(B_2) < s_{end}\} \\
&= \{t_1 < first(B_1), t_1 < s_{end}, Dec(B_2, s_{end}), \\
&\quad last(t_4) < s_{end}\} \\
&= \{t_1 < cs, t_1 < s_{end}, Dec(B_2, s_{end}), t_4 < s_{end}\}
\end{aligned}$$
(5.27)

The function call with block B_2 applies the resolution of the sequence $B^{(B_1, t_4)}$ on the basis of Def. 4.7 and of the single task block B^{t_4} on the basis of Def. 4.6.

$$\begin{aligned}
Dec(B_2, s_{end}) &= Dec(B^{(B_1, t_4)}, s_{end}) \\
&= \{last(B_1) < first(t_4), Dec(B_1, s_{end}), Dec(B^{t_4}, s_{end}), \\
&\quad last(t_4) < s_{end}\} \\
&= \{cj < t_4, Dec(B_1, s_{end}), t_4 < s_{end}, t_4 < s_{end}\}
\end{aligned}$$
(5.28)

Lastly, the transformation function for the control-flow block B_1 needs to be resolved for the sequence $B_{AND}^{(t_2, t_3)}$ on the basis of Def. 4.8 and for the blocks B^{t_2} and B^{t_3} on the basis of Def. 4.6.

$$\begin{aligned}
Dec(B_1, s_{end}) &= Dec(B_{AND}^{(t_2, t_3)}, s_{end}) \\
&= \{cs < first(t_2), last(t_2) < cj, Dec(B^{t_2}, s_{end}), \\
&\quad cs < first(t_3), last(t_3) < cj, Dec(B^{t_3}, s_{end}), cj < s_{end}\} \\
&= \{cs < t_2, t_2 < cj, t_2 < s_{end}, \\
&\quad cs < t_3, t_3 < cj, t_3 < s_{end}, cj < s_{end}\}
\end{aligned}$$
(5.29)

Now that the CSP is defined, work items can be determined. In Table 5.2 two runs of Algorithm 5.1 are exemplified. The values of some variables that change or that are of interest are indicated at the time of the start of the workflow and after the execution of the first proposed work item t_1.

At the start of the workflow, the node and edge sets are both empty. Derived from that, the starting position *current* in the de facto workflow is 1. For each decision variable, a solution is searched

5.4. WORKFLOW ENGINE

Table 5.2. Exemplary Computation of Work Items according to Algorithm 5.1, 1st and 2nd Iteration

	At Start	After Execution of t_1
N_F^S	$\emptyset$	$\{t_1\}$
E_F^C	$\emptyset$	$\emptyset$
current	1	2
sol for $x =$		
t_1	($\mathbf{t_1 = 1}, cs = 2, t_2 = 3,$ $cj = 4, t_4 = 5)$ $s_{end} = 6, t_3 = 7)$	–
t_2	$\emptyset$	$\emptyset$
t_3	$\emptyset$	$\emptyset$
t_4	$\emptyset$	$\emptyset$
s_{end}	$\emptyset$	$\emptyset$
cs	$\emptyset$	$(t_1 = 1, \mathbf{cs = 2}, t_2 = 3,$ $cj = 4, t_4 = 5,$ $s_{end} = 6, t_3 = 7)$
cj	$\emptyset$	$\emptyset$
workItems	$\{t_1\}$	$\{cs\}$

under the assumption that the *current* value is assigned. Only for t_1 a solution exists (see row 6 in Tab. 5.2). Consequently, t_1 is added to the set of work items.

The third column in Tab. 5.2 shows the values after the execution of t_1. The nodes of the de facto workflow are supplemented with t_1 and the position of the possible subsequent task is increased by 1, such that *current* = 2. Solutions are then again assessed for all decision variables, except t_1, as this task has already been executed. In this case, only for cs a solution is found (see Tab. 5.2). No other decision variable could be assigned the value 2 and still lead to a valid solution. Hence, the list of work items consists solely of cs after the execution of t_1.

5.4.3. Loop Handling

So far, the flexible workflow approach is limited to a singular execution of tasks and not incorporating loop constructs or considering deviations like redoing a task. Prerequisites as well as an algorithm to be able to handle the previously mentioned scenarios are explained in the following section.

First, the loop construct is formally defined as a workflow block.

Definition 5.9 (Loop Control-Flow Block). *A loop control-flow block $B = B_{LOOP}^{B_1}$, with $B_1 = (N_{B_1}^S, E_{B_1}^C)$ as workflow block of B contains an opening control-flow node $cs \in N_B^C$ (control-flow split) with an out-degree of two, one branch incoming to cs, containing a workflow block (B_1), whose incoming control-flow is outgoing from a matching closing control-flow node $cj \in N_B^C$ (control-flow join) with an in-degree of two and an empty path that leads back from the opening control-flow node cs to the closing node cj. The control-flow nodes and block elements are connected through the following set of edges: $E_B^{C'} = \{(cj, first(B_1)), (last(B_1), cs), (cs, cj)\} \subseteq E_B^C$. Thus, $E_B^C = E_B^{C'} \cup E_{B_1}^C$ and $N_B^S = \{cs\} \cup \{cj\} \cup N_{B_1}^S$. First and last elements are the control-flow nodes: $first(B) = cj$ and $last(B) = cs$.*

Fig. 5.10 shows an exemplary loop control-flow block. Loop control-flow nodes are marked with an "×". On the first sight it looks rather similar to a single-path exclusive control-flow pattern, but the straight edge between the two control-flow nodes is reversed. Therefore, in a loop block, the control-flow nodes are reversed compared to other control-flow block types. The first one is a join node cj as it joins the path prior to the loop block with the connection from the previous loop run. The loop ends with a split node cs, as two ways to continue are possible, either resulting in an additional loop run or leading to the subsequent path. This described loop control-flow block corresponds to the control flow pattern named *structured loop* with a "post-test" [205, p. 138ff] that refers to a do-while-loop. This restriction is necessary to adhere to block-orientation.

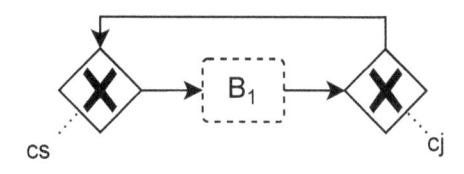

Figure 5.10. Loop Control-Flow Block

To differentiate between individual task instances in case of a repeated enactment, the decision variables that represent task nodes $\{s_n | s_n \in X \wedge s \in N_J^T\}$ are extended with a second index variable l, e.g. $s_{(n,l)}$, denoting the numbering of task instances referencing one single task, here s_n, of the de jure workflow.

5.4. WORKFLOW ENGINE

This second index also simplifies the validation of the constraint $Absence(s_1, x)$, because x might be compared to the second index l of the tasks that have already been executed. Thus, for each such constraint $Absence(s_1, x)$ the following formula needs to be checked during constraint validation: $\forall s_{(n,l)} \in N_F^T : l \leq x$. If this evaluates to false, the corresponding $Absence$ constraint is violated.

For including recurring tasks in the CSP algorithm, another algorithm is needed which alters the input sets for Algo. 5.1. The trigger for this processing (cf. Algo. 5.2) is an enactment of task s_n of the de jure workflow.

Algorithm 5.2: extendCSP(s_n)

Input : Task s_n
Output: X, D, C

1 **if** $s_{(n,l)} \notin X \setminus N_F^T$ **then**
2 $\quad$ find $s_{(n,l)}$ in N_F^T;
3 $\quad$ **if** $s_n \in N_{B_1}^T$ with $N_{B_1}^T \in B_1$ and $B = B_{LOOP}^{B_1}$ **then**
4 $\quad\quad$ integrateNewLoopRun($s_{(n,l)}$);
5 $\quad$ **else**
6 $\quad\quad$ $X \leftarrow X \cup \{s_{(n,l+1)}\}$;
7 $\quad\quad$ **foreach** $D_{s_i} \in D$ **do** $D_{s_i} \leftarrow D_{s_i} \cup \{max(D_{s_i}) + 1\}$;
8 **else if** $isLastNodeInLoop(s_n)$ **then**
9 $\quad$ integrateNewLoopRun($s_{(n,l)}$);

At first it is evaluated if a variable $s_{(n,l)}$ corresponding to task s_n exists in the set of variables that were not executed yet (see line 1 in Algo. 5.2). If such a variable does not exist, it is an unexpected repetition of a task, thus a deviation. Hence, the previous execution of the specific task needs to be found in order to determine the index number (see line 2 in Algo. 5.2). If the variable is part of a loop construct (see line 3 in Algo. 5.2), a possible new loop run has to be integrated in the constraint problem (see line 4 in Algo. 5.2), as explained in Algo. 5.3. Otherwise, as Algo. 5.1 has to cope with unexpected repeated enactments as well, a new variable with an increased index $l + 1$ has to be created and added to X (see line 6 in Algo. 5.2). Domains of the variable of the sequence nodes s_i have to be extended with one additional value for the new variable (see line 7 in Algo. 5.2). Therefore, the maximum value in the domain is searched; this value is then increased by one and added. The last condition checks in case the corresponding variable exists and hence, no deviation occurred, whether the executed task was the last node of a loop construct (see line 8 in Algo. 5.2). Thus, a new possible regular loop run has to be integrated in the constraint problem, which is implemented by Algo. 5.3.

Algorithm 5.3: integrateNewLoopRun($s_{(n,l)}$)

Input   : Task $s_{(n,l)}$
Output: X, D, C
1 **foreach** $s_m \in N_{B_1}^T$ with $N_{B_1}^T \in B_1$ and $B = B_{LOOP}^{B_1}$ **do**
2 $\quad$ $X \leftarrow X \cup \{s_{(m,l+1)}\}$;
3 $\quad$ **foreach** $D_{s_i} \in D$ **do**
4 $\quad\quad$ $D_{s_i} = D_{s_i} \cup \{max(D_{s_i}) + 1\}$;
5 $\quad$ addConstraints();

For each task s_m in the loop a new decision variable $s_{(m,l+1)}$ is included with an increased index variable $(l+1)$ (see line 2 in Algo. 5.3). Domains have to be expanded (see line 4 in Algo. 5.3) and constraints considering the new loop tasks have to be incorporated. The method *addConstraints()* considers three important aspects. A second loop run itself should be constrained regarding the workflow block within the control-flow block. Furthermore, the first loop needs to terminate before the second iteration is allowed to start. Hence, this dependency needs to be established. Moreover, if a second iteration is entered, this loop sequence needs to terminate before the workflow block subsequent to the loop block can be activated. Nevertheless, a second iteration should be optional with regard to continuing after the loop block and executing the remaining tasks.

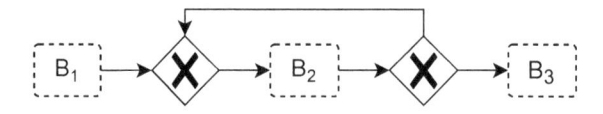

Figure 5.11. Exemplary Workflow Block with a Loop

Table 5.3 shows the generated constraint set that is added by the function *addConstraints()* for the abstract block-oriented workflow with a loop control-flow block shown in Fig. 5.11. All of the constraints in the right column are added to the set C^M. For a better understanding the table is subdivided into several lines, whose constraint subsets serve different purposes.

Table 5.3. Mapping Loop Pattern to Logical Formula with Possible Second Iteration (addConstraints())

Purpose	Constraints
no 2nd iteration	$\{(not(B_{2,2}, s_{end}) \wedge not(cj_2, s_{end}) \wedge not(cs_2, s_{end})) \vee$
2nd iteration pre-condition post-condition	$(cj_2 < first(B_{2,2}) \wedge Dec(B_{2,2}, s_{end}) \wedge$ $last(B_{2,2}) < cs_2 \wedge$ $cs_1 < cj_2 \wedge$ $cs_2 < first(B_3))\}$

The first row describes that a possible second iteration is not executed, therefore preventing the execution of all elements from this second iteration with the function $not(B, s_{end})$. As alternative and hence connected with a logical "or", the remaining rows in contrast consider the execution of the second iteration. This formula contains three subsets. The content of the loop itself is specified in row 2 that corresponds to a sequential connection of control-flow nodes and the block $B_{2,2}$. The pre-condition defines that the control-flow split node cs_1 of the first iteration has to terminate before the control-flow join node of the second iteration cj_2 can be activated. The post-condition represents the fact that the workflow block within the loop needs to be completed, and thus, in this case the last node cs_2, before the subsequent block B_3 can be started.

5.5. Deviation Handling

Up to now the constraint-based workflow engine was described and the used language based on logical formulae was specified. Algorithms were defined that exploit CSP solving for identifying valid work items. Deviations that lead to an inconsistent constraint net have not been regarded so far. The defined functionality does not differ from a traditional workflow engine. In the following sections on the one hand an algorithm that detects deviations and identifies affected constraints is introduced, and on the other hand some simple strategies are presented that restore consistency in the constraint net and allow the workflow engine to resume its duty by leaving the exceptional state and re-enabling CSP solving.

A task enactment first triggers an update of different data objects of the workflow instance. After this update, deviations can be detected. Therefore an algorithm is introduced that is responsible for this update and that furthermore links all previously explained algorithms in an appropriate invocation order.

Algorithm 5.4: updateCSP(s, F, CSP_W)

Input : Task s, F, CSP_W
1 $N_F^S \leftarrow N_F^S \cup \{s\}$;
2 $E_F^C \leftarrow E_F^C \cup (last(F), s)$;
3 $current \leftarrow D_s[|N_F^S|]$;
4 **if** $isPrecedentToCFNode(s)$ **then**
5 $\quad$ **foreach** $cFNode$ **do**
6 $\quad\quad$ $N_F^S \leftarrow N_F^S \cup \{cFNode\}$;
7 $\quad\quad$ $E_F^C \leftarrow E_F^C \cup (last(F), cFNode)$;
8 $\quad\quad$ $current \leftarrow D_s[|N_F^S|]$;
9 $\quad\quad$ $C \leftarrow C \cup \{cFNode = current\}$;
10 $C \leftarrow C \cup \{s = current\}$;
11 $detectDeviations(s, F, CSP_W)$;
12 $computeWorkItems(CSP_W, F)$;
13 $extendCSP(s)$;

The currently enacted task s, the de facto workflow F and the CSP serve as input. First, the task enactment triggers an update of different data. The corresponding sequence node s is included in the de facto workflow F (see line 1 in Algo. 5.4), as well as an edge connecting the previous last element with the new sequence element (see line 2 in Algo. 5.4). Next, the length of the de facto workflow needs to be determined. The value in the domain at this position identifies the assigned value to the variable of the currently enacted task within the CSP (see line 3 in Algo. 5.4). After this update concerning enacted task it needs to be checked if control-flow nodes are involved. If a control-flow node is directly precedent to the task s in the de jure workflow, each of these control-flow nodes are integrated into the de facto workflow (see lines 4-7 in Algo. 5.4) and an instance constraint is added, as the position of the control-flow element is thus determined (see lines 8,9 in Algo. 5.4). Constraints are extended with the value assignment of *current* to s (see line 10 in Algo. 5.4). Subsequently, deviations can be detected (see line 11 in Algo. 5.5), work items can be computed (see line 12 in Algo. 5.1) and the CSP can be checked for a necessary extension concerning repeated tasks or loop executions (see line 13 in Algo. 5.3).

5.5.1. Deviation Detection

How deviations are detected and violated constraints are identified is described by the algorithm that is introduced in the following. Deviations can only occur if a task has been enacted that was not part of the worklist. Algorithm 5.5 illustrates this procedure.

As prerequisite, an additional attribute for each constraint needs to be introduced, namely its status, that can be assigned three different values. The function *Status* specifies this property.

$$Status : C \to \{indefinite, valid, violated\} \quad (5.30)$$

The algorithm is triggered after a task enactment, as this might result in a constraint violation, and consequently, in an inconsistent workflow state. Therefore, all constraints need to be evaluated. This can simply be achieved through searching for a solution to the updated CSP (see line 1 in Algo. 5.5). If no solution is found, the violated constraint or even a set of constraints needs to be identified and retracted from C to restore consistency.

Algorithm 5.5: detectDeviations(s, F, CSP)

Input : Task s, F, CSP_W
1 **if** $!solveCSP(X,D,C)$ **then**
2 | inconsistent $\leftarrow$ true;
3 **foreach** $C_i \in C$ **do**
4 | **if** $Status(C_i) = indefinite \wedge C_i = s_1 < s_2$ **then**
5 | | **if** $s_1 = s$ **then**
6 | | | $Status(C_i) \leftarrow valid$;
7 | | **else if** $s_2 = s$ **then**
8 | | | $Status(C_i) \leftarrow violated$;
9 **if** *inconsistent* **then**
10 | restoreConsistency();

Therefore after each task enactment, the status of single constraints in the constraint set can be assigned in order to prevent unnecessary computations. Based on the value assignments due to the de facto workflow, which will never change for a workflow instance, some constraints will always resolve to true, while other parts always resolve to false, even without constraint violations, e.g. disjunctive associated propositions.

At the initialization of the CSP the default value for each constraint is *indefinite*. When a constraint status is updated to *valid* or *violated*, this status is definite and will not change, as it depends on the value assignments derived from the de facto workflow.

Assuming that the constraint set is available in conjunctive normal form $C = C_1 \wedge ... \wedge C_n$, clauses C_i are linked conjunctively and each clause represents a disjunction of literals $C_i = l_1 \vee ... \vee l_n$. The literals mostly result from the transformation of declarative workflow constructs to logical representations and thus, relate two tasks with the ordering relation "<". Other literals may be equations, such as $t_1 = 0$, depicting the de facto workflow, or *alldifferent(S)* due to the construction of the CSP. The literals of interest for the status assignment are the first ones. Thus, the constraint set is scanned for constraints that have an indefinite status and the following form: $C_i = s_1 < s_2$ (see line 4 in Algo. 5.5).

If a task enactment of task s occurs, the status of all clauses with s on the left side (e.g. $s < s_2$) in one of the literals can be marked as *valid*, as this clause will resolve to true in any case. Furthermore, single literals that contain s on the right side, e.g. $s_1 < s$, are *violated*. Those will never be fulfilled, but the remaining literals in the clause have to be.

One impact of this status changing strategy after each task enactment is that violated constraints can be determined easily. A clause consisting of a single literal, e.g. $s_1 < s$, where the currently enacted task s is on the right side, is *violated* as s_1 has not yet been enacted, otherwise the clause would have been assigned a *valid* status previously and thus, would be excluded during this check.

As violated constraints have been identified, they can simply be retracted in order to allow the workflow engine to compute work items on the basis of remaining constraints that form a consistent constraint net (see function *restoreConsistency()* in line 10 in Algo. 5.5). However, impacts of simply omitting one small part in a complex formula based on disjunctive and conjunctive connected subformulae are hardly predictable. Therefore the next section introduces two different scenarios with specific deviations that are related to different strategies of how to restore consistency.

5.5.2. Strategies for Restoring Consistency

Two different and very simple constraint violation scenarios will be presented in combination with strategies, which are implemented, for restoring consistency in the CSP.

5.5.2.1. Sequential Constraint Violation

For handling detected deviations in a simple sequential workflow or in sequential parts of a workflow, two different strategies are developed for restoring consistency. Consider the example in Fig. 5.12, where the first row shows the initial situation and the second row represents one step further with an additional executed task. Rectangles indicate tasks, whereas edges represent the execution order. Blue-coloured

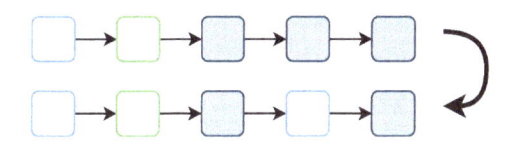

Figure 5.12. Exemplary Sequential Workflow with Deviation

nodes were already executed, green ones are currently recommended and grey nodes are not activated yet. In the lower row there is a task executed that is not in a valid order, meaning a deviation occurred. This situation can be detected in case a literal consists of a single constraint in the following form: $C_i = s_1 < s_2$. The cause of the violation is not explicit without semantic knowledge and can only be specified by the process participant. Without necessary intervention of the process participant two possible reasons can be derived, which are handled in different strategies.

1. **Skipped Tasks.** Tasks either have become obsolete and are therefore skipped or have been executed but without notice of the system (cf. Fig. 5.13a). All constraints concerning skipped tasks are irrelevant for continuing with the workflow and simply may be omitted.

2. **Changed Order.** Task order may have changed due to unknown reasons. Remaining tasks need to be connected sequentially, as if the current executed task (second blue one) had been inserted after the last executed one (first blue one, cf. new

edges in Fig. 5.13b). Therefore, the constraint set needs to be extended to map the newly introduced sequential dependencies.

(a) Skipped Tasks

(b) Changed Order

Figure 5.13. Possible Strategies for Handling Sequential Deviations

Which strategy is applied needs to be determined either prior to the start of a workflow or at run time. If the applied strategies differ for single deviations of the same type, further interaction from the process participant is necessary for each occurrence at run time, which reduces the advantages of allowed flexibility and an additional obstacle for an easy-to-use system emerges.

5.5.2.2. Exclusive Constraint Violation

Another exemplary scenario of a simple violation that might occur is depicted in Fig. 5.14. In this simplified sketch at first both exclusive paths might be chosen, followed by the execution of the upper task, which implies the exclusion of the lower tasks. The deviation occurs in the last step, as nevertheless a task of the lower path has been executed.

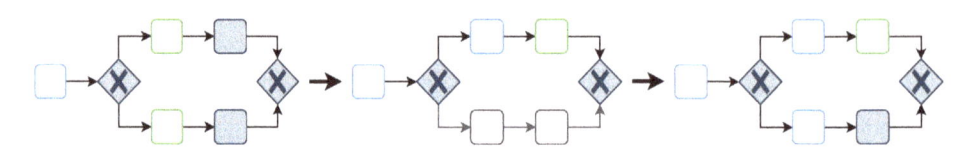

Figure 5.14. Exemplary Workflow with Exclusive Pattern and Deviation

Which path should be pursued for workflow continuation without further knowledge can only be guessed by the system. Possible reasons are that either some task was completed by mistake or eventually certain circumstances changed that demand an adjustment and caused the execution of an excluded task or rather whole path. Constraints need to be adapted in case of such a violation according to one of the strategies pointed out in Fig. 5.15a and 5.15b that draw new sequential

5.5. DEVIATION HANDLING

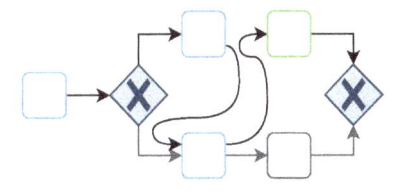

(a) Continuing with the Upper Path

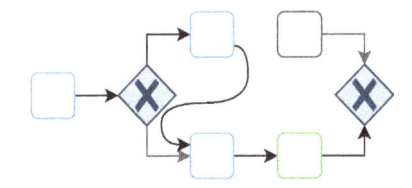

(b) Continuing with the Lower Path

Figure 5.15. Possible Strategies for Handling Deviations in Exclusive Patterns

connections. The same issues arise compared to the first scenario. Deciding which strategy to apply is not reasonably possible without further knowledge about the cause and purpose of the deviation. Expertise or up-to-date knowledge about the current situation is necessary that most likely will be introduced by process participants.

The described scenarios have shown two types of deviations and thus constraint violations with a simple structure and a limited number of resolving possibilities. These strategies are straight-forward and easy to implement, but require interaction from the process participant. Besides, deviations might lead to additional deviations or even might be more complex from ground up, which makes it impossible to determine similar strategies to handle all possible deviation scenarios. Furthermore, the intention of this work is not to construct strategies that need to be picked by the process participant. The objective is rather to construct methods that can be applied in an automated manner and support the process participant invisibly without the need of manual intervention. As further knowledge about a possible cause and the purpose of the deviation is necessary to make a well-founded decision for choosing a strategy, the next chapter introduces an approach that focuses on case-based reasoning as technique to overcome the previously mentioned disadvantages.

Nevertheless, the proposed deviation detection and handling approach addresses research question **RQ1.3** (see Section 1.2) with the limitation of a partial automation due to the necessary manual choice of applied strategies.

5.6. Related Work

Using constraints in the context of workflow management is prevalent and research in manifold directions exists. Constraints serve different purposes and address various aspects. They are foremost utilized for a specification of the formal basis for a WfMS or for an enhancement of traditional approaches.

The most popular declarative workflow approach, DECLARE [135, 184, 207], uses the *ConDec* language for the description, evaluation, and execution of constraint models [136, 137]. The formal basis are LTL formulae representing constraints. These LTL formulae are further transformed into finite-state automata, which are used for constraint validation and consequently as workflow engine. Though there is a differentiation between mandatory and optional constraints, and optional constraints may be violated, a possibility to retract constraints is not specified and therefore no unforeseen situations can be handled flexibly.

The concept of *Dynamic Condition Response (DCR) graphs* [70] is a declarative process model that is based on a mapping of these special graphs, which contain four different relations, to Büchi automata similar to DECLARE. The approach is described as offering more flexibility, but also has no possibility to restore consistency after deviations.

In later work Maggi et al. [100] developed an approach called *Mobucon* that is based on colored automata. Main advantages are the ability to detect deviations and to support continuously through various strategies. A drawback of this approach is that these strategies need to be determined beforehand and cannot be changed during run time, as the construction of a new automaton would take too long (for 30-50 constraints 5-10 seconds) [100]. Algorithms developed by Westergaard [206] improve this issue with efficient run time modifications, e.g. models with up to 50 constraints are handled in fewer seconds.

A main drawback of approaches that base on LTL is a poor scalability. When models are expanded, the state space increases exponentially with the consequences of a decreased efficiency [33]. The approach *ReFlex* tries to solve this issue with an efficient graph based rule engine [33]. Models are specified based on ConDec constraints that are compiled to graphs. During execution the rule engine interacts with the graph for updating activity states and verifying the rules that

5.6. RELATED WORK

are mapped in this graph [33]. Runtime changes are not supported, but on the basis of the presented runtime environment and a clear distinction of modelling and execution phase, rules would need to be adapted manually, compiled again to a graph, which would then be utilized by the rule engine to propose activities. Therefore, achieving flexibility by deviation through this declarative approach is rather tedious.

This significant drawback of existing declarative approaches for flexibility by deviation is solved in the presented work. The aim is to achieve efficient automated runtime modifications. Constraints can be added or retracted ad-hoc, without the need of a time-consuming recompilation of the model. Consistent models can then be used for a determination of the worklist through the formulated CSP. Here, the bottleneck concerning computation time is the solving of several CSPs, whereas it has been shown that the necessary time is acceptable for realistic scenarios [58]. A main aspect of this approach, foremost for the suitability for inexperienced process participants and a preservation of intuitive workflow modelling, is the transformation of procedurally modelled workflows to a declarative representation. Some related approaches exist.

Wedemeijer [202] presents an approach that transforms imperative workflow models to declarative business rules on the basis of relation algebra. At run time the rule set can be adapted, either by removing or adding some of the rules. Here, a high effort is necessary to evaluate the rules.

Ständer et al. [175] describe an approach for adaptive workflows in smart environments, where imperative and declarative workflow models are combined and also translated into each other to achieve flexibility when modelling the behaviour of a smart item. This combination and integration of distinct modelling paradigms sounds rather similar to the presented workflow concept. Unfortunately published research only consists of a very abstract description and lacks concrete specification. Therefore a profound comparison is impossible.

Declarative workflow approaches that incorporate constraints have been part of research for several years. Some approaches that relate in some way to the proposed constraint-based workflow concept are briefly described in the following.

Grambow et al. introduce a method for an automated semantically driven workflow generation using declarative modelling [54]. The user specifies single constraints, more complex building blocks and a set of activities. On this basis and depending on the current situation, the system automatically derives valid workflows on the fly through ontology reasoning. Single dependencies of elements need to be specified prior to execution, which is why usability is doubtful, at least for inexperienced users.

The Declarative Process Intermediate Language (DPIL) uses a rule-based model to specify multi-perspective constraints [168]. Three different perspectives are considered: control-flow, data, resources. Furthermore a distinction is made between mandatory ("ensure") and recommended ("advice") constraints.

Constraints are exploited for different aspects. Some approaches are presented that focus on improving flexibility.

Lu et al. [96] utilize constraints for defining temporal aspects considering scheduling through temporal constraint networks in order to increase workflow flexibility. "Instance customization" is allowed through a remodelling by the process participant, whereas the constraint network is used to validate consistency.

Another approach by Lu et al. [95] allows for specifying constraints at build time that describe selection dependencies of tasks for process adaptation at instance level. Task selection is coded in a rather simple fashion by tuples of 0 and 1 that can be combined through some operators, increasing the expressiveness.

The Process Constraint Ontology (ProContO) and the Process Constraint Language (PCL) use constraints in order to concern non-functional or domain-specific requirements such as geospatial dependencies [93]. These semantic technologies are applied alongside traditional WfMS. Constraints are connected to involved process elements and specified through PCL on the basis of concepts defined in ProContO.

Kuziemsky et al. [89] propose a data-driven and flexible approach for clinical practice guidelines. Constraints are used for the prevention of data incompleteness and inconsistencies in these guidelines for each patient. Missing or corrected data is suggested to the user as solution in order to improve data quality. Ultimately, this should assist the medical professional in choosing an adequate or even optimal treatment.

Barba et al. [11] enhance the ConDec Language through temporal aspects. The proposed language *TConDec-R* includes properties such as deadlines or limited validity of a process element in order to optimize the run time through generating enactment plans.

Chapter 6

Case-Based Deviation Management

To improve the user support for workflow flexibility by deviation, the presented approach, which consists of a constraint-based workflow engine up to here, is complemented with a case-based deviation management. To this end, previous experiences are exploited for a sophisticated decision process on how to continue with the workflow execution after a deviation occurred. This case-based approach is regarded as learning component of the presented flexible workflow concept. The main idea and the necessary similarity measures have been presented in previous work [57, 162, 163]. Both are adopted to a great extent and described in more detail in this work. Additionally, the case-based approach for deviation management is enhanced by adaptation algorithms.

This chapter starts with necessary preliminaries, which is followed by a description of the overall concept. Subsequently, concrete realizations such as the specification of the similarity measures, adaptation methods, and associated algorithms are presented. In the first Section 6.1, the foundations on case-based reasoning as such and process-oriented case-based reasoning as a special form are introduced. Subsequently, fundamentals on time-series similarity measures are presented in Section 6.2. In Section 6.3, the envisioned concept of a deviation management is contextualized with the CBR cycle. As integral part of this approach, the two phases of retrieval and reuse are introduced. The similarity measure is conceived and specified in Section 6.4. In this context, some algorithms are explained, which includes a pre-processing of the case base. In addition, two adaptation methods are defined in Section 6.5 that allow for an identification of work items. This encompasses a null adaptation and a generative variant that exploits the constraint set resulting from the workflow engine during execution. The chapter concludes in Section 6.6 with an overview of related approaches that exploit CBR methods for flexible workflows and similar research work concerning deviation handling.

6.1. Foundations on Case-Based Reasoning

Case-Based Reasoning (CBR) [149] is a powerful problem solving methodology in the field of AI that can be implemented through different technologies, e.g. neural networks or CSP [198]. It is broadly applicable as the underlying idea corresponds to natural problem solving, which is inspired by human thinking. Therefore, it is an intuitive methodology that benefits from available resources that machines provide, such as memory and speed [149, p. 3]. CBR intends "to solve a new problem by remembering a previous similar situation and by reusing information and knowledge of that situation" [1]. The methodology is based on the assumption that similar problems have similar solutions [13]. Summarized concisely, CBR fulfils the task of "problem solving and learning from experiences" [1].

CBR is prevalent and applied in various domains in order to solve manifold issues. Recent developments include for instance optimization of training plans in sports [47], proposing treatments in healthcare [10], and even identifying countermeasures to crop failure due to climate change [178].

In contrast to other AI approaches that solely build upon predefined general knowledge, CBR foremost considers experiential knowledge [1]. As integral part, this entails continuous learning and thus, self-improvement [1]. Encountered problems that were solved through CBR are integrated as experiential knowledge to increase the informativeness [13]. Compared to other AI approaches, such as deep learning, which require a huge amount of training data in order to produce a generally applicable model, a small data set suffices for CBR, as it is an instance-based approach. Besides, the learning process is much more simple and efficient, since only one new experience needs to be integrated in the data set when one problem is solved. This contrasts with other approaches where a completely new model needs to be trained. Consequently, a main advantage of CBR is that the effortful knowledge acquisition process becomes superfluous, as the main data

6.1. FOUNDATIONS ON CASE-BASED REASONING

basis is build upon experiences that emerge during operation [117].

6.1.1. Case Representation

An experience of a problem is considered a *case*. A case usually consists of a problem and a solution part. Cases can be separated in positive cases C^+ and negative cases C^- [149, p. 20]. Positive cases were handled successfully and can be reused. Negative ones failed in solving the problem, which can also help in deciding about a solution for a new problem, foremost to prevent the identical failure.

All cases are stored in a *case base CB*. The actually regarded problem case, for which a solution is searched, is denoted as *query*.

A successful problem solving with CBR, which implies effectiveness and efficiency at the same time, mainly depends on the representation of the cases and, in particular, on which properties that are relevant for obtaining similar cases are stored, as well as their organization in or the structure of the case base [1].

There are three main types of case representations that differ depending on aspects of the considered problem and concerning their solving strategy. Structural CBR handles structured cases that can be for instance attribute-value pairs, object-oriented representations, graphs or a set of atomic formulae [13]. Textual CBR considers natural language in text form, e.g. in documents, which additionally requires information retrieval and other text processing methods [91]. Conversational CBR involves the user through a list of questions that need to be answered. The resulting question answer pairs form the cases and are utilized in order to find an adequate solution [13].

6.1.2. CBR Cycle

The traditional CBR process consists of four sequential steps. Summarized, these are denoted as CBR cycle, since they are performed iteratively as one solved problem influences the handling of a subsequent issue by retaining these made experiences. This CBR cycle with its four phases is shown in Fig. 6.1.

The substantial parts, which are accessed by each of the process steps, are the knowledge containers. They consist of previously experienced cases, the *case base*, and general domain-specific knowledge, e.g. taxonomies or rules. These are explained in more detail in Subsect. 6.1.3.

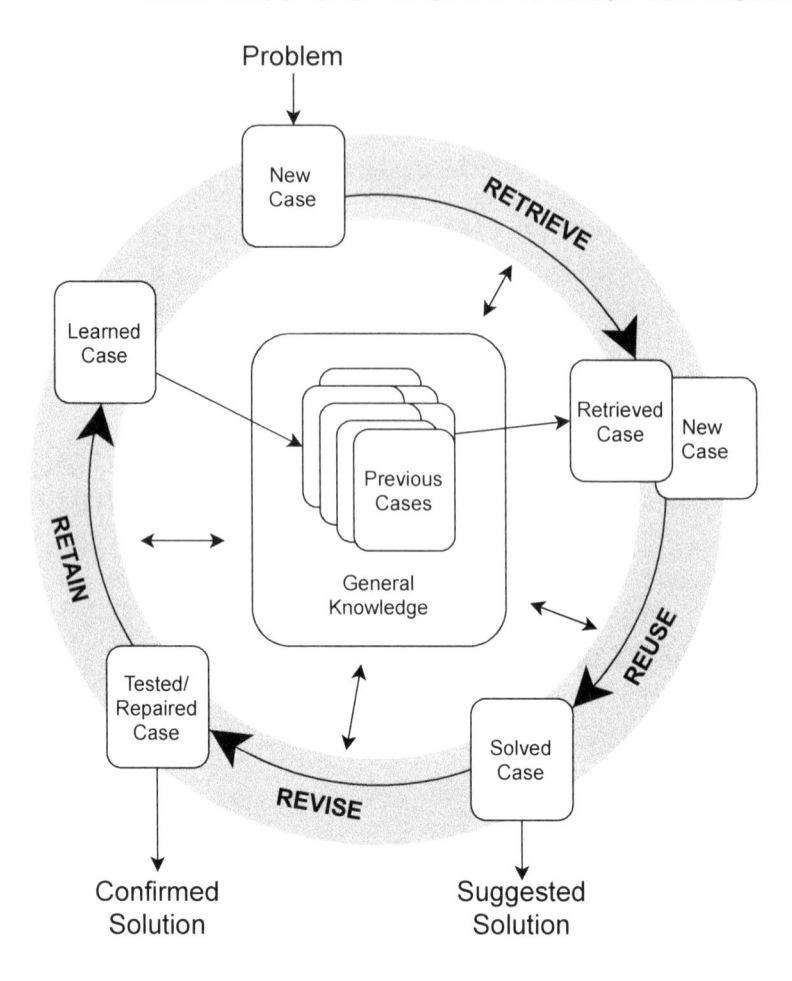

Figure 6.1. CBR Cycle by Aamodt and Plaza [1]

The starting point in the CBR cycle is the formulation of a problem that needs to be solved. Ideally, this query is specified in the same representation format as the elements in the case base. Each of the four steps, also denoted as the four "RE's", is described in the following.

6.1.2.1. Retrieve

In the retrieval phase, a case search and matching is performed [1]. In the simplest form, this is done via a k-nearest neighbour algorithm. The result can be either the most similar case, or k most similar cases, or even all cases that have at least a similarity higher than a specified value x [149, p. 168]. Several strategies for this search can be applied. A brute force technique simply compares all cases sequentially, which can lead to inefficiencies, in particular when considering large case bases. Improvements can be achieved through a two-level retrieval. Popular methods are clustering of cases or a MAC/FAC ("many are called but few are chosen") approach, where a first selection process concentrates on one specific property, whereas a complete similarity assessment is performed on this reduced set of cases [17],[149, p. 171f].

Similarity, as an integral part of the retrieval phase, is presented in more detail in Subsect. 6.1.4.

6.1.2.2. Reuse

The most similar cases, which result from the retrieval, are reused for finding a solution to the new case. The reuse principle is displayed in Fig. 6.2, where an old problem is retrieved. Its solution is further adapted to fit the new problem. If the similarity of the new case and the retrieved case is at maximum, meaning that they are equal, the solution can be easily transferred. Otherwise, in case of a lower similarity value, the old solution needs to be adapted to fit the new problem. The reuse step results in a suggested solution.

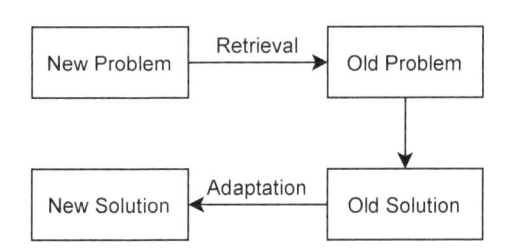

Figure 6.2. Reuse Principle by Richter and Weber [149, p. 30]

More details about adaptation are given in Subsect. 6.1.5.

6.1.2.3. Revise

In the revise phase, the outcome or rather success of the adapted solution that was applied to the new problem is evaluated. This can be done manually or in an automated manner. If the solution failed, it eventually is repaired, to learn from the mistakes that were made. Hence, the tested or repaired case results in a confirmed solution.

6.1.2.4. Retain

The last phase of the CBR cycle retains the learned case. It is not necessarily reasonable to store all upcoming cases in the case base, as this increases the size of the case base, possibly leads to redundancy and as a result decelerates the retrieval phase and ultimately decreases efficiency. Therefore a trade-off should be made between a necessary minimum amount of cases and the informativeness. Some methods exist, such as generalization of cases, that decrease the size of the case base, e.g. through abstracting and clustering or rather aggregating cases, but nevertheless preserve information content. In addition, the retain phase can include the learning of knowledge concerning similarity and adaptation, e.g. through applying machine learning algorithms.

6.1.3. Knowledge Containers

Besides this process view of CBR, the knowledge view is essential. The different knowledge containers, which are shown as one block in the middle of the CBR cycle in Fig. 6.1, are accessed and combined for the different phases and used for manifold purposes. In Fig. 6.3, the knowledge is split up into four distinct parts.

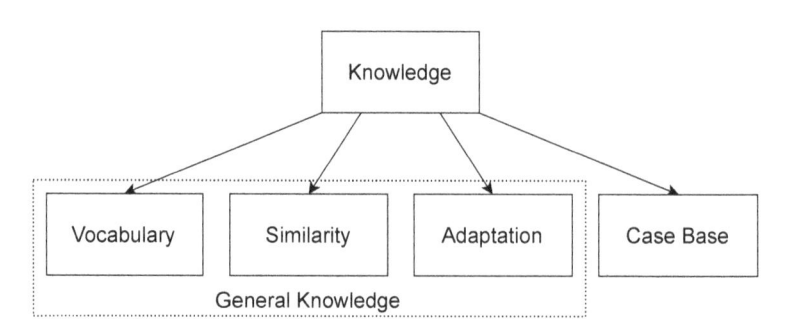

Figure 6.3. CBR Knowledge Containers by Richter and Weber [149, p. 34]

The knowledge can be stored explicitly or implicitly, for instance in form of algorithms [149, p. 34].

6.1.3.1. Case Base

The case base comprises past experiences and is quite naturally domain-specific. As previously mentioned, it includes positive and successful cases, as well as negative, failed ones. These cases can originate from a real context, they can be variations from these real cases or even completely consist of synthetically generated data [149, p. 36]. The case base is involved foremost in the retrieval phase and eventually in the retain phase, if the learned case is preserved in order to be used in future problem solving.

General knowledge can be split up into three individual containers: vocabulary, similarity, and adaptation.

6.1.3.2. Vocabulary

The vocabulary contains knowledge about the elements of the cases and their structure. This can be for instance an ontology that defines the value range of one attribute and their relationships [13]. The vocabulary is particularly utilized to support the similarity assessment and adaptation strategies.

6.1.3.3. Similarity Measures

Knowledge about how to assess the similarity of two cases is essential for the retrieval phase. Similarity measures need to be defined for the cases as such, as well as for each element type of one case, if it is a composite object. Usually, the similarity is formalized as a function with two input parameters, i.e. the two cases that are to be compared, that results in a real value $sim \in [0, 1]$ [13]. More details are given in Subsection 6.1.4.

6.1.3.4. Adaptation Knowledge

The adaptation knowledge is accessed in the reuse phase, where the solution of the retrieved case is transferred to the new case. If this solution is not directly applicable, because the cases are not equal, adaptation becomes necessary. Therefore, the existence of adaptation knowledge leads to a reduced amount of cases that is required for an effective problem solving. More details about adaptation are given in Subsect. 6.1.5.

6.1.4. Similarity

For finding the most suitable problem in the case base compared to the currently regarded problem, the similarity is decisive [149]. To this end, the specification of similarity and how it is measured are essential for retrieving a useful case. It is usually formalized as a function that compares two cases. A high value implies a high similarity, whereas a low value indicates nearly no similarity at all. The values are mapped to an interval between 0 and 1.

$$sim : CB \times CB \rightarrow [0,1] \tag{6.1}$$

The similarity value ultimately indicates utility and preference [13]. The concrete resulting value has no meaning but rather indicates a preference through an ordering of cases. Similarity assessment can be done in a number of ways and it is dependent on the type of data and the element structures. Bergmann proposes several similarity measures not only for rather simple types, such as numeric attributes, but also for object-oriented and graph representations [12].

A simple example for assessing the similarity of two integer values a, b is through calculating the absolute distance. To achieve a similarity result between 0 and 1, the value needs to be normalized through a division of the interval range (max-min). Furthermore, as distance has the opposite meaning compared to similarity (zero distance equals a high similarity), the resulting distance is subtracted from 1.

$$sim(a,b) = 1 - \frac{|a-b|}{max - min} \tag{6.2}$$

Thus, if two values 2 and 6 of the interval [0,10] are compared, the similarity value is $sim(2,6) = 1 - \frac{|2-6|}{10-0} = 1 - 0,4 = 0,6$.

An important technique for similarity assessment concerning cases that are composite objects and consist of more than one attribute is the local-global principle. Separate local similarity functions are used for each single attribute, whose results are then combined into one global similarity value. Therefore, an amalgamation function is used [149, p. 138]. This can be for instance in the simplest case a weighted average of all attributes, where the weights indicate the importance and the relevance of individual attributes [149, p. 28].

$$sim(a,b) = \sum_{i=1}^{n} w_i * sim_i(a_i, b_i) \tag{6.3}$$

where w_i defines a weight for each attribute and sim_i specifies the local similarity value of one attribute a_i and b_i [149, p. 134].

6.1. FOUNDATIONS ON CASE-BASED REASONING

When matching graphs, more elaborate techniques need to be applied. There are rather simple methods that investigate the property isomorphism, but the assessment result is binary and thus, restricted to either 0 or 1 [12, p. 132]. Another kind of graph similarity can be computed through the use of edit distances, which is transferred to nodes and edges in order to transform one graph into the other one [12, p. 134f]. However, this procedure is computationally expensive.

Similarity concerning processes will be regarded in Subsect. 6.1.6.2.

6.1.5. Adaptation

Since the resulting case from the retrieval phase is only approximately appropriate, adaptation is necessary in almost all cases. Further reasons why adaptation is indispensable are the probable lack of adequate cases and hence, a missing case that is sufficient similar; an approximate solution that was applied to the retained case; or an insufficient formulation of the query that leads to erroneously similar cases [149, p. 191].

Two main adaptation strategies are distinguished. Transformational reuse aims at applying the old solution with slight adjustments to fit the context of the new case. This can be for instance adaptation rules or operators [13][149, p. 36]. Generative or derivational adaptation makes use of analogies by replaying the solving strategy that was applied to the old case to the new case [1].

Generally, adaptation can vary from none, called "null adaptation", to the construction of a completely new solution [149, p. 191]. An appropriate adaptation technique allows for a rigorous decrease of the size of the case base [149, p. 36], as this lack of informativeness can be compensated.

6.1.6. Process-Oriented Case-Based Reasoning

A special type of CBR concerns procedural knowledge and is thus named Process-Oriented Case-Based Reasoning (POCBR) [114]. POCBR focusses on reasoning with workflows and allows for an integration of PAIS and CBR [15]. It is applied in various domains such as cooking [122], scientific workflows [214] or logistics [67].

The positive cases in a case base of a POCBR approach can be regarded as best practices, as they comprise only successfully terminated workflows of one specific domain [15]. The reasoning process aims at creating new workflows based on previous experiences, in this case terminated workflow instances, due to some demand that arises. The issue that is regarded in this work concerns an upcoming deviation, which requires an adapted workflow to enable worklist recommendations. The approach presented in this work can be classified as structural POCBR. Several case representations exist that can represent workflows. In this work, a specific graph-based structure is adopted, which is denoted as semantic workflows.

6.1.6.1. Semantic Workflows as Case Representation

Semantic workflows are used as case representation, as they allow for an enrichment of semantic descriptions for nodes, edges, and the workflow as such. Since the similarity assessment is additionally based on these semantic annotations, it is more sophisticated.

The utilized specification of semantic workflows is denoted as *NESTGraph*, which contains the same elements as block-oriented workflows, but is additionally enriched by semantic metadata. According to Bergmann and Gil [15], a NESTGraph is defined as follows:

Definition 6.1 (NESTGraph). *A semantic workflow graph, shortly denoted as NESTGraph, is a semantically labelled directed graph, specified as quadruple* $W = (N, E, S, T)$ *where*

- N *is a set of nodes and*

- $E \subseteq N \times N$ *is a set of edges.*

- $S : N \cup E \to \Sigma$ *associates to each node and each edge a semantic description from a semantic metadata language* Σ.

- $T : N \cup E \to \Omega$ *associates to each node and each edge a type from* Ω.

- Ω *contains the following types of nodes: workflow, task, data, control-flow node and the following types of edges: part-of, data-flow, control-flow and constraint edge.*

Fig. 6.4 shows an excerpt of a workflow instance, which is used for evaluating the presented approach. It is related to the workflow model illustrated in Fig. 3.2 - 3.5.

6.1. FOUNDATIONS ON CASE-BASED REASONING 131

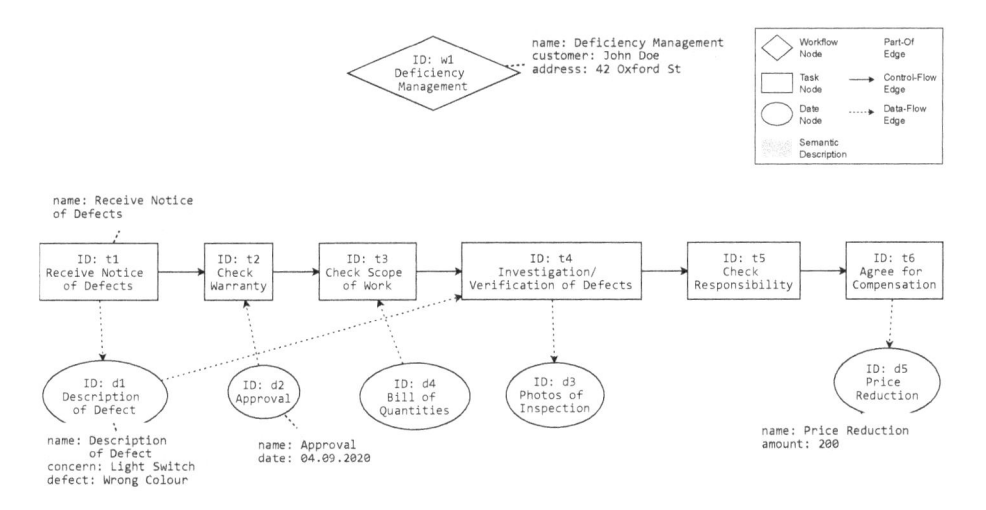

Figure 6.4. Exemplary Block-Oriented Semantic Workflow Graph

This workflow consists of six task nodes (rectangles), five data nodes (ovals) and one workflow node (rhombus), thus $N = \{w1, t1, t2, t3, t4, t5, t6, d1, d2, d3, d4, d5\}$. Control-flow nodes are missing in the example, as only a simple sequence is presented. Each node is labelled with its id (cf. "ID") and the name that is part of the semantic description. The edges denote either control-flow (solid black lines), data-flow (dashed lines, input/output relation) or part-of edges (solid grey lines) and jointly represent the set of edges E. Constraint edges are non-existent in the example.

Furthermore, each node is associated with a semantic description (grey rectangles), which contains additional information. In Fig. 6.4, some exemplary semantic descriptions are shown. The workflow node relates to some general information that concerns the whole workflow and not only individual task or data nodes. In the example, the customer name and the address of the concerned object is stored in this semantic description. The tasks' semantic descriptions only contain the name. The additional information of data nodes differ concerning the attributes. For instance in data node $d1$ further details are provided about the *description of defect* such as *concern* and *defect*, or in data object $d5$ the *amount* of price reduction is specified.

Another central aspect of each CBR approach is the applied similarity measure. For POCBR, a specific measure that is able to compare workflows is required.

6.1.6.2. Workflow Similarity

Besides local similarity measures that compare single attributes, the most interesting similarity measure for the presented approach concerns workflows. In research, many approaches exist that compare entire process models.

Workflows are represented through a complex structure and therefore, require more complex methods for retrieval and adaptation compared to simple case representations such as attribute-value pairs. As workflows are commonly represented in a graph-based structure, prevalent methods apply similarity measures for graph matching through a mapping of elements or through assessing the edit distance.

A mapping of two workflow models is created through assigning each element of the first model to an element of the second model. To this end, a local similarity function is used that compares individual elements to achieve the best possible mapping. Subsequently, these local similarity values for mapped elements can be aggregated to one global similarity score. There are various approaches that apply this method [15, 37, 128, 208]. These approaches generally give good results, however, finding the best mapping is non trivial and exhaustive search approaches are not feasible in most applications due to inefficiency. This issue can be limited by utilizing heuristics to find the best mapping [15, 213].

Besides graph matching, finding the edit distance between workflow models is a well-known approach, which is inspired by the Levenshtein distance [92] that is used to compare strings [90].

For semantic workflows, which were previously introduced as case representation, Bergmann and Gil propose a similarity measure that is based on an A*-search algorithm for finding the best possible mapping of graph elements [15]. This algorithm utilizes the local-global principle, where similarities of semantic descriptions are mainly used for mapping single elements and thus, substantially contribute to the global similarity value [15]. Nevertheless, A*-search is rather inefficient for large case bases.

However, de facto workflows constitute a special type of workflows, as they only consist of sequentially connected nodes. Thus, this restriction can be considered when evaluating adequate similarity measures. The myCBR system [176] provides a sequence similarity measure that was developed by Lupiani et al. [99]. Events are considered to be atomic and, consequently, an adapted Levenshtein distance is calculated between them [92]. Dijkman et al. developed a similar method [37].

6.1.6.3. Workflow Adaptation

Existing approaches for workflow adaptation mainly focus on the change of workflow models.

Minor et al. propose so-called *adaptation cases* that store knowledge about the transformation process of one workflow to a target workflow through adding or deleting certain workflow fragments [113].

Müller [120] investigated several adaptation methods for business workflows, such as structural and substitutional adaptation, which were transferred to the domain of scientific workflows by Zeyen et al. [214]. As a structural approach, workflow streams are extracted from workflow models that represent significant subworkflows with a certain input and output [121]. These workflow streams can be exchanged through subworkflows with similar properties.

Substitutional adaptation mainly depends on generalization and specialization of certain elements of the case [123]. Knowledge about the possible state space that is represented as taxonomies are exploited for the adaptation itself.

In the proposed approach for workflow flexibility, the focus is on comparing de facto workflows. These workflows can be interpreted as event sequences, where single tasks represent one event. Event sequences resemble time series and therefore, related similarity measures are considered. Before the designed similarity measure is presented, necessary foundations on some time-series similarity measures that are adopted are explained.

6.2. Foundations on Time-Series Similarity Measures

For comparing time series, most of the existing approaches can be distinguished into two categories. Similar to graph matching algorithms, some approaches directly compare the two objects by searching for the alignment while comparing individual elements. Similarity assessment is subsequently realised through the local-global principle, by aggregating local similarity values of single aligned elements into one global score. Prevalent approaches that follow this method are Dynamic Time Warping (DTW) [160] and the Smith-Waterman-

Algorithm (SWA) [172]. A similar approach that applies the SWA is called Trace-Based Reasoning (TBR) [112].

The second type of time-series similarity measures transform these series into a different representation format, such as an n-dimensional vector. Subsequently, adequate similarity measures, e.g. cosine similarity for vectors, can then be applied. Hence, the similarity assessment can be accomplished in a much more efficient way, but nevertheless some information might get lost due to the transformation into a simpler structure.

The main intention of these methods is to limit the series' complexities in order to subsequently compare the representations with a very efficient established measure. For instance, Agrawal et al. [5] apply the Discrete Fourier Transform to extract some features from a series and subsequently only compare a small number of the extracted features. Gundersen [61] uses a vector representation that specifies the temporal distribution of events in the series. Through a weighting factor, events with a greater temporal distance have lower influence on the similarity outcome than those with temporal proximity.

These related and promising approaches will be introduced in more detail in the following sections.

6.2.1. Dynamic Time Warping

Dynamic Time Warping (DTW) was originally developed in the context of speech recognition in order to properly align distorted time series data that is collected from voice recordings [18, 160]. Conventional methods for comparing time series only assess the similarity between elements with the same timestamp, whereas DTW allows elements to be warped onto elements with different timestamps, but nevertheless preserving the sequential order of elements. Therefore, this similarity measure is resistant to noise, e.g. to compression and stretching.

DTW is already applied in various CBR approaches, for instance for patient case matching in the medical domain [180].

The DTW algorithm is able to compare two sequences X with $|X| = n$ and $n \in \mathbb{N}$, and Y with $|Y| = m$ and $m \in \mathbb{N}$ and consists of the following steps:

1. Determine a local distance or similarity function.

2. Initialize the scoring matrix.

3. Calculate the remaining entries in the scoring matrix on the basis of the initial starting values and the defined local similarity measure.

4. Find the highest similarity value and the ideal warping path through backtracking.

To exemplify the algorithm, these steps are explained in detail on the basis of two string sequences $X_D = \langle a, b, c, d, e \rangle$ with $|X_D| = 5$ and $Y_D = \langle a, f, b, c, e, g \rangle$ with $|Y_D| = 6$. The scoring matrix and its filling is illustrated in Fig. 6.5

1. Local Similarity Measure

Originally, DTW is defined using distance functions, however, since distances can be losslessly converted into similarity scores, the algorithm will be presented using a similarity function. For the sake of simplification, in this example a primitive local similarity measure is used that assigns a value of 1 if the two characters match, otherwise a value of 0. For all elements $x_i \in X_D$ and $y_j \in Y_D$ the similarity values are assessed as follows:

$$sim(x_i, y_j) = \begin{cases} 1 & \text{if } x_i = y_j \\ 0 & \text{otherwise} \end{cases} \tag{6.4}$$

In general, every similarity measure can be applied that is adequate for the elements of the time series. Ideally this should be optimized for the specific domain. In the context of de facto workflows, this local similarity measure should be able to compare tasks and their properties.

2. Initialization of the Scoring Matrix

A scoring matrix $H = (h_{i,j}) \in \mathbb{R}^{(n+1,m+1)}$ is constructed (see Fig. 6.5) with $n+1$ columns and $m+1$ rows. The columns represent an element of the first case, whereas the rows refer to elements of the second case. One additional row and column is needed for the initialization of the matrix (cf. '-' in Fig. 6.5). The first row and column are initialized with zero: $\forall i \in \{0, \ldots, n\}, j \in \{0, \ldots, m\} : h_{i,0} = h_{0,j} = 0$. In the remaining cells, one element of the first series is contrasted with an

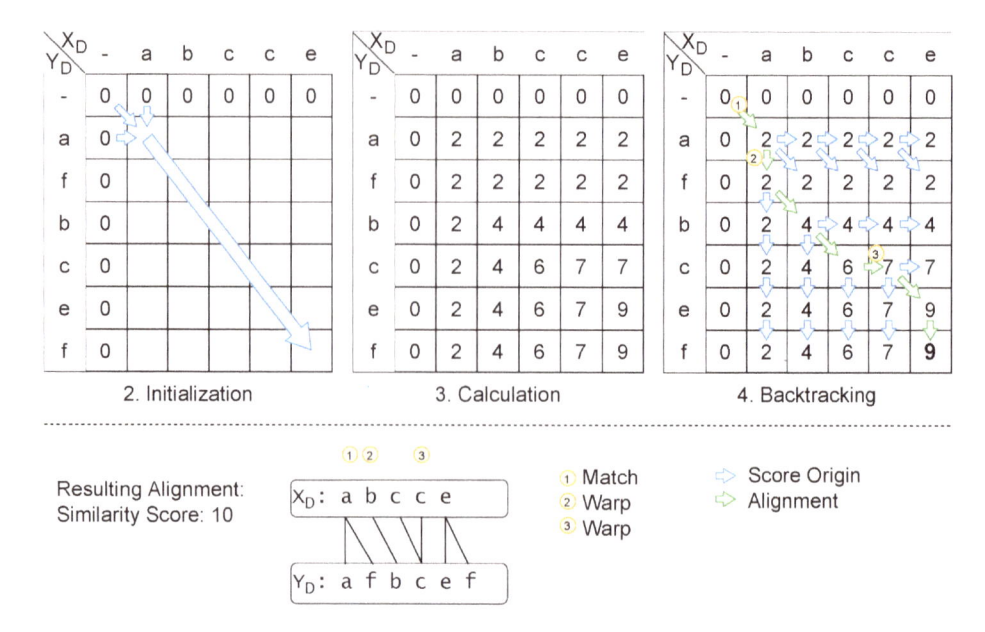

Figure 6.5. Exemplary Similarity Assessment with DTW based on Schake [162]

element of the second series. The calculation of these cells in the matrix is based on the initial values in the first row and column.

3. Calculation of the Scores in the Matrix

The entries in the scoring matrix H are computed by a recursive function. As a consequence, each cells' value is dependent on the previously assessed scores, which represent a comparison of subsequences up to the corresponding elements and therefore include all preceding mappings. Thus, one value in the matrix $h_{i,j}$ is either derived from a matching of elements (cf. diagonal step in the matrix, see ① in Fig. 6.5) or a warp either from an element of the second series to a previously matched element of the first series (cf. vertical step, see ② in Fig. 6.5 with $sim(a, f) = 0$) or from an element of the first series to a previously matched element of the second series (cf. horizontal step, see ③ in Fig. 6.5 with $sim(c, c) = 1$). For all of these cases the previous score depending on the operation (cf. *score origin* in Fig. 6.5) is added to the similarity of the currently regarded elements. If these elements are mapped onto each other, the similarity value is weighted twice in order to prefer this operation rather than a warp. The maximum value out of these three options determines the currently regarded cells' score:

$$h_{i,j} = \max \begin{cases} h_{i,j-1} + sim(x_i, y_j), & \text{warp (vertical)} \\ h_{i-1,j-1} + 2 * sim(x_i, y_j), & \text{mapping} \\ h_{i-1,j} + sim(x_i, y_j), & \text{warp (horizontal)} \\ 0 & \text{otherwise} \end{cases}$$

4. Similarity Value and Warping Path

The value of a cell $h_{i,j}$ in the matrix is interpreted as the similarity score between the subsequences $\langle x_1, x_2, \ldots, x_i \rangle$ and $\langle y_1, y_2, \ldots, y_j \rangle$. When the matrix is filled entirely, the cell with the maximum score determines the similarity value for the best matching subsequences. If the calculation of the scoring matrix is as presented here, this will be in all cases the right cell in the bottom row, as the scoring function only increases the values but never subtracts any values. In the example, the similarity value is $sim(X_D, Y_D) = 9$. Note that, since the value is not normalized, it is higher than 1.

The warping path can be reproduced by backtracking in the inverted direction of each cell's original calculation. Consequently, the alignment of both series can be determined by starting from the cell with the maximum score and subsequently backtracking to the cell of both first elements (see green *alignment* in 4. and the illustrated resulting alignment in the bottom of Fig. 6.5).

The complexity of DTW lies in $O(n^2)$ due to the construction of the matrix, but some algorithms exist that optimize the computation time [119].

6.2.2. Smith-Waterman-Algorithm

Another popular method for finding subsequence alignments is the Smith-Waterman-Algorithm (SWA) [172], which was originally invented for matching protein sequences in the context of DNA analysis. It was developed by Smith and Waterman in 1981 as an extension of the Needleman-Wunsch-Algorithm (NWA) [125]. The NWA finds global alignments through matching whole sequences, whereas the SWA is able to find local alignments through matching subsequences. Similar to the Levenshtein distance, the alignment is found by successively either matching, inserting, or deleting elements from one series in order to match the other series. Thus, compared to DTW, the interpretation of the alignment is slightly different. Instead of multiple warps from elements to one element, each element is either matched with an element or a *gap*, representing an insertion or a deletion.

The general proceeding is similar to DTW, with one additional parameter that is determined.

1. Determine a local distance or similarity function.

2. Determine a gap penalty function.

3. Initialize the scoring matrix.

4. Calculate the remaining entries in the scoring matrix on the basis of the initial starting values and the defined local similarity measure.

5. Find the highest similarity value and the optimal alignment through backtracking.

These steps are illustrated in Fig. 6.6 and described in more detail in the following on the basis of an example. The sequences of the previous example of DTW are slightly adjusted to $X_S = \langle a, b, c, d, e \rangle$ with $|X_S| = 5$ and $Y_S = \langle a, f, b, c, e, f \rangle$ with $|Y_S| = 6$.

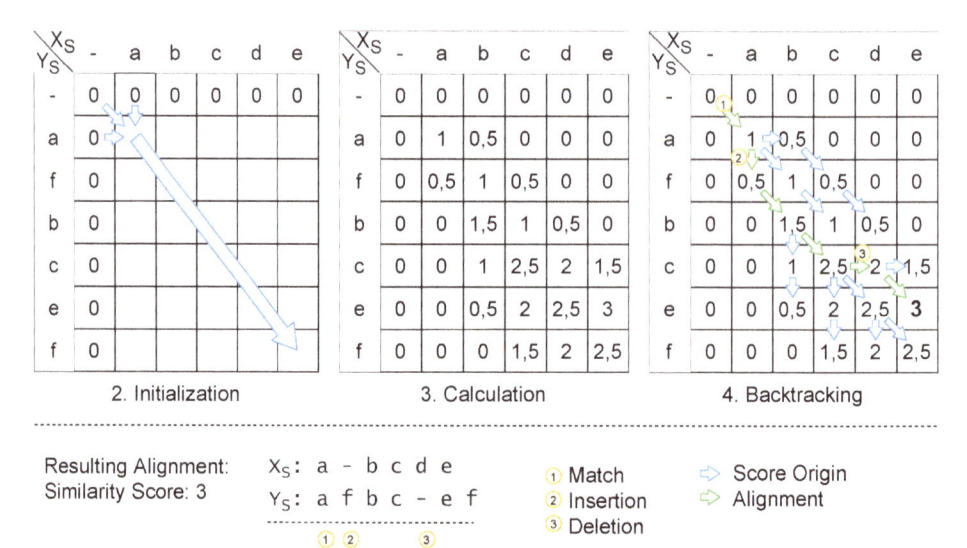

Figure 6.6. Exemplary Similarity Assessment with the SWA based on Schake [162]

1. Local Similarity Measure

To illustrate the operating principle of the SWA, the same simple local similarity measure that is used in the subsection about DTW is utilized. It assigns 1 if the two strings are equal and 0 in all other cases.

$$sim(x_i, y_j) = \begin{cases} 1 & \text{if } x_i = y_j \\ 0 & \text{otherwise} \end{cases} \quad (6.5)$$

2. Gap Penalty Function

As elements are not mapped in each case, compared to a warp when using DTW, a score needs to be determined that is integrated in the assessment when elements of the series are matched with a *gap*. This gap represents the insertion or deletion of an element. Therefore, the gap penalty function is introduced that is added instead of the similarity value of two elements. In this example a constant value G is used.

$$G = -0,5 \quad (6.6)$$

For each mapping with a gap, the similarity score is decreased by 0,5. Depending on the domain, functions can be utilized as gap penalty that depend on specific properties of the elements, such as their position in the sequence.

3. Initialization of the Scoring Matrix

The initialization of the scoring matrix $H = (h_{i,j})$ is conducted equivalently to DTW, as the values in the first column and the first row are set to 0 (see 2. in Fig. 6.5): $\forall i \in \{0, \ldots, n\}, j \in \{0, \ldots, m\} : h_{i,0} = h_{0,j} = 0$.

4. Calculation of the Scores in the Matrix

The calculation of the remaining scores in the matrix, however, differentiates the two approaches. Horizontal and vertical steps in the matrix represent either deletion or insertion (indels) of an element, while diagonal steps are interpreted as matching two elements. For any indel operation, the specified gap penalty is added to the preceding value, whereas the similarity score is added in case of a match. The scoring matrix is constructed in the following way:

$$H_{i,j} = \max \begin{cases} H_{i,j-1} + G, & \text{insertion} \\ H_{i-1,j-1} + sim(x_i, y_j), & \text{match/mismatch} \\ H_{i-1,j} + G, & \text{deletion} \\ 0 & \text{otherwise} \end{cases} \quad (6.7)$$

5. Similarity Value and Alignment

The similarity value is represented by the highest score in the matrix. In contrast to DTW, the alignment path, which can be found through backtracking, is not interpreted as mapping of elements, only diagonal steps represent an alignment. Values that originate from horizontal or vertical steps in the matrix indicate an insertion or deletion of elements concerning sequence X_S.

In the example in Fig. 6.6 the resulting similarity value is 3. The alignment is shown in the bottom line of Fig. 6.6.

Two main differences between the SWA and DTW are obvious. Whereas DTW matches all elements of both series on the basis of warping, the SWA omits elements at the end of one series if the mapping of the subsequence yields the best result. Moreover, some of the individual elements are mapped with a *gap* instead of a multiple mapping as in DTW. Thus, the SWA is noise-resistant. To this end, depending on the definition of the gap penalty, outliers can have a lower influence, whereas in DTW the rating is fix, as it bases on the similarity measure. Furthermore, this results in different interpretations of the alignments. DTW regards stretched or compressed sequences to be equal, whereas the SWA considers a subsequence to be equal to a sequence, if it is part of this sequence [163].

Both algorithms have in common that their output includes an alignment path besides the similarity score, which can be exploited in the reuse phase of CBR. Furthermore, computational complexity is not different, as it lies in $O(n^2)$ for both approaches.

Which algorithm fits best needs to be determined depending on the domain and use case. Both have specific properties that come with some advantages and disadvantages.

Both approaches can be adapted to specific needs of a domain, e.g. by altering the gap penalty function and local similarity measures. For the presented case-based deviation management, both will be evaluated according their suitability and are adopted to fit the characteristics of the pursued similarity measure.

Zarka et al. [212] adopt the SWA for an approach called trace-based reasoning.

6.2.3. Trace-Based Reasoning

TBR, which was first introduced by Mille [112], is a special form of case-based reasoning where traces serve as case base. An important aspect as extension to standard CBR is the introduction of a temporal aspect. In TBR similarity measures are used that base upon temporal sequences of elements, which are defined as *traces*. Cordier et al. [26] and Zarka [211] presented an approach with the objective of finding contextual recommendations for process participants that interact with web applications.

To this end, an algorithm was developed that is based on the SWA and was adapted for retrieving similar traces. The SWA is used for local sequence alignment and compares traces in all possible lengths. This characteristic perfectly matches the requirements of trace-based reasoning as terminated instances have to be compared to ongoing and not completed processes, which are only subsequences and will not match exactly considering the length. Several local similarity measures are used for each attribute of the observed elements, which are part of the traces. For each observed element a global similarity value is computed on the basis of local values with use of a weighted average function. These similarity values of single elements are furthermore used in the SWA to calculate the overall similarity of traces. This method can be transferred to the pursued deviation management, if de facto workflows are considered as traces, at least for retrieving the best matching cases.

As adaptation method, Zarka [211] proposes a simple extraction method that takes a subsequence of actions from the most similar retrieved case, which follows the part of the matched trace. Some values of this subsequence are adapted by more adequate ones on the basis of contextual information. As last step in the adaptation process, actions are filtered, e.g. invalid actions or unnecessary repetitions.

Zarka utilizes this method in order to find suggestions for workflow continuation in a mobile video editing suite by also incorporating a CBR approach. However, the context of deviations or adaptation methods are not considered by the authors [211].

Transferred to deviation management, this subsequence can be extracted from the retrieved de facto workflow and first tasks of this subsequence can then be recommended as work items. Furthermore, if case and query do not match exactly, edit steps, which are necessary for aligning query and case, are part of the solution of the SWA. These additional differences relate to previously happened deviations, but might be required for a successful completion of the workflow as well. Therefore, these edit steps possibly might be transformed adequately into additional work items to ultimately provide further workflow control.

A completely different approach is introduced by Gundersen [61].

6.2.4. Weighted Vector Similarity

Unlike the other two approaches that find series alignments through directly comparing the sequences, Gundersen adopts a similarity measure that transforms event sequences into a vector representation [61]. These vectors can then be compared with efficient vector similarity measures such as cosine similarity [61].

This approach was developed on the basis of requirements for recognizing failure causes and recommending adequate solutions in the oil-well drilling domain as part of a real-time analysis. As specific characteristics of this domain are addressed, the approach is not generally applicable, but some properties might be transferable.

This approach is based on the assumption that recent tasks to a certain point of interest are most important when comparing event sequences. The importance of events decreases the longer ago they occurred. This is realized by a weighting function that considers the position of events related to the start and end of a sequence. In the simplest case, the end of a sequence is regarded as point of interest. Consequently, the closer the occurrence of an event is to the end of a sequence, the higher the weight value. For each event type this weight is computed as sum of single weights of single event occurrences. These weights of event types are then combined into a vector, where each dimension represents one event. This vector can be compared to other sequences and their weight vectors.

The general proceeding includes the following steps:

1. Calculate the weight of each event.

2. Calculate the total weight for each event type.

3. Assess the similarity value by comparing the weight vectors.

The similarity assessment is explained in detail and exemplified through the comparison of two sequences $X_V = \langle a, b, c, c \rangle$ with $|X| = n \in \mathbb{N}$ and $Y_V = \langle a, c, b, c, d \rangle$ with $|Y| = m \in \mathbb{N}$.

1. Calculate Event Weight

A weight value w_i is assessed for each event in the sequence indicating its temporal position pos_i related to the end of the sequence. Let end be the last position in the sequence. Then, the weight is calculated as follows [61]:

$$w_i = \frac{1}{2^{\frac{end-pos_i}{h}}} \tag{6.8}$$

The halving distance h defines the position of an event related to the last element of the sequence, where its weight is 0,5, i.e. the half of the maximum weight value 1. Thus, the weight of an event at the end of the sequence is 1, the weight of an event i with $pos_i = end - h$ is 0,5, and for all events prior to the latter the weight is lower than 0,5 [162].

For the example, let $h = 2$. The weight variables for the characters c at position $pos_i = 3$ in X_V and for d in Y_V have the following values:

$$w_c = \frac{1}{2^{\frac{4-3}{2}}} = \frac{1}{2^{\frac{1}{2}}} \approx 0,71 \tag{6.9}$$

$$w_d = \frac{1}{2^{\frac{5-5}{2}}} = \frac{1}{2^{\frac{0}{2}}} = 1 \tag{6.10}$$

2. Calculate Total Weight

Each sequence is transformed to a vector V with l dimensions. The number of elements l of this vector results from the number of existing element types and is thus, completely independent from the size of the individual sequences, but each sequence is transformed to a vector with the same number of dimensions.

Consequently, derived from the individual elements' weights, a total weight for each event type needs to be assessed in order to build the vector. This total weight is computed as follows [61], where p is the number of weights in the sequence with the same event type k:

$$W_k = \sum_{i=1}^{p} w_i \tag{6.11}$$

Then, the vector V results and contains all total weights:

$$V = (W_1, W_2, ..., W_l) \tag{6.12}$$

Consequently for the exemplary sequences X and Y the following two vectors result:

$$V_X = \begin{pmatrix} W_a \\ W_b \\ W_c \\ W_d \end{pmatrix} = \begin{pmatrix} 0,35 \\ 0,5 \\ 1,71 \\ 0 \end{pmatrix} \tag{6.13}$$

$$V_Y = \begin{pmatrix} W_a \\ W_b \\ W_c \\ W_d \end{pmatrix} = \begin{pmatrix} 0,25 \\ 0,5 \\ 1,06 \\ 1 \end{pmatrix} \tag{6.14}$$

The value of event type d of the sequence Y_V conforms with the previously exemplary computation for the single event, as only one element of d occurs. In contrast, the value of event type c of sequence X_V is composed of the individual weights of both occurrences of c, and thus, is higher than the previously exemplary calculated one (cf. Equ. 6.9).

3. Similarity Assessment of Vectors

These weighted vector representations can now be compared by utilizing measures such as cosine similarity and relative component fraction [61]. Gundersen proposes a combination of both, as cosine does not differentiate magnitudes and parallel shifts [61].

For the exemplary sequences X and Y a similarity value of 0,76 is determined with the cosine similarity measure.

$$sim(X, Y) = cos(V_X, V_Y) = \frac{V_X \cdot V_Y}{||V_X|| \cdot ||V_Y||} \tag{6.15}$$

$$= \frac{2,15}{1,82 \cdot 1,56} = \frac{2,15}{2,84} = 0,76$$

The main strength of this measure is its efficiency due to its low computational complexity of $O(n)$. Major drawbacks however include that the approach lacks the possibility to obtain semantic similarity between single tasks, as only entire sequences are compared considering their properties of task occurrences. Only self-referential characteristics of tasks can be included in the single weights of tasks, like e.g. importance or severity. Moreover, similar to DTW, all elements of the sequences are compared, independent of their lengths.

Besides, one event type that is completely missing in the sequence has a strong influence on the similarity outcome, as this dimension is assigned a zero, whereas in DTW or the SWA a missing task can be compensated partly through warping or an indel operation. How heavy this difference is weighed is specified individually, depending on the gap penalty or the similarity assessment.

Furthermore depending on the use case, this vector representation does not necessarily incorporate all events since start of the sequence, but can also only integrate a specific time window from a certain point t until end of the sequence.

6.3. Case-Based Approach to Deviation Management

The methodology of CBR is transferred to the problem of deviation management. In order to support process participants during workflow execution, in particular when deviations occur, similar terminated workflow instances are searched and reused for recommending adequate work items despite these anomalies. Through this case-based approach, the tedious definition of strategies to overcome exceptional situations becomes superfluous. It is expected that the lack of expert knowledge can be compensated through a case-based deviation management that allows for a more sophisticated and individual situation-dependent decision. Thus, in contrast to existing approaches (see Section 6.6), this will be achieved without necessary user interaction or prior knowledge acquisition.

Before the overall concept is presented, the notion of deviation is shortly introduced, as it is used equivocally in research, and deviation management as such is abstractly sketched.

6.3.1. Deviation Management

The notion of deviation is not clearly defined and often included in the term exception, as a special type. To clarify the classification of exceptions and deviations in this work, several specifications will be quoted.

A process deviation is defined by da Silva et al. [29] as mismatch between executed process and process model. They state that deviations cannot be anticipated and explicitly put exceptional behaviour in contrast. According to Marrella et al. [106], exception handling is implemented manually at build time, whereas deviation handling requires ad-hoc changes at run time. Eder and Liebhart [43] describe unexpected exceptions, in their work denoted as deviations, as an important aspect that should be handled to gain possible benefits. Depaire et al. [35] categorize deviations into exceptions and anomalies, whereas explicit exceptions are implemented as part of the process model or defined as business rules. This definition does not conform with how it is used in the context of the presented work, as explicit exceptions are included in the notion *deviation*. In this work, the term *deviation* excludes explicit exceptions, as they are predictable, but includes implicit exceptions and anomalies as described by Depaire et al. [35].

Hence, the presented approach conforms with the specification of da Silva et al. [29], as the notion of deviation is regarded as a mismatch between process instance and process model that cannot be anticipated.

Deviation management in general can be split up into 3 phases: deviation detection, deviation handling and deviation analysis. In this work, the part of deviation detection as well as deviation handling, at least to a limited extent, has been presented in Section 5.5. The aim of this case-based approach is a more elaborate deviation handling. Deviation analysis is part of future work, as it refers to the last phase in the business process life cycle: *evaluation*. For that purpose, event logs are analyzed and exploited for improvements and optimization, foremost of the process model.

The notion *workaround* [8] is related to deviation, specifically how it is interpreted in this work, as unexpected situation. Outmazgin and Soffer describe a workaround as "incompliant behaviour, where employees intentionally decide to deviate" [131]. Thus, deviations can be workarounds themselves if no external trigger caused the deviation, but deviations in terms of changed circumstances require workarounds. The objective of the proposed approach is to support these workarounds or to make them unnecessary, as the system guides

6.3. CASE-BASED APPROACH TO DEVIATION MANAGEMENT

despite deviation.

6.3.2. Deviation Management in the Context of the CBR Cycle

The overall case-based approach that is pursued for a deviation management is sketched in Fig. 6.7.

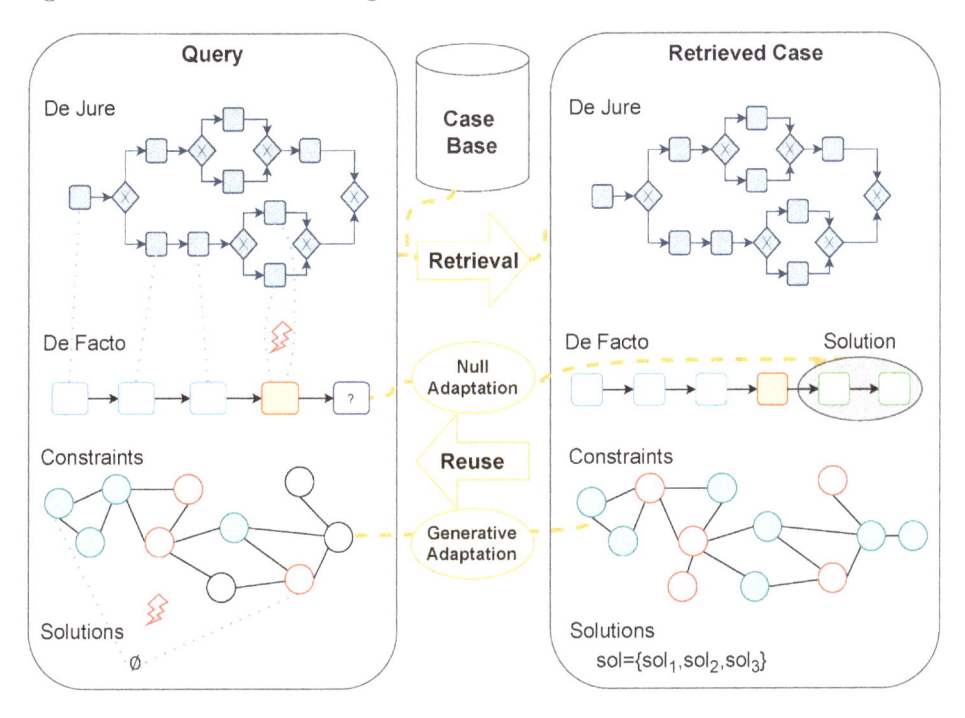

Figure 6.7. Case-Based Approach for Handling Deviations partially based on Grumbach and Bergmann [57]

6.3.2.1. Case Structure

Terminated workflows are regarded as cases. Each workflow case is a tuple $WC = (J_C, F_C, CSP_C, \text{sol}_C)$ with

- De jure workflow as NESTGraph J_C,
- De facto workflow as NESTGraph F_C,
- Constraint problem $CSP_C = (X_C, D_C, C_C)$ with
    - Decision variables X_C

- Set of domains D_C
- Constraints $C_C = \{alldifferent(S)\} \cup C^M \cup C^A \cup C^I$ and

- Set of solutions sol_C.

A workflow case contains the de jure workflow, which is the default for suggesting an execution order. Furthermore, the workflow instance is part of the workflow case and comprises a corresponding specific de facto workflow, the constraint set and its solutions. The de facto workflow represents one simple sequence of tasks that were traced at run time. Both the de jure workflow and the de facto workflow are represented as semantic workflows in the form of *NESTGraphs*. The constraint problem consists of the decision variables X_C, the set of domains D_C and the constraint set C_C with its different subsets, which were presented in Subsect. 5.4.1.

One would assume that for a terminated de facto workflow, where tasks have a specific position, the solution set consists of one single solution. However, some more valid solutions are possible when regarding the tasks that have not been enacted. Those are assigned a value higher than s_{end} and there still might be several valid variants.

The case base $CB = \{WC_1, WC_2, \ldots, WC_n\}$ consists of several workflow cases $WC_i = (J_C, F_C, CSP_C, \text{sol}_C)$ for $i \in \{1, \ldots, n\}$. Workflows both with or without deviations are included, as both cases might be useful for task recommendation.

6.3.2.2. Query

The problem to be solved with this CBR approach is the recommendation of adequate work items in case of a deviation. Hence, a running workflow with a de facto workflow that is not completed yet will be used as the query: $Q = (J_Q, F_Q, CSP_Q, \text{sol}_Q)$, where F_Q is not final and is continuously complemented with traced tasks and data nodes that served as input or output during execution. This instance is a subsequence of a completed de facto workflow and contains at least one deviation concerning its de jure workflow (see orange-coloured node in Fig. 6.7) that occurred at the time of the request. The associated de jure workflow is also available. In Fig 6.7, the executed trace in the de jure workflow is indicated through dotted lines that connect to the tasks of the de facto workflow. The lack of compliance and its resulting deviation is illustrated through the red-coloured flash symbol.

6.3. CASE-BASED APPROACH TO DEVIATION MANAGEMENT

Due to the occurred deviation, the constraint net, as part of the constraint problem CSP_Q, is inconsistent and no solution can be found, hence, $\text{sol}_Q = \emptyset$. Moreover, due to the running status of the workflow, some constraints can be assigned a definite status, while some constraints remain indefinite (see different colours for constraint nodes in Fig. 6.7, detailed explanations follow in Subsect. 6.5.2).

All phases of the CBR cycle are important for a holistic view of deviation management and lead to a self-learning system.

6.3.2.3. Retrieve

When a query is performed, the case base is searched through on the basis of an adequate similarity measure. The objective is to find similar de facto workflows whose subsequences match the current instance (see de facto workflows with blue and orange nodes in Fig. 6.7), containing a similar deviation (orange node) compared to the query. In the retrieved cases, the subsequences that succeed the deviation (see green-coloured nodes in Fig. 6.7) should not be considered when assessing the similarity, as this part is not existent in the query, but is rather a solution candidate.

6.3.2.4. Reuse

This most similar case or even several similar cases are then used to recommend tasks. One possibility is to propose those tasks of the case that followed the subsequence that ended with the deviation (see green-coloured nodes in Fig. 6.7), which is categorized as null adaptation. In some circumstances a simple transfer of the solution is not reasonable, but rather an adaptation of the recommended remaining workflow part is necessary. To this end, a constraint-based method is proposed as generative adaptation approach. Thereby, the constraint problems of case and query are aligned and adapted in order to re-enable the workflow engine to compute new solutions of the constraint problem for determining work items.

6.3.2.5. Revise

As tasks are only recommended and not strictly prescribed, the process participant is still able to execute a task that was not part of the solution resulting from the reuse step. Thus, by continuing the query workflow, the solution can be revised. But still, the final evaluation of the terminated workflow is pending. This assessment decides whether the revised case can be retained as successful or failed case.

6.3.2.6. Retain

When the query workflow has terminated, its de facto workflow, containing the actual execution, can be integrated in the case base. Ideally, some kind of validation, positive or negative, is stored with the case in order to draw the correct conclusions in subsequent reuse steps. Before integrating single cases, it needs to be evaluated whether the informativeness can be increased or whether this additional knowledge is already covered by adaptation methods. Nevertheless, the case base can be enhanced continuously, which ultimately leads to a learning system.

This work focusses on the retrieval and reuse phase. On account of this, a similarity measure and two adaptation methods are presented in the following. With this case-based approach, it is possible to recommend work items after deviations. This is done on the basis of a sophisticated decision that takes previously made experiences into account. The revise and retain phase are part of future work and are therefore only presented abstractly as idea.

6.4. Retrieving Similar Workflows for Flexibility by Deviation

For retrieving similar workflows that are adequate for a reuse in situations where deviations occur, a similarity measure has to be defined. In this section, this retrieval phase is described. First, in Subsect. 6.4.1, specific important characteristics of the flexible workflow approach are concretised and requirements for the similarity measure are derived on this basis. A pre-processing of the cases, which is part of achieving a meaningful comparison, is described in Subsect. 6.4.2. Subsequently, the developed similarity measure is introduced in detail in Subsect. 6.4.3. It combines, integrates and extends several properties of the previously presented similarity measures for time series (cf. Sect. 6.2), in order to create an adequate adoption and to fit the needs of the pursued case-based deviation management.

6.4.1. Characteristics of Similarity for Deviating Workflows

When designing a similarity measure, properties of the cases and the overall objective of the approach need to be considered. As prerequisite, the definition of similarity in this context needs to be defined. Specific properties of flexibility by deviation that are important for determining similarity are sketched. On this basis, requirements for the similarity measure can be derived.

In the proposed approach, the focus of assessing similarity solely lies on a comparison of the de facto workflows. This is a special type of a workflow, as it only contains traced tasks and consequently, is represented as sequentially ordered series of tasks without control-flow branches. Existing approaches for workflow similarity in most cases apply graph matching algorithms that tend to be rather inefficient, in particular for large graphs (see Subsect. 6.1.6.2). Due to the sequential structure of de facto workflows, which is much more simple, other types of similarity measures are more adequate and less complex. When abstracting from the workflow structure, de facto workflows resemble complex event sequences. Hence, they can be perceived as time series that consist of tasks with additional semantic information. Due to these reasons, the application of a time-series-based method seems to be promising (see Sect. 6.2).

Another important property of the de facto workflow of the query refers to its state. As the comparison is required during run time, the query comprises a running workflow. Consequently, its de facto workflow is incomplete, whereas all cases contain terminated workflows. The part of interest, which is the deviation itself, is situated at the end of the query, but possibly right in the middle of a case. The similarity measure has to deal with a subset relation between query and case, for which the support of partial mappings is required. An additional reason why only subsets of the case should be mapped concerns the reuse phase. Considering such a mapping of elements up to the deviation, the remaining sequence of the case workflow can be used to derive a solution or rather to propose work items. If all elements are mapped, no elements remain for a reuse.

Moreover, an important aspect of the pursued similarity is that under certain conditions some mismatches of subsequences of case and query should have low or rather no influence on the similarity score. This refers to two aspects.

On the one hand, it is assumed that differences with a greater temporal distance to the occurrence of the deviation should have a lower impact on the similarity, as they are less related.

On the other hand, a novel property of a case or query is incorporated that is introduced by the notion *model-consistency*. Any de facto workflow or any subsequence of a de facto workflow without a deviation, but conforming to the de jure workflow, is denoted as model-consistent. This property can be exploited to ignore some parts of the workflow during similarity assessment.

Consider a parallel workflow block, where two tasks are executed in parallel. During tracing of the de facto workflow, the first task that terminates is arranged sequentially prior to the second task, even if the point of termination only differed minimally and the execution took place primarily in parallel. If there are two cases containing opposite sequences of tasks, these two subsequences are nevertheless model-consistent. In this case, the omission of those tasks of the parallel workflow block during similarity assessment is reasonable, as the order of the tasks may have no relevance as most of the execution time was in parallel. Thus, through ignoring model-consistent parts in parallel workflow blocks, such inaccuracies can be eliminated that are introduced through the sequential tracing of tasks.

Besides, the similarity measure should comprise both task and data objects, as the data-flow between tasks contributes as much to the similarity value as the description of the tasks themselves, and hence, allows for a more significant comparison of workflows and its elements.

Summarized from these presented characteristics, the following requirements can be derived:

RS1 - Comparison of Sequences: The similarity measure should be able to compare sequences, as the de facto workflows consist of a sequence of tasks.

RS2 - Comparison of Subsequences: The similarity measure should be able to compare subsequences, as the running workflow is compared to terminated ones.

RS3 - Temporal Weighting: The similarity measure should be able to consider the temporal ordering of tasks and allow for a derived differentiated weighting.

6.4. RETRIEVING SIMILAR WORKFLOWS

RS4 - Exclusion of Model-Consistent Subsequences: The similarity measure should be able to detect model-consistent parts that are eliminated before the similarity is assessed.

RS5 - Comparison of Tasks and Data Objects: The similarity measure should be able to compare both task and data nodes.

Before the actual similarity assessment is explained in detail, a pre-processing algorithm that is applied to the case base and the query is introduced.

6.4.2. Pre-Processing

The pre-processing algorithm is used to identify irrelevant workflow blocks in case and query, which are excluded from similarity assessment by deleting these subsequences prior to comparison. This refers to requirement **RS4** (cf. Subsect. 6.4.1), in order to achieve an omission of model-consistent parts. The pre-processing of the case base results in reduced cases and consequently, similarity can be assessed faster and with lower complexity. Pre-processing can be done at build time, at least partially, such that retrieval time is not affected but rather accelerated. Besides, the size of the case base can be decreased potentially, as redundant cases might be the result of case reduction and can therefore be removed.

For a reasonable reduction of case and query and the subsequent similarity assessment, both workflows need to be based on the same de jure workflow, such subsequences that are derived from the corresponding subworkflow can be excluded.

First, the pre-processing algorithm enhances the cases in the case base with further information that is used for comparison and reduction when a query arises. As the overall approach is limited to block-oriented workflows, the block structuring is exploited for this purpose.

The pre-processing steps are listed abstractly in the following and described in detail subsequently:

1. Label elements of de jure workflow.

2. Transfer labels to de facto workflows.

3. Check for model-consistency.

4. Reduce workflows.

An example is presented in Fig. 6.8, which is used to exemplify each of the described steps.

1. Label Elements of De Jure Workflow

First, the nodes of the de jure workflow of each case are labelled to identify both the position of each task node within the workflow blocks that contain the task and what types of workflow blocks are involved. To this end, different labels are introduced. The set ids^b is a set of natural numbers that contains one unique id for each of the control-flow node pairs.

$$ids^b = \{1, \ldots, b\} \subseteq \mathbb{N} \text{ with } |ids^b| = b = \frac{|N_J^C|}{2} \qquad (6.16)$$

Each control-flow node pair, i.e. split cs and join node cj, is assigned a unique id id^b with $id^b \in ids^b$.

$$id^b : N_J^C \to ids^b \text{ with } id^b(cj) = id^b(cs) \qquad (6.17)$$

In the example in Fig. 6.8, only one control-flow block exists and therefore, the set of possible block ids has one element $ids^b = \{1\}$. This id is assigned to both contained control-flow nodes, as they comprise the split and join node of the same control-flow block, $id^b(cs) = id^b(cj) = 1$.

Furthermore, the task nodes are assigned two labels. This includes a set of ids, denoted as $levels$. These ids refer to the id id^b of each of the control-flow blocks they are nested in. This concerns not only the directly connected control-flow nodes, but also the ones that are on a higher hierarchical level, up to the highest level (start and end node of the workflow). Consequently, this includes the ids of all preceding control-flow split nodes that have not been joined until the currently regarded task node, as well as the value '0' for the top level, where no control-flow is split up yet and consequently, each task is subordinate.

$$levels : N_J^T \to \mathcal{P}(ids^b) \cup \{0\} \qquad (6.18)$$

The highest level is specified through the value '0', e.g. for task t_1 in Fig. 6.8 $levels(t_1) = \{0\}$. Tasks t_2 and t_3 additionally are assigned the value 1 as levels, as they are part of the parallel control-flow block with $id^b = 1$, hence, $levels(t_2) = levels(t_3) = \{0, 1\}$.

6.4. RETRIEVING SIMILAR WORKFLOWS 155

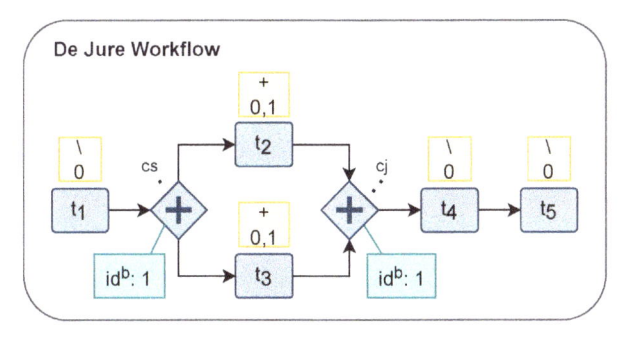

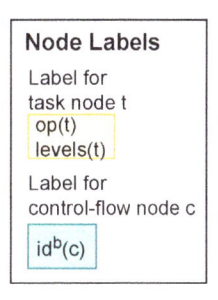

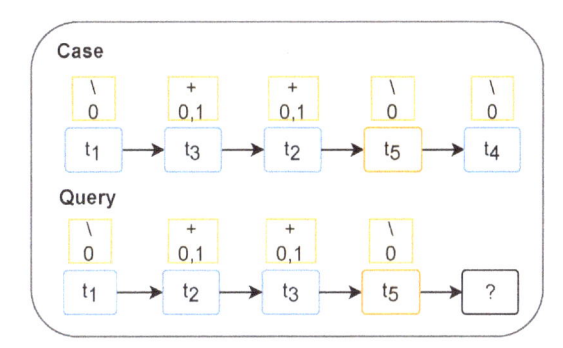

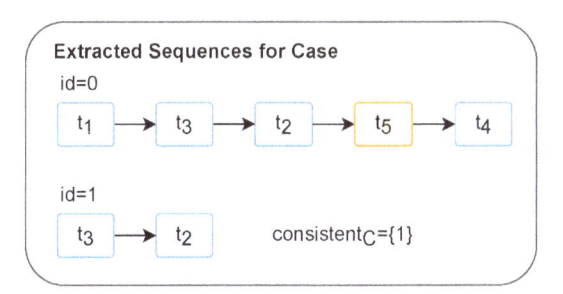

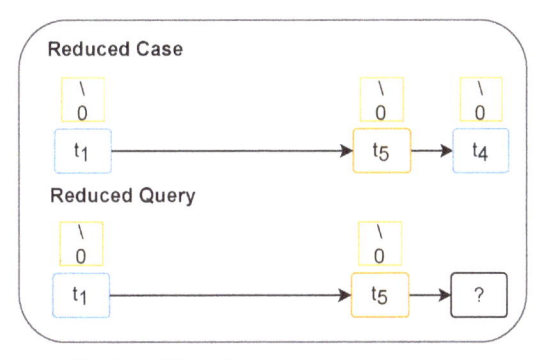

Figure 6.8. Exemplary Pre-Processing based on Schake et al. [163]

In addition to the ids of the levels, tasks are assigned the operator of the nearest control-flow block. The operator *op* specifies the type of control-flow block in which the task is directly nested. Hence, this results in the type of the nearest preceding control-flow node.

$$op : N_J^T \to \{+, \times, \circ, \backslash\} \qquad (6.19)$$

Parallel control-flow is specified through the symbol "+", exclusive control-flow is represented by "×", loop control-flow blocks are marked with "∘" and the highest level, where no control-flow block is involved, is labelled with "\". In the example in Fig. 6.8, the operator of t_2 and t_3 is '+', as both tasks are part of the control-flow that is directly connected to the parallel control-flow nodes without further interference of other control-flow nodes. All other tasks, that are not nested in any control-flow blocks but are on the highest level (cf. t_1, t_4, t_5) are allocated the operator '\'.

2. Transfer Labels to De Facto Workflows

These labels, which are complemented in the de jure workflow, are subsequently transferred to the de facto workflows of the cases. Each task in the de facto workflow is assigned the same labels as its corresponding task of the workflow model. This can be done easily, since each task node in the de facto contains a reference id of the specific task of the de jure workflow. This transfer step is illustrated in Fig. 6.8 as second step for the de facto workflows of an exemplary case and query. Note that the orange-coloured node indicates an existent deviation and as a result, the following task is left unclear in the query workflow.

3. Check for Model-Consistency

As soon as the nodes of the de facto workflows are labelled, model-consistency can be checked for the workflows. This property holds for subsequences of the de facto workflow due to their conformity to one workflow block of the de jure workflow. Therefore, for each level of workflow blocks, and thus for each value $id \in ids^b \cup \{0\}$, a set of tasks T_{id} from the de facto workflow is extracted that belong to this level.

$$T_{id} = \{t | t \in N_F^T \land id \in levels(t)\} \qquad (6.20)$$

Based on this subset of tasks of the original workflow, a reduced de facto workflow can be constructed. Edges are completely reset

6.4. RETRIEVING SIMILAR WORKFLOWS

and created newly on the basis of their order in the original de facto workflow. The result is a subsequence where the sequential order of tasks is preserved. These resulting workflow sequences (cf. for the exemplary case in Fig. 6.8, two sequences can be extracted, see 3.) can then be validated by the constraint-based workflow engine, which was introduced in Subsect. 5.4.1. If the workflow engine finds a solution for this reduced CSP, the subsequence is *model-consistent*. Consequently, every id of consistent control-flow blocks is stored in a set $consistent \subseteq ids^b \cup \{0\}$.

In the example in Fig. 6.8, this is illustrated for the case workflow. The sequence for $id = 0$ is not model-consistent, as a deviation is included (cf. position of t_5), whereas the subsequence for $id = 1$ is model-consistent, and consequently, this id is added to $consistent_C$. The same procedure will be applied to the de facto workflow of the query, resulting in the same set $consistent_Q = \{1\}$.

4. Reduce Workflows

The previously determined property of *model-consistency* can be used to reduce query and cases prior to similarity assessment. If any id coincides in the set $consistent$ of both query and case, every task t where $id \in level(t)$ can be deleted from the de facto workflows and the remaining tasks need to be reconnected sequentially, if this deletion concerns a part right in the middle. Hence, the deleted tasks do not affect the similarity score.

In the following, these adapted elements are formally specified for the de facto workflow. $N_F^{consistent}$ represents the set of tasks, that can be deleted.

$$N_F^{consistent} = \{t | t \in N_F^T : \exists id \in consistent : id \in levels(t)\} \quad (6.21)$$

Thus, the original set of nodes is reduced by this set and results in a reduced set.

$$N_F^{reduced} = N_F \setminus N_F^{consistent} \quad (6.22)$$

Subsequently, the edges need to be adjusted, as some nodes of edges are not existent any more, and in order to reconnect the control-flow, some edges need to be integrated, which is abstractly specified as $E_F^{reconnected}$.

$$E_F^{reduced} = E_F \setminus \{(t_1, t_2) | t_1 \in N_F^{consistent} \vee t_2 \in N_F^{consistent}\} \cup E_F^{reconnected} \quad (6.23)$$

Consequently, the reduced de facto workflow is composed as follows:

$$F^{reduced} = (N_F^{reduced}, E_F^{reduced}, S_F, T_F) \qquad (6.24)$$

In the example in Fig. 6.8, $id = 1 \in consistent_C = consistent_Q$ and thus, t_2 and t_3 are deleted from both de facto workflows and t_1 and t_5 are reconnected through a new edge. In this case, the omission of tasks of the parallel workflow block is reasonable, since the order of the tasks may only differ due to the sequential tracing of terminated tasks, whereas in reality in both cases tasks t_2 and t_3 might be executed in parallel. Thus, this pre-processing is able to eliminate the inaccuracies that are introduced through the sequential tracing of tasks. Furthermore, as the deviation does not occur until after the parallel block, the difference in the preceding part might have no impact on the deviation and the right choice to continue. Therefore, this partial mismatch is simply ignored when assessing the similarity.

The example showed a parallel control-flow block. But even in case of another type of control-flow block, e.g. an exclusive pattern with $f_3 = \langle t_1, t_2, t_4 \rangle$ and $f_4 = \langle t_1, t_3, t_4 \rangle$, both sequences could be regarded as highly similar. It is assumed, that the deviation is foremost related to the elements in the specific workflow block where the deviation occurs. If other workflow blocks are concluded prior to the deviation, those are probably irrelevant. Thus, in the proposed approach no differentiation is made between different kinds of control-flow blocks for reducing cases. Nevertheless, if additional requirements concerning a necessary differentiation arise in a certain domain, a condition can be integrated in order to reduce cases and query only for specific operators such as parallel control-flow blocks, using the introduced label op.

Steps 1-3 of the pre-processing as exemplified in Fig. 6.8 can be made offline before the start of the workflow engine, when a case base is available. The retraction of workflow parts needs to be done depending on the query and its model-consistent subsequences. This can be done during workflow execution with progressing state of the workflows. Consequently, model-consistent parts that emerge prior to the deviation, can be reduced earlier on as well. Through pre-processing, computation time is not influenced severely.

6.4. RETRIEVING SIMILAR WORKFLOWS

6.4.3. Similarity Assessment

For the actual similarity assessment between two de facto workflows, which are represented in the NESTGraph format, query $F_Q = (N_{F_Q}, E_{F_Q}, S_{F_Q}, T_{F_Q})$ with $|N_{F_Q}^T| = n$ and case $F_C = (N_{F_C}, E_{F_C}, S_{F_C}, T_{F_C})$ with $|N_{F_C}^T| = m$, a combined approach of the previously mentioned techniques is proposed in order to take advantage of each algorithm's specific strengths and address all specified requirements. This includes a dynamic programming approach that utilizes either the SWA or DTW, which both meet requirement **RS1** (cf. Subsect. 6.4.1), as the similarity measures compare sequences. Comparing subsequences, which is demanded by requirement **RS2** (cf. Subsect. 6.4.1), is implicitly done by using the SWA and can also be achieved through a slight modification of DTW.

Moreover, an extension is made to DTW and the SWA that comprises the idea of a weighting function considering temporal ordering to address requirement **RS3** (cf. Subsect. 6.4.1). Furthermore, local task similarities include data-flow and semantic information for a more sophisticated comparison of single elements, which responds to requirement **RS5** (cf. Subsect. 6.4.1).

The similarity assessment can either be applied to reduced cases or non-reduced ones depending on the importance of every single difference or a rather block-oriented view.

6.4.3.1. Local Task Similarity

The local task similarity, which is used during the calculation of the cell values in the scoring matrix, is composed of different values.

As prerequisite, local node similarity is defined according to Bergmann and Gil [15]. It is assessed by comparing the semantic descriptions of both nodes. Let $n^Q \in N_{F_Q}$ and $n^C \in N_{F_C}$ with semantic descriptors $S_Q(n^Q), S_C(n^C) \in \Sigma$. sim_Σ depicts the similarity value when comparing two semantic descriptors $S_Q(n^Q)$ and $S_C(n^C)$.

$$sim_\Sigma : \Sigma \times \Sigma \to [0, 1] \qquad (6.25)$$

Node similarity sim_N adopts this similarity of the semantic description in case the types of the nodes correspond. Otherwise the similarity is zero, as the elements cannot be mapped.

$$sim_N(n^Q, n^C) = \begin{cases} sim_\Sigma(S_Q(n^Q), S_C(n^C)) & \text{if } T(n^Q) = T(n^C) \\ 0 & \text{otherwise} \end{cases}$$
(6.26)

Additional to this narrow focus on the task description itself, data-flow is included in the local similarity measure for tasks. This is necessary to increase the significance of the global similarity result, as the similarity assessment of the whole sequences with either DTW or the SWA is limited to the comparison of sequential elements. This solely comprises the tasks when transferring this paradigm to de facto workflows. Thus, referring to requirement **RS5** (cf. Subsect. 6.4.1), the similarity of data objects that are connected to the tasks influence the local similarity values of the tasks. To this end, the sets of incoming and outgoing data nodes of one task are defined as follows:

$$N_t^{D_{in}} = \{d | d \in N^D \exists t \in N^T : (d, t) \in E^D\}$$
(6.27)
$$N_t^{D_{out}} = \{d | d \in N^D \exists t \in N^T : (t, d) \in E^D\}$$
(6.28)

The similarity of data-flow is defined as sim_D and maps two sets of data nodes:

$$sim_D : \mathcal{P}(N^D) \times \mathcal{P}(N^D) \to [0, 1]$$
(6.29)

Both sets are compared by finding the best mapping of nodes. To this end, each of the query nodes is mapped to one similar case node, but one case node cannot be mapped to several query nodes in order to achieve a unique mapping. Subsequently, local data node similarities, determined through sim_N, are aggregated and normalized to a final similarity value, which is between 0 and 1. Local task similarity sim_T of two task nodes $t^Q \in N_{F_Q}^T$ and $t^C \in N_{F_C}^T$ is then defined as follows [162]:

$$sim_T(t^Q, t^C) = \frac{l_t * sim_N(t^Q, t^C) + l_i * sim_D(N_{t^Q}^{D_{in}}, N_{t^C}^{D_{in}}) + l_o * sim_D(N_{t^Q}^{D_{out}}, N_{t^C}^{D_{out}})}{l_t + l_i + l_o}$$
(6.30)

This value is composed of the similarity of the task itself, its input and output objects, each assigned a respective weight $l_t, l_i, l_o \in \mathbb{R}^+$ for adapting the importance of the individual scores. sim_N represents

6.4. RETRIEVING SIMILAR WORKFLOWS

an aggregated similarity score of the semantic description of the task nodes, as specified in Equation 6.26. sim_D describes the similarity of input and output data nodes, which is calculated as described previously on the basis of the mapping of data nodes as specified in Equation 6.29. The local task similarity consists of the sum of these three weighted local similarities, which are normalized through the aggregated weights.

This local task similarity is subsequently used to determine the values in the scoring matrix for the SWA and DTW.

6.4.3.2. Scoring Matrix

The optimal alignment of the two de facto workflows is computed through the scoring matrix $H = (h_{i,j}) \in \mathbb{R}^{n+1,m+1}$. The values within are determined either on the basis of DTW or the SWA, similar to the traditional specification presented in Subsections 6.2.1 and 6.2.2. A slight modification, in order to optimally fit the scenario of upcoming deviations, is the combination with a temporal weighting factor $wTemp_i$. This fits the requirement **RS3** (cf. Subsect. 6.4.1) in order to lower the impact of dissimilarities that are more distant in time. To this end, a similar weighting function that was proposed by Gundersen [61] is adopted.

For DTW, the values in the matrix are calculated as follows:

$$h_{i,j}^{DTW} = \max \begin{cases} h_{i,j-1}^{DTW} + wTemp_i * sim_T(t_i^Q, t_j^C), & \text{warp (vertical)} \\ h_{i-1,j-1}^{DTW} + wTemp_i * 2 * sim_T(t_i^Q, t_j^C), & \text{mapping} \\ h_{i-1,j}^{DTW} + wTemp_i * sim_T(t_i^Q, t_j^C), & \text{warp (horizontal)} \\ 0 & \text{otherwise} \end{cases}$$

(6.31)

For the SWA the values in the matrix are calculated as follows:

$$h_{i,j}^{SWA} = \max \begin{cases} h_{i,j-1}^{SWA} + wTemp_i * penaltyInsertion(t_i^Q), & \text{insertion} \\ h_{i-1,j-1}^{SWA} + wTemp_i * sim_T(t_i^Q, t_j^C), & \text{match/mismatch} \\ h_{i-1,j}^{SWA} + wTemp_i * penaltyDeletion(t_i^C), & \text{deletion} \\ 0 & \text{otherwise} \end{cases}$$

(6.32)

The gap penalties *penaltyInsertion* and *penaltyDeletion* can be specified as needed, e.g. as constant or function. In previous experiments with two domains where different values were evaluated, a penalty value of -0,2 for both insertion and deletion turned out to lead to the best results [162].

The local similarity scores as well as the gap penalty are further multiplied by the weight depending on temporal distance. Therefore, equation 6.8 will be adapted as follows. Here, n is the length of the query, as this workflow should be mapped completely during the similarity calculation. The halving time as a parameter is assigned a value $h \in [0, n]$. Again, previous experiments that evaluated different values for this parameter showed that $h = 0,2n$, which means 20 % of length of the query, to lead to the best results [162].

$$wTemp_i = \frac{1}{2^{\frac{n-i}{h}}} \qquad (6.33)$$

6.4.3.3. Similarity Score

The maximum value in the last row of the matrix represents the non-normalized global similarity score sim_{raw}. In order to ensure that the alignment ends with the last task of the query and remaining elements of the case are not mapped any more, the search of this maximum value is restricted to $h_{n,j}$ for $0 < j \leq m$ [162].

$$sim_{raw}(F_Q, F_C) = \max_{0 < j \leq m} h_{n,j} \qquad (6.34)$$

To normalize the obtained score, it must be divided by the maximum possible score with regard to the query. The SWA only aggregates local similarity values, when elements are matched and thus, originate from a diagonal step in the matrix. Consequently, the maximum similarity score that is possible can be computed through the number of diagonal steps in the alignment [162]. In contrast, DTW adds a positive value to the score when stepping in either direction, even twice the value if elements are mapped [163].

The alignment can be found according to the original implementation of the SWA and DTW. Beginning from the cell that contains the maximum value in the last row up to a cell of the first row, while the origin of the computation of the value is decisive for backtracking.

Let $align = \{(0,0), \ldots, (n,k)\}$ denote all cells from the alignment path. Let $diag = \{(i_0, j_0), \ldots, (i_p, j_p)\} \subseteq align$ include all cells that

6.5. REUSE FOR DERIVING WORK ITEMS

origin from a diagonal step and let $other = align \setminus diag$ denote all cells with assignments resulting from vertical or horizontal steps. It is assumed that the local similarity values are all normalized to an interval of [0,1]. Then, normalized similarity for two de facto workflows sim_F is calculated as follows [163]:

$$sim_F^{SWA}(F_Q, F_C) = \frac{sim_{raw}(F_Q, F_C)}{\sum_{(i,j) \in diag} wTemp_i} \quad (6.35)$$

$$sim_F^{DTW}(F_Q, F_C) = \frac{sim_{raw}(F_Q, F_C)}{\sum_{(i,j) \in diag} 2 * wTemp_i + \sum_{(i,j) \in other} wTemp_i} \quad (6.36)$$

Based on these assessed similarity values, the k most similar cases can then be determined.[9]

Consequently, this designed similarity measure in two different forms addresses research question **RQ2.1** (see Section 1.2), as based on the results from the retrieval some terminated processes are identified to be reused in a subsequent step.

6.5. Reuse for Deriving Work Items

Based on these retrieved cases, whose de facto workflow is similar to the de facto workflow of the query, a solution can be derived. The objective of this reuse is to determine work items that can be proposed to the process participant for workflow continuation. To this end, an adaptation method is required that fulfils the following requirements:

RA1 - Reuse of Work Items: The adaptation method should allow for a reuse of work items in order to support the process participant in continuing with the workflow in case of a deviation.

RA2 - Re-Enable the Workflow Engine: The adaptation method should re-enable the workflow engine by resolving inconsistencies and providing a consistent constraint net in order to support the process participant until termination of the workflow.

---
[9] Note that, in the presented concept, a precondition for a case to be retrieved is that the de jure workflows of query and case are equal, as the similarity assessment is solely based on the de facto workflow, while the workflow model is not included therein.

RA3 - Restore Flexibility: The adaptation method should restore flexibility, which is reflected by the number of work items or rather number of execution paths that can be proposed as solution for terminating the workflow.

RA4 - Retain Unaffected Constraints: The adaptation method should retain constraints of the query workflow that are not affected by the deviation in order to preserve the initially specified relations.

To address these requirements, two different adaptation methods are proposed. The first one is classified as null adaptation, whereas the second one applies a generative adaptation strategy. The null adaptation directly applies the solution of the case to the query. To this end, the mapping of tasks that results from the similarity assessment is considered and the tasks that follow the last mapped element are proposed as work items (cf. green-coloured nodes in Fig. 6.7). This method is presented in detail in Subsect. 6.5.1.

The generative adaptation pursues a different approach, which is elaborated in Subsect. 6.5.2. The constraint problems of query and case are compared and some constraints from the case are added to the query, whereas some constraints of the query are excluded. Thereby, the constraint problem regains consistency and the constraint-based workflow engine can be reactivated for the support of the continuation of the workflow until termination. In contrast, through applying the null adaptation method, for every task execution a retrieval and adaptation has to be done. The generative method transfers order relations without prescribing fixed positions of constraints and thus, creates more variety, but still preserves existing constraints. In the following, both methods are presented in detail.

6.5.1. Null Adaptation

With the previously presented similarity measure, sim_F, the most similar terminated workflow or a set of workflows can be retrieved from the case base. This can also include several distinct cases with the same similarity score. Let $retrieved_Q$ be the set of retrieved cases with the highest similarity values. From these case workflows, work items can be derived.

6.5. REUSE FOR DERIVING WORK ITEMS

Let $WC_i \in retrieved_Q$ be one of the similar cases. Then, one work item can be derived from the alignment in the scoring matrix. The position in the de facto workflow of the case that was aligned with the deviating task of the query needs to be determined (cf. orange-coloured node in Fig. 6.7). Let $align = \{(0,0), \ldots, (n,k)\}$ denote the alignment path. Then, the task $t_{last}^C \in N_{FC}^T$ with position $pos(t_{last}^C) = k$ is the task of the case workflow that was the last to be aligned with an element of the query workflow. All tasks that are subsequent to t_{last}^C were not aligned to tasks of the query. The next one of these tasks can be recommended to the process participant as the next task, thus at $pos(t_{next}) = k+1$ (cf. green-coloured nodes in Fig. 6.7).

$$workItems = \{t_{next} | t_{next} \in N_C^T \wedge pos(t_{next}) = pos(t_{last}^C) + 1 \wedge \\ WC_i = ((N_C^T, E, S, T), F_C, CSP_C, \text{sol}_C) \in retrieved_Q\} \quad (6.37)$$

Consider the example in Fig. 6.6 that demonstrated the SWA, where simple string sequences are used instead of tasks. When the issue of deriving work items is transferred to this example, it can be determined which string should be appended to the end of the query. Let $X_S = \langle a, b, c, d, e \rangle$ be the query and $Y_S = \langle a, f, b, c, e, f \rangle$ the case. Then, the last element of case and query that was aligned is the e. The following element in the case can be proposed as next element, in this case f.

This adaptation method is efficient, as it simply bases on the mapping that origins from the retrieval phase without requiring additional handling. However, it only fulfils requirement **RA1**, as a proposal of work items is enabled. Moreover, this presented method of determining work items only temporarily solves the problem that arises when a deviation occurs. The constraint set and thus, the model that is used by the workflow engine remains inconsistent. After executing the derived work item, the constraint-based workflow engine continues to be in a deadlock, as no solution can be found. Thus, after executing the proposed task, the retrieval and reuse step needs to be repeated for determining new work items until termination. Alternatively, instead of proposing only one single work item, a whole subsequence of tasks can be derived from the retrieved case. This can be done by additionally extracting those tasks that follow the work item until workflow termination. However, this results in a limited variety of execution possibilities of exactly one and ultimately decreases the overall goal of flexibility.

Furthermore, as the retrieved similar cases are most probable not exactly the same as the query, proposing to end the workflow with the exact same subsequence of tasks is rather limited and might not be adequate.

Another drawback of this straightforward approach is that differences between case and query are not regarded. Consider the following example with two execution paths of query $F(F_Q) = \langle a, b, c, e, f \rangle$ and retrieved case $F(F_C) = \langle a, b, c, f, e, g \rangle$, where f is the deviating task. The following mapping results from applying the SWA:

$$F(F_Q): \quad \text{a} \quad \text{b} \quad \text{c} \quad \text{e} \quad \text{f}$$
$$F(F_C): \quad \text{a} \quad \text{b} \quad \text{c} \quad - \quad \text{f} \quad \text{e} \quad \text{g}$$

The mapping ends with the task f, with the result that the following task from the case e will be proposed as work item. However, the task e might then be executed redundantly, as it is already part of the de facto workflow of the query. Therefore, slight adjustments of the derived work items might be necessary and a more sophisticated adaptation method is proposed, in order to fulfil the remaining requirements (**RA2-RA4**).

6.5.2. Generative Adaptation

Adaptation in general is applied to transfer the solution of a previous case to the currently regarded problem, the query. In this proposed generative constraint-based adaptation, the objective is to restore consistency in the constraint net of the running workflow instance after a deviation occurred. This is a prerequisite for re-enabling the workflow engine to compute and propose work items without leading to an exceptional state. Its purpose is similar to the deviation handling that is described in Section 5.5, but in contrast to those predefined strategies, this approach is based on experiential knowledge in form of terminated workflows.

The restoration process is implemented through the adaptation of the constraint net of the query. For this purpose, the constraint net of the most similar case, which has been retrieved on the basis of the previously presented similarity measures, is reused. This constraint net is adopted such that some constraints are transferred to the

6.5. REUSE FOR DERIVING WORK ITEMS

constraints of the query. Thereby, parts of the solution strategy of the case are applied on the query, and the problem solver in form of the constraint-based workflow engine is able to find a solution. Hence, this constraint-based adaptation method can be classified as generative adaptation.

It is assumed that this leads to some improvements compared to the determination of work items on the basis of the alignment of either the SWA or DTW. The adaptation method is supposed to extend the locally limited and rigid recommendation of work items or a single subsequence that is suggested to continue and terminate the workflow. It is assumed that the state space can be increased as through the adapted constraint set more execution paths become valid. Consequently, flexibility may be restored.

Another main difference regarding the strategy of the null adaptation is that the generative adaptation approach adopts constraints that constitute relations instead of simply proposing tasks for a fixed position in the de facto workflow. To illustrate one resulting benefit, the previous example with $F(F_Q)$ and $F(F_C)$ is considered. Considering the de facto workflows, the following instance constraints are part of the respective constraint sets:

$$C_Q^I = \{a = 1, b = 2, c = 3, e = 4, f = 5\}$$
$$C_C^I = \{a = 1, b = 2, c = 3, f = 4, e = 5, g = 6\}$$

Instead of proposing predefined sequential orders that follow the last mapped element in the de facto workflow of the retrieved case (in the example $\langle f, e, g \rangle$), this subsequence is transferred as constraints. Hence following the deviating task f, a dependency of e and g would be derived as constraint $con = e < g$. This constraint is then transferred to the query, while violated ones are removed, and the constraint-based workflow engine is activated to compute work items. According to Algorithm 5.1 in the current situation of the example, each task is assigned the value 6 once and a solution is searched. For task g, a solution can be found as con is fulfilled, since e with $e = 4$ is already part of the de facto workflow. Thus, the worklist consists of g, and e is not proposed redundantly.

To this end, a generative adaptation approach based on the constraint net of the workflows is proposed to reactivate the workflow engine and propose a wider variety of possible workflow completions, ultimately increasing flexibility.

Furthermore, the adaptation of the constraint net seems to be promising in terms of complexity and efficiency, as no structural adaptation of a procedural workflow model needs to be done, which is non-trivial and rather time-consuming. The insertion or deletion of constraints is rather simple and resource-saving. Thus, the workflow engine can still base upon the constraint-based workflow representation and flexibility is retained.

Figure 6.7 schematically shows the generative adaptation and its integration in the case-based approach. The deviation not only leads to an inconsistency between de jure and de facto workflow as indicated by the red flash symbol, but also to an empty set of solutions due to an inconsistent constraint set. Besides that, Fig. 6.7 shows that not all constraints of the query have a definite state due to the incomplete de facto workflow (indicated by a red for *violated* or turquoise fill for *valid* in contrast to blank nodes that have an *indefinite* status), whereas in the constraint net of the retrieved case all constraints have a definite state. Furthermore, it is possible that both sets differ in terms of which constraints are contained, e.g. due to additionally added constraints.

Before the actual generative adaptation method is introduced in detail, some related work that concerns the integration of CBR and CSP is sketched.

6.5.2.1. Integrating CBR and CSP

There are several approaches that combine CSP and CBR methods in different ways and for different purposes, e.g. [104, 140, 190].

Marling et al. identify two ways of combining CBR with CSP [104]. On the one hand, this includes utilizing CBR techniques for the initialization of a CSP [104]. Through a pre-selection of promising value assignments on the basis of similar cases, the solution space can be reduced, leading to an increased efficiency. Thus, a case retrieval is applied for supporting or rather simplifying the constraint solving process. On the other hand, CSP methods can be exploited during adaptation in CBR [104]. In this approach, CSP is seen as part of the reuse phase of CBR.

The objective of the presented work is to find a technique for case adaptation where cases consist of CSPs, in order to restore consistency in the query's CSP. Thus, this issue is correlated to the second type of integration of CSP and CBR. But few related approaches exist in

6.5. REUSE FOR DERIVING WORK ITEMS

research. To this end, a repair algorithm is required that considers similar cases and possibly combines several cases or rather parts of them.

Purvis and Pu [140] developed an approach that combines several CSPs into one, called *case combination*. They evaluate the approach in the domain of assembly sequences, but assume their approach to be generally applicable. From these several cases that are integrated, each fits partially to the regarded problem and a solution exists for each case. However, in case a solution cannot be applied to a combined CSP, they apply the minimum conflicts algorithm [116]. This is a repair algorithm for a CSP with a given solution, where constraints have changed or been added. New constraints are added one by one and the solution is validated. If the solution becomes unsuitable, the values of the variables are modified in order to adapt the solution in such a way that a maximum number of constraints can be fulfilled. It is regarded as a heuristic to find a solution, as the search space is reduced. Consequently, one found solution is sufficient.

The objective to somehow try to repair an inconsistent CSP is similar to the use case regarded here, but nevertheless slightly different concerning its purpose and the necessary adaptation.

There are several reasons why the minimum conflicts algorithm is not adequate in this case. The trigger that requires an adaptation differs. An upcoming task that is added to the de facto workflow entails a value assignment to the specific variable of the task. This causes the solver to be unable to find a solution to the CSP, which results in a required adaptation of the constraints. This is necessary in order to again fit this partial immutable solution and to be able to assess several solutions for determining work items. The solution that is the result of the adaptation is a consistent constraint net, in contrast to one valid solution for the CSP that is the outcome of the proposed adaptation of Purvis and Pu [140].

Furthermore, different elements of the CSP need to be adapted. Some variables have fixed assignments and hence, some constraints and their status are immutable. Consequently, a part of the solution is unchangeable. In this case, it is the set of constraints that needs to be adapted such that several solutions can be found, rather than adapting the solution in order to fulfil as many constraints as possible according to the approach by Purvis and Pu [140].

Eventually, the goal of the required adaptation step is to fulfil the maximum number of relevant constraints when combining case and query. This means choosing adequate ones from the case to add and choosing adequate ones from the query to retract.

Nevertheless, retracting or adding constraints simply based on the criterion of how many constraints are dependent and thus, violated, might be not adequate. Therefore, a deviation-dependent approach is proposed.

To enable a constraint-based adaptation method, the query and case format has to be extended.

6.5.2.2. Constraint-Based Adaptation

For the constraint-based adaptation approach, the query and case structure is identical to the one presented in Subsect. 6.3.2.1.

The query as a special form of a case has some peculiarities. As mentioned before, the presented approach is limited to cases that share the same de jure workflow. Consequently, $J_Q = J_C$. Furthermore, the de facto workflow is not terminated. As the workflow is in an exceptional state, the workflow engine is not able to determine a solution to the CSP, hence, $sol_Q = \emptyset$. Nevertheless, a partial solution is existent as well as a part of the instance constraint set (cf. C_Q^I), due to the subsequence of the de facto workflow prior to the deviation.

The intended output of the adaptation algorithm is a modified constraint problem of the query CSP_Q^*, to re-enable the computation of solutions and ultimately, to offer task recommendations. The set of solutions of the query is affected indirectly, as, through the altered set of constraints, some valid solutions result in opposition to the previously empty set of solutions.

To this end, constraints that are dependent on the deviating task are adapted. Constraints that are directly related to those constraints, i.e. through contained tasks, are transferred from the case to the query. This can be propagated for arbitrary levels of related constraints, which is explained in the following subsection.

This re-enables the workflow engine to compute work items and find new solutions. First, the approach is described abstractly and a detailed formalization is presented subsequently. For each of the steps, a small example is given that is based on the sequential workflow model J and two de facto workflows of query F_Q and case F_C, presented in Fig. 6.9. As the adaptation is initiated during workflow execution in order to compute work items when a deviation occurs, the currently

6.5. REUSE FOR DERIVING WORK ITEMS

regarded deviating task of the query in this example is t_4. One previous deviation exists in F_Q, as t_2 and t_1 are switched in order, but this deviation was handled earlier. In the example, it is assumed that F_C has been retrieved as similar case and is used for adaptation. Query and case were chosen in the example in such a way that the adaptation can be illustrated in the best possible way.

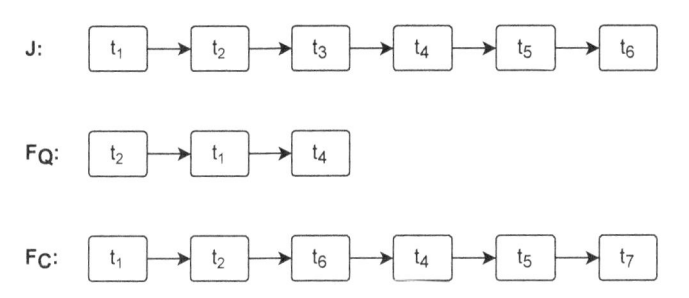

Figure 6.9. Exemplary De Jure Workflow with Query and Case

The following steps are applied in order to obtain an adapted constraint net of the query:

1. **Initialization**
   In the initialization phase, the constraints that describe the fixed assignments of values in the de facto workflows are transformed to abstract order relations.

   (a) *Create derived constraint set for query and case.*
   For both constraint sets an additional set, denoted as derived constraints C^D, is generated and added. This set represents the order of tasks in the de facto workflow. For this purpose, an order relation is added for each two consecutive tasks.
   For the exemplary de facto workflows in Fig. 6.9, the following constraints are derived: $C_Q^D = \{t_2 < t_1, t_1 < t_4\}$ and $C_C^D = \{t_1 < t_2, t_2 < t_6, t_6 < t_4, t_4 < t_5, t_5 < t_7\}$. Hence, the de facto workflow is included in the constraint set as relational dependencies between tasks, which may be reused in the constraint net of the query.

   (b) *Exclude instance constraint set of case.*
   In contrast to the addition of derived constraints, the instance constraints (cf. C^I in Subsect. 5.4.1) of the case are

excluded. Transferring instance constraints to the query would assign a fixed position to some tasks, even to ones that were not executed. When case and query do not conform to each other exactly, a transfer of instance constraints would lead to conflicts. Furthermore, this is not reasonable, since the presented workflow approach should allow a flexible execution, which is contradicting the fixed assignments.

For the example in Fig. 6.9, the following instance constraint sets exist: $C_Q^I = \{t_2 = 1, t_1 = 2, t_4 = 3\}$ and $C_C^I = \{t_1 = 1, t_2 = 2, t_6 = 3, t_4 = 4, t_5 = 5, t_7 = 6\}$. If those constraint sets are combined, a conflict would arise immediately, as task positions do not conform to each other, e.g. $t_2 = 1$ holds for the query, while $t_2 = 2$ holds for the case.

2. **Pre-Processing**

   The pre-processing phase is responsible for aligning the sets of decision variables and corresponding domains. Constraints from the case that conflict the constraints of the queries are excluded from adaptation.

   (a) *Extend set of decision variables and corresponding domains.*

   In case the tasks of case and query do not correspond exactly, e.g., due to a repeated task execution or an unexpected task that was not part of the de jure workflow, the CSP of the query needs to be aligned to allow for these additional deviations that are part of the retrieved case and for a possible adoption of constraints that regard these additional tasks. This concerns the set of decision variables that needs to be complemented by missing variables and, correspondingly, the domains of the task variables that need to be extended.

   In the example in Fig. 6.9, the de facto workflow of the case contains an additional task t_7 that was not part of the de jure workflow. Thus, the set of decision variables as well as the set of domains of the query need to be extended

6.5. REUSE FOR DERIVING WORK ITEMS

in the following way:

$$X_Q^* = X_Q \cup \{t_7\} = \{t_1, t_2, t_3, t_4, t_5, t_6, t_7\}$$
$$D_Q^* = D_Q \cup \{7\} = \{1, 2, 3, 4, 5, 6, 7\}$$

(b) *Ignore conflicting constraints.*
As the query workflow has been executed partially, some constraints already have a definite and valid status. All constraints of the case that contradict these valid constraints are no candidate for transfer, as they would simply add inconsistencies and prevent finding a solution for the CSP of the query. To this end, these valid constraints are extracted from the constraint net of the query and each of the case constraints are validated against this constraint set. If no solution can be found when adding such a case constraint to this valid set of constraints of the query, then this case constraint is excluded from adaptation.

In the example in Fig. 6.9, this is applicable to the constraint $(t_1 < t_2) \in C_C^D$. If this constraint is combined with the constraint set of the query $C_Q^D = \{t_2 < t_1, t_1 < t_4\}$[10], no solution can be found, as $(t_1 < t_2)$ and $(t_2 < t_1)$ contradict each other. Thus, $(t_1 < t_2)$ is excluded from a possible transfer during adaptation.

3. **Adaptation**
In the actual adaptation phase, some constraints of the retrieved case are directly transferred to the constraint set of the query, while some constraints derived from existing ones are added, whereas others are deleted from the original constraint set of the query. This transfer of relations of tasks, instead of fixed positions, ensures a higher flexibility and hence, addresses requirement **RA3** (cf. Section 6.5). The adaptation results in an adapted and consistent constraint net of the query, which re-enables the constraint-based workflow engine to compute work items and thus, requirement **RA2** (cf. Section 6.5) is fulfilled.

(a) *Insertion of directly related constraints.*

---

[10] Note that the constraints that are derived from the de facto workflow always have a valid status. For the sake of simplification, only the set of derived constraints is regarded in this example.

From these filtered case constraints that result from preprocessing, constraints can be chosen that directly involve the deviating task and that are therefore most likely related to the deviation. These constraints are added to the constraint set of the query.

In the example in Fig. 6.9, the regarded deviating task of the query workflow is t_4. Considering the derived constraint set of the case, such a directly related constraint where t_4 is involved is $(t_4 < t_5)$. Thus, $(t_4 < t_5)$ can be transferred to the set of constraints of the query.

(b) *Insertion of constraints that include directly related tasks.*
Constraints that are directly related to the deviating task involve other tasks that are indirectly related to the deviating task. These indirectly related tasks can be extracted and, subsequently, valid constraints that include these indirectly related tasks can be extracted and used for a transfer to the set of constraints of the query.

In the example in Fig. 6.9, constraints that involve the task t_5 are transferred. This concerns the constraint $(t_5 < t_7) \in C_C^D$.

(c) *Insertion of negation of violated constraints that include directly related tasks.*
Constraints of the case that involve the previously described indirectly related tasks but have a violated status can also be used for an adaptation of the constraint set of the query. It is assumed that the opposite of violated constraints should apply, as this held in the case with the same deviating task. To this end, the extracted constraints of the case with a violated status are reversed and added to the constraint set of the query. Thus, additional deviations that result from the de facto workflow of the case are induced, as they are supposed to be related to the currently regarded deviating task and are considered as a contribution that leads to a successful termination of the workflow.

In the example in Fig. 6.9, this concerns the constraint $(t_5 < t_6) \in C_C^M$, as task t_6 is executed before t_5. Hence, the opposite of this constraint $(t_6 < t_5)$ is added to the constraint set of the query.

(d) *Removal of violated constraints that result from insertion.* For the constraint set that was added previously and results from the reversed violated constraints, the original constraints need to be retracted from the constraint set of the query.

In the example in Fig. 6.9, the violated constraint $(t_5 < t_6)$, which was determined in the previous step, needs to be deleted from the constraint set of the query.

So far, the description of the adaptation only involved the transfer of constraints that are either directly related to the deviating task or indirectly related via a transitive relation. This transitivity can be exploited to transfer further constraints, starting from the indirectly related constraints and their contained tasks.

In the presented work, this transfer of constraints is limited to the directly and indirectly related constraints concerning the deviating task and its transitive relations, because it is assumed that directly related constraints are more important than those with a higher temporal distance. Analogously to the temporal weighting factor that is integrated in the proposed similarity measure and that concerns the past, this relatedness-level-based adaptation influences the future outcome. Moreover, the effect of the adaptation is locally limited and not arbitrary, as it regards related constraints but preserves parts of the original CSP that are unrelated to the deviation. Hence, requirement **RA4** (cf. Section 6.5) is fulfilled. In case all constraints in the transitive closure are regarded for a transfer, the complete de facto workflow of the case would also be prescribed in the query, which results in neglecting flexibility.

In the following, each of the previously described phases is explained in more detail based on formal descriptions.

1. Initialization

    a) In the initialization phase, the set of derived constraints (cf. Equ. 6.38) is created for both query and case and added to the constraints of the CSP respectively.

    This set C^D is derived from the de facto workflow and represents implicitly the same as C^I, but in an abstract way, as it only specifies dependencies instead of specific positions or concrete value assignments. These constraints are defined as follows:

$$C^D = \{t_1 < t_2 | t_1, t_2 \in N_F^T \wedge (t_1, t_2) \in E_F^C\} \quad (6.38)$$

The constraint sets of query and case then both are extended with this set of derived constraints, leading to an extended constraint set $C_C^{extended}$ and $C_Q^{extended}$.

$$C_C^{extended} = C_C \cup C_C^D \quad (6.39)$$

$$C_Q^{extended} = C_Q \cup C_Q^D \quad (6.40)$$

b) The instance constraints of the case will be excluded, as they specify the exact positions of tasks in the de facto workflow of the case and hence, very likely contradict the de facto workflow of the query, except if both are equal. Consequently, they are irrelevant for adaptation, as the objective is not to transfer the exact sequential position of tasks to the query, but rather relational interdependencies.

$$C_C^{relational} = C_C^{extended} \setminus C_C^I \quad (6.41)$$

After the initialization, the constraint sets are adjusted. Subsequently, some pre-processing steps are performed that exclude single constraints from a possible reuse.

2. Pre-Processing

Prior to combining parts of both constraint sets, each constraint is assigned two additional attributes that declare its origin and its type. These properties are utilized in order to distinguish those constraints in the integrated set during adaptation such that they can be handled differently. To this end, the function $Orig$ specifies whether the constraint was originally part of the query or case.

$$Orig : C \to \{query, case\} \quad (6.42)$$

$Type$ indicates for which purpose the constraint was created, relating to the different sets that $C^{extended}$ consists of.

$$Type : C \to \{model, additional, instance, derived\} \text{ with}$$

$$\forall c \in C : Type(c) = \begin{cases} model & \text{if } c \in C^M \\ additional & \text{if } c \in C^A \\ instance & \text{if } c \in C^I \\ derived & \text{if } c \in C^D \end{cases} \quad (6.43)$$

6.5. REUSE FOR DERIVING WORK ITEMS

a) As prerequisite for combining parts of both constraint sets, the set of decision variables and corresponding domains need to be aligned. It is possible that there are some additional variables in either of these sets, due to repetitions of tasks or newly introduced tasks. Thus, the set of decision variables of the query needs to be complemented with further variables that only exist in the set of decision variables of the case.

$$X_Q^* = X_Q \cup X_C \tag{6.44}$$

Furthermore, the domains of the task variables need to be adjusted to the newly created decision variables. Therefore, the extended domains are simply instantiated completely new and contain ascending values with the same number as variables.

$$D_Q^* = \{1, \ldots, |X_Q^*|\} \tag{6.45}$$

b) Before parts of both constraint sets can be combined, each of the constraints in the case that is possibly transferred needs to be checked for compliance with those constraints of the query that have a definite and valid status. Only those constraints of the case are validated that have a valid status, as violated constraints will not be adopted anyway. Furthermore, this concerns solely constraints that were derived from the workflow instance of the case or additionally modelled constraints, as all other constraints, which originate from the de jure workflow, are equal in case and query.

To this end, a constraint net is extracted from the query that contains all constraints with $status = valid$.

$$C_Q^{valid} = \{c | c \in C_Q \wedge Status(c) = valid\} \tag{6.46}$$

On this basis, it can be checked if any constraint of the remaining case constraints, which are possibly transferred, conflicts this set of valid constraints of the query. Therefore, each case constraint is added once to the valid query constraints and the resulting CSP is validated. If no solution can be found, this specific case constraint contradicts the valid constraints of the query, and consequently, this constraint does not constitute a candidate for transfer. All constraints that conflict these *valid* constraints of the query are ignored and hence, removed from the case constraints.

$$\begin{aligned} C_C^{conflicting} = & \{c | c \in C_C^{relational} \land Status(c) = valid \\ & \land \texttt{sol}(Q) = \emptyset \} \\ & \text{with } CSP_Q = (X_Q, D_Q, C_Q^{valid} \cup c) \text{ for } \texttt{sol}(Q) \end{aligned}$$
(6.47)

All conflicting constraints are removed from the case constraints, leading to the residual constraints $C_C^{validated}$.

$$C_C^{validated} = C_C^{relational} \setminus C_C^{conflicting} \qquad (6.48)$$

These constraints are candidates for an adoption in the constraint set of the query. The adaptation method is based on this extracted set of transferable, validated constraints of the case.

3. Adaptation

The starting point for the adaptation are the two sets $C_C^{validated}$ and $C_Q^{extended}$. The idea is to add some of the constraints that are related and dependent on the deviating task, which is generally known in constraint programming as "restriction" of the solution set, while some are removed from the set of constraints, denoted as "relaxation"[34].

An adaptation method based on a generally applicable method from the constraint programming field, such as finding Minimal Unsatisfiable Cores (MUCs) [66] of an inconsistent constraint net when combining the set of case and query constraints, can be implemented. However, an adaption on the basis of such a method would not lead to adequate results, as explained below. Applying finding MUCs would result in a retraction of randomly picked conflicting constraints and would not consider any dependencies. In the worst case, this would either lead to a complete adoption of derived constraints of the case, which only allows for an exact repetition of this task sequence, or to simply retaining the model constraints, which would result in ignoring deviations in the case that occurred after the regarded deviation.

For developing the similarity measure, the assumption was made that differences close to the deviation are more severe than those in far distance. Similarly, it is assumed that tasks nearby a deviation are related to a greater extent and should more likely be proposed

6.5. REUSE FOR DERIVING WORK ITEMS

than those far away. Therefore, a local adaptation with a customizable extent is proposed, originating from the deviation itself and its dependencies.

a) In a first step, case constraints that are directly related to the deviating task $devTask$ are transferred to the set of query constraints.

$$C_C^{directlyRelated} = \{c | c \in C_C^{validated} : \exists s \in N_C^T : c = (devTask < s) \\ \wedge Status(c) = valid\} \tag{6.49}$$

b) Subsequently, tasks are extracted that are part of these constraints and are therefore related to the deviating task.

$$N_C^{T_{directlyRelated}} = \{t | t \in N_C^T : \exists s \in N_C^T : (s < t) \in C_C^{directlyRelated}\} \tag{6.50}$$

Derived from that, all constraints that are related to those tasks can be extracted and transferred to the constraint set of the query. This relates only to constraints that are valid in the set of constraints of the case.

$$C_C^{related+} = \{c | c \in C_C^{validated} : \exists t \in N_C^{T_{directlyRelated}} \exists s \in N_C^T : \\ c = (t < s) \wedge Status(c) = valid\} \tag{6.51}$$

When adding each constraint from the case to the constraint net of the query, the CSP needs to be checked for consistency, as the new constraint may contradict existing dependencies. If no solution can be found after an addition, conflicting constraints need to be retracted. This is done through applying a simplified version of the algorithm for finding minimum unsatisfiable cores of a constraint problem. In the regarded scenario, only some of the constraints need to be considered to eliminate conflicts. Let $(t_1 < t_2)$ be a constraint that was transferred from the constraint net of the case to the constraint net of the query, then those constraints of the query that contain either t_1 or t_2 are considered for retraction, as other constraints are not concerned, at least primarily.

c) Violated constraints from the case can also be transferred to the query in such a way that their opposite is added. In this regard as well, only constraints that involve deviation-related tasks are transferred.

$$\begin{aligned} C_C^{related-} = \{(s < t) | t \in N_C^{T_{directly Related}} \land s \in N_C^T : \\ \exists c \in C_C^{validated} : c = (t < s) \land \\ Status(c) = violated\} \end{aligned} \quad (6.52)$$

d) Additionally, those constraints for which the opposite has been added need to be retracted from the constraints of the query, if they exist. Therefore, the set of these violated constraints is extracted from the query.

$$\begin{aligned} C_Q^{violated} = \{c | c \in C_C^{validated} \land c \in C_Q : \exists t \in N_C^{T_{directly Related}} \\ \exists s \in N_C^T : c = (t < s) \land Status(c) = violated\} \end{aligned} \quad (6.53)$$

Consequently, the following adapted constraint net arises, when combining the previously defined sets.

$$C_Q^* = C_Q \cup C_C^{directly Related} \cup C_C^{related+} \cup C_C^{related-} \setminus C_Q^{violated} \quad (6.54)$$

This consistent constraint set can be used as input for the constraint-based workflow engine, in order to compute work items.

The previously mentioned propagation extent can be customized according to the use case. If more than one level of transitively related constraints starting from the deviating task should be considered for adaptation, the extraction of the previously describes constraint sets can be repeated on the basis of previously extracted tasks in constraints (cf. Equation 6.50, 6.51, and 6.52).

6.5.2.3. Selection Criterion

As the retrieval results in several similar cases, a selection criterion needs to be defined that decides which case is adopted to solve the query. To this end, several strategies are conceivable.

6.5.2.4. Adaptability

The adaptability of the query concerning the case can be measured through compatibility of the partial solution of the query with the constraint net of each case. Therefore, it is checked whether a solution can be found for the CSP of each case that also incorporates the derived constraint set of the query.

$$C'_C = C_C \cup C_Q^D \tag{6.55}$$

With this combined set of constraints, it can be evaluated whether the constraint set of the case can be transferred to the de facto workflow without contradictions. If a solution to the adapted CSP exists, the previously stated condition holds.

$$\texttt{sol} \neq \emptyset \text{ for } CSP = (X_C, D_C, C'_C) \tag{6.56}$$

In case the solution set is empty, the comparison can be made based upon the number of conflicts that arise when searching for a solution. The case with a minimum number of conflicts might then be the most adequate case to be reused for a solution of the query. The number of conflicts is determined through applying the algorithm for finding MUCs [66].

If, however, no best choice can be identified based on the presented properties, one case can be chosen at random.

6.5.2.5. Frequency

On the other hand, the least conflicting case might not be the best choice, as the extent of adaptation may not be an indicator for the quality and success of the outcome. A different property of cases that might influence the selection is the frequency. The most frequent workflow of the most similar ones should be chosen for adaptation, as it has been established and possibly represents a "best practice" workflow.

Additional ideas, which are part of future work, include a more elaborated selection of those constraints that are transferred, instead of choosing randomly at one specific point in the adaptation process which constraints to retain and which ones to discard.

A differentiation could be made based upon the constraint origins. A violation of those that result from data dependencies might be more severe than those which are simply derived from sequential control-flow.

Furthermore, a prioritisation of constraints could also be possible. Constraints that are not directly affected by the deviation-dependent choice could be integrated as optional constraints and further influence the weighting of conflicts and hence, those constraints that are discarded.

Both of the proposed adaptation methods address research question **RQ2.2** (see Section 1.2) through transferring valuable process execution characteristics from one or several retrieved workflow cases. Concerning the null adaptation this transfer solely consists of work items, whereas the generative adaptation combines and integrates the constraint sets.

6.6. Related Work

In this section related work is presented. All known approaches consider manually created knowledge or even require manual intervention in a running workflow for the management of deviations. As the addressed target group in this work are SMEs, where employees have low experience of process modelling, the presented case-based approach aims at automatically adapting to changing circumstances without the need of modelling process fragments or adaptation knowledge in any form. Consequently, the approach relies on experience, which means previously executed workflows, and the exploitation of available data to provide further workflow control and recommendations of work items even in unexpected situations.

The most important aspect of flexibility by deviation, which is essential for a successful support of the process participant, is the management of deviations, i.e. deviation detection, handling and analysis. The presented work focusses mainly on deviation handling strategies.

Several related approaches exist in research; most of these works focus on the detection and handling of deviations by either adapting running workflow instances or proposing corrective measures. Furthermore, the type of regarded deviations varies. In the presented work foremost deviations in control-flow, considering the order of tasks, are regarded, whereas some of the related work refer to other perspectives

6.6. RELATED WORK

of the workflow model, such as exceeded deadlines or non-conforming context variables.

PROSYT represents an early approach that is related to flexibility by deviation, as the focus lies on support of unexpected deviations without adapting the model at run time [28]. Processes are modelled on the basis of an artifact-based language that is enhanced through finite-state machines. Four types of deviations are distinguished, such that for each type one out of five policies can be determined. When encountering such a deviation, this policy is consequently triggered.

Several existing approaches utilise ECA rules [22, 40, 72, 124] to determine a reaction to detected deviations. However, these rules need to be specified at build time, which is a time-consuming and knowledge-intensive task.

As advancement to these simple ECA rules, Grambow et al. [53] present a flexible variant of ECA rules, which is enhanced through contextual semantic information and reasoning. Actions to perform are additionally adapted on the basis of semantic knowledge through the use of an ontology, a reasoner and Semantic Web Rule Language (SWRL) rules. Nevertheless, this approach requires a tedious manual specification of applicable knowledge.

Luo et al. [98] propose an extension of ECA rules to justified ECA, abbreviated as JECA, rules that are able to map uncertain parts. Through these rules, the workflow itself and possible exceptions are specified as graph structure. Moreover, they integrate a CBR component that is able to retrieve similar exception handlers.

Döhring and Zimmermann [39] developed an extension to BPMN called *vBPMN* (variant BPMN). Adaptation patterns can be applied thereon that are specified through ECA rules. vBPMN is widely applicable, as it is BPMN2 compliant due to an existing model transformation [38].

Another rule-based approach is pursued by Da Silva et al. [29]. Logical formulae are used as rule basis for the detection of deviations. Correction plans are subsequently created by a planning algorithm and recommended to guide the process participant to fix the workflow. In addition, they implemented a risk assessment that is able to determine the impact of an unhandled deviation to the goal of the process in order to prioritize necessary corrective measures.

A similar approach is developed by Adams et al. [4]. The manual handling of deviation is circumvented by so-called *worklets*, which represent exception handling patterns that are inserted automatically in running workflow instances on the basis of contextual information.

Marrella et al. [105, 106] developed a planner that integrates recovery procedures when deviations occur. In this approach, which was developed in the context of cyber-physical systems, pre-specified domain knowledge is necessary, which needs to be modelled manually.

Mourão and Antunes [118] focus on a collaborative way of handling unexpected exceptions. They propose to integrate recovery as well as monitoring actions at the same time and regard the resolving of exceptions as an iterative process. Changes to the deviating process are applied manually and consequently can only be made by experienced employees.

Zhu et al. [215] developed a process behaviour space expression based on algebra to identify deviations and provide simple methods like tolerating or adjusting deviations that handle such exceptions to a limited extent.

A novel approach that completely dispenses workflow models, but still enables detecting deviations, is presented by Lu et al. [97]. They propose an approach that is solely based on event logs, foremost applicable in the case where no model exists. To this end, event logs are transformed to execution graphs that are used as case representation. Common behaviour and derived from that deviating tasks, which occur rather infrequently in a specific context, are identified through a mapping and clustering of execution graphs.

Depaire et al. [35] focus on deviation diagnosis or as they refer to the "managerial view". They investigate and analyse characteristics of deviations on purpose of searching for control weaknesses. Workflow instances are mined and business rules representing the deviations are derived subsequently. This results in a drastically reduced amount of data, which in turn may be analysed.

Eder and Liebhart [43] developed the transaction-oriented workflow activity model (WAMO), where expected exceptions can be integrated directly into the workflow model through compensation tasks.

Klein and Dellarocas [82] propose an approach where exception handling is integrated during workflow modelling. These exception patterns, which are reflected by knowledge about which exceptions exist, how to detect and how to handle them, needs to be specified at build time in a time-consuming and effortful manner. Furthermore, solely anticipated deviations can be integrated, which distinguishes it

6.6. RELATED WORK

from the approach that is pursued by this work.

These are two of several approaches that focus on expected exceptions. As this is not the type of deviations that are handled by the proposed approach, more related approaches are not listed in this work.

Samiri et al. [161] propose an approach for automated adaptation of workflows that is based on reinforcement learning and forecasting controlled through a collaborative multi-agent system.

CBRFlow [200, 201] is a system that exploits conversational CBR to react to changing circumstances. In this approach a case base is combined with a rule base. Cases consist of question-answer pairs that describe the reasons for the deviations and the corresponding performed actions. Business rules are used to model necessary run time changes of workflows and may then be recommended in similar future situations. Nevertheless, the process participant has to intervene manually to trigger a deviation and to resolve the issues.

Montani [117] presents an approach that combines workflow management and CBR methods as well. Cases are represented through hierarchical graphs and are stored after a generalization step to so-called *prototypes*. Through retrieving a similar process schema at run time, end users are enabled and supported in changing the process instance ad-hoc. A drawback of this approach is that process participants are burdened with the remodelling task, which can lead to excessive demands and an avoidable intricacy.

A related approach that solely concerns the restoration of a consistent model is pursued by Di Ciccio et al. [24]. They propose an approach that resolves inconsistencies that arise during declarative process discovery. They therefore apply techniques that base on automata-product monoid, as LTL constructs are used as formal language that can be translated to automata. Though, compared to the presented approach, the use case is quite distinct and the underlying formalisation differs.

Chapter 7

Prototype

This chapter gives an overview of the prototypical implementation of the presented flexible workflow approach. The envisioned concept for a flexible workflow system that is able to handle deviations including all previously presented functionalities is sketched in the context of the process cycle in Section 7.1. Furthermore, an architecture is proposed in Section 7.2 which serves as basis for the prototypical implementation. Concluding, implementation details, utilized frameworks, and libraries are introduced in Section 7.3.

7.1. Flexible Workflow Approach

Summing up all previously presented components, the overall flexible workflow approach with different alternative methods for deviation handling is presented in Fig. 7.1 from a user perspective, as extension of Fig. 5.1. Necessary interactions of process engineers and the process participants are shown as well as the functionalities of the flexible workflow system. The first step where the system is incorporated in the workflow process is when the process engineer sets up the workflow model, called de jure workflow, and possibly additional constraints (see (1)). This procedurally modelled workflow is transformed by the system to a constraint-based workflow language, which builds the formal foundation for the developed methods (see ⓐ). This transformation function is explained in more detail in Subsection 5.4.2. The de jure workflow and constraint net together form the model. These steps constitute the design phase.

At the time at which the workflow execution is triggered, the model is instantiated, to be more specific, the constraint net is initialized (see (2)). This instantiated constraint net is then used as input (see (3)) for the constraint algorithm (see ⓑ) that is designed to compute the worklist, which consists of those tasks that represent a valid next execution step (see (4)). This algorithm is presented in Subsection 5.4.1. These work items are suggested to the process participant (see (5)). Normally, the process participant chooses one of those tasks to execute (see (6)). In the proposed flexible workflow system, the executed tasks are simply traced. This recorded sequence of tasks represents the de facto workflow. Furthermore, the task enactment affects the constraint net, as variable values are set and influence possible remaining variable assignments (see (7)).

Afterwards, the workflow engine is activated again and the cycle starts all over (from step (3) to (7)), until the workflow terminates. When the end of the workflow is reached, its trace is stored in the event log (see (8)). The event log, which contains multiple terminated workflow instances, is used by the process engineer (see (9)) for performance analysis and optimization of the workflow model (see (10)). This overall procedure holds for standard operations without exceptional situations.

As deviations during workflow executions are allowed in this approach, the executed task may not match the ones contained in the worklist. Such a deviation triggers the workflow engine (see (11)), as the constraint net has become inconsistent and the initial constraint algorithm cannot find a solution any more and therefore proposes an empty worklist. In this work three different deviation handling approaches are proposed (see ⓒ, ⓓ, ⓔ). The first approach (see ⓒ) is simply based on the constraint net and proposes different strategies to restore consistency by retracting violated constraints and possibly adding some others. Thus, the constraint net is adapted (see (12)) and the initial constraint algorithm is subsequently re-enabled to compute the worklist (see (3)). These strategies are explained in Subsection 5.5.2.

The case-based deviation management constitutes the two other approaches, which are both adaptation methods with a retrieval phase as precondition. In this retrieval phase, a similarity measure using time series comparison is used to find the most similar terminated process in the event logs (see (13)). The principle of the similarity measure is

7.1. FLEXIBLE WORKFLOW APPROACH

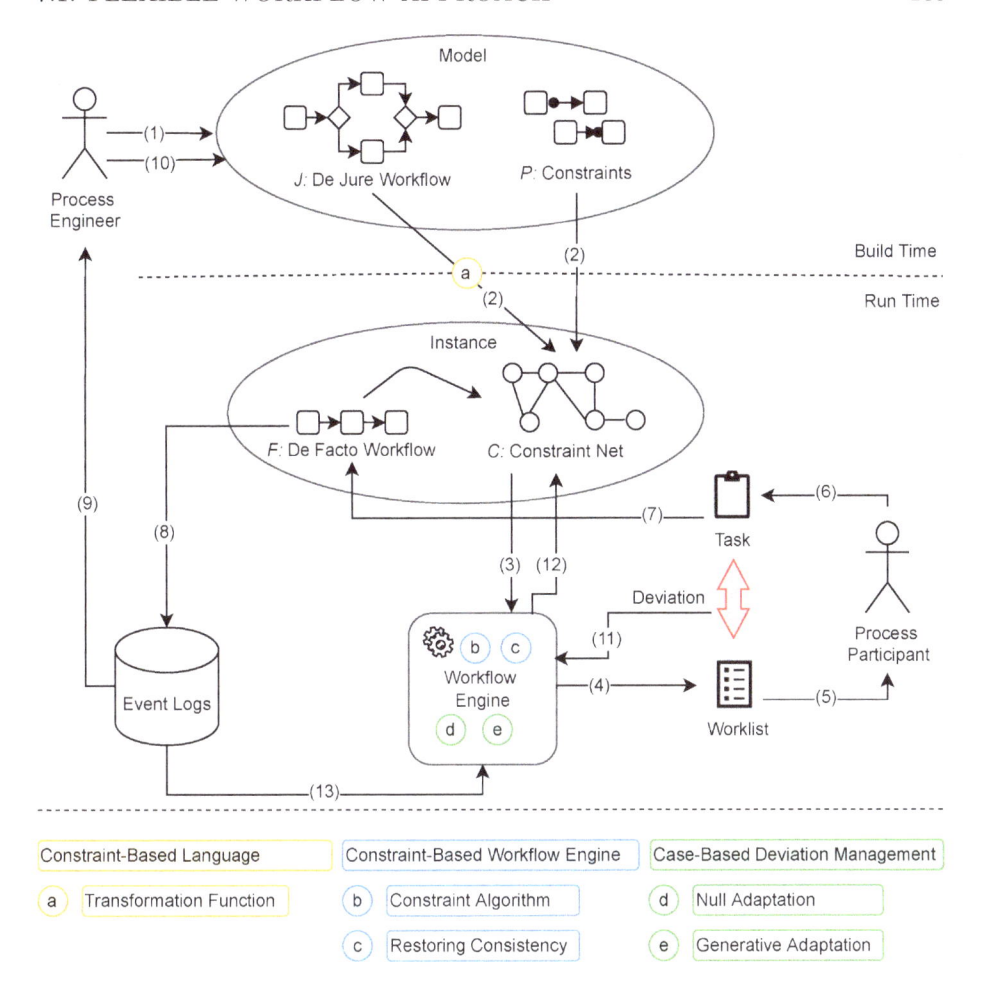

Figure 7.1. Flexible Workflow System for Handling Deviations

presented in Section 6.4. Based on this most similar workflow trace, new work items can be derived. This can be done via a rather simple method denoted as null adaptation (see ⓓ), which is introduced in Subsect. 6.5.1, whereas the generative constraint-based adaptation (see ⓔ), which is presented in Subsection 6.5.2, is more sophisticated. It takes several most similar workflow traces into account and adapts the constraint net of the regarded workflow instance accordingly. Thus, more information influences the computation of the work items, leading to a restoration of consistency and the ability to use this adapted constraint net until termination of the workflow, whereas after retrieval and null adaptation only single work items are exchanged and the constraint net is left untouched and thus, still inconsistent. Hence, after task execution another interference of the workflow engine is necessary.

7.2. Architecture

As architecture for a flexible workflow system that is able to handle deviations, a client-server model is proposed. The structure with its single components, which are distributed on three different layers, is shown in Fig. 7.2.

The presentation layer on the client side contains different user interfaces for providing basic functionality of a WfMS. The client communicates with the server through requesting specific information. The application layer is addressed first and accesses data from the knowledge layer in order to compute return values.

7.2.1. Presentation Layer

The presentation layer consists of several Graphical User Interfaces (GUIs) for different purposes that meet the demands of distinct users:

- **Editor:** The editor view can be used by the process engineer who is responsible for specifying or adapting a process model.

- **Worklist:** The worklist is primarily used by the process participant who is assigned activated tasks and subsequently is enabled to execute them. The functionality provided for the worklist, thus, computing work items, is the main focus of the presented work.

- **Monitoring:** The monitoring view can be utilized by the process engineer for supervising running and terminated workflows, for analysing arising issues or inefficiencies, and ultimately for identifying optimization potentials.

7.2.2. Application Layer

The application layer consists of several components that handle the execution of a workflow. This essentially includes three parts, which are highlighted in Fig. 7.2 in the same colour as in the illustration of the process cycle (cf. Fig. 7.1).

7.2. ARCHITECTURE

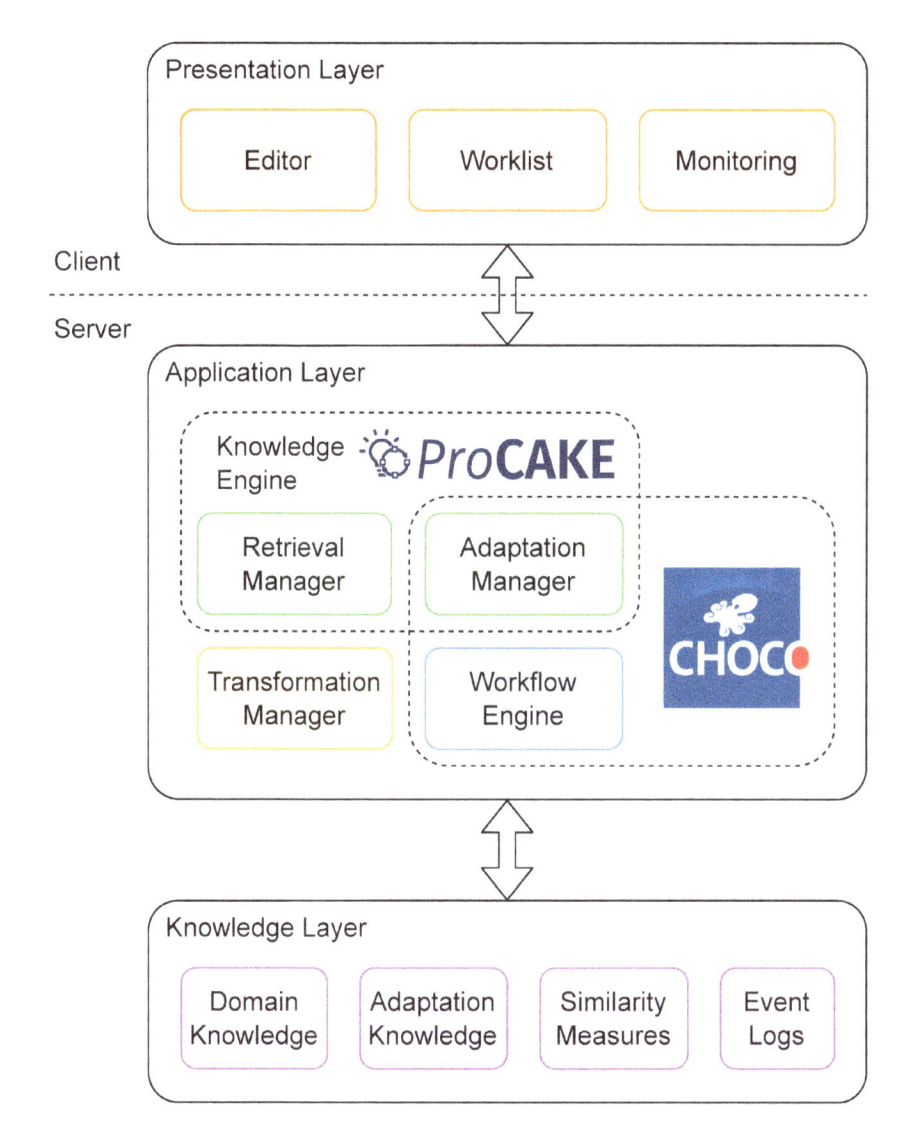

Figure 7.2. Architecture of the Prototypical Implementation of a Flexible Workflow System for Handling Deviations

- **Transformation Manager:** The transformation manager is responsible for transforming defined de jure workflows, including additionally specified constraints, into one declarative formula according to equation 5.4.

- **Knowledge Engine:** The knowledge engine includes two substantial case-based components, which are the retrieval and the adaptation manager that apply a time-series based similarity measure and two adaptation methods, null and generative.

- **Workflow Engine:** The workflow engine is part of the application layer as essential component for controlling workflow execution and consequently, computing of the worklist.

The application layer is mainly supported by the integration of two external libraries. The knowledge engine is based on the Process-Oriented Case-Based Knowledge Engine (ProCAKE) framework, whereas Choco-Solver is applied for constraint solving. Both are explained in more detail in the subsequent section about implementation details.

7.2.3. Knowledge Layer

The knowledge layer comprises the four knowledge containers of CBR. This includes as vocabulary some domain knowledge about the workflow itself, including its tasks and data objects. Besides, the structure of the cases is specified. Furthermore, necessary knowledge for adaptation methods and similarity measures are persisted, as well as the event logs that contain terminated workflows and are accordingly used as case base.

7.3. Prototypical Implementation

The presented concept for a flexible workflow system is realized as prototype that complies with the proposed architecture. The prototypical implementation is generic and can be adopted in any specific domain. The domain of deficiency management in construction, as introduced in Sect. 3.1, is utilized for an exemplification of the proposed approach and for evaluation purposes.

The client is realized as a web application, which is implemented in JavaScript. The application layer is fully implemented in Java,

7.3. PROTOTYPICAL IMPLEMENTATION

whereas data persistence is ensured through Extensible Markup Language (XML) or JavaScript Object Notation (JSON) files. The communication between client and server is completely based on an Application Programming Interface (API) that is based on the Representational State Transfer (REST) principle to ensure separation of concerns. As serialization of data that is send to and from the client, JSON is used as easy way to translate java objects.

In this section two external libraries, *Choco-Solver* and *ProCAKE*, which are used by the prototype, are introduced. Implementation details and an overview of selected GUIs are given in the following subsections.

7.3.1. Choco-Solver

Choco-Solver[11] is an open-source java library for constraint programming [139]. It provides basic functionality for constraint modelling and solving as well as interfaces for integrating custom implementations such as propagators or search heuristics.

For a specific use case, necessary variables, domains, and constraints need to be defined in a central model object. Some data types are provided such as *IntVar* for integer values or *BoolVar* for boolean variables. Bounded domains for integer variables can be specified by simply declaring two values that limit the interval through a minimum and maximum number. The domain of boolean variables is self-explanatorily predetermined as *true* or *false*.

For constraint specification, various options are offered, such as arithmetical relations between two numerical variables or even scheduling constraints that restrict the start, end, or duration of a task variable. Furthermore, boolean variables or constraints can be linked through a logical expression and again form a constraint. A differentiation between mandatory and optional constraints is not possible, but through reifying, constraints can be associated with boolean variables and consequently, the state of the constraint is part of the solution.

Choco-Solver offers a constraint propagation algorithm that enables a reduction of domains without assigning values to variables. This allows for a preliminary check for contradictions of constraints that

---

[11] https://choco-solver.org/ - In the prototypical implementation, version 4.10.2 is used.

indicate an inconsistent constraint net and ultimately, for determining the impossibility of solving the problem.

Based on this specified model, a solver can be created and initiated. The default search strategy for finding a solution is creating a binary search tree based on depth first search. Nevertheless, some other heuristics and search strategies are implemented and can be chosen. Those are responsible for identifying the next variable that is assigned a value or determining the value to be assigned based on a certain criteria. Besides available selectors, custom ones can be implemented and embedded through provided interfaces. The solving process can additionally include an optimization goal, through specifying the objective in context of a variable, e.g. maximization. Moreover, a multi-threaded resolution can be deployed, where different search strategies are applied to the problem in parallel, which during the process share some significant information in order to increase efficiency.

Choco-Solver also offers a statistics component, which allows for an analysis of the search that happened during the solving process. Several information can be retrieved, such as the number of backtracks, fails, or the depth of the search tree.

7.3.2. ProCAKE

ProCAKE[12] is a domain-independent framework for structural and process-oriented CBR [16]. It is developed at the Department of Business Information Systems II at the Trier University and evolved throughout several research projects. ProCAKE was extracted as the core knowledge engine of the Collaborative Agile Knowledge Engine (CAKE) [14] and is applied in prototypes of various research projects of different domains, such as social workflows [52], cooking workflows [120], scientific workflows [214], or even adaptive production processes in the context of Industry 4.0 and cyber-physical systems [101].

ProCAKE includes miscellaneous syntactic and semantic similarity measures as well as several retrieval algorithms. For defining the structure of the case representation, ProCAKE provides a data model that contains several data types. For a domain model, these predefined

---

[12]http://procake.uni-trier.de - In the prototypical implementation, version 1.3.1 is used.

7.3.2.1. Data Model

Maximini developed the *CAKE data model* that consists of basic data types, such as string or integers [108]. In Fig. 7.3, this data model is shown with the inheritance hierarchy of the data types. All types are based on the abstract root class *Data* and split up into *Atomic* and compound types such as *Collection* or *Interval*.

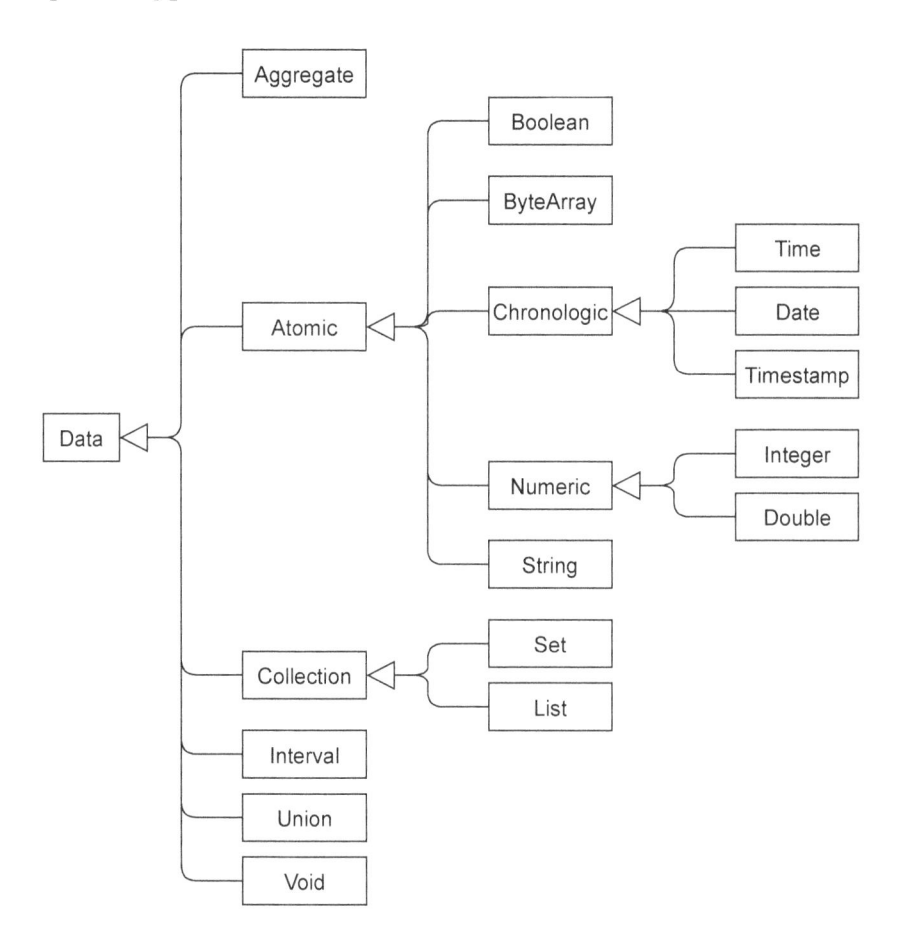

Figure 7.3. System Classes of the CAKE Data Model according to Maximini [108]

For an object-oriented structure *Aggregate* classes can be utilized that allow for a specification of composite data objects, by assembling attributes that are either of those simple data types or aggregate objects again. Thus, an arbitrary nesting of attributes is possible.

These system classes were extended later with the *NESTGraph* and its elements to handle semantic workflows. Figure 7.4 shows these elements and their hierarchy, except different forms of *NESTControlflowNode* for the sake of simplification.

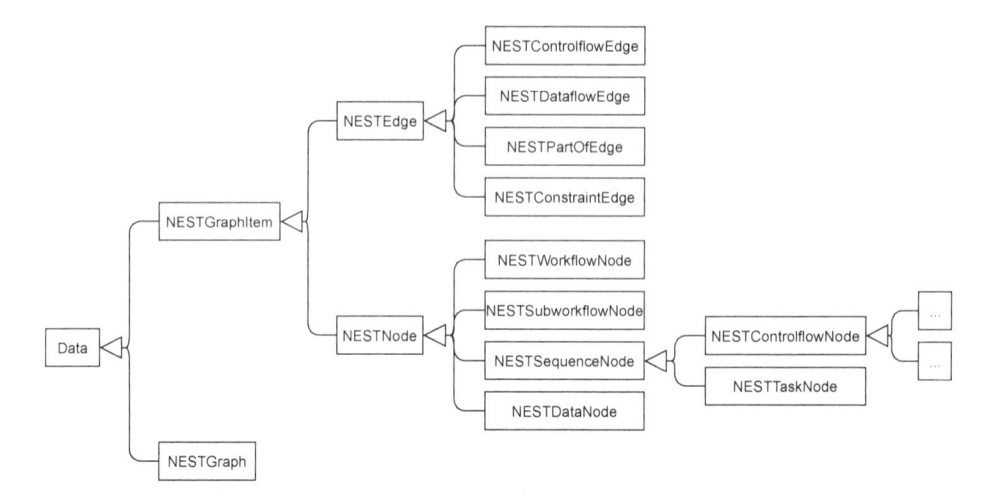

Figure 7.4. Extension of the System Classes of the CAKE Data Model with *NESTGraph* elements

The *NESTGraph* itself and its elements as *NESTGraphItem* are defined. *NESTGraphItem* further splits into nodes and edges, *NESTNode* and *NESTEdge*, and their different manifestations. Each of these elements can be linked to a so-called semantic description that is specified as object of a user-defined class. As substantial part of a semantic workflow, these descriptions are mainly used for comparison during similarity assessment.

7.3.2.2. Similarity and Retrieval

ProCAKE provides manifold similarity measures for each of these data types, which can be chosen to be applied during retrieval. To name but two, this ranges from a simple *StringEquals* measure, which delivers a binary result as it only evaluates equality, to complex mapping algorithms for *NESTGraphs* such as *A**.

Several retrieval algorithms can be utilized, where the most important ones comprise a simple *LinearRetriever*, a *ParallelRetriever*,

7.3. PROTOTYPICAL IMPLEMENTATION

which uses multiple cores concurrently for a more efficient retrieval, and a *MACFACRetriever*, which applies a filtering method based on a predefined characteristic in a first step in order to reduce the retrieval time for evaluating the complete remaining case base in the second step.

Adaptation methods are not part of the generic ProCAKE framework so far, as only domain-specific methods were implemented during past research projects. Nevertheless, own implementations can be integrated by connecting them to the interface of the provisioned adaptation manager.

The configuration of an instance of ProCAKE, which consists of the used data types, the similarity measures with the parameters that are applied for the cases and their attributes, and the case base itself for a specific domain, can be specified through XML files.

7.3.3. Web Application

The user interface of the prototypical implementation of the presented flexible workflow approach is implemented as web application, using different libraries, such as Angular[13] for the main structure and *vis.js*[14] for visualizing the workflow graphs. This web application contains four different views. At start, an overview of all running workflow instances and all workflow models is shown, as overview for the process engineer (see Fig. 7.5).

In this view, workflows can be started through choosing and initializing a workflow model, and new workflow models can be created. Furthermore, the detail views can be accessed. By clicking on a workflow model, the editor is opened. When selecting a workflow instance, the execution view is shown, which contains the worklist among other aspects. Besides, through this view, the monitoring page can be accessed.

7.3.3.1. Editor

The editor component shows one selected workflow model and is divided into a main view for the de jure workflow and a tab for

---
[13] https://angular.io/
[14] https://visjs.org/

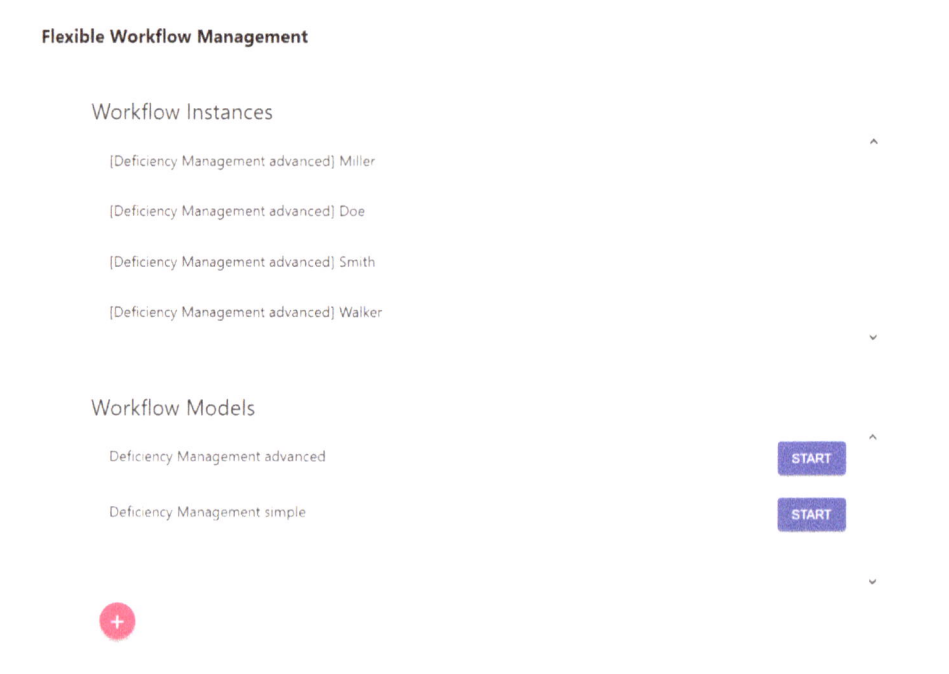

Figure 7.5. Start Page of the Web Application - GUI with a List of Workflow Models and Instances

constraint specification, which can be folded out sidewards from the right.

The main view in Fig. 7.6 shows the block-oriented de jure workflow. For a modification of this workflow graph, buttons in the upper left corner can be used to insert different nodes into the graph. Existent nodes can be deleted through selecting a specific node which activates a delete button. Descriptions of nodes or edges can be modified through double-clicking. In this case, a dialogue for editing appears. An overview of the de jure workflow can be seen in the lower right corner, which is helpful when editing large graphs. Through this map, the current position is apparent and the focussed section can be shifted.

The expandable tab on the right side, where constraints can be specified, modified or deleted, is shown in Fig. 7.7. These constraints refer to the additional DECLARE constraints of the set C^A, which is described on page 98. A simple table represents this constraint set, where each row represents one stored constraint. In the bottom row, new constraints can be added.

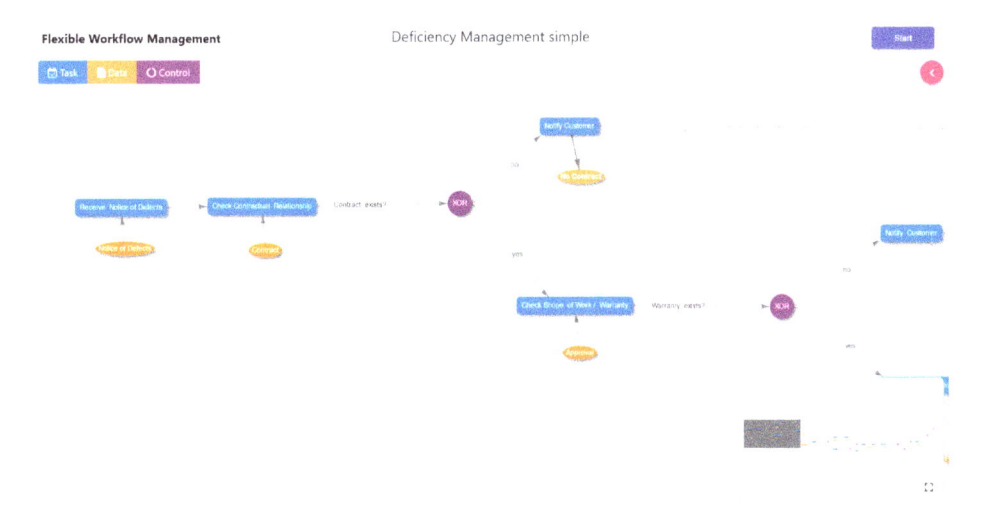

Figure 7.6. Editor View for Modelling De Jure Workflows

An integrated view for the workflow graph and the constraints in the main graphical view exists and can be toggled. The constraints are shown thereupon integrated in the workflow graph indicated as additional edges, at least *Precedence*, *Response* through green-coloured directed edges and *Non-Existence* through red-coloured bidirectional edges. In Fig. 7.7, an exemplary constraint is added and can be seen in the workflow graph as green-coloured edge.

7.3.3.2. Worklist

The GUI that is foremost used by the process participant and that controls the execution of the process contains an overview of the workflow model and the worklist (see Fig. 7.8). The de jure workflow is shown in the editor view with an adapted colouring of nodes depending on the execution state of the workflow. In this example, the first task has been executed and is coloured in green, whereas all other tasks remain to be executed and are coloured in grey. The worklist is presented in the right tab view in a table format. In this specific case, where flexibility by deviation should be allowed, the worklist contains on the one hand the determined work items that are ideally executed next. Consequently, they are positioned at the top and highlighted with yellow colour. On the other hand, a list of the remaining tasks complements these work items, as they can nevertheless be enacted, which then leads to a deviation. Furthermore, tasks that were already

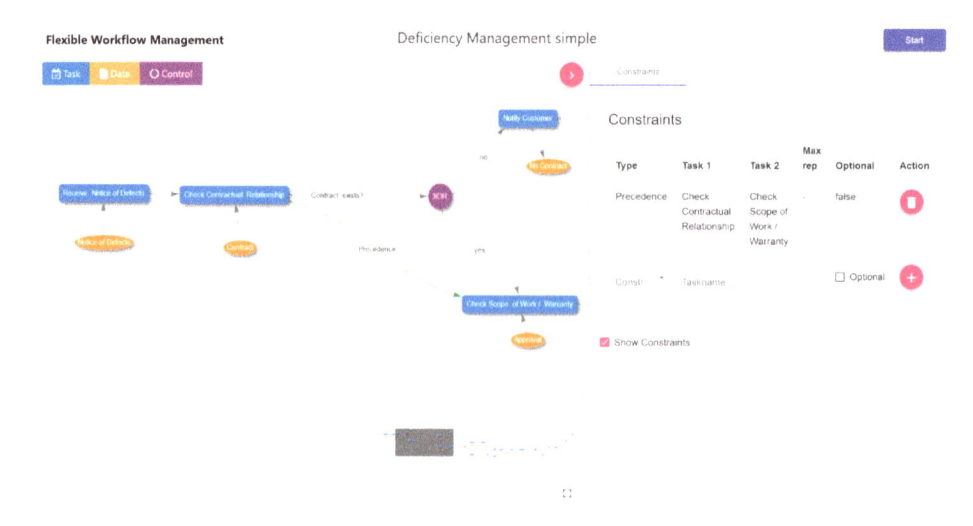

Figure 7.7. Editor View for Modelling De Jure Workflows with Constraint Tab

enacted remain part of the worklist, but with a changed action label in the button, named *Reenact* to indicate the potential repeated execution (cf. row 4, task: *Receive Notice of Defects*).

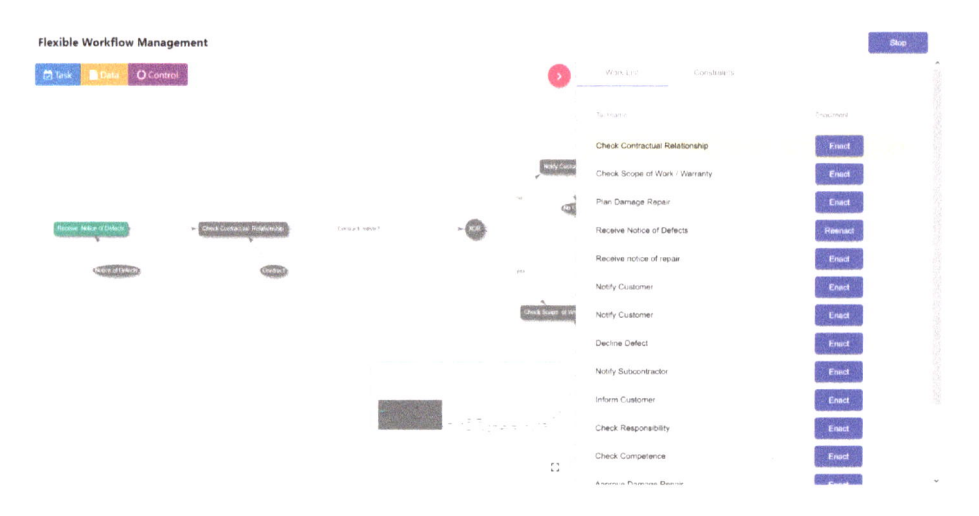

Figure 7.8. Execution View with Worklist and De Jure Workflow

This design choice was made in this prototypical implementation, as there is no other possibility to become aware of executed and deviating task in case only valid work items can be chosen by the process participant. As intended in the SEMAFLEX project, where for instance an update about an execution of a specific task is derived from

7.3. PROTOTYPICAL IMPLEMENTATION

incoming documents that are classified and from which information is extracted, it is reasonable to only show valid work items in order to not actively mislead process participants to deviate.

7.3.3.3. Monitoring

The monitoring view (see Fig. 7.9) contains various details about one workflow instance. The view can either be invoked after termination of the workflow or during execution. The de facto workflow is shown as well as the de jure workflow. Furthermore, the worklist is shown as in the execution view and a list of all constraints that are part of the generated CSP, including their current status, is presented.

Figure 7.9. Monitoring View with Information about the Workflow Instance

Two functions for further analysis are implemented in the prototype. With the button *Enhance* in the de facto view, the sequence of tasks of the de facto workflow can be enhanced by control-flow nodes, that were on the path when replaying the de facto on the de jure workflow. Besides, *Color Nodes* in the de jure view allows for a mapping of the de facto workflow to be integrated into the view of de jure workflow. Here, the nodes in the de jure workflow are coloured depending on their execution status (green for correctly executed, yellow for deviations concerning order, grey for not executed yet). In the example in Fig. 7.9, this function is activated and the two first tasks are executed in the correct order, as can be seen in the de jure view.

The client communicates with the server through a REST API. The implementation on the server side is also supported by the use of some frameworks, such as RestEasy[15] for the REST API or Jetty[16] as web server. Thus, the client interacts via requests with the server, which activates the specific components with the required functionality. Each of these components is subsequently explained in detail.

7.3.4. Transformation Manager

The first component on the application layer that is triggered when initializing a workflow instance is the transformation manager. During run time, the block-oriented de jure workflow, which is specified as *NESTGraph*, is translated to a *Formula* object. The class structure which is used for this purpose is presented in Fig. 7.10. The formula consists of either a *Term* or an atomic *Constraint*. A term comprises several formulae that are linked with a conjunctive or disjunctive connector *con*. This allows for an arbitrary encapsulation of terms and atomic constraints.

These atomic constraints can be of different types and have some specific attributes that are necessary for an adequate handling of the workflow as described in previous chapters. Besides the DECLARE constraints, an additional constraint *EqualsConstraint* is provided to enable the mapping of control variables and their value assignments. The transformation of sequential dependencies into order relations is mapped through *PrecedenceConstraints*, as the semantic is equal. Consequently, the relation $(t_1 < t_2)$ for two sequential tasks t_1 and t_2, which possibly results from the transformation function *Dec* (cf. Subsect. 5.4.2), is stored as *PrecedenceConstraint* with the *NESTTaskNodeObject* of t_1 as *firstTask* and the *NESTTaskNodeObject* of t_2 as *secondTask*.

The formula is stored independent from the constraint representation that is used by the constraint solver in order to allow for storing the additionally defined attributes, such as type and status. Furthermore, not all constraints are part of the CSP, but it is determined depending on the status of the constraint whether a constraint is included in the CSP and thus, in the solving process. The originally

---

[15] https://resteasy.dev/
[16] https://www.eclipse.org/jetty/

7.3. PROTOTYPICAL IMPLEMENTATION

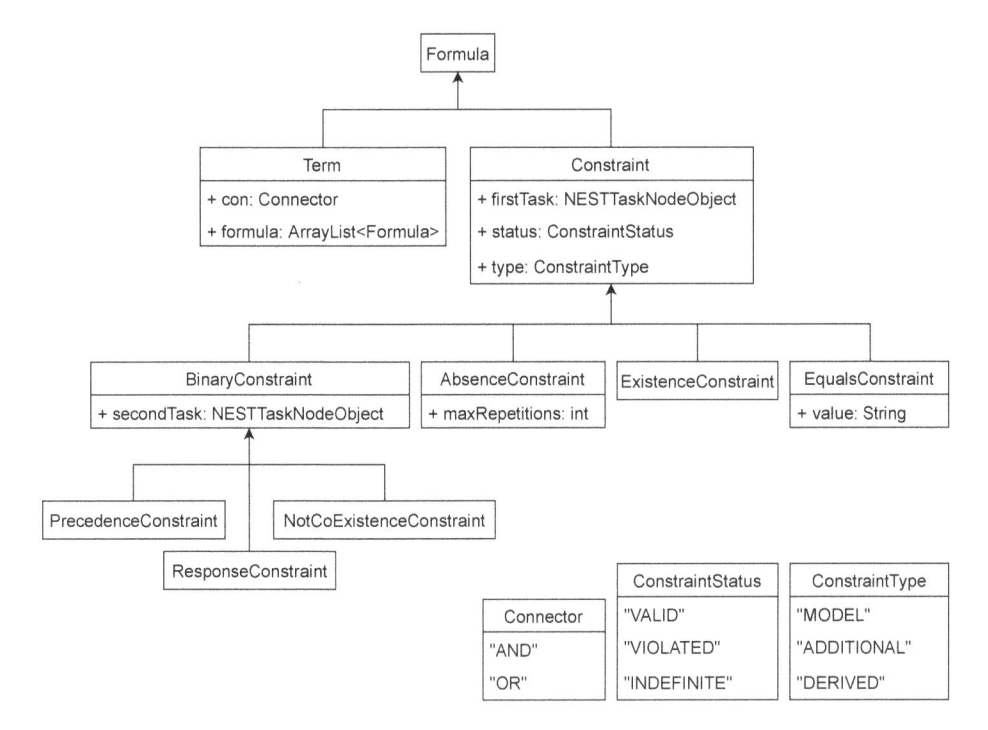

Figure 7.10. Class Diagram of the Declarative Formula for Transformation Process

created constraints can still be accessed through the formula object.

7.3.5. Workflow Engine

As the essential part of the workflow engine is the CSP which is used for determining work items, this component is mainly based on a constraint solver. To this end, Choco-Solver [139] is utilized.

The model object is initialized according to the specification of the CSP_W in Subsect. 5.4.1. As variables, $IntVar$ is used for the elements of the set of sequence tasks S and $BoolVar$ for the control variables A. Domains are set up appropriately. Based on the previously presented $Formula$ object, constraints are generated in the respective representation that the solver can handle and use for finding a solution.

To determine work items, the solver runs several times with a varying set of constraints, where in each of the runs one constraint is added to evaluate if one task is a valid candidate for next task execution. During workflow progress, the sets of the CSP_W may also be extended, which is done through a new model object, as no dynamic extension or reduction is possible in Choco-Solver. The solution search is started with the default configuration, which means a binary search tree with depth first search.[17]

During workflow progress, the de facto workflow is enhanced by traced executed tasks, which is done by extending the respective *NESTGraph* object during run time. Terminated workflows are persisted in XML files to serve as case base for a further processing by the knowledge engine. Their structure is explained in subsequent sections concerning the knowledge layer.

7.3.6. Knowledge Engine

The two components of the knowledge engine are responsible for the case-based deviation management and essentially base on the ProCAKE framework. To this end, ProCAKE was extended with a similarity measure in two different forms (cf. Section 6.4) and two adaptation algorithms (cf. Section 6.5).

The retrieval manager is responsible for initiating the preprocessing algorithm. For calculating the similarity between de facto workflows, the two similarity measures *SMGraphSWA* and *SMGraphDTW* are provided.[18]. A simple linear retriever is used for retrieval.[19]

The specification of all knowledge containers that are used by the knowledge engine are presented in the following section.

7.3.7. Knowledge Layer

The knowledge layer contains several components that are used to initialize ProCAKE. Each of these configuration files is persisted in XML format and at run time deserialized to objects.

---

[17]Note that, as the focus of this work is not performance optimization, there is room for improvement in future work. To this end, different search strategies and heuristics can be validated and compared concerning their run time.

[18]Both similarity measures are available in the public repository of ProCAKE (see https://gitlab.rlp.net/procake/procake-framework). Furthermore, a generalized version of both measures exists, to compare sequences of arbitrary elements (see *SMListSWA* and *SMListDTW*).

[19]Note that the focus of this work is not to optimize the computation time. Different retrievers can be evaluated in future work in order to gain improvements. For instance, a *ParallelRetriever* that is offered by ProCAKE could be applied and exchanged with low effort.

7.3. PROTOTYPICAL IMPLEMENTATION

The case structure is stored in a *model* object. An excerpt of the specified domain model is shown in Listing 7.1.

In the domain of flexible workflows, a case constitutes a workflow instance. It is represented by a composite object *DeviatingWorkflow*, which consists of the workflow model *wfModel* and the de facto workflow *deFacto*, which is a *NESTGraph* object (see lines 1-4 in Listing 7.1). The de jure workflow *deJure* as *NESTGraph* object and a set of constraints *constraints* together form the workflow model (see lines 6-9 in Listing 7.1). Constraints can have different types, which conform with the available classes on the application layer, with some common but also some distinct attributes. All specific constraints therefore inherit from the super class *Constraint* (see line 15-19 in Listing 7.1) and relate to one task *firstTask*, a *status* and a *type*, where values of the classes *ConstraintStatus* and *ConstraintType* are predefined (see lines 33-39 and 41-47 in Listing 7.1). Two exemplary specific constraint types are shown in Listing 7.1 (see lines 21-31). *PrecedenceConstraint* has an additional attribute *secondTask* that refers to the second involved task, whereas *EqualsConstraint* requires the specification of the *value* of the task.

Listing 7.1. Excerpt from the Domain Model representing the Case Structure for Flexible Workflows

```
1  <AggregateClass name="DeviatingWorkflow">
2    <Attribute name="wfModel" class="WorkflowModel"/>
3    <Attribute name="deFacto" class="NESTGraph"/>
4  </AggregateClass>
5
6  <AggregateClass name="WorkflowModel">
7    <Attribute name="deJure" class="NESTGraph"/>
8    <Attribute name="constraints" class="
         ConstraintSet"/>
9  </AggregateClass>
10
11 <SetClass name="ConstraintSet">
12   <ElementClass name="Constraint"/>
13 </SetClass>
14
15 <AggregateClass name="Constraint">
16   <Attribute name="firstTask" class="String"/>
```

```
17      <Attribute name="status" class="ConstraintStatus"
             />
18      <Attribute name="type" class="ConstraintType"/>
19   </AggregateClass>
20
21   <AggregateClass name="PrecedenceConstraint"
22                          superClass="Constraint">
23      <Attribute name="secondTask" class="String"/>
24   </AggregateClass>
25              .
26              .
27              .
28   <AggregateClass name="EqualsConstraint"
29                          superClass="Constraint">
30   <Attribute name="value" class="Integer"/>
31   </AggregateClass>
32
33   <StringClass name="ConstraintStatus">
34      <InstanceEnumerationPredicate>
35        <Value v="VALID"/>
36        <Value v="VIOLATED"/>
37        <Value v="INDEFINITE"/>
38      </InstanceEnumerationPredicate>
39   </StringClass>
40
41   <StringClass name="ConstraintType">
42      <InstanceEnumerationPredicate>
43           <Value v="MODEL"/>
44           <Value v="ADDITIONAL"/>
45           <Value v="DERIVED"/>
46      </InstanceEnumerationPredicate>
47   </StringClass>
```

The constraints are only persisted as set without logical connections, because the point of interest is their status. The logical formulae can be rebuild by the transformation manager on the basis of the de jure workflow and hence, each constraint status can be retrieved for elements of this formula at run time. Compared to the constraint objects in the formula implementation, here only a reference id of the tasks is stored, as the task node is part of the de jure workflow and thus, a redundant persistence is prevented. Other constraint types

7.3. PROTOTYPICAL IMPLEMENTATION

are specified analogously to *PrecedenceConstraint*.

In addition to defining the case structure as such, each contained element of the *NESTGraph* is connected to a semantic description that needs to be specified in the domain model. Whereas the case structure of flexible workflows is generic and applicable in every domain, these semantic descriptions are domain-specific. They represent the properties of nodes and edges, which are substantial for similarity assessment. The composition is shown in Listing 7.2.

Listing 7.2. Excerpt from the Domain Model for Flexible Workflows with Semantic Descriptions for NESTGraph Elements

```
1  <AggregateClass name="WorkflowSemantic">
2    <Attribute name="name" class="String"/>
3  </AggregateClass>
4
5  <AggregateClass name="TaskSemantic">
6    <Attribute name="name" class="String"/>
7  </AggregateClass>
8
9  <AggregateClass name="ExecutedTaskSemantic"
       superClass="TaskSemantic">
10   <Attribute name="deJureId" class="String"/>
11   <Attribute name="index" class="String"/>
12 </AggregateClass>
13
14 <AggregateClass name="DataSemantic">
15   <Attribute name="data" class="DataflowElement"/>
16 </AggregateClass>
17
18 <AggregateClass name="DataflowElement">
19   <Attribute name="name" class="String"/>
20 </AggregateClass>
21
22 <AggregateClass name="DataValue" superClass="
       DataflowElement">
23   <Attribute name="value" class="String"/>
24 </AggregateClass>
25
26 <AggregateClass name="ControlEdgeSemantic">
27   <Attribute name="description" class="String"/>
```

28 |</AggregateClass>

TaskSemantic refers to the description of task nodes (see lines 5-7 in Listing 7.2). In the domain model for deficiency management in construction only the name of the task itself is stored as simple string. A special form of this semantic description, which is generally applicable, is represented by *ExecutedTaskSemantic* (see lines 9-12 in Listing 7.2), which stores details about tasks of a de facto workflow, where additionally the reference id of the task in the de jure workflow *deJureId* and its *index* are stored.

DataSemantic (see lines 14-16 in Listing 7.2) for data nodes is encapsulated into a *DataflowElement* that can contain only a *name* (see lines 18-20 in Listing 7.2), but can also be an object of its subclass *DataValue*, which describes a concrete information with a *value* (see lines 22-24 in Listing 7.2).

Control-flow edges can contain additional information that refer to the control variables of control-flow nodes, specified as *ControlEdgeSemantic* (see lines 26-28 in Listing 7.2).

In the domain model for deficiency management in construction, simple strings are used for task and data descriptions. Nevertheless, with slight modifications it is possible to use semantic information that is stored in a taxonomy or an ontology. In ProCAKE, several similarity measures for both data types exist, such that this extension can be adopted very easily by modifying the data types in the domain model, specifying the semantic model and determining applied similarity measures.

In the similarity model, the similarity measures that are applied during retrieval, including used parameters, are determined for each of the data types that are defined in the domain model. Listing 7.3 shows an excerpt of the similarity model for flexible workflows.

The similarity model contains both generally applicable measures for all types of flexible workflows, referring to the *NESTGraph* similarity measures, as well as domain-specific, chosen similarity measures concerning domain-specific parts of the model, such as *DataSemantic*.

The most important similarity measures are those for *NESTGraphs*. In the similarity model three different definitions are made for the measures that are based on A*, the SWA and DTW. As A* measure, the third variant is applied that uses a specific heuristic [213] and

7.3. PROTOTYPICAL IMPLEMENTATION

the maximum used queue size is set to five (see line 6 in Listing 7.3). For both the SWA and DTW (see lines 7 and 8 in Listing 7.3), the similarity measure that is used for comparing data or task nodes is specified (cf. *taskSimName, dataSimName*). It is further specified that the alignment ends with the query, such that following tasks in the case are not considered in the similarity assessment (cf. *endWithQuery*). The SWA requires a value for the penalties for insertion and deletion, as well as for the halving distance, which is also defined for DTW.

String attributes are compared on the basis of the Levenshtein distance (see line 14 in Listing 7.3).

Listing 7.3. Excerpt from the Similarity Model for Flexible Workflows

```
1  <AggregateAverage name="wfSemSim"
2          class="WorkflowSemantic">
3    <AggWeight att="name" weight="1"/>
4  </AggregateAverage>
5
6  <GraphAStarThree name="SMGraph" class="NESTGraph"
       maxQueueSize="5"/>
7  <GraphSWA class="NESTGraph" name="GraphSWA"
       taskSimName="taskSim" dataSimName="dataSim"
       constInsertionPenalty="-0.5"
       constDeletionPenalty="-0.5" halvingDist="0.5"
       endWithQuery="false"/>
8  <GraphDTW class="NESTGraph" name="GraphDTW"
       taskSimName="taskSim" dataSimName="dataSim"
       halvingDist="0.5" endWithQuery="false"/>
9
10 <AggregateAverage name="dataSim" class="
       DataSemantic">
11   <AggWeight att="data" weight="1"/>
12 </AggregateAverage>
13
14 <StringLevenshtein name="stringSim" class="String"
       caseSensitive="false"/>
```

The cases as such are also persisted in an XML file, which is used as in- and output of ProCAKE. Listing 7.4 represents an excerpt of a case base, denoted as event log in Fig. 7.2, with the de jure workflow of deficiency management in construction shown in Fig. 3.1. Different nodes and edges are included with their semantic description according to the previously shown definitions. The structure of the *NESTGraph* definition is generic, but is exemplified with the regarded use case of deficiency management in construction.

Listing 7.4. Excerpt from the Case Base for Flexible Workflows

```
1  <nest:NESTGraph id="Deficiency Management" c="
       NESTWorkflow">
2   <nest:Nodes>
3    <nest:Node id="END_20" c="NESTXorEndNode" refId="
        20"></nest:Node>
4    <nest:Node id="t14" c="NESTTaskNode">
5     <cdol:Agg c="TaskSemantic">
6      <cdol:AA n="name" v="Notify Subcontractor">
7      </cdol:AA>
8     </cdol:Agg>
9    </nest:Node>
10   <nest:Node id="d6" c="NESTDataNode">
11    <cdol:Agg c="DataSemantic">
12     <cdol:OA n="data">
13      <cdol:Agg>
14       <cdol:AA n="name" v="Approval"></cdol:AA>
15      </cdol:Agg>
16     </cdol:OA>
17    </cdol:Agg>
18   </nest:Node>
19   <nest:Node id="t12" c="NESTTaskNode">
20    <cdol:Agg c="TaskSemantic">
21     <cdol:AA n="name" v="Decline Defect"></cdol:AA>
22    </cdol:Agg>
23   </nest:Node>
24   <nest:Node id="d16" c="NESTDataNode">
25    <cdol:Agg c="DataSemantic">
26     <cdol:OA n="data">
27      <cdol:Agg>
28       <cdol:AA n="name" v="No Repair"></cdol:AA>
29      </cdol:Agg>
30     </cdol:OA>
31    </cdol:Agg>
32   </nest:Node>
```

```
33       .
34       .
35       .
36   </nest:Nodes>
37   <nest:Edges>
38    <nest:Edge id="e22" pre="d14" post="t16" c="
         NESTDataflowEdge"></nest:Edge>
39    <nest:Edge id="e83" pre="t10" post="WORKFLOW_27"
         c="NESTPartOfEdge"></nest:Edge>
40    <nest:Edge id="e61" pre="23" post="t10" c="
         NESTControlflowEdge">
41     <cdol:Agg c="ControlEdgeSemantic">
42      <cdol:AA n="description" v="no"></cdol:AA>
43     </cdol:Agg>
44    </nest:Edge>
45       .
46       .
47       .
48   </nest:Edges>
49  </nest:NESTGraph>
```

Each element is identified through a unique identifier *id* and a *class* for specifying the type of the element. Moreover, edges include the ids of the preceding and subsequent node (*pre* and *post*).

An evaluation, which is presented in the next chapter, is done based on this prototypical implementation and the use case *deficiency management in construction*.

Chapter 8
Evaluation

Design science research creates artifacts that represent solutions to some specific issues [133]. Consequently, an evaluation is necessary to "observe and measure how well the artifact supports a solution to the problem" [133]. Different criteria should be subject of investigation, such as functionality, performance, usability and many more [69]. The evaluation of the presented constraint-based workflow engine with a case-based deviation management is subject of this chapter. Parts of the approach were assessed in previous experiments [58, 163], whereas this evaluation focuses on the utility of the overall flexible workflow approach. To this end, a technical experiment in combination with an illustrative scenario [132] on the basis of synthetic data was performed.

This chapter introduces the evaluation setup and stated hypotheses, and analyses the results and their implications. First, as a short recap, the contributions of the presented work are subsumed in Section 8.1. The initial main research question is subsequently taken up in Section 8.2 and it is addressed how some requirements of a flexible workflow approach for SMEs are met. The criteria that are investigated in the evaluation are presented in Section 8.3. On this basis, several hypotheses that address different aspects are formulated in Section 8.4. Section 8.5 describes the generation of synthetic data, which is derived from a real-world use case, and the performed experiments, which consist of a simulation of workflow executions for several specified types of process participants. Subsequently, in Section 8.6, the results of the experiments are shown, analysed and interpreted. Section 8.7 concludes the chapter with a summary of the findings resulting from the evaluation of the proposed approach.

8.1. Contributions

This section briefly recaps the created artifacts of the presented work, which are subject of the evaluation.

One essential characteristic of a developed artifact that needs to be evaluated is its utility. The utility of the proposed flexible workflow approach mainly results from the work items that are produced. To this end, three different variants for flexible workflows with deviation management and a continuous support of the process participant have been developed. This encompasses the following artifacts:

- **Constraint-Based Workflow Engine**
  The designed constraint-based workflow engine includes a method that detects deviations in terms of violated constraints, which are removed from the constraint net in order to restore consistency. The result is a reduced constraint net that serves as input for the CSP and, consequently, re-enables the workflow engine to compute work items.

- **Null Adaptation Based on a Retrieved Case Using a Sequence Similarity Measure**
  The sequence similarity measures based on DTW or the SWA can both be used to compare de facto workflows, more precisely to search for the most similar terminated workflow on the basis of the currently running workflow where a deviation has occurred. A subsequence of tasks or one task of this retrieved case can then be extracted and suggested to the process participant for workflow continuation.

- **Generative Constraint-Based Adaptation Based on a Retrieved Case Using a Sequence Similarity Measure**
  The generative adaptation method builds upon one of the two previously mentioned approaches for similarity assessment. As input, the case retrieved on the basis of the sequence similarity measure, either the SWA or DTW, is used. Its constraint net is aligned with the constraint net of the query, resulting in a consistent, adapted constraint net. The latter can be used by the constraint-based workflow engine to compute work items.

Minor artifacts such as the translation function are a means to an end and are included in or rather are prerequisites for these major artifacts.

With this evaluation, it is shown to which extent all of these three variants of flexibly computing work items can support a process participant in successfully terminating workflows. This includes both conforming and deviating workflow executions. Each of the different methods considers distinct input, such as the constraint-based transformation function, experiential knowledge in form of workflow traces, or rules for constraint set combination.

A main motivation behind this approach is to enable flexibility by deviation, in order to supersede flexibility by design and change through intelligent methods such as CSP and CBR.

8.2. Research Question RQ0

The key research question of this work **RQ0** (see Section 1.2) has been left open to be answered until now. The requirements of SMEs were presented in Subsect. 3.2.3. Concluding from the presented concepts, these requirements are fulfilled by the different methods of the presented flexible workflow engine. This concerns the following aspects:

RE1: Flexibility

Requirement **RE1** is met by all of the proposed variants of the flexible workflow engine. Each of them allows for deviations from the prescribed model at run time without entering an exceptional state. Despite these deviations, work items are proposed subsequently. Therefore, continuous support is guaranteed.

RE2: Knowledge Transfer

Knowledge transfer is enabled through the case-base methods, as experiential knowledge is integrated into the decisions of the workflow engine. Through the retain step of the CBR cycle, terminated workflows can be included in the case base and are preserved for future access. As these workflows serve as cases for the null or generative adaptation, they are simultaneously shared and reused for work item proposal. Consequently, requirement **RE2** is fulfilled by the case-based modes of the workflow engine.

RE3: Low Effort

The presented approach is likewise usable for experienced as well as inexperienced process participants, as no manual interference of the user is necessary, e.g. to handle deviations, such that low effort (cf. requirement **RE3**) is required in order to be able to adopt this flexible workflow system. Furthermore through the retain phase, terminated workflow instances are integrated automatically without the need of manual interaction, such that the necessary effort for maintenance is minimized. Through the integrated workflow model, which combines procedural and declarative aspects, and through the transformation function, the most intuitive paradigm according to the specific process engineer can be chosen in order to ease the modelling effort.

8.3. Evaluation Criteria

In order to be able to assess what has been achieved by the presented research, different criteria are investigated in this evaluation. The main objective is to prove the utility of the created artifacts. Various aspects that have non-functional influence on usability or work capability are observed, such as computation time. Other properties that deliver valuable feedback and have an impact on the utility, such as the necessary size of the case base, are inspected. Each of these regarded criteria is presented in more detail in the following.

8.3.1. Computation Time

The computation time is an essential aspect to ensure the applicability in practical use and to counteract an instant rejection of a newly introduced system, at least when considering WfMSs as interactive systems. It should rather encourage the willingness of a process participant to use the system. A workflow approach should support her/him through controlling and guiding the execution of tasks. If the necessary computations for generating a worklist are too time-consuming, the process participant is apt to circumvent the system.

According to Nielsen [126], 10 seconds is the limit for a response time of a system, such that the user is not distracted, but keeps the focus. Longer waiting times are perceived as unreliable and the user will turn to another task. Consequently, a maximum of 10 seconds can be seen as a guideline for the computation of the work items for

8.3. EVALUATION CRITERIA

an immediate response of the system, such that the waiting time is reduced to a minimum after a process participant executed a task.[20]

8.3.2. Utility

The second essential criteria is the *utility*, which is interpreted in this domain of flexible workflows as the degree to which the workflow can be terminated successfully in standard cases or even despite deviations. The overall utility can be determined through measuring the utility of work items during execution. To assess this property, various types of process participants need to be taken into account in order to investigate and evaluate different behaviour of process participants and the corresponding reaction of the system. Consequently, the criteria of utility needs to be evaluated in a differentiated way. Before describing the derived utility definitions, these distinct types of process participants are presented.

8.3.2.1. Types of Process Participants

- *Experienced*

  The experienced process participant constitutes an expert and knows how to handle any situation during process execution. This not only includes the ideal way of completing a workflow, but also recovering after deviations in case the WfMS is in an exceptional state without proper task suggestions. Her/his expectations of a flexible workflow system concern the support of those workflow instances that s/he would produce, foremost in terms of traceability and reporting. In case the system offers no support, a circumvention of the system would be hazarded or even triggered.

- *Inexperienced*

  The inexperienced process participant, who can be regarded as a novice, relies on the support of the workflow engine, as s/he

---

[20] In this evaluation the computation time will be investigated on the basis of an exemplary use case that is simulated on only one machine. However, as the computation time depends on several parameters, such as size of the workflows, number of constraints, amount of cases in the case base and the performance of the machine where the workflow system is deployed on, the results are not generally valid but can only indicate a rough guide.

is not aware of the correct workflow execution and does not know how to handle unexpected situations and how to continue after deviations. Each workflow instance executed by him/her is strictly adhering the suggested work items. This concerns both ways of completing a workflow, either conforming to the model or continuing after a deviation. Consequently, the success of an inexperienced process participant completely depends on the appropriateness of the work items proposed by the workflow engine.

- *Non-Conforming*

    The non-conforming process participant executes his workflows in a non-conforming way, which includes executing tasks that are not within the proposed list of work items, thus causing deviations from the de jure workflow with unknown consequences. This might happen on purpose, unintentionally or even unknowingly. The expectation of using a flexible workflow system is that, when encountering one of those undesired deviations, the guidance leads to a better outcome.

On the basis of these types of process participants, a more sophisticated definition of utility is specified correspondingly.

8.3.2.2. Utility for the Experienced Process Participant

The workflow engine is useful for the experienced process participant if the proposed work items correspond to the task executions s/he has in mind. Hence, utility of the workflow engine is measured as amount of support in contrast to misguidance. This is assessed by comparing the pursued task execution of the experienced process participant with the proposed work items of the workflow engine. If the task is not among the list of proposed work items, the workflow engine would lead to a miscontrol, which is not useful. The utility can then be assessed on the basis of the ratio of the number of miscontrols ($nrOfMiscontrols$) and the number of task executions ($nrOfTasks$) in a workflow as degree of support:

$$utility_{experienced} = 1 - \frac{nrOfMiscontrols}{nrOfTasks} \qquad (8.1)$$

8.3. EVALUATION CRITERIA

8.3.2.3. Utility for the Inexperienced Process Participant

As the inexperienced process participant completely relies on the workflow engine, the workflow instances that can result from the execution of proposed work items are the basis to assess the degree of utility. Therefore, these resulting workflow instances can be compared to valid workflow instances. The minimum edit distance [92] gives information about the amount of conformance. Relating this edit distance ($editDistance$) to the total number of executed tasks ($nrOfTasks$) in the workflow instance indicates the utility of one proposed workflow instance:

$$utility_{inexperienced} = 1 - \frac{editDistance}{nrOfTasks} \quad (8.2)$$

8.3.2.4. Utility for the Non-Conforming Process Participant

Successfully supporting a non-conforming process participant is interpreted as putting him/her back on the right track. The workflow engine should provide work items in order to recover from an undesired deviation. Taking a workflow instance with more than one deviation as starting point and letting the process participant complete the workflow instance, always following the work items proposed by the workflow engine after the first deviation, an adapted workflow instance emerges. In this case utility is defined as the improvement with respect to the workflow instance the user would create without support of the workflow engine, indicated by the reduction of necessary edit steps. Therefore, the minimum edit distance to a valid workflow of both the workflow instances that emerge with and without support of the workflow engine can be compared.

$$utility_{non-conforming} = 1 - \frac{\left(\frac{editDistanceNew}{nrOfTasksNew}\right)}{\left(\frac{editDistanceOriginal}{nrOfTasksOriginal}\right)} \quad (8.3)$$

Conforming workflow instances should be supported as well as deviating ones. The objective of this approach is to overcome the need for flexibility by design and flexibility by change through implementing flexibility by deviation. In this context, *utility* means that with a simple model as input for the designed workflow approach and the use of previous made experiences, a support for an extended set of workflow instances is offered, superseding a tedious modelling of the workflow model through flexibility by design or a necessary manual remodelling with flexibility by change, as deviations are handled automatically.

8.4. Hypotheses

The following hypotheses constitute the assumptions and reflect the goals that are pursued in this research work. These are investigated during the evaluation for the different variants of the workflow engine[21].

H1 (*Computation Time*): The computation of the worklist completes sufficiently fast for interactive systems.

For a usable interactive system, the work items should be computed in real-time to be of adequate value for the process participant. If the determination of task suggestions takes too long, it might have several negative impacts. The acceptance to use the system, as well as the trust in the system for being a support might be decreased. The risk that the system is circumvented and detached decisions are taken by the process participant might increase and ultimately might lead to an ineffective or failed result of the workflow. Thus, the computation of work items should be completed in a timely manner. The limit for a user to keep focus without distraction is 10 seconds [126], as described in Subsection 8.3.1.

H2 (*Experienced Process Participant*): When replaying a valid workflow, the executed tasks are mostly proposed by the workflow engine. Consequently, the workflow engine achieves a high utility for the experienced process participant.

The workflow engine is assumed to support various types of process participants. In SMEs, best practices that manifested over time through the work of experienced employees are mostly implicitly accepted, but might not be depicted by the workflow model. The proposed workflow approach should support these best practices and even propose them to inexperienced process participants. To this end, the expertise, in form of experiential knowledge, which in this case consists of previous workflow executions, should be considered and integrated when computing work items.

---

[21]Note that if a hypothesis refers to the workflow engine or computing work items and this is not further differentiated, it refers to all variants of the workflow engine, where each of them is evaluated separately.

8.4. HYPOTHESES

H3 (*Inexperienced Process Participant*): After a deviation from the workflow model, workflows can be terminated similarly to valid workflows based on the suggestions of the workflow engine. Consequently, the edit distance of proposed workflow instances compared to the most similar case of valid previous executions is small, which leads to a high utility for the inexperienced process participant.

The workflow approach should be robust in order to still propose an adequate termination of the workflow in case of a deviation. This concerns foremost the support of inexperienced process participants who are not aware of successful alternatives, lack experience, and cannot help themselves out of such a situation.

H4 (*Non-Conforming Process Participant*): The workflow engine can improve the outcome of workflow instances that have been terminated previously leading to an invalid workflow. Workflow instances that are terminated according to the proposed work items by the workflow engine after the first deviation have a smaller edit distance to the most similar valid workflow than the original workflow instance. Consequently, the utility for the non-conforming process participant is high.

This hypothesis considers a process participant who deviated in a non-conforming way for whatever reasons. First and foremost, if this deviation was unintentional, the workflow approach should be able to recover and still propose a good way of ending the workflow if such a solution exists.

H5 (*Comparison of Computation Time and Utility Concerning Different Variants of the Workflow Engine*): The utility for each type of process participant is significantly higher with the case-based methods of the workflow engine than with the constraint-based workflow engine, whereas the computation time is not significantly higher.

The case-based deviation management in form of either null or generative adaptation to determine work items originates out of the pursuit to better adapt the needs of the process participant by means of exploiting experiential knowledge. In order to achieve an improvement, the computation time of the case-based methods should be equal to or lower than that of the constraint-based workflow engine, whereas the utility of the work items of the case-based methods should be significantly higher than that of the constraint-based workflow engine.

H6 (*Comparison of Utility Concerning Sizes of the Case Base*): The utility of the case-based deviation management when using 50 % of all known valid workflow instance as input is significantly higher than with a smaller case base (10 %), but not significantly worse than with a larger case base (e.g. 90 %).

With this hypothesis it is elaborated how many of all valid workflow instances are needed as case base for the case-based deviation management to achieve high utility values. In a real-world scenario a high coverage of all valid workflow executions is not possible at launch of the flexible workflow system, as the experiential knowledge needs to be build up through the learning of cases. The variety of workflow instances increases by itself with the period of use. Thus, this hypothesis aims at evaluating the learning curve of the system and with which size of the case base the system can be deployed to provide benefit to the process participant.

8.5. Setup

To evaluate the presented hypotheses, a technical experiment in combination with an illustrative scenario is conducted [132]. To this end, a synthetic data set is generated that represents possible de facto workflows. Based on this data set, a ten-fold cross validation is performed. The de facto workflows of the test set are simulated through a trace replay, while the training set is used as case base. The trace replays are carried out several times in different ways, representing distinct types of process participants, in order to cover all usual real-world usage scenarios.

8.5.1. Data Generation

As described in Section 3.1, a workflow from the exemplary domain of deficiency management in construction is used to demonstrate the application of the proposed flexible workflow approach. A simple

8.5. SETUP

workflow model that represents the ideal handling of deficiencies was defined first (cf. Fig. 3.1). In consultation with an architect as domain expert, this model was refined and extended by all alternative cases (cf. Fig. 3.2 - 3.5) that are conceivable and represent a correct handling.

When implementing flexibility by design, this extended workflow model would need to be modelled at build time, whereas the incomplete and simplified ideal workflow would be used as model in order to realize flexibility by change. Nevertheless in the latter case, when encountering irregularities during execution, the workflow model would need to be modified manually at run time in order to support the process participant.

The objective of flexibility by deviation is to avoid both of these drawbacks such that neither an extensive modelling phase is required, nor a manual remodelling is necessary.

Reusing the diagram that relates declarative and imperative paradigms for modelling workflows (cf. Fig. 2.7), the simple and extended model and the different paradigms can be put into relation (cf. Fig. 8.1).

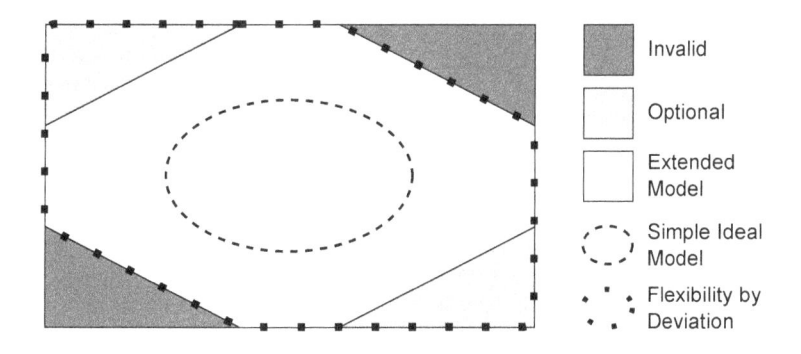

Figure 8.1. De Facto Workflow Spectrum related to Fig. 2.7 based on Pešić [134]

The simple ideal model represents only a subset of all possible valid workflow instances (cf. oval with dashed line in Fig. 8.1). In contrast, the extended model is assumed to map all valid workflow instances (cf. white-coloured shape in Fig. 8.1), which would need to be modelled when applying the approach of flexibility by design. Nevertheless, as it is not possible to think of all valid alternatives at build time, some de facto workflows remain unknown, but should be supported with flexibility by deviation (cf. shape with dotted line in Fig. 8.1).

In the presented evaluation, the implementation of the advantages of flexibility by deviation are validated. To this end, the simple ideal workflow model is used as workflow model by the flexible workflow approach, whereas all or some possible de facto workflows of the extended model are only fed as experiential knowledge to the case-based methods. This is done in order to evaluate the capability of the proposed approach to automatically support valid de facto workflows of the extended model.

As prerequisite for the conducted experiment, all possible valid de facto workflows of the extended model were generated through the constraint-based workflow engine. Furthermore, the simple model was slightly adjusted by integrating some deviations, which leads to a manipulated workflow model. Thus, few negative cases are generated as well (cf. dark grey triangles denoted as invalid in Fig. 8.1). To this end, the simple workflow model for deficiency management in construction was manipulated through integrating two deviations[22]. Several modified models arise from this with different deviations. By generating all possible traces from these models, negative traces were created.

Based on this synthetic data set, a validation of the workflow engine was conducted. Ultimately, five workflow instances were generated out of the simple model, 2.184 traces of the extended model and 12 negative cases.

8.5.2. Experiment

The experiments were made on a laptop with (QuadCore) Intel(R) Core(TM) i7-10510U CPU @ 1.80GHz 2.30 GHz and 16 GB RAM on a 64 bit system and Windows 10.

Figure 8.2 shows the overall setting of the experimental evaluation. Based on previously generated de facto workflows, workflow executions are simulated for different types of process participants and the different modes of the workflow engine. Additionally, different sizes of the case base are used as input for the retrieval phase of the case-based variants, and positive as well as negative cases are used as queries. The resulting event log contains various information that is analysed regarding the evaluation criteria and the assumed hypotheses.

---

[22]This was done in several ways, e.g. switching the order of tasks for two different task pairs, omitting two tasks or integrating unknown tasks.

8.5. SETUP

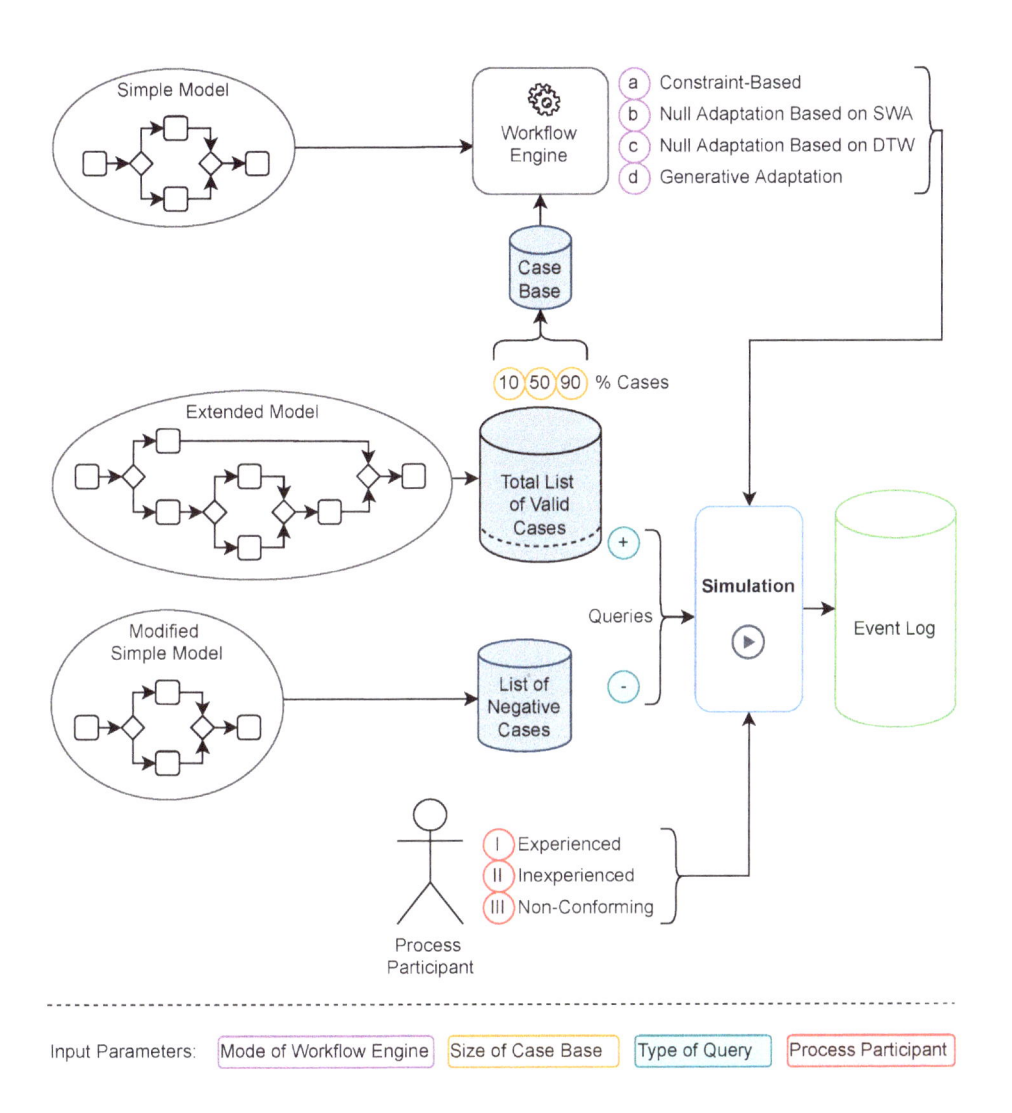

Figure 8.2. Setup of Simulation Experiments

As described in Subsection 8.5.1, the *total list of valid cases* that is shown in the centre of Fig. 8.2 contains all possible de facto workflow traces that were generated based on the *extended model* of deficiency management in construction (cf. Fig. 3.2 - 3.5). The experiment is done as a ten-fold cross validation, such that for each single validation run 10 % of the cases in the total list of cases form the test set, which are used as queries. The remaining cases serve as the training data set, which is used as *case base*. Each query is simulated as a trace replay several times with different parameters. These parameters include:

- Mode of Workflow Engine (ⓐ-ⓓ)
- Size of Case Base (10/50/90 %)
- Type of Query (⊕/⊖)
- Type of Process Participant ((I)/(II)/(III))

This simulation produces an event log that is analysed concerning the assumed hypotheses. Each of the parameters is explained in more detail in the following.

8.5.2.1. Mode of Workflow Engine

During the trace replay of one query, the worklist is computed after each task, for each of the different methods that are able to compute work items, denoted here as modes of the workflow engine:

> ⓐ Constraint-Based Workflow Engine
>
> ⓑ Null Adaptation Based on a Retrieved Case using the SWA
>
> ⓒ Null Adaptation Based on a Retrieved Case using DTW
>
> ⓓ Workflow Engine with Generative Constraint-Based Adaptation using the SWA during Retrieval

The resulting worklist is stored in the event log for a comparison of tasks in the de facto workflow and the corresponding work items. In some cases the trace replay is influenced by the items contained in the worklist, which is explained later when introducing the different types of process participants.

8.5. SETUP

These modes of the workflow engine only use the simple model of deficiency management in construction (cf. Fig. 3.1) and the remaining training data set of the case base as input, see component *workflow engine* in Fig. 8.2.

In this experiment, the null adaptation variants consider all cases with the highest similarity for reuse. The generative adaptation uses the retrieved cases with highest similarity on the basis of the SWA, while one case is chosen randomly for reuse if there are several with the same similarity value.

8.5.2.2. Size of Case Base

For the three modes of the workflow engine that include case-based methods (ⓑ-ⓓ), the size of the case base is varied and the simulation is done for each of these different sizes, in order to investigate which size is required to achieve good results. This involves the following sizes of the training data set in relation to the total list of valid cases:

- 10 %
- 50 %
- 90 %

For a reasonable comparison, the test data set consists of the same 10 % of the remaining case base for each of the different sizes.

8.5.2.3. Type of Query

In the experiment, two different lists of cases are used for simulations, that have a specific type:

⊕ Positive

⊖ Negative

As mentioned before, the type of the query depends on its origin, either the extended model or the modified simple model. They are used to differentiate between different types of process participants. *Positively* rated queries are simulated for the *experienced* and *inexperienced* process participants, whereas *negatively* rated queries are simulated for the *non-conforming* process participant.

8.5.2.4. Process Participant

The trace replay of the queries is conducted in several distinct ways, to evaluate the behaviour of the workflow engine in different situations and its support for all kinds of process participants. To this end, different types of *process participants* that react differently when facing a deviation are specified based on realistic assumptions, as described in Subsection 8.3.2.1.

(I) Experienced

(II) Inexperienced

(III) Non-Conforming

8.5.2.4.1. Experienced The proposed flexible workflow approach supports the experienced process participant if the proposals of the workflow engine are conforming to his/her previously executed workflow instances, as they are most likely equal to those that will be executed in the future. These previously terminated instances are part of the case base as experiential knowledge. To validate this assumption, a replay of the cases in the test set is simulated as presented in Fig. 8.3.

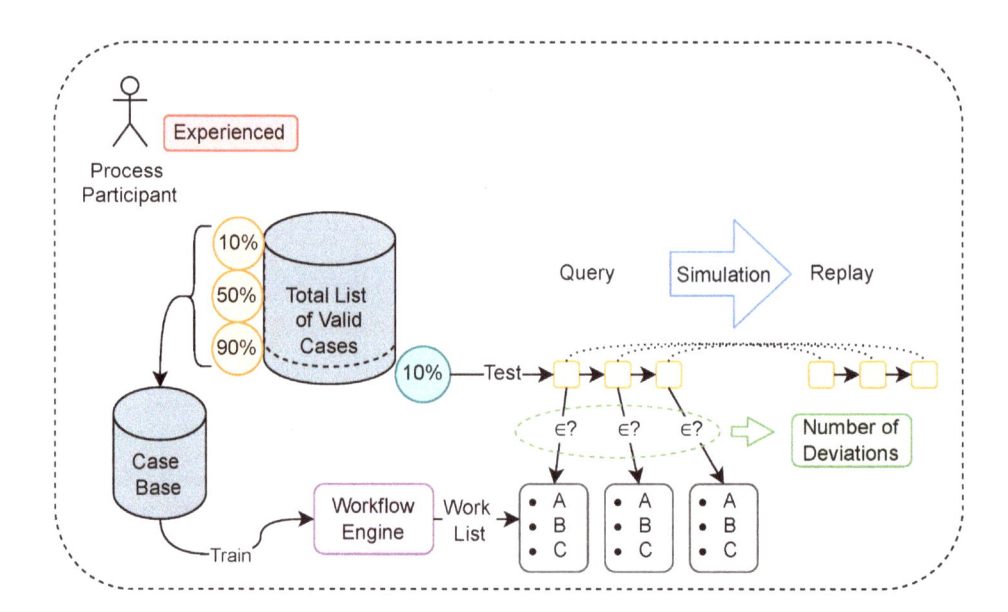

Figure 8.3. Experiential Evaluation for the Experienced Process Participant

8.5. SETUP

For the experienced process participant, the exact trace is replayed for each query. During this trace replay, for each task that is replayed and added to the de facto workflow, it is checked if it is contained in the proposed work items of the workflow engine. When the trace replay terminates, the utility for experienced process participants is computed, denoting the number of deviations.

8.5.2.4.2. Inexperienced The *inexperienced* process participant mainly profits from the proposed work items of the workflow engine. To investigate this resulting utility, the trace replay is conducted differently compared to the experienced process participant. The simulation is visualized in Fig. 8.4.

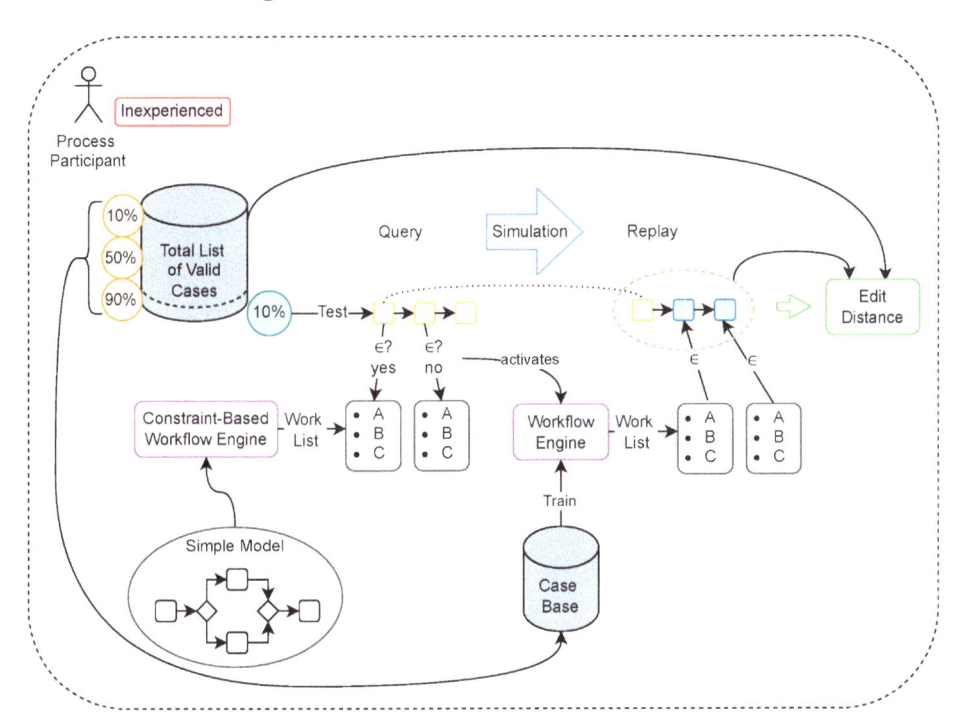

Figure 8.4. Experiential Evaluation for the Inexperienced Process Participant

In a first step, the query workflows are re-enacted as trace replay. For this purpose, the constraint-based workflow engine is used as ideal workflow execution reference using the simple model as input. The point of investigation concerning utility starts when a deviation occurs, in terms of a task in the replay that is not part of the work items proposed on the basis of the simple model. At this point in time, the proposed novel modes of the workflow engine are activated and simulate the replay until the end. Thus, the replay is completed following the suggestions of the worklist for each of the solve modes (see blue-coloured nodes of *Replay* in Fig. 8.4). Work items are picked randomly. When the worklist is empty, the workflow instance concludes. This emerging workflow instance, which results from the replay considering the proposed work items, can be rated considering its similarity compared to the total list of valid cases. As objective and quantifiable similarity measure, the edit distance based on Levenshtein distance [92] is chosen, that indicates the utility for the inexperienced process participant as described previously.

8.5.2.4.3. Non-Conforming The non-conforming process participant executes workflow instances with unknown or unwanted deviations. Thus, the simulation is not based on the test set of the total list of valid cases that resulted from the extended workflow model, but the regarded query workflows are negative cases that were generated on the basis of the manipulated simple workflow model (see Fig. 8.5).

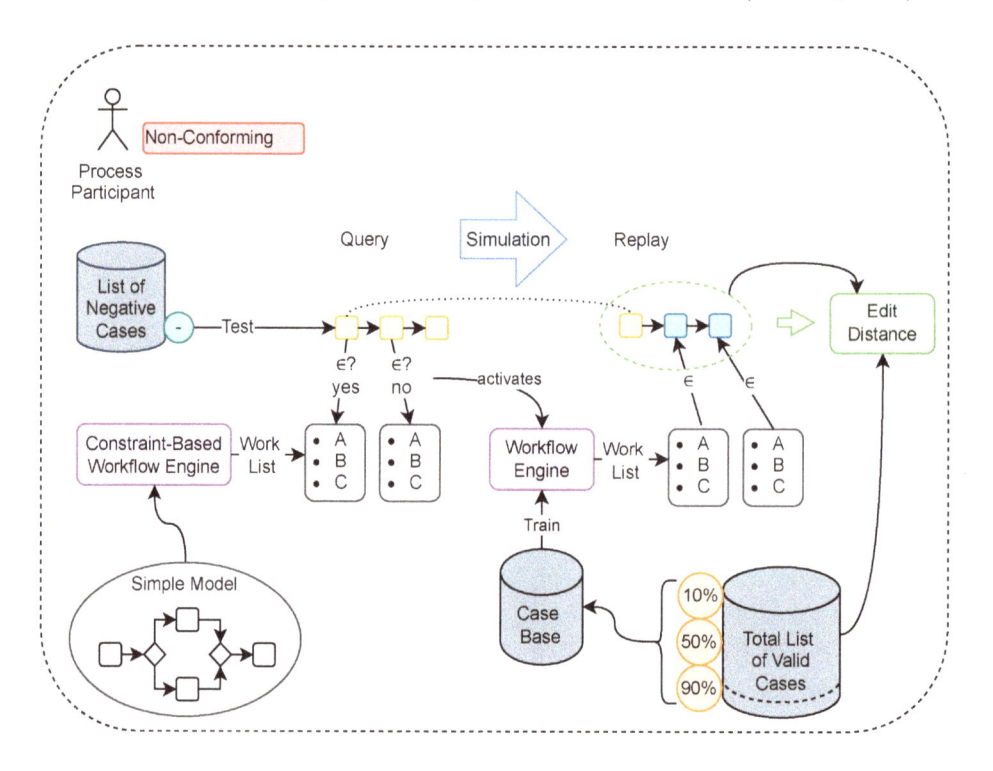

Figure 8.5. Experiential Evaluation for the Non-Conforming Process Participant

8.5. SETUP

The simulation itself is done in the same way as for the inexperienced process participant. The query workflow is replayed until a deviation occurs, according to the constraint-based workflow engine with the simple model as input. After this deviation, the workflow instance is completed by randomly picking work items generated by the workflow engine until termination of the workflow. This is done for each of the modes of the workflow engine. The similarity of the emerging workflow instance can then be assessed compared to the total list of valid cases. Again, the edit distance is chosen as similarity measure. Here, the resulting value can be compared to the edit distance of the original query and the improvement can be quantified, which leads to the utility assessment.

8.5.2.5. Simulation of the Process Participant

The *simulation* component (cf. Fig. 8.2) takes all these parameters as input and performs the trace replay according to the previous description. The simulation is done as ten-fold cross validation with an overall number of 2.184 positively rated traces and 12 negatively rated traces. Thus, the test set consists for six folds out of 218 traces and for four folds out of 219 traces positively rated traces, adding in each case the 12 negatively rated traces as queries.

8.5.2.6. Event Log

During the simulation, log files are generated that trace all set parameters, all events, and different upcoming or computed values, such as similarity values, computation time, or simply the conformance of a task to a worklist, to allow for an in-depth analysis. Derived from that, average values can be assessed or proportional relations can be determined.

8.6. Simulation Results

In summary, 44.880 trace replays resulted from the experiment in which the process participants were simulated with the previously described parameters, which are combined in all possible ways.[23]

---

[23] Note that the constraint-based workflow engine was not simulated with different sizes of the cases, as the case base is no input for this mode of the workflow engine, and therefore varying sizes make no difference.

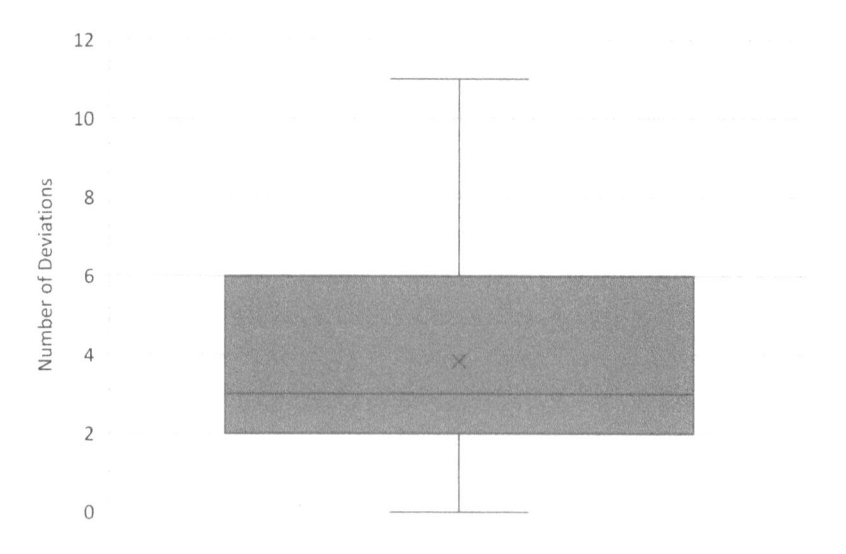

Figure 8.6. Number of Tasks for Each Replay

Fig. 8.6 shows the distribution of number of task enactments for each of the trace replays. Here, the values are outlined in a box plot where the main distribution of data points becomes obvious. The box itself visualizes 50 % of the middle data points with the cross in the middle representing the mean and the line representing the median. In addition, the whiskers represent the majority of the remaining 50 % of all values, whereas they solely include data points within a distance of one and a half times the range of the box at maximum, while some dots occurring outside these lines mark outliers. Considering task enactments in Fig. 8.6, ten tasks were replayed on average, at maximum 26 and at least two tasks.

In order to validate the assumed hypotheses, the logged traces and additional data are analysed with regard to the evaluation criteria. The results are presented in the following.

8.6.1. Computation Time

During the trace replays and for each task enactment, computation times that indicate how long it takes to determine a worklist are logged.

Fig. 8.7 shows the distribution of the maximum computation times in milliseconds for each replay when using a size of the case base of 10 %. The values range from almost 0 to 55 seconds. As can be seen in

8.6. SIMULATION RESULTS

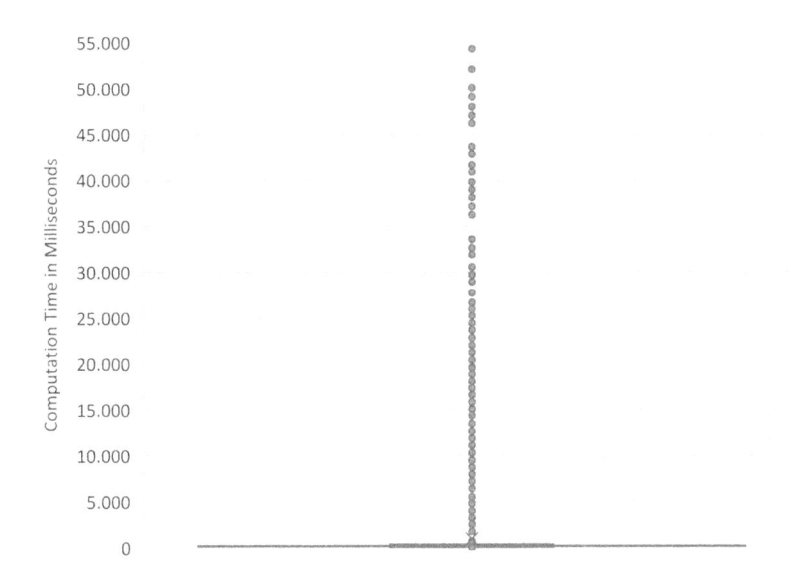

Figure 8.7. Maximum Computation Time for Each Replay

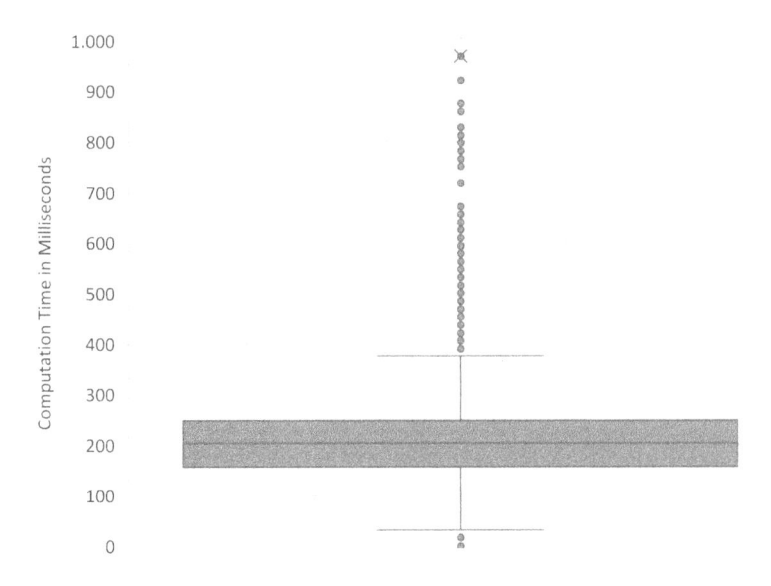

Figure 8.8. Maximum Computation Time for Each Replay Zoomed in on 0 - 1.000 ms

Fig. 8.8 where the y-axis is limited to 1.000 ms, the main distribution of values is concentrated on the segment of 150 ms to 250 ms, which indicates an immediate response of the system.

Splitting this set up concerning different parameters, some differentiations can be made concerning the modes of the workflow engine. In Fig. 8.9 this data is broken down for each of the modes of the

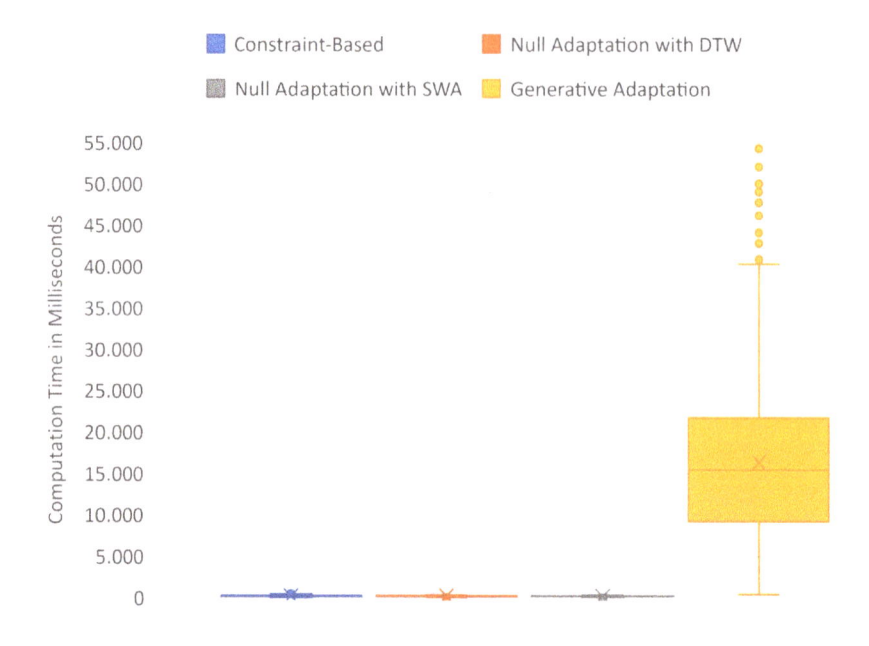

Figure 8.9. Maximum Computation Time for Each Replay for All Different Modes of the Workflow Engine

workflow engine in form of box plots.

The results of one method clearly stand out. This distinction exposes much higher maximum values for the generative adaptation (see yellow bar and points in Fig. 8.9) compared to the remaining modes of the workflow engine. Consequently, process participants would have to wait up to one minute in the worst case for a worklist to be computed, which completely thwarts the practical suitability. These comparatively high computation times result from the multiple necessary computations of a solution for the different CSPs during the adaptation process.

Nevertheless, this method should not be excluded from further investigation solely concluding from this property. As the focus of the presented work was finding a valuable solution rather than optimizing

8.6. SIMULATION RESULTS

the computation time, this aspect can still be improved in future work.

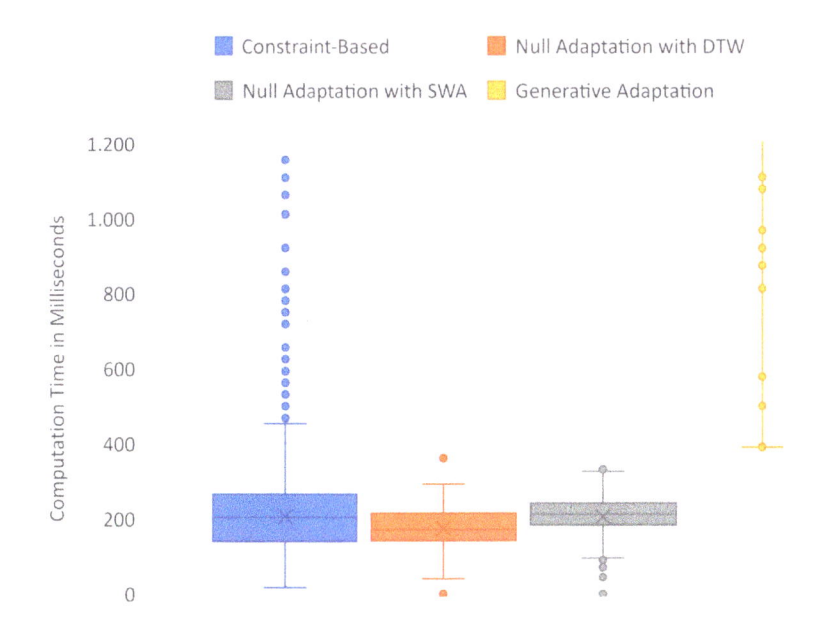

Figure 8.10. Maximum Computation Time for Each Replay for Different Modes of the Workflow Engine Zoomed in on 0 - 1.200 ms

Fig. 8.10 shows the maximum values for all remaining modes of the workflow engine, zoomed in to the interval of 0 - 1.200 ms.

This more detailed comparison indicates that the maximum of both null adaptation methods is slightly lower, exactly under 400 milliseconds, whereas the vast majority of maximum values of all modes are under 400 ms. The constraint-based workflow engine has maximum computation times of up to 1.200 ms, which is still quite low.

Thus, for the constraint-based workflow engine and both methods that apply null adaptation either with the SWA or DTW computation times are low. Each computation of work items takes at most 1.200 milliseconds and consequently, a fast feedback to the process participant with work item proposals is possible. Hence, hypothesis **H1** is confirmed for those methods. Furthermore, it provides operational capability and prevents a circumvention of the system. For the generative adaptation, the computation times are much too high and the process participants will be distracted or focus on other tasks. Thus, hypothesis **H1** is partly rejected. However, this might be no disadvantage depending on the domain or the organisation of work. For instance, in case one employee is not only concerned with the execution of one process, but with several ones at the same time, the chance that her/his worklist is empty is rather low.

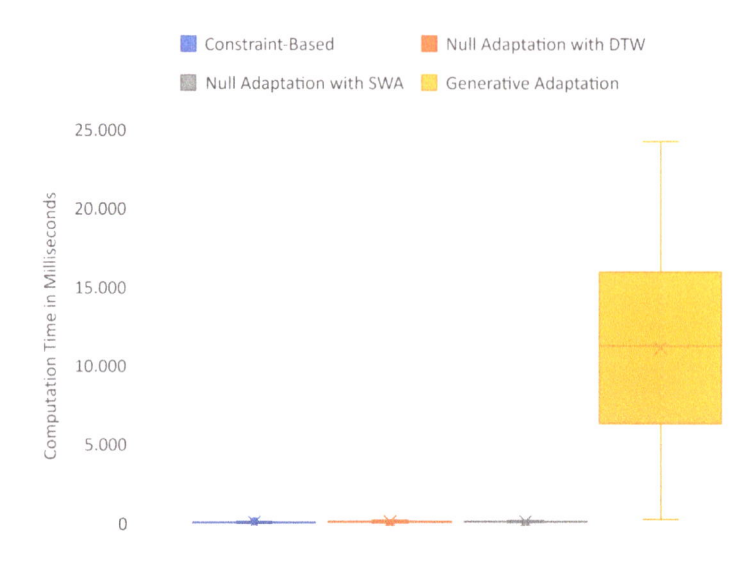

Figure 8.11. Average Computation Time for Each Replay for Different Modes of the Workflow Engine

So far, only maximum values of one replay were regarded. To reinforce these low computation times, Fig. 8.11 additionally indicates the average computation times for determining work items for the different solve modes. Analogously to the maximum computation times, the mode of generative adaptation performs much poorer than the other methods with an average computation time of 11 seconds.

Zooming in to the interval of 0-300 ms (see Fig. 8.12), the constraint-based workflow engine is faster on average. As all values are lower than 200 ms, the difference is not perceivable by the process participant when using the system. No waiting time occurs, as at most 200 ms is close to an immediate response.

While both null adaptation methods are slower on average, the maximum computation time is considerably lower than the computation time of the constraint-based workflow engine. Nevertheless, the range of computation times is overall acceptable except for the generative adaptation, meaning under one second, and thus, does not cause idle time for the process participant or contradict usability or

8.6. SIMULATION RESULTS

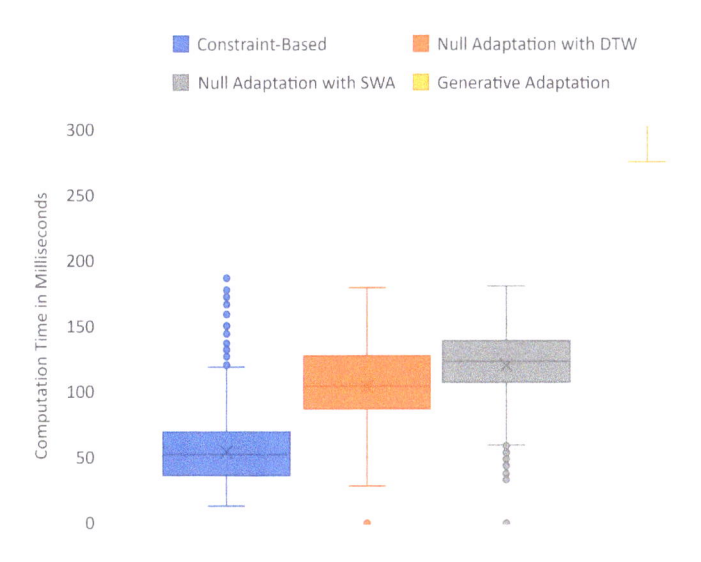

Figure 8.12. Average Computation Time for Each Replay for Different Modes of the Workflow Engine Zoomed in on 0 - 300 ms

acceptance.

For the case-based methods, different sizes of the case base were used as input for the simulation of the process participant.

Fig. 8.13 shows the average and maximum computation times for computing work items for different sizes of the case base, both null adaptation methods of either the SWA or DTW are included. The generative adaptation is not part of this comparison, as it builds upon the retrieval with either the SWA or DTW, which is compared in Fig. 8.13, but adds some CSP solving for the adaptation part, whose computation time is not influenced by the size of the case base.

The average computation time still lies under one second even for a case base of 90 %, but the maximum increases to nearly three seconds, which might impact the behaviour of the process participant and induce a circumvention of the system in some individual cases.

8.6.2. Utility for the Experienced Process Participant

For the experienced process participant, it is essential that the workflow engine supplying work items supports the best practices that are enacted by her/him. To this end, the traces are replayed and each task in the replay is compared to the suggestions of the workflow engine.

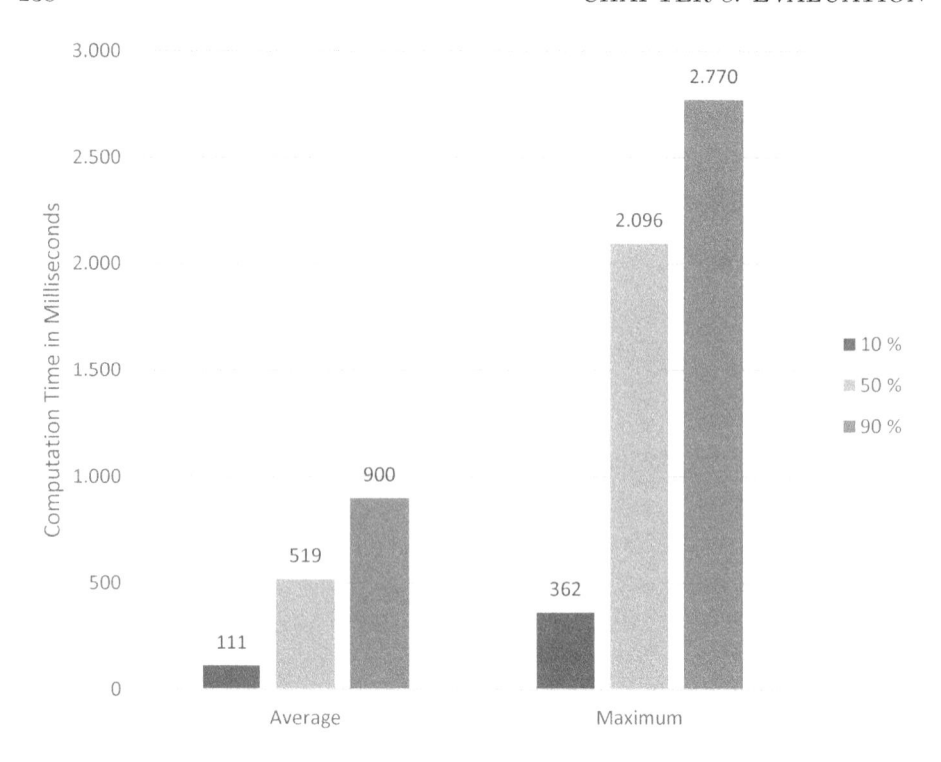

Figure 8.13. Average and Maximum Computation Time for Different Sizes of the Case Base for Both Null Adaptation Variants

Fig. 8.14 shows the total number of occurring deviations per replay as a box plot, where a deviation is defined as a task in the trace not being part of the suggested worklist during the trace replay.

The number of deviations range from 0 to 11, with an average of four deviations.

Fig. 8.15 shows the single distributions of values regarding the different modes of the workflow engine. It can be seen that the proposals of the null adaptation with the SWA show the most conformance with the traces, as the number of deviations is lower than for the other three methods for determining work items.

Based on this, the utility for the experienced process participant ($utility_{experienced}$, see Equation 8.1) can be computed. Fig. 8.16 shows the results, which confirm the previously made observations.

For the null adaptation method based on a retrieval with the SWA, the utility is very high, as in most cases over 80 % of the tasks were proposed by the workflow engine, whereas this holds for only 45 % on average when computing the worklist on the basis of the constraint-

8.6. SIMULATION RESULTS

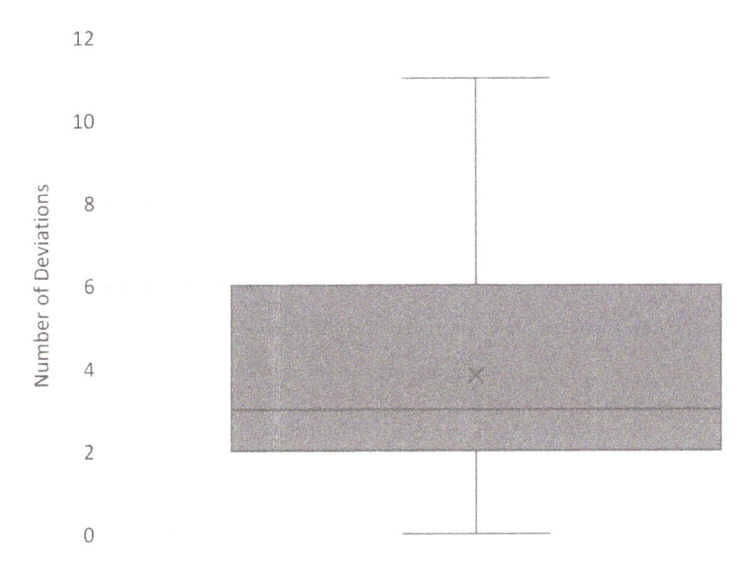

Figure 8.14. Total Number of Deviations for Each Replay for the Experienced Process Participant

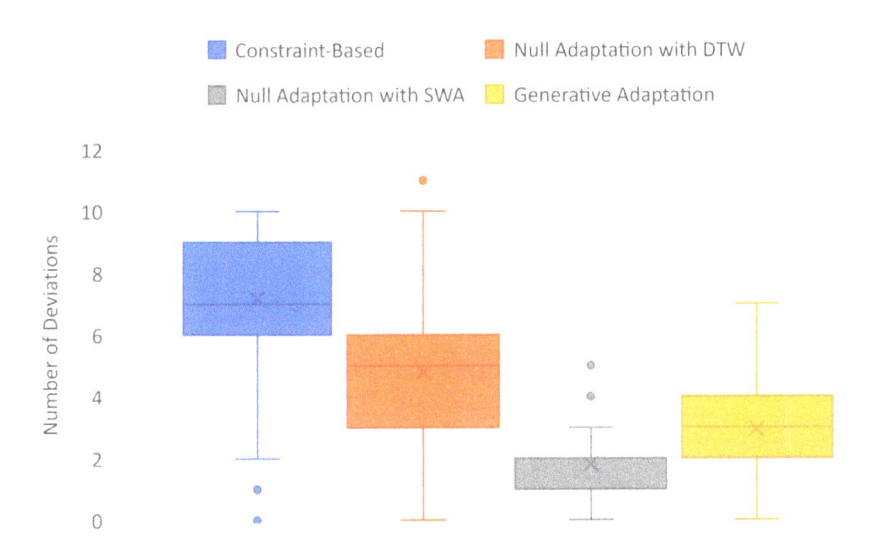

Figure 8.15. Total Number of Deviations for Each Replay for Different Modes of the Workflow Engine for the Experienced Process Participant

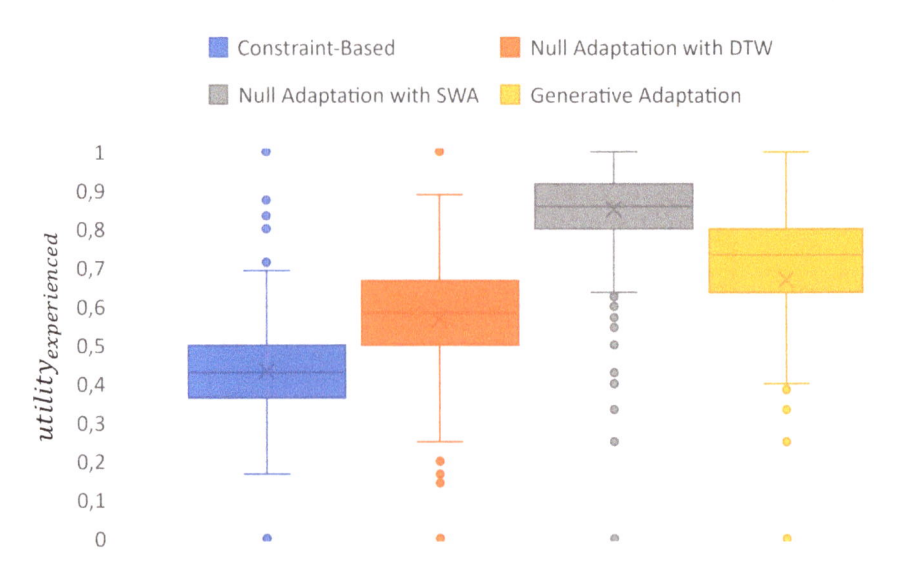

Figure 8.16. Utility for the Experienced Process Participant for Each Replay for Different Modes of the Workflow Engine

based workflow engine. The utility is also high for the generative adaptation and slightly lower for the null adaptation with DTW.

The poor performance of the constraint-based workflow engine concerning deviations can be explained due to the differing inputs of the methods. The only input for the constraint-based approach is the simplified workflow model with a reduced set of tasks compared to the extended model. Consequently, work items are only derived from this reduced set, while all additional tasks are not part of the build CSPs and therefore cannot be part of the solution. In contrast, all other methods rely on the experiential knowledge in form of workflow traces, which includes all tasks of the extended model.

Hence, hypothesis **H2** is predominantly confirmed, excluding the constraint-based workflow engine. However, especially for the null adaptation with the SWA, the workflow traces are largely compliant with the proposed work items, which verifies a great support for the experienced process participants.

The case-based modes of the workflow engine clearly outperform the constraint-based workflow engine, as they incorporate the previous experiences better and are able to propose those. Consequently, for the experienced process participant the case-based methods offer a higher utility of work items and a better support. Hence, hypothesis

8.6. SIMULATION RESULTS

H5 is confirmed for the experienced process participant.

Fig. 8.17 shows the average utility value split up concerning sizes of the case base. The average utility slightly increases with a larger

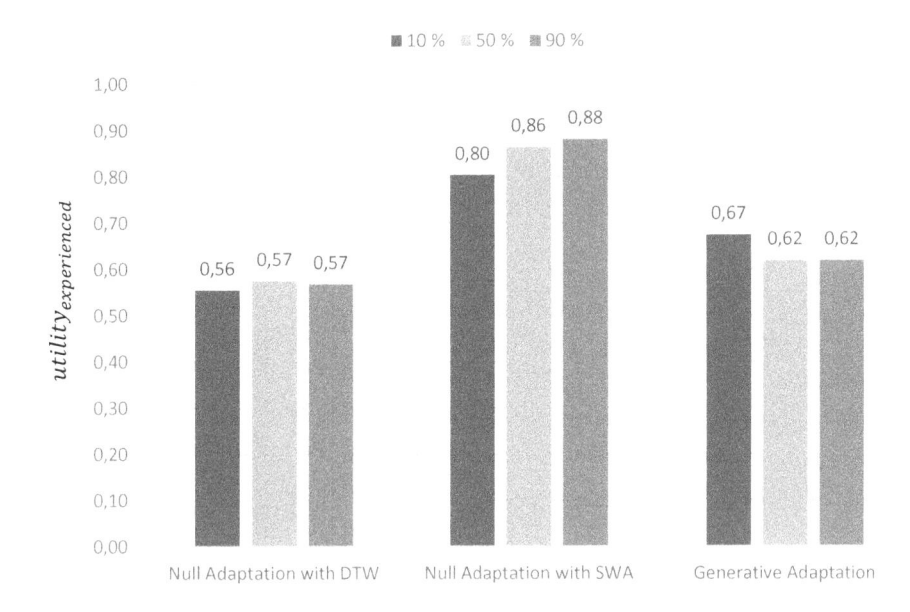

Figure 8.17. Average Utility for the Experienced Process Participant for Different Case-Based Modes of the Workflow Engine and Different Sizes of the Case Base

case base of 50 % for the null adaptation with DTW, while the value for the null adaptation with the SWA increases significantly by 0,06. In contrast, the average utility decreases for the generative adaptation when considering larger case bases. Hence, hypothesis **H6** can be confirmed for the null adaptation with the SWA, but is rejected for the generative adaptation. For the null adaptation with DTW, the size of the case base has no influence on the outcome, as the average utility remains relatively static. Nevertheless, absolutely speaking, the generative adaptation performs slightly better than the DTW but worse than the SWA.

8.6.3. Utility for the Inexperienced Process Participant

The inexperienced process participant follows the work items after facing a deviation, as s/he is not aware of how to continue the workflow. Thus, the criteria of interest is the resulting trace when following the work item suggestions. To this end, the traces are replayed on the basis of the simple workflow model until a deviation occurs and are afterwards completed on the basis of the work item suggestions of the different modes of the workflow engine. The resulting trace can be compared to the total list of valid cases and the edit distance of the most similar case can be assessed in order to determine the utility.

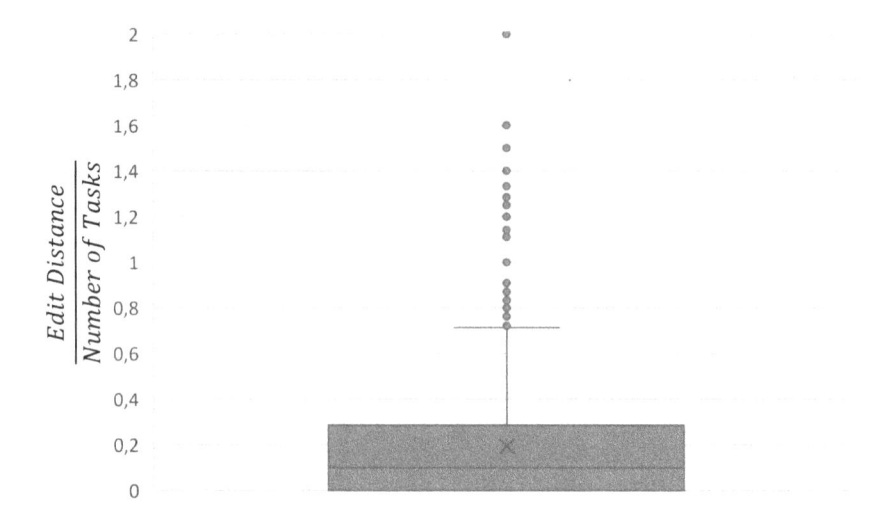

Figure 8.18. Edit Distance in Relation to Number of Executed Tasks for the Inexperienced Process Participant for Each Replay

Fig. 8.18 shows the ratio of the edit distance and number of executed tasks for all replays for the simulation of the inexperienced process participant. The assessed amount of necessary edit steps compared to number of tasks is quite low with a main distribution of values in between 0 and 0,3, which means that at maximum one third of all tasks needed to be edited in order to align the de facto workflows. This indicates an overall high similarity between resulting traces and the total list of valid cases containing all possible traces from the extended workflow model. Nevertheless, some outliers are visible with a maximum ratio of 2, meaning that the most similar trace might have a length three times that of the original query trace.

Fig. 8.19 shows the derived utility value for each trace ($utility_{inexperienced}$, see Equation 8.2), split up for the different modes of the workflow engine. With an average value of more than 0,85 for both null adaptation variants, the utility is high and consequently, hypothesis **H3** is confirmed for those two methods.

In contrast, the constraint-based workflow engine and the genera-

8.6. SIMULATION RESULTS

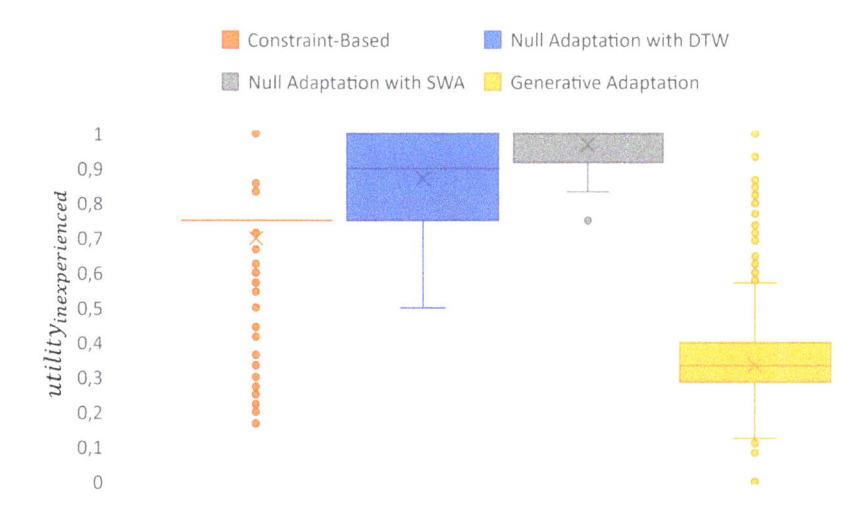

Figure 8.19. Utility for the Inexperienced Process Participant of Each Replay and Different Modes of the Workflow Engine

tive adaptation perform not as good concerning this aspect. With an average value of 0,7, the constraint-based workflow engine still works better than the generative adaptation with an average similarity of 0,35, which is quite low in comparison. Furthermore, the values of both methods have a higher variance, which decreases the reliability. Consequently, hypothesis **H3** is rejected for the constraint-based workflow engine and the generative adaptation. However, hypothesis **H5** is partially confirmed, since both null adaptation methods perform significantly better than the two remaining methods.

Fig. 8.20 shows the average utility for the different sizes of the case base and the different case-based modes of the workflow engine. The values do not differ significantly. A slight increase for a case base size of 50 % can be seen for the null adaptation with DTW and the generative adaptation, but only of about 2 or 3 %. However, the average utility slightly decreases for case bases of 90 %. This may be explained by an increased variance of work items when considering more cases for similarity assessment and therefore the resulting traces differ to a higher degree, as work items are chosen randomly. Consequently, hypothesis **H6** is not confirmed for the inexperienced process participant, as the size of the case base does not lead to any significant difference in results.

Derived from that, one can argue that both null adaptation vari-

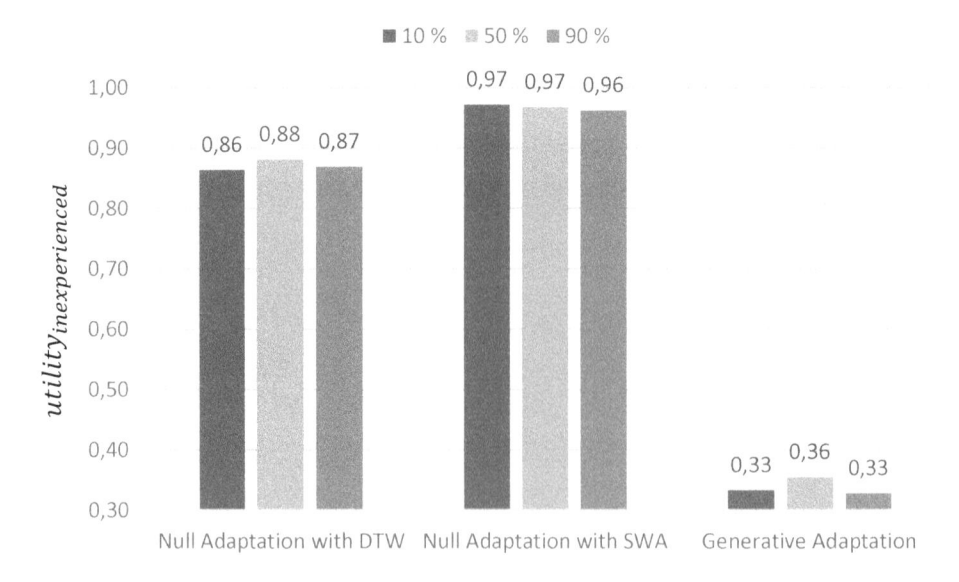

Figure 8.20. Average Utility for the Inexperienced Process Participant for Different Case-Based Modes of the Workflow Engine and Different Sizes of the Case Base

ants, foremost the one applying the SWA, can achieve a high utility even with a small case base and thus, are able to support an inexperienced process participant at an early stage of deploying the flexible workflow approach where only a few workflows have been terminated, at least in this exemplary domain.

8.6.4. Utility for the Non-Conforming Process Participant

The non-conforming process participant deviated multiple times from the suggested tasks in the past. When replaying these workflows, it is validated if the proposals of the workflow engine lead to workflow traces with a higher similarity to the total list of valid cases, which is assessed through computing the edit distance. Similar to the simulation of the inexperienced process participant, the queries, in this case resulting from the modified simple workflow model, are replayed and after the first occurring deviation, the work item suggestions of the workflow engine were followed, resulting in new traces. These traces were then compared to the total list of valid cases and the resulting similarity values are assumed to improve in contrast to the similarity value of the original query trace. On this basis, the utility can be computed.

8.6. SIMULATION RESULTS

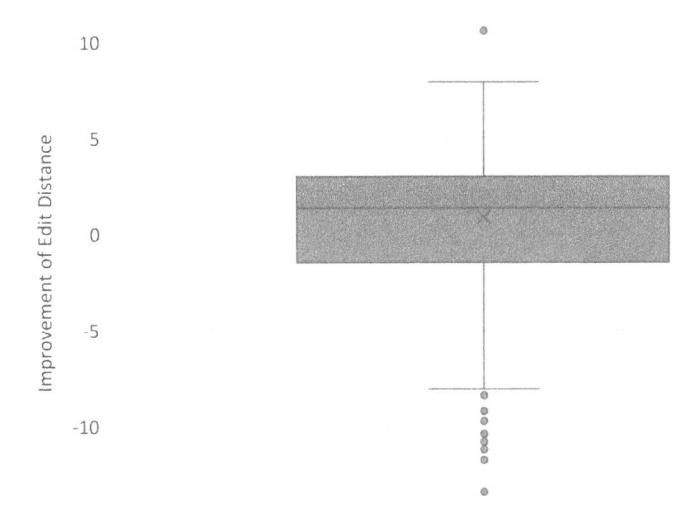

Figure 8.21. Improvement of the Edit Distance and Number of Executed Tasks for the Non-Conforming Process Participant for Each Replay

Fig. 8.21 shows the distribution of the improvement of the edit distance. Here, positive values indicate an improvement through the workflow engine, meaning less necessary edit steps, while negative ones reveal the opposite, meaning more necessary edit steps. As can be seen, there are several improvements, but also some deterioration. Nevertheless, the average value is slightly positive, around 1, indicating a tendency.

Fig. 8.22 differentiates the results according to the different modes of the workflow engine and shows the derived utility ($utility_{non-conforming}$, see Equation 8.3). Both null adaptation variants with either the SWA or DTW yield overall high utility values around 0,5 and higher. The constraint-based workflow engine and the generative adaptation mostly lead to a negative utility value, which means both are tending to decrease the similarity value or increase the edit distance slightly, resulting in an impairment of the support for the non-conforming process participant, as the original trace is more similar to the most similar valid workflow. Consequently, hypothesis **H4** can be confirmed for both null adaptation methods, but is denied for the constraint-based workflow engine and the generative adaptation. However, similar to the inexperienced process participant, hypothesis **H5** can only be partially confirmed for both null adaptation methods as they clearly create high utility, whereas the generative adaptation

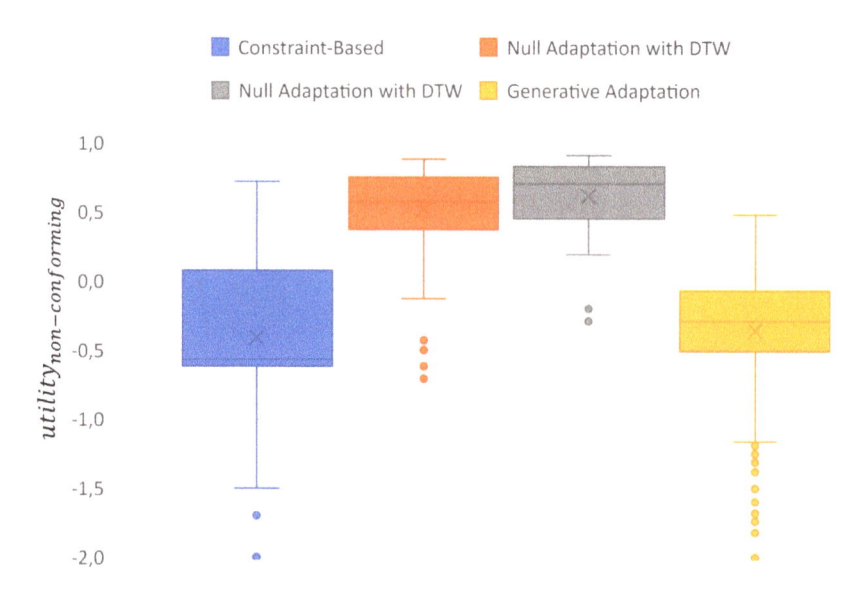

Figure 8.22. Utility for the Non-Conforming Process Participant for Each Replay for Different Modes of the Workflow Engine

is even worse than the constraint-based workflow engine.

Average utility values split up for different sizes of the case base and the different modes of the workflow engine are presented in Fig. 8.23. Concerning the null adaptation variant with DTW, an increase of 0,08 for the average utility can be identified, when comparing a size of 10 and 50 % of the case base. The same direction holds for the generative adaptation. Nevertheless, for the null adaptation with the SWA, the average utility value slightly decreases by 0,03, but not significantly. Moreover, no impact of the sizes of the case base of 50 and 90 % is recognized. Consequently, the 50 % increase is worth it and can significantly improve the utility foremost for the null adaptation with DTW, whereas 90 % yields no significant improvement, which confirms hypothesis **H6** partially.

8.7. Conclusion of Evaluation

In summary, the results of the evaluation are promising, as all hypotheses can be confirmed, some completely and others partially.

Concerning utility of work items, the null adaptation with the SWA achieved the best results and outperformed the three other methods for all types of process participants. The null adaptation with DTW

8.7. CONCLUSION OF EVALUATION

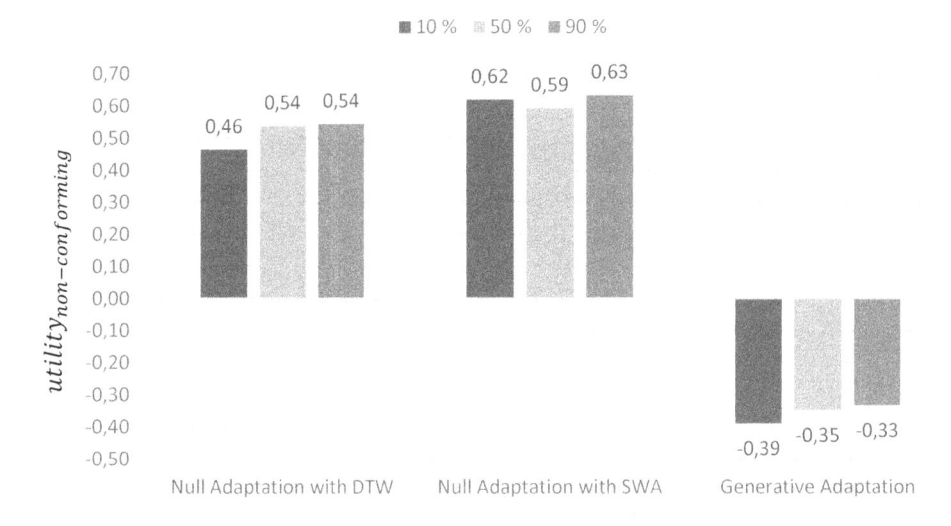

Figure 8.23. Average Utility for the Non-Conforming Process Participant for Different Case-Based Modes of the Workflow Engine and Different Sizes of the Case Base

was slightly but not significantly worse, which might result from the domain and be different for other domains.

For both null adaptation methods, a 50 % coverage of all valid traces as case base is sufficient to lead to good results for a support for the process participant through work items. 90 % coverage yields no significant improvement, but requires a much higher effort for knowledge acquisition, e.g. time for learning new experiences in form of adding cases to the case base.

An unexpected result of the experiment was the relatively poor performance of the generative adaptation, as it originally was developed in order to improve the null adaptation variants. Consequently, the generative adaptation needs some major improvements to be of utility for the process participant. On the one hand, the method requires a huge decrease of the computation time to be applicable in practice. This bad performance mainly stems from the multiple solving of CSPs, which has not been optimized considering runtime. Hence, there is still potential, such that this is not a valid criteria to abandon the proposed generative adaptation method.

On the other hand, a further in-depth analysis of the adaptation strategy is necessary to achieve an improvement of utility, as results concerning proposed work items get worse compared to the null adaptation, even though the same retrieved cases are used.

One limitation of the experiment for the generative adaptation, which can be used to explain the poor performance, is that only one retrieved case with the highest similarity was reused. It is assumed that results will improve when all cases with the highest similarity are adapted. Hence, all single worklists that result from solving each of the adapted CSPs can be combined. However, this will entail an increase of the computation time by a multiple of the number of retrieved cases.

Nevertheless, when regarding the experienced process participant, results are not bad. This indicates a broad mapping of possible work items. In contrast, the similarity values of the trace replays from the simulated inexperienced process participant are not high. Both results indicate a vast variance of the work item proposals, which is confirmed when analysing the size of the generated worklists. The generative adaptation produces a higher number of work items, on average 8, compared to the constraint-based workflow engine and both null adaptation variants, which compute two work items on average.

Taking a closer look at these work items, it can be observed that tasks from workflow blocks which are positioned further away are allowed much earlier than expected. The constraint-based adaptation method only includes constraints that are related to the deviating task and constraints that are related to those constraints. Transitive dependencies are not re-established and the nested structure of the constraint formula is ignored. This results in the disconnection of some relations and preconditions and, consequently, in larger worklists with unexpected work items.

Future work should therefore focus on modifying constraints within the formula and restoring transitive dependencies in order to remove those undesired side effects. Hence, the concept of the constraint-based adaptation should be more restrictive.

Chapter 9
Conclusion

Most of the existing flexible workflow approaches either require comprising knowledge about all possible execution paths at build time or demand a remodelling at run time. When considering users without expert knowledge concerning process management, both of these aspects are drawbacks and impossible to handle. Nevertheless, the possibility of a flexible handling of processes at run time in order to react to unpredictable circumstances or customer needs is important, which holds foremost for all SMEs.

This thesis proposes a novel workflow approach for flexibility by deviation that tries to overcome these disadvantages. The main objectives are allowing flexible deviations at run time, while still offering continuous support for the process participant without the need of a manual intervention.

This chapter summarizes the main contributions in Section 9.1 and proposes research perspectives in Section 9.2.

9.1. Summary

Only few workflow approaches exist in research that implement *flexibility by deviation*. The automated handling of deviations is rather limited, as either knowledge needs to be modelled manually or process participants need to actively intervene in order to achieve deviations, as described in Sections 5.6 and 6.6.

9.1.1. Contributions

The main contribution of this thesis is a novel concept for workflow flexibility by deviation that consists of several artifacts and addresses the overall research question **RQ0** (see Section 1.2). The conducted research complies with the design-science research methodology, as described in Section 1.3. Rigor is ensured, as two renowned AI methods, Constraint Satisfaction Problem (CSP) solving and Case-Based Reasoning (CBR), are applied as theoretical foundation in the proposed concept.

During the analysis phase, requirements for an approach that suits SMEs best were identified. This includes foremost flexibility, knowledge transfer, and low effort. Additionally, an analysis was made for the single artifacts of the case-based deviation management, where requirements were derived from the specific characteristics and needs of flexibility by deviation, defined in Sections 6.4.1 and 6.5.

To meet these requirements, several artifacts were designed that incorporate specific features. One developed artifact is the constraint-based workflow engine, which itself combines other artifacts. The constraint-based workflow model, which is described in Sections 5.2 and 5.4, combines procedural and declarative models that allow for an intuitive modelling without required expert knowledge. Referring to research question **RQ1.1** (see Section 1.2), the model allows for deviations without leading to an exceptional state, as declarative models implicitly offer flexibility and violated constraints can simply be retracted in order to restore consistency.

An important contribution in this context is the transformation function, defined in Subsection 5.4.2, that converts procedurally modelled workflows, limited to block-oriented ones, into declarative formulae. This is a prerequisite for a combination of procedural and declarative models, and to allow for an automated handling through a CSP. This transformation function, which is applied to a block-oriented workflow in combination with additionally specified constraints, gives an answer to the formulated research question **RQ1.2** (see Section 1.2), as the resulting combined constraint set is used as input by the workflow engine.

On this basis, another artifact was developed. The workflow engine, which is defined in Section 5.4, builds upon the established method of CSP solving and exploits the sequential tracing of flexibility

9.1. SUMMARY

by deviation in combination with the introduced constraint-based workflow model.

The transformation function represents a novel contribution in the field of workflow management. Most of the related work that applies a constraint-based approach and allows deviations utilize LTL and finite-state-automata as theoretical foundation [136, 137]. Converting block-oriented workflows and additional constraints to one overall constraint set and the CSP model, which is constructed for the determination of work items, is a novel perspective in workflow management and has not been considered in research so far.

On top of this workflow engine, deviation handling strategies are presented in order to resolve occurring inconsistencies. This deviation management presented in Section 5.5 solves research question **RQ1.3** (see Section 1.2) to a limited extent, as an intervention of the process participant is necessary.

Therefore, the constraint-based workflow engine has been complemented with a case-based deviation management to achieve improvements. For a more sophisticated decision about handling deviations, experiential knowledge is integrated.

To identify reusable knowledge in form of similar previous workflow instances, a similarity measure in two different forms has been developed, which resolves research question **RQ2.1** (see Section 1.2). For the comparison of workflows, several approaches, particularly based on graph matching, exist in research. However, the workflow instances that need to be compared in this scenario have a much simpler structure due to the sequential tracing of task executions and therefore, resemble time series. Consequently, a similarity measure based on sequence similarity has been designed, which is presented in Section 6.4. This sophisticated comparison of sequentially traced workflows, integrating specific characteristics of the approach of flexibility by deviation through utilizing trace-based reasoning in combination with a vector similarity measure for event sequences, constitutes a novel contribution in the field of POCBR.

To exploit the retrieved cases, two adaptation methods have been designed as artifacts that allow for a proposal of work items based on experiential knowledge, addressing research question **RQ2.2** (see Section 1.2). The null adaptation, which is explained in Subsection 6.5.1, directly applies the solution of the similar case in form of work items to the running workflow instance, whereas the generative adaptation, which is specified in Subsection 6.5.2, combines both constraint nets, offering a consistent input for the constraint-based workflow engine. The constraint-based adaptation was assumed to achieve better results than the null adaptation, which proved to be wrong. In order to achieve an improvement of the generative adaptation, an in-depth analysis is necessary. However, some weaknesses and starting points have already been identified. Nevertheless, both adaptation methods allow for a continuous support of the process participant after a deviation by providing a more informed decision than the constraint-based workflow engine as such.

The combination of CSP solving and CBR is primarily applied in research to the domain of product configuration. This integration of both methods concerning the proposed generative adaptation represents a novel contribution in the context of POCBR as well as flexible workflow management.

So far, the developed artifacts have been evaluated in a simulated environment and promising results could be achieved, as presented in Chapter 8. The main object of investigation was the utility for the process participant, which consists of the support of the workflow engine during workflow execution in form of proposed work items. In different scenarios, it was foremost the null adaptation variant that proposes similar workflow execution paths compared to synthetically generated terminated workflows, which represent previously made experiences. However, the generative adaptation method performed worse compared to the constraint-based workflow engine and the null adaptation variants, demanding a redesign in order to improve its utility.

9.1.2. Exemplary Use Cases

In Subsection 3.2.2, two exemplary use cases were sketched in combination with the pursued concept. After presenting the proposed approach, these use cases and how they are covered can be addressed directly.

The first use case described the skipping of tasks that were implicitly handled due to the knowledge of the process participant. The explicit task enactment traced by the system starts later than the workflow model expects and proposes. Nevertheless, it is intended that the flexible workflow system notices this deviation in form of skipped tasks and instead proposes the subsequent tasks concerning the currently enacted one. The proposed constraint-based workflow engine is capable to react and offer support accordingly. With the enactment of the task, deviation resolving strategies are triggered and the respective strategy that interprets this situation of a task being executed too early as skipped previous tasks can be chosen, which will suggest tasks that follow the deviating task in order to eliminate the exception.

The second use case focuses on providing execution alternatives on the basis of experiential knowledge. In this case, the process participant is confronted with a deviation that consists of a task that is not included in the workflow model. A traditional workflow system would cause an exception and would stop providing support for the process participant. However, in case this task is part of terminated workflows that have been enacted previously, it is included as knowledge for the proposed case-based approach. Nevertheless, work items can be suggested on this basis thereby reactivating the support of the process participant.

Consequently, both exemplary use cases are addressed by the proposed flexible workflow approach.

9.2. Research Perspectives

The results of the evaluation revealed some shortcomings of the presented artifacts. Some apparent potential improvements and promising evolutions were simply out of the scope of this research work, but could be regarded in future work. This concerns various aspects that are outlined in the following.

9.2.1. Case-Based Deviation Management

The case-based deviation management can be evolved and improved concerning several characteristics.

Due to the bad results of the generative adaptation, this method needs a major revision to be applicable and, in particular, to be useful in practice. The constraint transfer needs to be integrated into the formula that is generated by the transformation function in order to restore connections between single workflow blocks that get lost through the constraint violations occurring due to a deviation. To this end, an in-depth analysis is necessary.

A further promising improvement can be derived from the applied similarity measure that applies the SWA. The alignment resulting from the computation can be exploited to propose corrective measures, as it produces edit steps. Deletion steps, which are part of the alignment, can deliver valuable information. For a simple example, consider these two execution paths of query $F(F_Q) = \langle a, b, c, e, f \rangle$ and retrieved case $F(F_C) = \langle a, b, c, f, e, g \rangle$, where f is the deviating task. If the tasks subsequent to the deviation are proposed without adaptation, the task e might be executed redundantly, as it is already part of the de facto workflow of the query. Therefore, slight adjustments of the derived work items might be necessary in certain circumstances.

In contrast, insertion steps can initiate to catch up on a skipped task in the query that was executed in the similar case. Consider the two execution paths of the query $F(F_Q) = \langle a, b, d \rangle$ and case $F(F_C) = \langle a, b, c, d, e \rangle$. In this example, d constitutes the deviation. According to the case, e would be suggested as next task for execution. An additional difference between the two execution paths is the lack of task c in the query. It is possible that c and e are interdependent and e requires a prior execution of c. Consequently, in some cases it might be reasonable to first propose such tasks that are part of insertion steps of the alignment. In the presented example, c could be suggested as work item as well. However, these further proposals are not based on experiential knowledge; they are simply proposed tasks that were omitted in the query workflow, but occurred in the case workflow up to the deviation. The decision about when to suggest such tasks needs to base on further knowledge, e.g. about dependencies of tasks and data.

Furthermore, in the described approach it is assumed that the case base only consists of successfully terminated workflows that share the same workflow model. But workflows that were terminated without success can also deliver valuable information, as they prove how workflow instances should not be executed. Instead the opposite should hold and thus, constraints can be derived and transferred to the running workflow instance. Considering workflow traces from other workflow models during workflow retrieval can help in finding the correct model, if e.g. an inexperienced process participant unintentionally chose the wrong model for instantiation. In such a case, the instantiated workflow model could be exchanged and consistency could be restored easily.

Another potential, which can be investigated in future work, is a possible optimization of the worklist through using the proposed case-based methods even if no deviation occurs, e.g. through a priorization and ranking of work items. Potentially, deviations could even be triggered explicitly.

9.2.2. Extension of the Constraint-Based Model

The constraint-based model is substantial as input for the workflow engine. Up to now, when regarding the transformation of a procedural workflow, it focusses on the valid sequential order of tasks and only indirectly considers dependencies that arise from data- and control-flow decisions. As the data-flow indicates substantial preconditions and restrictions, it should be integrated in the constraint-based approach more thoroughly. The remaining workflow perspectives that have not been regarded in this thesis, namely the organizational, operational and time perspective, could support this integration. For instance resource constraints, which result from data input and output relations, might have an extensive impact on valid task execution sequences. For a holistic approach of focusing data-flow besides control-flow, the case-based deviation management should integrate this perspective as well by extending the similarity measure and the adaptation methods.

Furthermore, only five constraints from the DECLARE language can be used as manually modelled constraints. This set of possible constraint types can be extended by more complex constraints to provide a higher flexibility during workflow modelling. Nevertheless, this needs to be analysed in more detail and compatibility with the defined CSP algorithm needs to be checked.

The differentiation between mandatory and optional constraints should be incorporated into the approach as well, in order to increase the flexibility of workflow modelling and to allow for diversification of possible reactions to different types of constraint violations. This can involve a severity specification, a warning message or even a proposed recovery measure. Furthermore, this distinction of mandatory and optional constraints can be integrated in the generative adaptation aiming at different transfer strategies concerning this constraint property.

9.2.3. Holistic View of the Business Process Life Cycle

The remaining phases of the business process life cycle, which have not been focussed in this work, should be elaborated in more detail. A monitoring of running workflow instances should be provided to the process engineer in order to analyse occurring deviations. To this end, a concise and expressive visualization of workflow model and instance in contrast depicting the deviations is required. In the prototypical implementation, a rudimentary illustration is integrated, which needs further elaboration. Existing approaches [49, 102] should be considered and analysed for their suitability.

This monitoring view considers the online phase of workflow management, whereas offline analysis of terminated workflows pursues an optimization of the workflow model. Process mining techniques address this objective. Thus, deviations that occur on a regular basis can be identified and, in case they are valid, be integrated in the workflow model, such that they become part of the work items. Moreover, additional information could be derived from process mining to improve the workflow model, e.g. enhancing control-flow decisions. Regarding a data perspective, the method of decision mining, which derives decision relevant knowledge from historic process information, seems promising. First results in this context [171] can be evolved and further elaborated.

9.2.4. Combination with Document Management

In order to exploit the full potential of flexibility by deviation following the approach of the SEMAFLEX project, an integration with methods from document management could be beneficial. By automatically classifying upcoming documents and, derived from that, reasoning about task executions, deviations could be detected automatically. To this end, an integration of the proposed flexible workflow approach with the work of Schwinn [170] could be pursued. Additionally integrating methods from text mining, which could for instance analyse the contents of received mails, would further enhance the approach.

9.2.5. Evaluation

Despite the promising results of the conducted technical experiment with synthetically generated data and simulated process participants,

9.2. RESEARCH PERSPECTIVES

the utility in a real-world scenario still needs to be proven. This requires an elaborate user study in a real-world environment. Furthermore, the experiment solely handled the demonstration use case of deficiency management in construction, such that a transferability to other domains needs further investigation. A generally applicable approach should be pursued in future work.

Concluding, the proposed approach addressing workflow flexibility by deviation combines two renowned AI methods, and the currently designed integration of a constraint-based workflow engine with a case-based deviation management can be seen as a starting point for various optimizations and enhancements in different directions and for specializations considering manifold domains and types of process participants.

Appendix A

Proof of Trace Equivalence

As the function $Dec(B, s_{end})$ should express the same execution orders as procedurally modelled block-oriented workflows, it should be proven that resulting traces are equivalent. Hence, with a proof it will be verified that for a block-oriented workflow B the execution path set $\mathcal{F}(B)$ cf. Def. 4.18 - 4.22 is equivalent to solutions $\texttt{sol}(B)$ of $CSP_B = (S, D, Dec(C, s_{end}))$ cf. Def. 5.4 - 5.8.

Prior to the actual proof some necessary ancillary definitions and corollaries are introduced.

Solution $\texttt{sol}_m(B)$ to CSP_B

A solution $\texttt{sol}_m(B)$ to CSP_B according to Def. 5.2 with $C = Dec(B, s_{end})$ is an assignment of all variables $S = \{s_1, \ldots, s_n, s_{end}\}$. Hereby $[s_i]^{sol}$ and $[s_{end}]^{sol}$ denote the value of the variable assignments in $\texttt{sol}_m(B)$ with $[s_i]^{sol} \in D_i \subseteq \mathbb{N}$ with $D_i \geq |n+1|$. $\texttt{sol}(B)$ represents the set of all possible solutions of the workflow block B.

Adapted Solution sol*

Any solution $\texttt{sol}$ or a part of $\texttt{sol}$ to CSP_B as well as its domains $D_i \in D$ can be "shifted" and still preserve validity and completeness in terms of workflow execution. Constraints only express relations between variables and these remain unchanged, when either the absolute distance of assigned values is increased or all assigned values are increased by the same value. A shift can be made through adding a constant value $k \in \mathbb{N}$ to all variables in the solution or a subset of the solution, but this subset must not be arbitrary but needs to fulfil a certain property. When adapting a solution through such a "shift", all domains D_i are increased by this offset and enhanced with k values. Furthermore, all variables, or variables that are assigned a value over a certain threshold b are incremented by the constant k in order to preserve the sequential relations. This adapted solution sol* is defined as follows.

Definition A.1 (Adapted CSP_B*). Let $\text{sol}_m(B)$ be a solution to $CSP_B = (S, D, Dec(B, s_{end}))$ with $S = \{s_1, ..., s_n, s_{end}\}$ and $D_i = \{d_1, ..., d_n, d_{n+1}\}$. Adapting sol with offset $k \in \mathbb{N}$ and threshold $b \in \mathbb{N}$ results in extended domains $D_i{}^* = \{d_1, ..., d_n, d_{n+1}, ..., d_{n+k+1}\}$ and an adapted solution $\text{sol}_m{}^*(B, b, k)$ for which holds $\forall [s_i]^{sol}$ with $s_i \in S$ and $[s_i]^{sol} \geq b$, k is added to the former values of the solution assignments: $[s_i]^{sol}{}^* = [s_i]^{sol} + k$.

For example, let $\text{sol}_m(B) = ([s_1]^{sol} = 0, [s_2]^{sol} = 1, [s_3]^{sol} = 2, [s_4]^{sol} = 3)$ with $D_i = \{0, 1, 2, 3\}$. If all values on and above the threshold $b = 2$ in this solution are shifted by the constant value $k = 3$, the adapted solution $\text{sol}_m{}^*(B, 2, 3) = ([s_1]^{sol}{}^* = 0, [s_2]^{sol}{}^* = 1, [s_3]^{sol}{}^* = 5, [s_4]^{sol}{}^* = 6)$ with $D_i{}^* = \{0, 1, 2, 3, 4, 5, 6\}$ remains valid, as the relational ordering is left untouched (cf. valid execution path in both cases $F(B) = \langle s_1, s_2, s_3, s_4 \rangle$).

Considering Definitions 4.10, 5.1, 5.2, 5.3 and 5.4-5.8 three corollaries can be derived.

Corollary A.1. Let B be a workflow block and sol a solution to CSP_B. It holds $\forall s \in N_B^S \setminus \{first(B)\} : [first(B)]^{sol} < [s]^{sol}$.

Corollary A.2. Let B be a workflow block and sol a solution to CSP_B. It holds $\forall s \in N_B^S \setminus \{last(B)\} : [s]^{sol} < [last(B)]^{sol} \lor [s_{end}]^{sol} < [s]^{sol}$.

Corollary A.3. Let B be a workflow block and sol a solution to $not(B, s_{end})$. It holds $\forall s \in N_B^S : [s_{end}]^{sol} < [s]^{sol}$

To prove the trace equivalence of block-oriented workflows and the generated logical formula that is used by CSP_B, the following theorem has to be proven.

Theorem 1 ($CSP_B \iff \mathcal{F}(B)$). Let $B = (N, E)$ be a block-oriented workflow with sequence nodes $N_B^S = \{s_1, ..., s_n\}$. Let $M \subseteq \mathbb{N}$ be a set of natural numbers with $|M| \geq n + 1$.

$sol_q(B) = (s_1 = [s_1]^{sol}, \ldots, s_n = [s_n]^{sol}, s_{end} = [s_{end}]^{sol}) \in sol(B)$ with $\forall i \in \{1, \ldots, n\} : D_i(s_i) = M$, i.e. is a solution to CSP_B, iff an execution path $F_j(B) = \langle s_{j_1}, \ldots, s_{j_k} \rangle \in \mathcal{F}(B)$ exists, such that
(Condition 1)[24] $\forall l \in \{1, \ldots, k-1\} : [s_{j_l}]^{sol} < [s_{j_{l+1}}]^{sol} < [s_{end}]^{sol} \wedge$
(Condition 2)[25] $\forall p \in \{1, \ldots, n\} \setminus \{j_1, \ldots, j_k\} : [s_p]^{sol} > [s_{end}]^{sol}$.

To prove Theorem 1, the proof is divided into two parts. As $X \Leftrightarrow Y$ corresponds to $X \Rightarrow Y \wedge X \Leftarrow Y$, these single implications are to be proven.

Proof of Theorem 1

Due to the recursive structure of block oriented workflows, the proof will be conducted by induction starting with the base case that B consists of a single task. In the induction step, equality will be shown for all possible remaining block elements according to Def. 4.5.

Part 1 ($X \Rightarrow Y$: $\forall sol_q(B) \in sol(B) \exists F_j(B) \in \mathcal{F}(B)$). Let $B = (N, E)$ be a block-oriented workflow with sequence nodes $N_B^S = \{s_1, \ldots, s_n\}$.
Let $M \subseteq \mathbb{N}$ be a set of natural numbers with $|M| \geq n+1$.
Let $sol_q(B) = (s_1 = [s_1]^{sol}, \ldots, s_n = [s_n]^{sol}, s_{end} = [s_{end}]^{sol}) \in sol(B)$ with $\forall i \in \{1, \ldots, n\} : D_i(s_i) = M$, i.e. is a solution to CSP_B.
Then, there exists an execution path $F_j(B) = \langle s_{j_1}, \ldots, s_{j_k} \rangle \in \mathcal{F}(B)$ such that
(Condition 1) $\forall l \in \{1, \ldots, k-1\} : [s_{j_l}]^{sol} < [s_{j_{l+1}}]^{sol} < [s_{end}]^{sol} \wedge$
(Condition 2) $\forall p \in \{1, \ldots, n\} \setminus \{j_1, \ldots, j_k\} : [s_p]^{sol} > [s_{end}]^{sol}$.

Case 1: $B = B^t$. Let B be a single task, thus $N_B^S = \{t\}$.

- According to Definition 5.4, $Dec(B^t, s_{end}) = \{t < s_{end}\}$ and thus $C = \{alldifferent(\{t, s_{end}\})\} \cup \{t < s_{end}\}$.

- For $sol_1(B) = ([t]^{sol} = 1, [s_{end}]^{sol} = 2)$, it holds $[t]^{sol} < [s_{end}]^{sol}$.

- Thus, $sol_1(B) \in sol(B)$.

- According to Definition 4.18, the only valid execution path for $B = B^t$ is $F(B) = \langle t \rangle$.

---
[24]Condition 1: The order of tasks match.
[25]Condition 2: Variables whose assigned values are higher than the value of s_{end} do not occur in the execution path.

- Thus, conditions 1 and 2 hold.

□

Case 2: $B = B^{(B_1, B_2)}$. Let B be a sequence of two workflow blocks B_1 with $|N_{B_1}^S| = n_1$ and B_2 with $|N_{B_2}^S| = n_2$.

- According to Definition 5.5, $Dec(B, s_{end}) = Dec(B^{(B_1,B_2)}, s_{end}) = \{last(B_1) < first(B_2), Dec(B_1, s_{end}), Dec(B_2, s_{end}), last(B_2) < s_{end}\}$.

- Let $\text{sol}_1(B)$ be a solution to CSP_B with $C = Dec(B, s_{end}) \cup \{alldifferent(N_B^S \cup s_{end})\}$.

- $\text{sol}_1(B)$ comprises a solution to CSP_{B_1} and CSP_{B_2}.

- Due to the induction hypothesis, an execution path $F(B_1) = \langle s_{j_1}, \ldots, s_{j_v} \rangle \in \mathcal{F}(B_1)$ exists, such that conditions 1 and 2 hold:
$\forall l \in \{1, \ldots, v-1\} : [s_{j_l}]^{sol} < [s_{j_{l+1}}]^{sol} < [s_{end}]^{sol} \wedge$ and
$\forall p \in \{1, \ldots, n_1\} \setminus \{j_1, \ldots, j_v\} : [s_p]^{sol} > [s_{end}]^{sol}$.

- Accordingly, an execution path $F(B_2) = \langle s_{j_{v+1}}, \ldots, s_{j_w} \rangle \in \mathcal{F}(B_2)$ exists, such that conditions 1 and 2 hold:
$\forall l \in \{v+1, \ldots, w-1\} : [s_{j_l}]^{sol} < [s_{j_{l+1}}]^{sol} < [s_{end}]^{sol}$ and
$\forall p \in \{1, \ldots, n_2\} \setminus \{j_{v+1}, \ldots, j_w\} : [s_p]^{sol} > [s_{end}]^{sol}$.

- As $last(B_1) < first(B_2)$ must be fulfilled, it follows $[s_{j_v}]^{sol} < [s_{j_{v+1}}]^{sol}$.

- As $last(B_2) < s_{end}$ holds, it follows $[s_{j_w}]^{sol} < [s_{end}]^{sol}$.

- Thus, the combined execution path is $F(B) = \langle s_{j_1}, \ldots, s_{j_w} \rangle = F(B_1) \circ F(B_2) \in \mathcal{F}(B) = \mathcal{F}(B^{(B_1,B_2)})$.

- Then, condition 1 holds for the execution path $F(B)$: $\forall l \in \{1, \ldots, v-1\} : [s_{j_l}]^{sol} < [s_{j_{l+1}}]^{sol} < [s_{end}]^{sol}$.

- Further, condition 2: $\forall p \in \{1, \ldots, n\} \setminus \{j_1, \ldots, j_w\} : [s_p]^{sol} > [s_{end}]^{sol}$ holds for the combined execution path, as the condition holds for workflow blocks B_1 and B_2 respectively.

□

Case 3: $B = B_{XOR}^{(B_1,B_2)}$. Let B be an exclusive control-flow block containing two workflow blocks B_1 with $|N_{B_1}^S| = n_1$ and B_2 with $|N_{B_2}^S| = n_2$.

- According to Definition 5.6, $Dec(B, s_{end}) = Dec(B_{XOR}^{(B_1,B_2)}, s_{end}) = \{((cs < first(B_1) \land last(B_1) < cj \land Dec(B_1, s_{end}) \land not(B_2, s_{end})) \lor (cs < first(B_2) \land last(B_2) < cj \land Dec(B_2, s_{end}) \land not(B_1, s_{end}))), cj < s_{end}\}$.

- Let $\text{sol}_1(B)$ be a solution to CSP_B with $C = Dec(B, s_{end}) \cup \{alldifferent(N_B^S \cup s_{end})\}$.

- $Dec(B, s_{end})$ can be split up into two cases. Thus, it holds either

  (i) $\{cs < first(B_1), last(B_1) < cj, Dec(B_1, s_{end}), not(B_2, s_{end}), cj < s_{end}\}$, or it holds

  (ii) $\{cs < first(B_2), last(B_2) < cj, Dec(B_2, s_{end}), not(B_1, s_{end}), cj < s_{end}\}$,

  but never both.

- For case (i):

  a) $\text{sol}_1(B)$ is a solution to (i).

  b) Thus, $\text{sol}_1(B)$ fulfils all constraints of $Dec(B_1, s_{end})$ and comprises a solution to B_1.

  c) Due to the induction hypothesis, an execution path $F(B_1) = \langle s_{j_1}, \ldots, s_{j_v} \rangle \in \mathcal{F}(B_1)$ exists, such that conditions 1 and 2 hold:
  $\forall l \in \{1, \ldots, v-1\}: [s_{j_l}]^{sol} < [s_{j_{l+1}}]^{sol} < [s_{end}]^{sol}$ and
  $\forall p \in \{1, \ldots, n_1\} \setminus \{j_1, \ldots, j_v\}: [s_p]^{sol} > [s_{end}]^{sol}$.

  d) As $cs < first(B_1)$ must be fulfilled, it follows $[cs]^{sol} < [s_{j_1}]^{sol}$.

  e) As $last(B_1) < cj$ must be fulfilled, it follows $[s_{j_v}]^{sol} < [cj]^{sol}$.

  f) As $cj < s_{end}$ holds, it follows $[cj]^{sol} < [s_{end}]^{sol}$.

  g) As $not(B_2, s_{end})$ must be fulfilled and according to Cor. A.3 it holds, that $\forall s \in N_{B_2}^S : [s_{end}]^{sol} < [s]^{sol}$.

  h) Thus, B_2 is not part of the execution path.

264   APPENDIX A. PROOF OF TRACE EQUIVALENCE

   i) Thus, the combined execution path is
      $F(B) = \langle cs, s_{j_1}, \ldots, s_{j_v}, cj \rangle = \langle cs \rangle \circ F(B_1) \circ \langle cj \rangle$.

   j) Considering d)-f) and that condition 1 is valid for $F(B_1)$, condition 1 holds as well for the combined execution path $F(B)$.

   k) Further, condition 2 holds for the combined execution path $F(B)$, as condition 2 holds for the execution path $F(B_1)$ and due to g): $\forall s \in N_B^S \setminus \{cs, cj, s_{j_1}, \ldots, s_{j_v}\} : [s]^{sol} > [s_{end}]^{sol}$.

- For case (ii) the argumentation is analogously to case (i) with B_1 and B_2 switched.

  $\square$

Case 4: $B = B_{AND}^{(B_1, B_2)}$. Let B be a parallel control-flow block containing two workflow blocks B_1 with $|N_{B_1}^S| = n_1$ and B_2 with $|N_{B_2}^S| = n_2$.

- According to Definition 5.7, $Dec(B, s_{end}) = Dec(B_{AND}^{(B_1,B_2)}, s_{end}) = \{cs < first(B_1), last(B_1) < cj, Dec(B_1, s_{end}), cs < first(B_2), last(B_2) < cj, Dec(B_2, s_{end}), cj < s_{end}\}$.

- Let $\texttt{sol}_1(B)$ be a solution to CSP_B with $C = Dec(B, s_{end}) \cup \{alldifferent(N_B^S \cup s_{end})\}$.

- $\texttt{sol}_1(B)$ comprises a solution to CSP_{B_1} and CSP_{B_2}.

- Due to the induction hypothesis, an execution path $F(B_1) = \langle s_{j_1}, \ldots, s_{j_v} \rangle \in \mathcal{F}(B_1)$ exists, such that conditions 1 and 2 hold:
  $\forall l \in \{1, \ldots, v-1\} : [s_{j_l}]^{sol} < [s_{j_{l+1}}]^{sol} < [s_{end}]^{sol} \wedge$ and
  $\forall p \in \{1, \ldots, n_1\} \setminus \{j_1, \ldots, j_v\} : [s_p]^{sol} > [s_{end}]^{sol}$.

- Accordingly, an execution path $F(B_2) = \langle s_{j_{v+1}}, \ldots, s_{j_w} \rangle \in \mathcal{F}(B_2)$ exists, such that conditions 1 and 2 hold:
  $\forall l \in \{v+1, \ldots, w-1\} : [s_{j_l}]^{sol} < [s_{j_{l+1}}]^{sol} < [s_{end}]^{sol} \wedge$ and
  $\forall p \in \{1, \ldots, n_2\} \setminus \{j_{v+1}, \ldots, j_w\} : [s_p]^{sol} > [s_{end}]^{sol}$.

- As $\{cs < first(B_1), last(B_1) < cj\}$ must be fulfilled, it follows $[cs]^{sol} < [s_{j_1}]^{sol}$ and $[s_{j_v}]^{sol} < [cj]^{sol}$.

- As $\{cs < first(B_2), last(B_2) < cj\}$ must be fulfilled, it follows $[cs]^{sol} < [s_{j_{v+1}}]^{sol}$ and $[s_{j_w}]^{sol} < [cj]^{sol}$.

- As $cj < s_{end}$ holds, it follows $[cj]^{sol} < [s_{end}]^{sol}$.

- Thus, the combined execution path is $F(B) = \langle cs, s_1, \ldots, s_k, cj \rangle$ with $\forall i \in \{1, \ldots, k\} : s_i \in F(B_1) \lor s_i \in F(B_2)$.

- It follows $\langle s_1, \ldots, s_k \rangle \in F(B_1) \bowtie F(B_2)$.

- By induction hypothesis holds $F(B_1) \in \mathcal{F}(B_1)$ and $F(B_2) \in \mathcal{F}(B_2)$, thus, $F(B) \in \{\langle cs \rangle\} \odot \mathcal{F}(B_1) | \mathcal{F}(B_2) \odot \{\langle cj \rangle\}$.

- Then, condition 1 holds for the execution path $F(B)$: $\forall l \in \{1, \ldots, k-1\} : [s_l]^{sol} < [s_{l+1}]^{sol} < [s_{end}]^{sol}$.

- Further, condition 2: $\forall p \in \{1, \ldots, n\} \setminus \{j_1, \ldots, j_w\} : [s_p]^{sol} > [s_{end}]^{sol}$ holds for the combined execution path, as the condition holds for workflow blocks B_1 and B_2 respectively.

$\square$

Case 5: $B = B_{XOR}^{B_1}$. Let B be a single-branch exclusive control-flow block containing one workflow block B_1 with $|N_{B_1}^S| = n_1$.

- According to Definition 5.8, $Dec(B, s_{end}) = Dec(B_{XOR}^{(B_1)}, s_{end}) = \{((cs < cj \land not(B_1, s_{end})) \lor (cs < first(B_1) \land last(B_1) < cj \land Dec(B_1, s_{end}))), cj < s_{end}\}$.

- Let $\text{sol}_1(B)$ be a solution to CSP_B with $C = Dec(B, s_{end}) \cup \{alldifferent(N_B^S \cup s_{end})\}$.

- $Dec(B, s_{end})$ can be split up into two cases. Thus, it holds either

  (i) $\{cs < cj, not(B_1, s_{end}), cj < s_{end}\}$, or it holds
  (ii) $\{cs < first(B_1), last(B_1) < cj, Dec(B_1, s_{end}), cj < s_{end}\}$.

  but never both.

- For case (i):

    a) As $cs < cj$ must be fulfilled, it follows $[cs]^{sol} < [cj]^{sol}$.
    b) As $cj < s_{end}$ must be fulfilled, it follows $[cj]^{sol} < [s_{end}]^{sol}$.
    c) Thus, the execution path is $F(B) = \langle cs, cj \rangle$.
    d) Condition 1 holds for $F(B)$, as $[cs]^{sol} < [cj]^{sol} < [s_{end}]^{sol}$.

e) As $not(B_1, s_{end})$ must be fulfilled and according to Cor. A.3 it holds, that $\forall s \in N_{B_1}^S : [s_{end}]^{sol} < [s]^{sol}$. Thus, condition 2 is fulfilled for $F(B)$.

- For case (ii):

  a) $\mathtt{sol}_1(B)$ is a solution to (i).

  b) Thus, $\mathtt{sol}_1(B)$ fulfils all constraints of $Dec(B_1, s_{end})$ and comprises a solution to B_1.

  c) Due to the induction hypothesis, an execution path $F(B_1) = \langle s_{j_1}, \ldots, s_{j_v} \rangle \in \mathcal{F}(B_1)$ exists, such that conditions 1 and 2 hold: $\forall l \in \{1, \ldots, v-1\} : [s_{j_l}]^{sol} < [s_{j_{l+1}}]^{sol} < [s_{end}]^{sol} \wedge$ and $\forall p \in \{1, \ldots, n_1\} \setminus \{j_1, \ldots, j_v\} : [s_p]^{sol} > [s_{end}]^{sol}$.

  d) As $cs < first(B_1)$ must be fulfilled, it follows $[cs]^{sol} < [s_{j_1}]^{sol}$.

  e) As $last(B_1) < cj$ must be fulfilled, it follows $[s_{j_v}]^{sol} < [cj]^{sol}$.

  f) As $cj < s_{end}$ holds, it follows $[cj]^{sol} < [s_{end}]^{sol}$.

  g) Thus, the combined execution path is
  $F(B) = \langle cs, s_{j_1}, \ldots, s_{j_v}, cj \rangle = \langle cs \rangle \circ F(B_1) \circ \langle cj \rangle$.

  h) Considering d)-f) and that condition 1 is valid for $F(B_1)$, condition 1 holds as well for the combined execution path $F(B)$.

  i) Further, condition 2 holds for the combined execution path $F(B)$, as condition 2 holds for the execution path $F(B_1)$ and B contains no more sequence nodes other than cs, cj which are part of $F(B)$: $N_B^S \setminus (N_{B_1}^S \cup \{cs, cj\}) = \emptyset$.

□

Part 2 ($Y \Rightarrow X : \forall F_j(B) \in \mathcal{F}(B) \exists \text{sol}_q(B) \in \text{sol}(B)$). Let $B = (N, E)$ be a block-oriented workflow with sequence nodes $N_B^S = \{s_1, \ldots, s_n\}$.
Let $M \subseteq \mathbb{N}$ be a set of natural numbers with $|M| \geq n + 1$.
Let $F_j(B) = \langle s_{j_1}, \ldots, s_{j_k} \rangle \in \mathcal{F}(B)$ be a valid execution path.
Then, there exists a solution $\text{sol}_q(B) = (s_1 = [s_1]^{sol}, \ldots, s_n = [s_n]^{sol}, s_{end} = [s_{end}]^{sol}) \in \text{sol}(B)$
with $\forall i \in \{1, \ldots, n\} : D_i(s_i) = M$ to CSP_B such that
(Condition 1) $\forall l \in \{1, \ldots, k-1\} : [s_{j_l}]^{sol} < [s_{j_{l+1}}]^{sol} < [s_{end}]^{sol} \wedge$
(Condition 2) $\forall p \in \{1, \ldots, n\} \setminus \{j_1, \ldots, j_k\} : [s_p]^{sol} > [s_{end}]^{sol}$.

Case 1: $B = B^t$. Let B be single task, thus $N_B^S = \{t\}$.

- Let $F(B) \in \mathcal{F}(B)$, then $F(B) = \langle t \rangle$, according to Definition 4.18.

- According to Definition 5.4, $Dec(B^t, s_{end}) = \{t < s_{end}\}$.

- Thus, $[t]^{sol} = a$ and $[s_{end}]^{sol} = a + b$ with $a, b \in \mathbb{N}$, $M = \{a, a+b\}$ and $|M| = 2$ is a solution to CSP_B.

- Therefore, conditions 1 and 2 hold.

□

Case 2: $B = B^{(B_1, B_2)}$. Let B be a sequence of two workflow blocks B_1 with $|N_{B_1}^S| = n_1$ and B_2 with $|N_{B_2}^S| = n_2$.

- Let $F(B) \in \mathcal{F}(B) := \mathcal{F}(B_1) \odot \mathcal{F}(B_2)$, then $F(B) = F(B_1) \circ F(B_2)$ with $F(B_1) \in \mathcal{F}(B_1)$ and $F(B_2) \in \mathcal{F}(B_2)$, according to Definition 4.19.

- Let $F(B_1) = \langle s_1^{B_1}, \ldots, s_q^{B_1} \rangle$ and $F(B_2) = \langle s_1^{B_2}, \ldots, s_r^{B_2} \rangle$ and thus, $F(B) = \langle s_1^{B_1}, \ldots, s_q^{B_1}, s_1^{B_2}, \ldots, s_r^{B_2} \rangle$.

- Due to the induction hypothesis, there exists a solution $\text{sol}_1(B_1) = ([s_1^{B_1}]^{sol} = a_1^{B_1}, \ldots, [s_q^{B_1}]^{sol} = a_q^{B_1}, [s_{end}^{B_1}]^{sol} = a_{end}^{B_1}, [s_{q+2}^{B_1}]^{sol} = a_{q+2}^{B_1}, \ldots, [s_{n_1}^{B_1}]^{sol} = a_{n_1}^{B_1})$ to CSP_{B_1} with $M_1 = \{a_1^{B_1}, \ldots, a_{n_1}^{B_1}\} \subseteq \mathbb{N}$, such that conditions 1 and 2 hold, as $\forall l \in \{1, \ldots, q-1\} : a_l < a_{l+1} < a_{end}$ and $\forall p \in \{1, \ldots, n_1\} \setminus \{1, \ldots, q\} : a_p > a_{end}$.

- Accordingly, a solution $\mathtt{sol}_2(B_2) = ([s_1^{B_2}]^{sol} = a_1^{B_2}, \ldots, [s_r^{B_2}]^{sol} = a_r^{B_2}, [s_{end}^{B_2}]^{sol} = a_{end}^{B_2}, [s_{r+2}^{B_2}]^{sol} = a_{r+2}^{B_2}, \ldots, [s_{n_2}^{B_2}]^{sol} = a_{n_2}^{B_2})$ to CSP_{B_2} with $M_2 = \{a_1^{B_2}, \ldots, a_{n_2}^{B_2}\} \subseteq \mathbb{N}$ exists, such that conditions 1 and 2 hold, as $\forall l \in \{1, \ldots, r-1\} : a_l < a_{l+1} < a_{end}$ and $\forall p \in \{1, \ldots, n_2\} \setminus \{1, \ldots, r\} : a_p > a_{end}$.

- In order to create a combined solution $\mathtt{sol}(B)$ for the overall execution path $F(B)$ that fulfils the necessary conditions and constraints, several shifts of the single solutions for B_1 and B_2 are required.

- $\mathtt{sol}_2(B_2)$ is shifted by an offset $k_1 = [s_q^{B_1}]^{sol}$ and threshold $b_1 = [s_1^{B_2}]$, such that all contained elements of path $F(B_2)$ are assigned higher values than the elements of $F(B_1)$ in the solution.
  This results in an adapted solution
  $\mathtt{sol}_2{*}(B_2, b_1, k_1) = \mathtt{sol}_2{*}(B_2, [s_1^{B_2}], [s_q^{B_1}]^{sol}) =$
  $([s_1^{B_2}]^{sol*} = a_1^{B_2} + [s_q^{B_1}]^{sol}, \ldots, [s_r^{B_2}]^{sol*} = a_r^{B_2} + [s_q^{B_1}]^{sol},$
  $[s_{end}^{B_2}]^{sol*} = a_{end}^{B_2} + [s_q^{B_1}]^{sol}, [s_{r+2}^{B_2}]^{sol*} = a_{r+2}^{B_2} + [s_q^{B_1}]^{sol}, \ldots,$
  $[s_{n_2}^{B_2}]^{sol*} = a_{n_2}^{B_2} + [s_q^{B_1}]^{sol})$
  to CSP_{B_2} with $M_2{*} = \{a_1^{B_2}, \ldots, a_{n_2}^{B_2}, \ldots, a_{n_2}^{B_2} + [s_q^{B_1}]^{sol}\} \subseteq \mathbb{N}$, such that condition 1 can be adhered to, when combining single solutions of B_1 and B_2.

- $\mathtt{sol}_1(B_1)$ is shifted by an offset $k_2 = [s_{n_2}^{B_2}]^{sol} + [s_q^{B_1}]^{sol}$ and threshold $b_2 = [s_{q+2}^{B_1}]^{sol}$, such that all elements of B_1 not contained in the execution path $F(B_1)$ are assigned higher values of all elements of B_2.
  This results in an adapted solution
  $\mathtt{sol}_1{*}(B_1, b_2, k_2) = \mathtt{sol}_1{*}(B_1, [s_{q+2}^{B_1}]^{sol}, [s_{n_2}^{B_2}]^{sol} + [s_q^{B_1}]^{sol}) =$
  $([s_1^{B_1}]^{sol*} = a_1^{B_1}, \ldots, [s_q^{B_1}]^{sol*} = a_q^{B_1}, [s_{end}^{B_1}]^{sol*} = a_{end}^{B_1},$
  $[s_{q+2}^{B_1}]^{sol*} = a_{q+2}^{B_1} + [s_{n_2}^{B_2}]^{sol} + [s_q^{B_1}]^{sol}, \ldots,$
  $[s_{n_1}^{B_1}]^{sol*} = a_{n_1}^{B_1} + [s_{n_2}^{B_2}]^{sol} + [s_q^{B_1}]^{sol})$ to CSP_{B_1}
  with $M_1{*} = \{a_1^{B_1}, \ldots, a_{n_1}^{B_1}, \ldots, a_{n_1}^{B_1} + [s_{n_2}^{B_2}]^{sol} + [s_q^{B_1}]^{sol}\} \subseteq \mathbb{N}$, such that $alldifferent(N_{B_1}^S \cup N_{B_2}^S)$ holds.

- In the combined solution only one variable is necessary, that marks the end of the de facto workflow. Thus, $s_{end}^{B_1}$ is ignored.

- The overall solution $\text{sol}_0(B)$ is constructed by
$\text{sol}_0(B) = (\text{sol}_1*(B_1, b_2, k_2) \setminus \{[s_{end}^{B_1}]^{sol*}\}) \cup \text{sol}_2*(B_2, b_1, k_1) =$
$([s_1^{B_1}]^{sol*} = a_1^{B_1}, \ldots, [s_q^{B_1}]^{sol*} = a_q^{B_1}, [s_1^{B_2}]^{sol*} = a_1^{B_2} + [s_q^{B_1}]^{sol}, \ldots,$
$[s_r^{B_2}]^{sol*} = a_r^{B_2} + [s_q^{B_1}]^{sol}, [s_{end}^{B_2}]^{sol*} = a_{end}^{B_2} + [s_q^{B_1}]^{sol},$
$[s_{r+2}^{B_2}]^{sol*} = a_{r+2}^{B_2} + [s_q^{B_1}]^{sol}, \ldots, [s_{n_2}^{B_2}]^{sol*} = a_{n_2}^{B_2} + [s_q^{B_1}]^{sol},$
$[s_{q+2}^{B_1}]^{sol*} = a_{q+2}^{B_1} + [s_q^{B_2}]^{sol} + [s_q^{B_1}]^{sol}, \ldots,$
$[s_{n_1}^{B_1}]^{sol*} = a_{n_1}^{B_1} + [s_{n_2}^{B_2}]^{sol} + [s_q^{B_1}]^{sol})$ to CSP_B with
$M = M_1* \cup M_2* = \{a_1^{B_2}, \ldots, a_{n_2}^{B_2}, \ldots, a_{n_2}^{B_2} + [s_q^{B_1}]^{sol}, a_1^{B_1}, \ldots,$
$a_{n_1}^{B_1}, \ldots, a_{n_1}^{B_1} + [s_{n_2}^{B_2}]^{sol} + [s_q^{B_1}]^{sol}\} \subseteq \mathbb{N}$ such that conditions 1 and 2 hold.

$\square$

Case 3: $B = B_{XOR}^{(B_1, B_2)}$. Let B be an exclusive control-flow block containing two workflow blocks B_1 with $|N_{B_1}^S| = n_1$ and B_2 with $|N_{B_2}^S| = n_2$.

- Let $F(B) \in \mathcal{F}(B) := \{\langle cs \rangle\} \odot \mathcal{F}(B_1) \odot \{\langle cj \rangle\} \cup \{\langle cs \rangle\} \odot \mathcal{F}(B_2) \odot \{\langle cj \rangle\}$ according to Definition 4.20, then either

    (i) $F(B) = \langle cs \rangle \circ F(B_1) \circ \langle cj \rangle$ or
    (ii) $F(B) = \langle cs \rangle \circ F(B_2) \circ \langle cj \rangle$

    with $F(B_1) \in \mathcal{F}(B_1)$ and $F(B_2) \in \mathcal{F}(B_2)$ but never both.

- Let $F(B_1) = \langle s_1^{B_1}, \ldots, s_q^{B_1} \rangle$ and $F(B_2) = \langle s_1^{B_2}, \ldots, s_r^{B_2} \rangle$.

- Due to the induction hypothesis, there exists a solution $\text{sol}_1(B_1) = ([s_1^{B_1}]^{sol} = a_1^{B_1}, \ldots, [s_q^{B_1}]^{sol} = a_q^{B_1}, [s_{end}^{B_1}]^{sol} = a_{end}^{B_1},$
$[s_{q+2}^{B_1}]^{sol} = a_{q+2}^{B_1}, \ldots, [s_{n_1}^{B_1}]^{sol} = a_{n_1}^{B_1})$ to CSP_{B_1} with $M_1 = \{a_1^{B_1}, \ldots, a_{n_1}^{B_1}\} \subseteq \mathbb{N}$, such that conditions 1 and 2 hold, as $\forall l \in \{1, \ldots, q-1\} : a_l < a_{l+1} < a_{end}$ and $\forall p \in \{1, \ldots, n_1\} \setminus \{1, \ldots, q\} : a_p > a_{end}$.

- Accordingly, a solution $\text{sol}_2(B_2) = ([s_1^{B_2}]^{sol} = a_1^{B_2}, \ldots, [s_r^{B_2}]^{sol} = a_r^{B_2}, [s_{end}^{B_2}]^{sol} = a_{end}^{B_2}, [s_{r+2}^{B_2}]^{sol} = a_{r+2}^{B_2}, \ldots, [s_{n_2}^{B_2}]^{sol} = a_{n_2}^{B_2})$ to CSP_{B_2} with $M_2 = \{a_1^{B_2}, \ldots, a_{n_2}^{B_2}\} \subseteq \mathbb{N}$ exists, such that conditions 1 and 2 hold, as $\forall l \in \{1, \ldots, r-1\} : a_l < a_{l+1} < a_{end}$ and $\forall p \in \{1, \ldots, n_2\} \setminus \{1, \ldots, r\} : a_p > a_{end}$.

- For case (i):

a) The combined execution path is:
$$F(B) = \langle cs, s_1^{B_1}, \ldots, s_q^{B_1}, cj \rangle.$$

b) In order to create a combined solution $\text{sol}(B)$ for the overall execution path $F(B)$ that fulfils the necessary conditions and constraints, several shifts of the single solutions for B_1 and B_2 are required.

c) $\text{sol}_1(B_1)$ is shifted by an offset $k_1 = 1$ and threshold $b_1 = [s_1^{B_1}]^{sol}$, such that cs can be assigned the value 1 in the combined solution and all values of the elements of B_1 are higher than this value.
This results in an adapted solution
$\text{sol}_1{}^*(B_1, b_1, k_1) = \text{sol}_1{}^*(B_1, [s_1^{B_1}]^{sol}, 1) =$
$([s_1^{B_1}]^{sol*} = a_1^{B_1} + 1, \ldots, [s_q^{B_1}]^{sol*} = a_q^{B_1} + 1,$
$[s_{end}^{B_1}]^{sol*} = a_{end}^{B_1} + 1, [s_{q+2}^{B_1}]^{sol*} = a_{q+2}^{B_1} + 1, \ldots,$
$[s_{n_1}^{B_1}]^{sol*} = a_{n_1}^{B_1} + 1)$ to CSP_{B_1}
with $M_1{}^* = \{a_1^{B_1}, \ldots, a_{n_1}^{B_1} + 1\} \subseteq \mathbb{N}$.

d) $\text{sol}_1{}^*(B_1, b_1, k_1)$ is again shifted by an offset $k_2 = 1$ and threshold $b_2 = [s_{end}^{B_1}]^{sol*}$, such that cj can be assigned the value $[s_q^{B_1}]^{sol*} + 1$ in the combined solution and the values of all elements that are not part of $F(B_1)$ are increased by one to ensure the *alldifferent* constraint.
This results in an adapted solution
$\text{sol}_1{}^{**}(B_1, b_2, k_2) = \text{sol}_1{}^{**}(B_1, [s_{end}^{B_1}]^{sol*}, 1) =$
$([s_1^{B_1}]^{sol**} = a_1^{B_1} + 1, \ldots, [s_q^{B_1}]^{sol**} = a_q^{B_1} + 1,$
$[s_{end}^{B_1}]^{sol**} = a_{end}^{B_1} + 2, [s_{q+2}^{B_1}]^{sol**} = a_{q+2}^{B_1} + 2, \ldots,$
$[s_{n_1}^{B_1}]^{sol**} = a_{n_1}^{B_1} + 2)$ to CSP_{B_1}
with $M_1{}^{**} = \{a_1^{B_1}, \ldots, a_{n_1}^{B_1} + 2\} \subseteq \mathbb{N}$.

e) $\text{sol}_2(B_2)$ is shifted by an offset $k_3 = [s_{n_1}^{B_1}]^{sol**}$ and threshold $b_3 = [s_1^{B_2}]$, such that all elements of B_2 are assigned higher values than the elements of B_1.
This results in an adapted solution
$\text{sol}_2{}^*(B_2, b_3, k_3) = \text{sol}_2{}^*(B_2, [s_1^{B_2}], [s_{n_1}^{B_1}]^{sol**}) =$
$([s_1^{B_2}]^{sol*} = a_1^{B_2} + [s_{n_1}^{B_1}]^{sol**}, \ldots, [s_r^{B_2}]^{sol*} = a_r^{B_2} + [s_{n_1}^{B_1}]^{sol**},$
$[s_{end}^{B_2}]^{sol*} = a_{end}^{B_2} + [s_{n_1}^{B_1}]^{sol**}, [s_{r+2}^{B_2}]^{sol*} = a_{r+2}^{B_2} + [s_{n_1}^{B_1}]^{sol**}, \ldots$
$, [s_{n_2}^{B_2}]^{sol*} = a_{n_2}^{B_2} + [s_{n_1}^{B_1}]^{sol**})$ to CSP_{B_2}
with $M_2{}^* = \{a_1^{B_2}, \ldots, a_{n_2}^{B_2} + [s_{n_1}^{B_1}]^{sol**}\} \subseteq \mathbb{N}$.

f) In the combined solution only one variable is necessary,

that marks the end of the de facto workflow. Thus, $s_{end}^{B_2}$ is ignored and $s_{end}^{B_1}$ marks the end of the workflow.

g) The overall solution $\text{sol}_0(B)$ is constructed by
$\text{sol}_0(B) = \text{sol}_1^{**}(B_1, b_2, k_2) \cup (\text{sol}_2^*(B_2, b_3, k_3)$
$\setminus \{[s_{end}^{B_2}]^{sol*}\}) \cup \{[cs]^{sol} = 1, [cj]^{sol} = [s_q^{B_1}]^{sol} + 2\} =$
$([cs]^{sol} = 1, [s_1^{B_1}]^{sol**} = a_1^{B_1} + 1, \ldots, [s_q^{B_1}]^{sol**} = a_q^{B_1} + 1,$
$[cj]^{sol} = [s_q^{B_1}]^{sol} + 2, [s_{end}^{B_1}]^{sol**} = a_{end}^{B_1} + 2,$
$[s_{q+2}^{B_1}]^{sol**} = a_{q+2}^{B_1} + 2, \ldots, [s_{n_1}^{B_1}]^{sol**} = a_{n_1}^{B_1} + 2,$
$[s_1^{B_2}]^{sol*} = a_1^{B_2} + [s_{n_1}^{B_1}]^{sol**}, \ldots, [s_r^{B_2}]^{sol*} = a_r^{B_2} + [s_{n_1}^{B_1}]^{sol**},$
$[s_{r+2}^{B_2}]^{sol*} = a_{r+2}^{B_2} + [s_{n_1}^{B_1}]^{sol**}, \ldots, [s_{n_2}^{B_2}]^{sol*} = a_{n_2}^{B_2} + [s_{n_1}^{B_1}]^{sol**})$
to CSP_B with $M = M_1^{**} \cup M_2^* \cup \{1\} =$
$\{1, a_1^{B_1}, \ldots, a_{n_1}^{B_1} + 2, a_1^{B_2}, \ldots, a_{n_2}^{B_2} + [s_{n_1}^{B_1}]^{sol**}\} \subseteq \mathbb{N}$ such that conditions 1 and 2 hold.

- For case (ii) the argumentation is analogously to case (i) with B_1 and B_2 switched.

□

Case 4: $B = B_{AND}^{(B_1, B_2)}$. Let B be a parallel control-flow block containing two workflow blocks B_1 with $|N_{B_1}^S| = n_1$ and B_2 with $|N_{B_2}^S| = n_2$.

- Let $F(B) \in \mathcal{F}(B) := \{\langle cs \rangle\} \odot \mathcal{F}(B_1) | \mathcal{F}(B_2) \odot \{\langle cj \rangle\}$, then $F(B) \in \{cs\} \odot F(B_1) \bowtie F(B_2) \odot \{cj\}$ with $F(B_1) \in \mathcal{F}(B_1)$ and $F(B_2) \in \mathcal{F}(B_2)$, according to Definition 4.21.

- Let $F(B_1) = \langle s_1^{B_1}, \ldots, s_q^{B_1} \rangle$ and $F(B_2) = \langle s_1^{B_2}, \ldots, s_r^{B_2} \rangle$.

- Due to the induction hypothesis, there exists a solution $\text{sol}_1(B_1) = ([s_1^{B_1}]^{sol} = a_1^{B_1}, \ldots, [s_q^{B_1}]^{sol} = a_q^{B_1}, [s_{end}^{B_1}]^{sol} = a_{end}^{B_1}, [s_{q+2}^{B_1}]^{sol} = a_{q+2}^{B_1}, \ldots, [s_{n_1}^{B_1}]^{sol} = a_{n_1}^{B_1})$ to CSP_{B_1} with $M_1 = \{a_1^{B_1}, \ldots, a_{n_1}^{B_1}\} \subseteq \mathbb{N}$, such that conditions 1 and 2 hold, as $\forall l \in \{1, \ldots, q-1\} : a_l < a_{l+1} < a_{end}$ and $\forall p \in \{1, \ldots, n_1\} \setminus \{1, \ldots, q\} : a_p > a_{end}$.

- Accordingly, a solution $\text{sol}_2(B_2) = ([s_1^{B_2}]^{sol} = a_1^{B_2}, \ldots, [s_r^{B_2}]^{sol} = a_r^{B_2}, [s_{end}^{B_2}]^{sol} = a_{end}^{B_2}, [s_{r+2}^{B_2}]^{sol} = a_{r+2}^{B_2}, \ldots, [s_{n_2}^{B_2}]^{sol} = a_{n_2}^{B_2})$ to CSP_{B_2} with $M_2 = \{a_1^{B_2}, \ldots, a_{n_2}^{B_2}\} \subseteq \mathbb{N}$ exists, such that conditions 1 and 2 hold, as $\forall l \in \{1, \ldots, r-1\} : a_l < a_{l+1} < a_{end}$ and $\forall p \in \{1, \ldots, n_2\} \setminus \{1, \ldots, r\} : a_p > a_{end}$.

- In order to create a combined solution $\text{sol}(B)$ for the overall execution path $F(B)$ that fulfils the necessary conditions and constraints, several shifts of the single solutions for B_1 and B_2 are required.

- One shift of both $\text{sol}_1(B_1)$ and $\text{sol}_2(B_2)$ is necessary, such that cs can be assigned the value 1 in the combined solution and all values of the elements of B_1 and B_2 are higher than this value.

  a) $\text{sol}_1(B_1)$ is shifted by an offset $k_1 = 1$ and threshold $b_1 = [s_1^{B_1}]^{sol}$, which results in an adapted solution
  $\text{sol}_1^*(B_1, b_1, k_1) = \text{sol}_1^*(B_1, [s_1^{B_1}]^{sol}, 1) =$
  $([s_1^{B_1}]^{sol*} = a_1^{B_1} + 1, \ldots, [s_q^{B_1}]^{sol*} = a_q^{B_1} + 1,$
  $[s_{end}^{B_1}]^{sol*} = a_{end}^{B_1} + 1, [s_{q+2}^{B_1}]^{sol*} = a_{q+2}^{B_1} + 1, \ldots,$
  $[s_{n_1}^{B_1}]^{sol*} = a_{n_1}^{B_1} + 1)$ to CSP_{B_1}
  with $M_1^* = \{a_1^{B_1}, \ldots, a_{n_1}^{B_1} + 1\} \subseteq \mathbb{N}$.

  b) Analogously, $\text{sol}_2(B_2)$ is shifted by an offset $k_2 = 1$ and threshold $b_2 = [s_1^{B_2}]^{sol}$, which results in an adapted solution
  $\text{sol}_2^*(B_2, b_2, k_2) = \text{sol}_2^*(B_2, [s_1^{B_2}]^{sol}, 1) =$
  $([s_1^{B_2}]^{sol*} = a_1^{B_2} + 1, \ldots, [s_r^{B_2}]^{sol*} = a_r^{B_2} + 1,$
  $[s_{end}^{B_2}]^{sol*} = a_{end}^{B_2} + 1, [s_{r+2}^{B_2}]^{sol*} = a_{r+2}^{B_2} + 1, \ldots,$
  $[s_{n_2}^{B_2}]^{sol*} = a_{n_2}^{B_2} + 1)$ to CSP_{B_2}
  with $M_2^* = \{a_1^{B_2}, \ldots, a_{n_2}^{B_2} + 1\} \subseteq \mathbb{N}$.

- According to Def. 4.14 $F(B_1) \bowtie F(B_2)$ is resolved to either

  (i) $\{first(B_1) \circ rest_1 | rest_1 \in (F(B_1) \setminus first(B_1) \bowtie F(B_2))\}$
  or

  (ii) $\{first(B_2) \circ rest_2 | rest_2 \in (F(B_1) \bowtie F(B_2) \setminus first(B_2))\}$.

- For case (i):

  a) $\text{sol}_2^*(B_2)$ is shifted by an offset $k_3 = [first(B_1)]^{sol*}$ and threshold $b_3 = [first(B_2)]^{sol*}$, such that all elements of B_2 and all elements of B_1 except the first in $F(B_1)$ are assigned higher values than the first element of $F(B_1)$. This results in an adapted solution
  $\text{sol}_2^{**}(B_2, b_3, k_3) =$
  $\text{sol}_2^{**}(B_2, [first(B_2)]^{sol*}, [first(B_1)]^{sol*}) =$
  $([s_1^{B_2}]^{sol**} = a_1^{B_2} + 1 + [first(B_1)]^{sol*}, \ldots,$

$$[s_r^{B_2}]^{sol**} = a_r^{B_2} + 1 + [first(B_1)]^{sol*},$$
$$[s_{end}^{B_2}]^{sol**} = a_{end}^{B_2} + 1 + [first(B_1)]^{sol*},$$
$$[s_{r+2}^{B_2}]^{sol**} = a_{r+2}^{B_2} + 1 + [first(B_1)]^{sol*}, \ldots,$$
$$[s_{n_2}^{B_2}]^{sol**} = a_{n_2}^{B_2} + 1 + [first(B_1)]^{sol*}) \text{ to } CSP_{B_2} \text{ with}$$
$$M_2^{**} = \{a_1^{B_2}, \ldots, a_{n_2}^{B_2} + 1, a_{n_2}^{B_2} + 1 + [first(B_1)]^{sol*}\} \subseteq \mathbb{N}.$$

- For case (ii) the shift is done analogously to case (i) with B_1 and B_2 switched.

- These shifts for either case (i) or (ii) are repeated with (i) $F(B_1) \setminus first(B_1) \bowtie F(B_2)$ or (ii) $F(B_1) \bowtie F(B_2) \setminus first(B_2)$ until $rest_1, rest_2 = \emptyset$, such that all elements of $F(B_1)$ and $F(B_2)$ are assigned ascending and distinct values in the combined solution, resulting in solutions $\texttt{sol}_1^+(B_1, b_1^+, k_1^+)$ to CSP_{B_1} with M_1^+ and $\texttt{sol}_2^+(B_2, b_2^+, k_2^+)$ to CSP_{B_2} with M_2^+.

- Then, one partial shift of both $\texttt{sol}_1^+(B_1)$ and $\texttt{sol}_2^+(B_2)$ is necessary, such that $[cj]^{sol} = [s_{end}^{B_1}]^{sol+} + [s_{end}^{B_2}]^{sol+}$ in the combined solution and to ensure the *alldifferent* constraint:

  a) $\texttt{sol}_1^+(B_1, b_1^+, k_1^+)$ is shifted by an offset $k_4 = 1$ and threshold $b_4 = [s_{end}^{B_1}]^{sol+}$, such that all elements that are not part of $F(B_1)$ are assigned higher values than cj.
  This results in an adapted solution
  $\texttt{sol}_1^{++}(B_1, b_4, k_4) = \texttt{sol}_1^{++}(B_1, [s_{end}^{B_1}]^{sol+}, 1) =$
  $([s_1^{B_1}]^{sol++} = [s_1^{B_1}]^{sol+}, \ldots, [s_q^{B_1}]^{sol++} = [s_q^{B_1}]^{sol+},$
  $[s_{end}^{B_1}]^{sol++} = [s_{end}^{B_1}]^{sol+} + 1, [s_{q+2}^{B_1}]^{sol++} = [s_{q+2}^{B_1}]^{sol+} + 1, \ldots,$
  $[s_{n_1}^{B_1}]^{sol++} = [s_{n_1}^{B_1}]^{sol+} + 1)$
  to CSP_{B_1} with $M_1^{++} = \{a_1^{B_1}, \ldots, [s_{n_1}^{B_1}]^{sol+} + 1\} \subseteq \mathbb{N}$.

  b) Analogously, $\texttt{sol}_2^+(B_2, b_2^+, k_2^+)$ is shifted by an offset $k_5 = 1$ and threshold $b_5 = [s_{end}^{B_2}]^{sol+}$, such that all elements that are not part of $F(B_2)$ are assigned higher values than cj.
  This results in an adapted solution
  $\texttt{sol}_2^{++}(B_2, b_5, k_5) = \texttt{sol}_2^{++}(B_2, [s_{end}^{B_2}]^{sol+}, 1) =$
  $([s_1^{B_2}]^{sol++} = [s_1^{B_2}]^{sol+}, \ldots, [s_r^{B_2}]^{sol++} = [s_r^{B_2}]^{sol+},$
  $[s_{end}^{B_2}]^{sol++} = [s_{end}^{B_2}]^{sol+} + 1, [s_{r+2}^{B_2}]^{sol++} = [s_{r+2}^{B_2}]^{sol+} + 1, \ldots,$
  $[s_{n_2}^{B_2}]^{sol++} = [s_{n_2}^{B_2}]^{sol+} + 1)$
  to CSP_{B_2} with $M_2^{++} = \{a_1^{B_2}, \ldots, [s_{n_2}^{B_2}]^{sol+} + 1\} \subseteq \mathbb{N}$.

- Lastly, solution $\texttt{sol}_2^{++}(B_2, b_5, k_5)$ is shifted by an offset $k_6 = [s_{n_1}^{B_1}]^{sol++}$ and threshold $b_6 = [s_{end}^{B_2}]^{sol++}$, such that all elements

of B_2 that are not part of $F(B_2)$ are assigned higher values than the elements of B_1 to ensure the *alldifferent* constraint. This results in an adapted solution
$\text{sol}_2^{+++}(B_2, b_6, k_6) = \text{sol}_2^{+++}(B_2, [s_{end}^{B_2}]^{sol++}, [s_{n_1}^{B_1}]^{sol++}) =$
$([s_1^{B_2}]^{sol+++} = [s_1^{B_2}]^{sol+}, \ldots, [s_r^{B_2}]^{sol+++} = [s_r^{B_2}]^{sol+},$
$[s_{end}^{B_2}]^{sol+++} = [s_{end}^{B_2}]^{sol+} + 1 + [s_{n_1}^{B_1}]^{sol++},$
$[s_{r+2}^{B_2}]^{sol+++} = [s_{r+2}^{B_2}]^{sol+} + 1 + [s_{n_1}^{B_1}]^{sol++}, \ldots,$
$[s_{n_2}^{B_2}]^{sol+++} = [s_{n_2}^{B_2}]^{sol+} + 1 + [s_{n_1}^{B_1}]^{sol++})$ to CSP_{B_2}
with $M_2^{+++} = \{a_1^{B_2}, \ldots, [s_{n_2}^{B_2}]^{sol+} + 1 + [s_{n_1}^{B_1}]^{sol++}\} \subseteq \mathbb{N}$.

- In the combined solution only one variable is necessary, that marks the end of the de facto workflow. Thus, $s_{end}^{B_2}$ is ignored and $s_{end}^{B_1}$ marks the end of the workflow.

- The combined solution $\text{sol}_0(B)$ is constructed by
$\text{sol}_0(B) = \text{sol}_1^{++}(B_1, b_4, k_4) \cup (\text{sol}_2^{+++}(B_2, b_6, k_6) \setminus \{[s_{end}^{B_2}]^{sol+++}\}) \cup \{[cs]^{sol} = 1, [cj]^{sol} = [s_{end}^{B_1}]^{sol+} + [s_{end}^{B_2}]^{sol+}\}$
to CSP_B with $M = M_1^{++} \cup M_2^{+++} \cup \{1\} = \{1, a_1^{B_1}, \ldots, [s_{n_1}^{B_1}]^{sol+} + 1, a_1^{B_2}, \ldots, [s_{n_2}^{B_2}]^{sol+} + 1 + [s_{n_1}^{B_1}]^{sol++}\} \subseteq \mathbb{N}$
such that conditions 1 and 2 hold.

□

Case 5: $B = B_{XOR}^{B_1}$. Let B be a single-branch exclusive control-flow block containing one workflow block B_1 with $|N_{B_1}^S| = n_1$.

- Let $F(B) \in \mathcal{F}(B) := \{\langle cs, cj \rangle\} \cup \{\langle cs \rangle\} \odot \mathcal{F}(B_1) \odot \{\langle cj \rangle\}$, then either

  (i) $F(B) = \langle cs \rangle \circ \langle cj \rangle$ or

  (ii) $F(B) = \langle cs \rangle \circ F(B_1) \circ \langle cj \rangle$

  with $F(B_1) \in \mathcal{F}(B_1)$ but never both, according to Definition 4.22.

- Let $F(B_1) = \langle s_1^{B_1}, \ldots, s_q^{B_1} \rangle$.

- Due to the induction hypothesis, there exists a solution
$\text{sol}_1(B_1) = ([s_1^{B_1}]^{sol} = a_1^{B_1}, \ldots, [s_q^{B_1}]^{sol} = a_q^{B_1}, [s_{end}^{B_1}]^{sol} = a_{end}^{B_1},$
$[s_{q+2}^{B_1}]^{sol} = a_{q+2}^{B_1}, \ldots, [s_{n_1}^{B_1}]^{sol} = a_{n_1}^{B_1})$ to CSP_{B_1} with $M_1 = \{a_1^{B_1}, \ldots, a_{n_1}^{B_1}\} \subseteq \mathbb{N}$, such that conditions 1 and 2 hold, as $\forall l \in \{1, \ldots, q-1\} : a_l < a_{l+1} < a_{end}$ and $\forall p \in \{1, \ldots, n_1\} \setminus \{1, \ldots, q\} : a_p > a_{end}$.

- For case (i):

    a) The combined execution path is: $F(B) = \langle cs, cj \rangle$.

    b) To fulfil the necessary conditions, the solution $\text{sol}(B_1)$ is shifted.

    c) $\text{sol}_1(B_1)$ is shifted by an offset $k_1 = 3$ and threshold $b_1 = [s_1^{B_1}]^{sol}$, such that all elements of B_1 are assigned higher values than cj.
    This results in an adapted solution
    $\text{sol}_1^*(B_1, b_1, k_1) = \text{sol}_1^*(B_1, [s_1^{B_1}]^{sol}, 3) =$
    $([s_1^{B_1}]^{sol*} = a_1^{B_1} + 3, \ldots, [s_q^{B_1}]^{sol*} = a_q^{B_1} + 3,$
    $[s_{end}^{B_1}]^{sol*} = a_{end}^{B_1} + 3, [s_{q+2}^{B_1}]^{sol*} = a_{q+2}^{B_1} + 3, \ldots,$
    $[s_{n_1}^{B_1}]^{sol*} = a_{n_1}^{B_1} + 3)$
    to CSP_{B_1} with $M_1^* = \{a_1^{B_1}, \ldots, a_{n_1}^{B_1} + 3\} \subseteq \mathbb{N}$.

    d) For the combined solution, a new variable s_{end} is introduced that marks the end of the workflow instance, whereas $s_{end}^{B_1}$ is ignored.

    e) The overall solution $\text{sol}_0(B)$ is constructed by
    $\text{sol}_0(B) = (\text{sol}_1^*(B_1, b_1, k_1) \setminus \{[s_{end}^{B_2}]^{sol*}\}) \cup$
    $\{[cs]^{sol} = 1, [cj]^{sol} = 2, [s_{end}]^{sol} = 3\} =$
    $([cs]^{sol} = 1, [cj]^{sol} = 2, [s_{end}]^{sol} = 3, [s_1^{B_1}]^{sol*} = a_1^{B_1} + 3, \ldots,$
    $[s_q^{B_1}]^{sol*} = a_q^{B_1} + 3, [s_{end}^{B_1}]^{sol*} = a_{end}^{B_1} + 3, [s_{q+2}^{B_1}]^{sol*} = a_{q+2}^{B_1} + 3, \ldots, [s_{n_1}^{B_1}]^{sol*} = a_{n_1}^{B_1} + 3)$
    to CSP_B with $M = M_1^* \cup \{1, 2, 3\} \subseteq \mathbb{N}$ such that conditions 1 and 2 hold.

- For case (ii):

    a) The combined execution path is:
    $F(B) = \langle cs, s_1^{B_1}, \ldots, s_q^{B_1}, cj \rangle$.

    b) In order to create a combined solution $\text{sol}(B)$ for the overall execution path $F(B)$ that fulfils the necessary conditions and constraints, several shifts of the single solutions for B_1 are required.

    c) $\text{sol}_1(B_1)$ is shifted by an offset $k_1 = 1$ and threshold $b_1 = [s_1^{B_1}]^{sol}$, such that cs can be assigned the value 1 in the combined solution and all values of the elements of B_1 are higher than this value.

This results in an adapted solution
$\text{sol}_1^*(B_1, b_1, k_1) = \text{sol}_1^*(B_1, [s_1^{B_1}]^{sol}, 1) =$
$([s_1^{B_1}]^{sol*} = a_1^{B_1} + 1, \ldots, [s_q^{B_1}]^{sol*} = a_q^{B_1} + 1,$
$[s_{end}^{B_1}]^{sol*} = a_{end}^{B_1} + 1, [s_{q+2}^{B_1}]^{sol*} = a_{q+2}^{B_1} + 1, \ldots,$
$[s_{n_1}^{B_1}]^{sol*} = a_{n_1}^{B_1} + 1)$
to CSP_{B_1} with $M_1^* = \{a_1^{B_1}, \ldots, a_{n_1}^{B_1} + 1\} \subseteq \mathbb{N}$.

d) $\text{sol}_1^*(B_1, b_1, k_1)$ is again shifted by an offset $k_2 = 1$ and threshold $b_2 = [s_{end}^{B_1}]^{sol*}$, such that cj can be assigned the value $[s_q^{B_1}]^{sol*} + 1$ in the combined solution and the values of all elements that are not part of $F(B_1)$ are increased by one to ensure the *alldifferent* constraint.
This results in an adapted solution
$\text{sol}_1^{**}(B_1, b_2, k_2) = \text{sol}_1^{**}(B_1, [s_{end}^{B_1}]^{sol*}, 1) =$
$([s_1^{B_1}]^{sol**} = a_1^{B_1} + 1, \ldots, [s_q^{B_1}]^{sol**} = a_q^{B_1} + 1,$
$[s_{end}^{B_1}]^{sol**} = a_{end}^{B_1} + 2, [s_{q+2}^{B_1}]^{sol**} = a_{q+2}^{B_1} + 2, \ldots,$
$[s_{n_1}^{B_1}]^{sol**} = a_{n_1}^{B_1} + 2)$
to CSP_{B_1} with $M_1^{**} = \{a_1^{B_1}, \ldots, a_{n_1}^{B_1} + 2\} \subseteq \mathbb{N}$.

e) The overall solution $\text{sol}_0(B)$ is constructed by
$\text{sol}_0(B) = \text{sol}^{**}_1(B_1, b_2, k_2) \cup$
$\{[cs]^{sol} = 1, [cj]^{sol} = [s_q^{B_1}]^{sol} + 2\} = ([cs]^{sol} = 1,$
$[s_1^{B_1}]^{sol**} = a_1^{B_1} + 1, \ldots, [s_q^{B_1}]^{sol**} = a_q^{B_1} + 1,$
$[cj]^{sol} = a_q^{B_1} + 2, [s_{end}^{B_1}]^{sol**} = a_{end}^{B_1} + 2,$
$[s_{q+2}^{B_1}]^{sol**} = a_{q+2}^{B_1} + 2, \ldots, [s_{n_1}^{B_1}]^{sol**} = a_{n_1}^{B_1} + 2)$
to CSP_B with $M = M_1^{**} \cup \{1\} = \{1, a_1^{B_1}, \ldots, a_{n_1}^{B_1} + 2\} \subseteq \mathbb{N}$
such that conditions 1 and 2 hold.

□

Proof. As a block-oriented workflow W consists of a single root block element B, Theorem 1 holds for whole block-oriented workflows. □

Appendix B
List of Variables

Table B.1: Variable Descriptions of Chapter 4

Variable	Formula	Description	Reference
G	(N, E)	directed graph with nodes and edges	69
W	(N, E)	workflow with nodes and edges	70
N^T		task nodes	70
N^D		data nodes	70
N^C		control-flow nodes	70
N^S	$N^T \cup N^C$	sequence nodes	70
E^C		control-flow edges	70
E^D		data-flow edges	70
B	(N_B^S, E_B^C)	workflow block	71
B^t		single task block	72
$B^{(B_1, B_2)}$		sequence block	72
$B_{AND/XOR}^{(B_1, B_2)}$		control-flow block	73
$B_{XOR}^{B_1}$		single-branch exclusive block	73
F_i	$\langle f_1, \ldots, f_n \rangle$	execution path	75
$\mathcal{F}$	$\{F_1, \ldots, F_m\}$	execution path set	75
	$F_1 \circ F_2$	sequential execution paths	75
	$\mathcal{F}_1 \odot \mathcal{F}_2$	sequential combination of execution path sets	75
	$F_1 \bowtie F_2$	parallel execution paths	75
	$\mathcal{F}_1 | \mathcal{F}_2$	parallel combination of execution path sets	76
$\mathcal{F}(W)$		execution path set of workflows	76

Table B.2: Variable Descriptions of Chapter 5

Variable	Formula	Description	Reference
J	(N_J, E_J)	de jure workflow	83
P		constraints of workflow model	84
F	(N_F, E_F)	de facto workflow	89
CSP_W	(X, D, C)	constraint problem for workflow engine	90
S'	$\{s_i \mid s_i \in N_B^S\}$	decision variables for sequence nodes	91
S	$S' \cup \{s_{end}\}$	decision variables for sequential control-flow	91
D_{s_i}		domains for sequence nodes	93
C	$\{\text{alldifferent}(S)\} \cup C^M \cup C^A \cup C^I$	constraint net	95
C^M	$Dec(J) \cup C^{CF} \cup C^{DF}$	model constraints	96
C^{DF}		data-flow constraints	97
A	$\{a_1, \ldots, a_n\}$	control variables	97
X	$S \cup A$	decision variables	97
D_a	$\{true, false\}$	domains for control variables	97
C^{CF}		control-flow constraints	98
C^A		additional constraints of P	98
C^I		instance constraints	99
$not(B, s_{end})$		auxiliary function	99
$Dec(B, s_{end})$		transformation function	100
$B_{LOOP}^{B_1}$		loop block	106
$Status(c)$	$\in \{indefinite, valid, violated\}$	status of a constraint	111

Table B.3: Variable Descriptions of Chapter 6

Variable	Formula	Description	Reference
W	(N, E, S, T)	NESTGraph	130
J_C	(N_J, E_J, S_J, T_J)	de jure workflow of case as NESTGraph	147
WC	$(J_C, F_C, CSP_C, \text{sol}_C)$	workflow case	147
CB		case base	148
Q	$(J_Q, F_Q, CSP_Q, \text{sol}_Q)$	query	148
id^b		block ids	154
ids^b		block ids of task	154
op		block operators	156
$levels$		ids of levels for tasks	154
T_{id}		set of tasks for a specific id	156
$N_F^{consistent}$		model-consistent task nodes	157
$N_F^{reduced}$	$N_F \setminus N_F^{consistent}$	reduced node set of task nodes, not consistent	157
$E_F^{reduced}$		reduced and reconnected set of edges	157
$F^{reduced}$		reduced de facto workflow	158
$sim_N(n^Q, n^C)$		node similarity	160
$N_t^{D_{in}}$		set of incoming data nodes for a task	160
$N_t^{D_{out}}$		set of outgoing data nodes for a task	160
$sim_T(t^Q, t^C)$		local task similarity	160
H	$(h_{i,j})$	scoring matrix	161

$penaltyInsertion(t_i^Q)$		gap penalty for insertion	162
$penaltyDeletion(t_i^C)$		gap penalty for deletion	162
$wTemp_i$	$\frac{1}{2^{n-i}_h}$	temporal weighting factor	162
$sim_{raw}(F_Q, F_C)$		raw similarity score	162
$sim_F^{SWA/DTW}(F_Q, F_C)$		normalized similarity score	163
$workItems$		work items	165
C^D		derived constraints	176
$C_{C/Q}^{extended}$	$C_{C/Q} \cup C_{C/Q}^D$	extended set of constraints	176
$C_C^{relational}$	$C_C^{extended} \setminus C_C^I$	relational set of constraints	176
$Orig$	$\in \{query, case\}$	origin of constraint	176
$Type$	$\in \{model, additional, instance, derived\}$	type of constraint	176
X_Q^*	$X_Q \cup X_C$	extended set of decision variables	177
D_Q^*		extended domains	177
C_Q^{valid}		valid constraints	177
$C_C^{conflicting}$		conflicting constraints	178
$C_C^{validated}$	$C_C^{relational} \setminus C_C^{conflicting}$	validated constraints	178
$C_C^{directlyRelated}$		constraints directly related to deviating task	179
$N_C^{T_{directlyRelated}}$		tasks that are directly related to deviating task through constraints	179

$C_Q^{related+}$	related and valid constraints of case	179
$C_Q^{related-}$	related and violated constraints of case	180
$C_Q^{violated}$	violated constraints from query resulting from $C_Q^{related-}$	180
C_Q^*	adapted constraint net	180

Table B.4: Variable Descriptions of Appendix A

Variable	Formula	Description	Reference
$\text{sol}(B)$		solution	259
CSP_B^*		adapted CSP with	260
k		offset	260
b		threshold	260
$\text{sol}^*(B)$		adapted solution	260

Appendix C

Curriculum Vitae

Personal Details

Name	Lisa Grumbach
E-Mail	lisa.grumbach@dfki.de
ORCID	0000-0002-2247-8270

Work Experience

11/2021 - today   German Research Center for Artificial Intelligence, Branch Trier, Germany
Researcher at the Department of Smart Data & Knowledge Services, Topic Field: Experience-Based Learning Systems

07/2017 - 10/2021   Trier University of Applied Sciences, Environmental Campus Birkenfeld, Germany
Research Associate

09/2015 - 06/2017   Trier University, Trier, Germany
Research Associate at the Department of Business Information Systems II

10/2012 - 08/2015 Trier University of Applied Sciences, Trier, Germany
Assistant at the Department of Computer Science

Education

09/2012 - 07/2015 Trier University of Applied Sciences, Trier, Germany
Business Information Systems - Information Management Studies (**M.Sc.**)

08/2011 - 12/2011 University of Technology, Sydney, Australia
Study Abroad Semester in Computer Science

09/2009 - 09/2012 Trier University of Applied Sciences, Trier, Germany
Computer Science Studies (**B.Sc.**)

08/2000 - 03/2009 Angela-Merici-Gymnasium, Trier, Germany
Higher Education Entrance Qualification (**Abitur**)

Bibliography

[1] Agnar Aamodt and Enric Plaza. Case-Based Reasoning: Foundational Issues, Methodological Variations, and System Approaches. *AI Commun.*, 7(1):39–59, 1994.

[2] Michael Adams, Andreas V. Hense, and Arthur H. M. ter Hofstede. YAWL: an open source business process management system from science for science. *SoftwareX*, 12:100576, 2020.

[3] Michael Adams, Arthur H. M. ter Hofstede, David Edmond, and Wil M. P. van der Aalst. Worklets: A Service-Oriented Implementation of Dynamic Flexibility in Workflows. In Robert Meersman and Zahir Tari, editors, *On the Move to Meaningful Internet Systems 2006: CoopIS, DOA, GADA, and ODBASE, OTM Confederated International Conferences, CoopIS, DOA, GADA, and ODBASE 2006, Montpellier, France, October 29 - November 3, 2006. Proceedings, Part I*, volume 4275 of *Lecture Notes in Computer Science*, pages 291–308. Springer, 2006.

[4] Michael Adams, Arthur H. M. ter Hofstede, Wil M. P. van der Aalst, and David Edmond. Dynamic, Extensible and Context-Aware Exception Handling for Workflows. In Robert Meersman and Zahir Tari, editors, *On the Move to Meaningful Internet Systems 2007: CoopIS, DOA, ODBASE, GADA, and IS, OTM Confederated International Conferences CoopIS, DOA, ODBASE, GADA, and IS 2007, Vilamoura, Portugal, November 25-30, 2007, Proceedings, Part I*, volume 4803 of *Lecture Notes in Computer Science*, pages 95–112. Springer, 2007.

[5] Rakesh Agrawal, Christos Faloutsos, and Arun N. Swami. Efficient Similarity Search In Sequence Databases. In David B. Lomet, editor, *Foundations of Data Organization and Algorithms, 4th International Conference, FODO'93, Chicago, Illinois, USA,*

October 13-15, 1993, Proceedings, volume 730 of *Lecture Notes in Computer Science*, pages 69–84. Springer, 1993.

[6] European Digital SME Alliance. Manifesto for Europe's Digital Future - A Way Forward for the EU Mandate 2019-2024, 2019. https://www.eesc.europa.eu/sites/default/files/files/manifesto_for_eu_digital_future.pdf, accessed on 05 December 2022.

[7] Gustavo Alonso, Divyakant Agrawal, Amr El Abbadi, and C. Mohan. Functionality and Limitations of Current Workflow Management Systems. *IEEE Expert*, 12, 1997.

[8] Steven Alter. Theory of Workarounds. *CAIS*, 34:55, 2014.

[9] Tony Andrews, Francisco Curbera, Hitesh Dholakia, Yaron Goland, Johannes Klein, Frank Leymann, Kevin Liu, Dieter Roller, Doug Smith, Satish Thatte, Ivana Trickovic, and Sanjiva Weerawarana. Business Process Execution Language for Web Services, Version 1.1. Technical report, BEA Systems, International Business Machines Corporation, Microsoft Corporation, 2003.

[10] Kerstin Bach, Tomasz Szczepanski, Agnar Aamodt, Odd Erik Gundersen, and Paul Jarle Mork. Case Representation and Similarity Assessment in the selfBACK Decision Support System. In Ashok K. Goel, M. Belén Díaz-Agudo, and Thomas Roth-Berghofer, editors, *Case-Based Reasoning Research and Development - 24th International Conference, ICCBR 2016, Atlanta, GA, USA, October 31 - November 2, 2016, Proceedings*, volume 9969 of *Lecture Notes in Computer Science*, pages 32–46. Springer, 2016.

[11] Irene Barba, Andreas Lanz, Barbara Weber, Manfred Reichert, and Carmelo Del Valle. Optimized Time Management for Declarative Workflows. In Ilia Bider, Terry A. Halpin, John Krogstie, Selmin Nurcan, Erik Proper, Rainer Schmidt, Pnina Soffer, and Stanislaw Wrycza, editors, *Enterprise, Business-Process and Information Systems Modeling - 13th International Conference, BPMDS 2012, 17th International Conference, EMMSAD 2012, and 5th EuroSymposium, held at CAiSE 2012, Gdańsk, Poland, June 25-26, 2012. Proceedings*, volume 113 of *Lecture Notes in Business Information Processing*, pages 195–210. Springer, 2012.

[12] Ralph Bergmann. *Experience Management: Foundations, Development Methodology, and Internet-Based Applications*, volume 2432 of *Lecture Notes in Computer Science*. Springer, 2002.

[13] Ralph Bergmann, Klaus-Dieter Althoff, Mirjam Minor, Meike Reichle, and Kerstin Bach. Case-based reasoning. *Künstliche Intell.*, 23(1):5–11, 2009.

[14] Ralph Bergmann, Sarah Gessinger, Sebastian Görg, and Gilbert Müller. The Collaborative Agile Knowledge Engine CAKE. In Sean P. Goggins, Isa Jahnke, David W. McDonald, and Pernille Bjørn, editors, *Proceedings of the 18th International Conference on Supporting Group Work, Sanibel Island, FL, USA, November 09 - 12, 2014*, pages 281–284. ACM, 2014.

[15] Ralph Bergmann and Yolanda Gil. Similarity assessment and efficient retrieval of semantic workflows. *Inf. Syst.*, 40:115–127, 2014.

[16] Ralph Bergmann, Lisa Grumbach, Lukas Malburg, and Christian Zeyen. ProCAKE: A Process-Oriented Case-Based Reasoning Framework. In Stelios Kapetanakis and Hayley Borck, editors, *Workshops Proceedings for the Twenty-seventh International Conference on Case-Based Reasoning co-located with the Twenty-seventh International Conference on Case-Based Reasoning (ICCBR 2019), Otzenhausen, Germany, September 8-12, 2019*, volume 2567 of *CEUR Workshop Proceedings*, pages 156–161. CEUR-WS.org, 2019.

[17] Ralph Bergmann and Alexander Stromer. MAC/FAC Retrieval of Semantic Workflows. In Chutima Boonthum-Denecke and G. Michael Youngblood, editors, *Proceedings of the Twenty-Sixth International Florida Artificial Intelligence Research Society Conference, FLAIRS 2013, St. Pete Beach, Florida, USA, May 22-24, 2013*. AAAI Press, 2013.

[18] Donald J. Berndt and James Clifford. Using Dynamic Time Warping to Find Patterns in Time Series. In Usama M. Fayyad and Ramasamy Uthurusamy, editors, *Knowledge Discovery in Databases: Papers from the 1994 AAAI Workshop, Seattle, Washington, USA, July 1994. Technical Report WS-94-03*, pages 359–370. AAAI Press, 1994.

[19] Ilia Bider. Masking flexibility behind rigidity: Notes on how much flexibility people are willing to cope with. In *Proceedings of the Conference on Advanced Information Systems Engineering*, volume 5, pages 7–18, 2005.

[20] Thomas Burkhart and Peter Loos. Flexible Business Processes - Evaluation of Current Approaches. In Matthias Schumann, Lutz M. Kolbe, Michael H. Breitner, and Arne Frerichs, editors, *Multikonferenz Wirtschaftsinformatik, MKWI 2010, Göttingen, Deutschland, 23.-25.2.2010, Proceedings*, pages 1217–1228. Universitätsverlag Göttingen, 2010.

[21] Federico Cabitza and Carla Simone. "Drops Hollowing the Stone": Workarounds as Resources for Better Task-Artifact Fit. In Olav W. Bertelsen, Luigina Ciolfi, Maria Antonietta Grasso, and George Angelos Papadopoulos, editors, *ECSCW 2013: Proceedings of the 13th European Conference on Computer Supported Cooperative Work, 21-25 September 2013, Paphos, Cyprus*, pages 103–122. Springer, 2013.

[22] Fabio Casati, Stefano Ceri, Stefano Paraboschi, and Giuseppe Pozzi. Specification and Implementation of Exceptions in Workflow Management Systems. *ACM Trans. Database Syst.*, 24(3):405–451, 1999.

[23] Carolina Ming Chiao, Vera Künzle, and Manfred Reichert. Enhancing the Case Handling Paradigm to Support Object-aware Processes. In Rafael Accorsi, Paolo Ceravolo, and Philippe Cudré-Mauroux, editors, *Proceedings of the 3rd International Symposium on Data-driven Process Discovery and Analysis, Riva del Garda, Italy, August 30, 2013*, volume 1027 of *CEUR Workshop Proceedings*, pages 89–103. CEUR-WS.org, 2013.

[24] Claudio Di Ciccio, Fabrizio Maria Maggi, Marco Montali, and Jan Mendling. Resolving inconsistencies and redundancies in declarative process models. *Inf. Syst.*, 64:425–446, 2017.

[25] Claudio Di Ciccio, Andrea Marrella, and Alessandro Russo. Knowledge-Intensive Processes: Characteristics, Requirements and Analysis of Contemporary Approaches. *J. Data Semant.*, 4(1):29–57, 2015.

[26] Amélie Cordier, Marie Lefèvre, Pierre-Antoine Champin, Olivier L. Georgeon, and Alain Mille. Trace-Based Reason-

ing - Modeling Interaction Traces for Reasoning on Experiences. In Chutima Boonthum-Denecke and G. Michael Youngblood, editors, *Proceedings of the Twenty-Sixth International Florida Artificial Intelligence Research Society Conference, FLAIRS 2013, St. Pete Beach, Florida, USA, May 22-24, 2013*. AAAI Press, 2013.

[27] Thomas H. Cormen, Charles E. Leiserson, Ronald L. Rivest, and Clifford Stein. *Introduction to Algorithms, 3rd Edition*. MIT Press, 2009.

[28] Gianpaolo Cugola. Tolerating Deviations in Process Support Systems via Flexible Enactment of Process Models. *IEEE Transactions on Software Engineering*, 24(11):982–1001, 1998.

[29] Marcos Aurélio Almeida da Silva, Reda Bendraou, Jacques Robin, and Xavier Blanc. Flexible Deviation Handling during Software Process Enactment. In *Workshops Proceedings of the 15th IEEE International Enterprise Distributed Object Computing Conference, EDOCW 2011, Helsinki, Finland, August 29 - September 2, 2011*, pages 34–41. IEEE Computer Society, 2011.

[30] Peter Dadam, Manfred Reichert, Stefanie Rinderle, Martin Jurisch, Hilmar Acker, Kevin Göser, Ulrich Kreher, and Markus Lauer. Towards Truly Flexible and Adaptive Process-Aware Information Systems. In Roland H. Kaschek, Christian Kop, Claudia Steinberger, and Günther Fliedl, editors, *Information Systems and e-Business Technologies, 2nd International United Information Systems Conference, UNISCON 2008, Klagenfurt, Austria, April 22-25, 2008, Proceedings*, volume 5 of *Lecture Notes in Business Information Processing*, pages 72–83. Springer, 2008.

[31] Peter Dadam, Manfred Reichert, and Stefanie Rinderle-Ma. Prozessmanagementsysteme - Nur ein wenig Flexibilität wird nicht reichen. *Informatik Spektrum*, 34(4):364–376, 2011.

[32] Peter Dadam, Manfred Reichert, Stefanie Rinderle-Ma, Andreas Lanz, Rüdiger Pryss, Michael Predeschly, Jens Kolb, Linh Thao Ly, Martin Jurisch, Ulrich Kreher, and Kevin Göser. From ADEPT to AristaFlow BPM Suite: A Research Vision Has Become Reality. In Stefanie Rinderle-Ma, Shazia Wasim Sadiq, and Frank Leymann, editors, *Business Process Management*

Workshops, BPM 2009 International Workshops, Ulm, Germany, September 7, 2009. Revised Papers, volume 43 of *Lecture Notes in Business Information Processing*, pages 529–531. Springer, 2009.

[33] Renata Medeiros de Carvalho, Natália Cabral Silva, Ricardo Massa Ferreira Lima, and Márcio Cornélio. ReFlex: An Efficient Graph-Based Rule Engine to Execute Declarative Processes. In *IEEE International Conference on Systems, Man, and Cybernetics, Manchester, SMC 2013, United Kingdom, October 13-16, 2013*, pages 1379–1384. IEEE, 2013.

[34] Rina Dechter and Avi Dechter. Belief Maintenance in Dynamic Constraint Networks. In Howard E. Shrobe, Tom M. Mitchell, and Reid G. Smith, editors, *Proceedings of the 7th National Conference on Artificial Intelligence, St. Paul, MN, USA, August 21-26, 1988*, pages 37–42. AAAI Press / The MIT Press, 1988.

[35] Benoît Depaire, Jo Swinnen, Mieke Jans, and Koen Vanhoof. A Process Deviation Analysis Framework. In Marcello La Rosa and Pnina Soffer, editors, *Business Process Management Workshops - BPM 2012 International Workshops, Tallinn, Estonia, September 3, 2012. Revised Papers*, volume 132 of *Lecture Notes in Business Information Processing*, pages 701–706. Springer, 2012.

[36] Telekom Deutschland and techconsult. Digitalisierungsindex Mittelstand 2018, November 2018. `https://www.telekom.com/resource/blob/553602/e4618ce5f3eb5e4601979550b994a3d5/dl-digitalisierungsindex-2018-zusammenfassung-data.pdf`, accessed on 05 December 2022.

[37] Remco M. Dijkman, Marlon Dumas, Boudewijn F. van Dongen, Reina Käärik, and Jan Mendling. Similarity of business process models: Metrics and evaluation. *Inf. Syst.*, 36(2):498–516, 2011.

[38] Markus Döhring, Axel Schulz, and Ivan Galkin. Emulating Runtime Workflow Adaptation and Aspect Weaving by Recursive Rule-Based Sub-Process Selection - A Model Transformation Approach. In Chi-Hung Chi, Dragan Gasevic, and Willem-Jan van den Heuvel, editors, *16th IEEE International Enterprise Distributed Object Computing Conference, EDOC 2012, Beijing,*

China, September 10-14, 2012, pages 133–142. IEEE Computer Society, 2012.

[39] Markus Döhring and Birgit Zimmermann. vBPMN: Event-Aware Workflow Variants by Weaving BPMN2 and Business Rules. In Terry A. Halpin, Selmin Nurcan, John Krogstie, Pnina Soffer, Erik Proper, Rainer Schmidt, and Ilia Bider, editors, *Enterprise, Business-Process and Information Systems Modeling - 12th International Conference, BPMDS 2011, and 16th International Conference, EMMSAD 2011, held at CAiSE 2011, London, UK, June 20-21, 2011. Proceedings*, volume 81 of *Lecture Notes in Business Information Processing*, pages 332–341. Springer, 2011.

[40] Markus Döhring, Birgit Zimmermann, and Eicke Godehardt. Extended Workflow Flexibility using Rule-Based Adaptation Patterns with Eventing Semantics. In Klaus-Peter Fähnrich and Bogdan Franczyk, editors, *Informatik 2010: Service Science - Neue Perspektiven für die Informatik, Beiträge der 40. Jahrestagung der Gesellschaft für Informatik e.V. (GI), Band 1, 27.09. - 1.10.2010, Leipzig, Deutschland*, volume P-175 of *LNI*, pages 195–200. GI, 2010.

[41] Paul Dourish, Jim Holmes, Allan MacLean, Pernille Marqvardsen, and Alex Zbyslaw. Freeflow: Mediating Between Representation and Action in Workflow Systems. In Mark S. Ackerman, Gary M. Olson, and Judith S. Olson, editors, *CSCW '96, Proceedings of the ACM 1996 Conference on Computer Supported Cooperative Work, Boston, MA, USA, November 16-20, 1996*, pages 190–198. ACM, 1996.

[42] Marlon Dumas, Wil M. P. van der Aalst, and Arthur H. M. ter Hofstede, editors. *Process-Aware Information Systems: Bridging People and Software Through Process Technology*. Wiley, 2005.

[43] Johann Eder and Walter Liebhart. The Workflow Activity Model WAMO. In Steve Laufmann, Stefano Spaccapietra, and Toshio Yokoi, editors, *Proceedings of the Third International Conference on Cooperative Information Systems (CoopIS-95), May 9-12, 1995, Schloss Wilhelminenburg Hotel, Vienna, Austria*, pages 87–98, 1995.

[44] Gregor Engels, Alexander Förster, Reiko Heckel, and Sebastian Thöne. Process Modeling Using UML. In Marlon Dumas, Wil

M. P. van der Aalst, and Arthur H. M. ter Hofstede, editors, *Process-Aware Information Systems: Bridging People and Software Through Process Technology*, pages 83–117. Wiley, 2005.

[45] European Commission. What is an SME?, 2019. `https://ec.europa.eu/growth/smes/business-friendly-environment/sme-definition_en`, accessed on 05 December 2022.

[46] Dirk Fahland, Daniel Lübke, Jan Mendling, Hajo A. Reijers, Barbara Weber, Matthias Weidlich, and Stefan Zugal. Declarative versus Imperative Process Modeling Languages: The Issue of Understandability. In Terry A. Halpin, John Krogstie, Selmin Nurcan, Erik Proper, Rainer Schmidt, Pnina Soffer, and Roland Ukor, editors, *Enterprise, Business-Process and Information Systems Modeling, 10th International Workshop, BPMDS 2009, and 14th International Conference, EMMSAD 2009, held at CAiSE 2009, Amsterdam, The Netherlands, June 8-9, 2009. Proceedings*, volume 29 of *Lecture Notes in Business Information Processing*, pages 353–366. Springer, 2009.

[47] Ciara Feely, Brian Caulfield, Aonghus Lawlor, and Barry Smyth. Using Case-Based Reasoning to Predict Marathon Performance and Recommend Tailored Training Plans. In Ian Watson and Rosina O. Weber, editors, *Case-Based Reasoning Research and Development - 28th International Conference, ICCBR 2020, Salamanca, Spain, June 8-12, 2020, Proceedings*, volume 12311 of *Lecture Notes in Computer Science*, pages 67–81. Springer, 2020.

[48] Andreas Gadatsch. *Grundkurs Geschäftsprozess-Management*. Vieweg+Teubner Verlag, Wiesbaden, 2013.

[49] Manuel Gall, Günter Wallner, Simone Kriglstein, and Stefanie Rinderle-Ma. Differencegraph - A ProM Plugin for Calculating and Visualizing Differences between Processes. In Florian Daniel and Stefan Zugal, editors, *Proceedings of the BPM Demo Session 2015 Co-located with the 13th International Conference on Business Process Management (BPM 2015), Innsbruck, Austria, September 2, 2015*, volume 1418 of *CEUR Workshop Proceedings*, pages 65–69. CEUR-WS.org, 2015.

[50] Judith Gebauer and Franz Schober. Information System Flexibility and the Cost Efficiency of Business Processes. *J. Assoc. Inf. Syst.*, 7(3):8, 2006.

[51] Sarah Gessinger and Ralph Bergmann. Flexible Process-Aware Information Systems Deficiency Management in Construction. In Ralph Bergmann, Sebastian Görg, and Gilbert Müller, editors, *Proceedings of the LWA 2015 Workshops: KDML, FGWM, IR, and FGDB, Trier, Germany, October 7-9, 2015*, volume 1458 of *CEUR Workshop Proceedings*, pages 330–338. CEUR-WS.org, 2015.

[52] Sebastian Görg. *Foundations for a Social Workflow Platform*. Springer, 2016.

[53] Gregor Grambow, Roy Oberhauser, and Manfred Reichert. Event-Driven Exception Handling for Software Engineering Processes. In Florian Daniel, Kamel Barkaoui, and Schahram Dustdar, editors, *Business Process Management Workshops - BPM 2011 International Workshops, Clermont-Ferrand, France, August 29, 2011, Revised Selected Papers, Part I*, volume 99 of *Lecture Notes in Business Information Processing*, pages 414–426. Springer, 2011.

[54] Gregor Grambow, Roy Oberhauser, and Manfred Reichert. Semantically-Driven Workflow Generation Using Declarative Modeling for Processes in Software Engineering. In *Workshops Proceedings of the 15th IEEE International Enterprise Distributed Object Computing Conference, EDOCW 2011, Helsinki, Finland, August 29 - September 2, 2011*, pages 164–173. IEEE Computer Society, 2011.

[55] Lisa Grumbach and Ralph Bergmann. Using Constraint Satisfaction Problem Solving to Enable Workflow Flexibility by Deviation (Best Technical Paper). In Max Bramer and Miltos Petridis, editors, *Artificial Intelligence XXXIV - 37th SGAI International Conference on Artificial Intelligence, AI 2017, Cambridge, UK, December 12-14, 2017, Proceedings*, volume 10630 of *Lecture Notes in Computer Science*, pages 3–17. Springer, 2017.

[56] Lisa Grumbach and Ralph Bergmann. Workflow Flexibility by Deviation by means of Constraint Satisfaction Problem Solving. In Michael Leyer, editor, *Lernen, Wissen, Daten, Analysen*

(LWDA) Conference Proceedings, Rostock, Germany, September 11-13, 2017, volume 1917 of *CEUR Workshop Proceedings*, page 212. CEUR-WS.org, 2017.

[57] Lisa Grumbach and Ralph Bergmann. Towards Case-Based Deviation Management for Flexible Workflows. In Robert Jäschke and Matthias Weidlich, editors, *Proceedings of the Conference on "Lernen, Wissen, Daten, Analysen", Berlin, Germany, September 30 - October 2, 2019*, volume 2454 of *CEUR Workshop Proceedings*, pages 241–252. CEUR-WS.org, 2019.

[58] Lisa Grumbach and Ralph Bergmann. SEMAFLEX: A novel approach for implementing workflow flexibility by deviation based on constraint satisfaction problem solving. *Expert Systems - The Journal of Knowledge Engineering*, 38(7), 2021.

[59] Lisa Grumbach, Eric Rietzke, Markus Schwinn, Ralph Bergmann, and Norbert Kuhn. SEMAFLEX - Semantic Integration of Flexible Workflow and Document Management. In Ralf Krestel, Davide Mottin, and Emmanuel Müller, editors, *Proceedings of the Conference "Lernen, Wissen, Daten, Analysen", Potsdam, Germany, September 12-14, 2016.*, volume 1670 of *CEUR Workshop Proceedings*, pages 43–50. CEUR-WS.org, 2016.

[60] Lisa Grumbach, Eric Rietzke, Markus Schwinn, Ralph Bergmann, and Norbert Kuhn. SEMANAS - Semantic Support for Grant Application Processes. In Rainer Gemulla, Simone Paolo Ponzetto, Christian Bizer, Margret Keuper, and Heiner Stuckenschmidt, editors, *Proceedings of the Conference "Lernen, Wissen, Daten, Analysen", LWDA 2018, Mannheim, Germany, August 22-24, 2018.*, volume 2191 of *CEUR Workshop Proceedings*, pages 126–131. CEUR-WS.org, 2018.

[61] Odd Erik Gundersen. Toward Measuring the Similarity of Complex Event Sequences in Real-Time. In Belén Díaz-Agudo and Ian Watson, editors, *Case-Based Reasoning Research and Development - 20th International Conference, ICCBR 2012, Lyon, France, September 3-6, 2012. Proceedings*, volume 7466 of *Lecture Notes in Computer Science*, pages 107–121. Springer, 2012.

[62] Cornelia Haisjackl, Irene Barba, Stefan Zugal, Pnina Soffer, Irit Hadar, Manfred Reichert, Jakob Pinggera, and Barbara Weber.

Understanding Declare models: strategies, pitfalls, empirical results. *Softw. Syst. Model.*, 15(2):325–352, 2016.

[63] Michael Hammer. What is Business Process Management? In Jan vom Brocke and Michael Rosemann, editors, *Handbook on Business Process Management 1, Introduction, Methods, and Information Systems, 2nd Ed*, International Handbooks on Information Systems, pages 3–16. Springer, 2015.

[64] Yanbo Han, Amit Sheth, and Christoph Bussler. A taxonomy of adaptive workflow management. In *Workshop of the ACM 1998 Conference on Computer Supported Cooperative Work*, Seattle, WA, 1998.

[65] Petra Heinl, Stefan Horn, Stefan Jablonski, Jens Neeb, Katrin Stein, and Michael Teschke. A comprehensive approach to flexibility in workflow management systems. In *Proceedings of the international joint conference on Work activities coordination and collaboration 1999, San Francisco, California, USA, February 22-25, 1999*, pages 79–88. ACM, 1999.

[66] Fred Hemery, Christophe Lecoutre, Lakhdar Sais, and Frédéric Boussemart. Extracting MUCs from Constraint Networks. In Gerhard Brewka, Silvia Coradeschi, Anna Perini, and Paolo Traverso, editors, *ECAI 2006, 17th European Conference on Artificial Intelligence, August 29 - September 1, 2006, Riva del Garda, Italy, Including Prestigious Applications of Intelligent Systems (PAIS 2006), Proceedings*, volume 141 of *Frontiers in Artificial Intelligence and Applications*, pages 113–117. IOS Press, 2006.

[67] Miriam Herold and Mirjam Minor. Ontology-based transfer learning in the airport and warehouse logistics domains. In Stelios Kapetanakis and Hayley Borck, editors, *Workshops Proceedings for the Twenty-seventh International Conference on Case-Based Reasoning co-located with the Twenty-seventh International Conference on Case-Based Reasoning (ICCBR 2019), Otzenhausen, Germany, September 8-12, 2019*, volume 2567 of *CEUR Workshop Proceedings*, pages 63–73. CEUR-WS.org, 2019.

[68] Alan Hevner and Samir Chatterjee. *Design Research in Information Systems - Theory and Practice*, volume 22 of *Integrated Series in Information Systems*. Springer US, 2010.

[69] Alan R. Hevner, Salvatore T. March, Jinsoo Park, and Sudha Ram. Design Science in Information Systems Research. *MIS Quarterly*, 28(1):75–105, 2004.

[70] Thomas T. Hildebrandt and Raghava Rao Mukkamala. Declarative Event-Based Workflow as Distributed Dynamic Condition Response Graphs. In Kohei Honda and Alan Mycroft, editors, *Proceedings Third Workshop on Programming Language Approaches to Concurrency and communication-cEntric Software, PLACES 2010, Paphos, Cyprus, 21st March 2010*, volume 69 of *EPTCS*, pages 59–73, 2010.

[71] Carsten Huth, Ingo Erdmann, and Ludwig Nastansky. GroupProcess: Using Process Knowledge from the Participative Design and Practical Operation of ad hoc Processes for the Design of Structured Workflows. In *34th Annual Hawaii International Conference on System Sciences (HICSS-34), January 3-6, 2001, Maui, Hawaii, USA*. IEEE Computer Society, 2001.

[72] San-Yih Hwang and Jian Tang. Consulting past exceptions to facilitate workflow exception handling. *Decision Support Systems*, 37(1):49–69, 2004.

[73] Michael Igler, Paulo Moura, Michael Zeising, and Stefan Jablonski. ESProNa: Constraint-Based Declarative Business Process Modeling. In *Workshops Proceedings of the 14th IEEE International Enterprise Distributed Object Computing Conference, EDOCW 2010, Vitória, Brazil, 25-29 October 2010*, pages 91–98. IEEE Computer Society, 2010.

[74] Gregor Joeris. Defining Flexible Workflow Execution Behaviors. In Peter Dadam and Manfred Reichert, editors, *Workshop Informatik '99: Enterprise-wide and Cross-enterprise Workflow Management: Concepts, Systems, Applications, Paderborn, Germany, October 6, 1999*, volume 24 of *CEUR Workshop Proceedings*, pages 49–55. CEUR-WS.org, 1999.

[75] Håvard D. Jørgensen. Interaction as a framework for flexible workflow modelling. In *Proceedings of GROUP 2001, ACM 2001 International Conference on Supporting Group Work, September*

30 - October 3, 2001, Boulder, Colorado, USA, pages 32–41. ACM, 2001.

[76] Wolfram Jost and August-Wilhelm Scheer. *Geschäftsprozessmanagement: Kernaufgabe einer jeden Unternehmensorganisation*, pages 33–44. Springer Berlin Heidelberg, Berlin, Heidelberg, 2002.

[77] Gerhard Keller, Markus Nüttgens, and August-Wilhlem Scheer. *Semantische Prozessmodellierung auf der Grundlage "ereignisgesteuerter Prozessketten (EPK)"*. Veröffentlichungen des Instituts für Wirtschaftsinformatik. Inst. für Wirtschaftsinformatik Saarbrücken, 1992.

[78] KfW Bankengruppe. KfW-Digitalisierungsbericht Mittelstand 2018, April 2019. https://www.kfw.de/PDF/Download-Center/Konzernthemen/Research/PDF-Dokumente-Digitalisierungsbericht-Mittelstand/KfW-Digitalisierungsbericht-2018.pdf, accessed on 05 December 2022.

[79] Maxim Khomyakov and Ilia Bider. Achieving Workflow Flexibility through Taming the Chaos. In Dilip Patel, Islam Choudhury, Shushma Patel, and Sergio de Cesare, editors, *6th International Conference on Object Oriented Information Systems, OOIS 2000, London, UK, December 18-20, 2000. Proceedings*, pages 85–92. Springer, 2000.

[80] Bartek Kiepuszewski, Arthur H. M. ter Hofstede, and Christoph Bussler. On Structured Workflow Modelling. In Benkt Wangler and Lars Bergman, editors, *Advanced Information Systems Engineering, 12th International Conference CAiSE 2000, Stockholm, Sweden, June 5-9, 2000, Proceedings*, volume 1789 of *Lecture Notes in Computer Science*, pages 431–445. Springer, 2000.

[81] Kai Kittel, Stefan Sackmann, and Kevin Göser. Flexibility and Compliance in Workflow Systems - The KitCom Prototype. In Rébecca Deneckère and Henderik Alex Proper, editors, *Proceedings of the CAiSE'13 Forum at the 25th International Conference on Advanced Information Systems Engineering (CAiSE), Valencia, Spain, June 20th, 2013*, volume 998 of *CEUR Workshop Proceedings*, pages 154–160. CEUR-WS.org, 2013.

[82] Mark Klein and Chrysanthos Dellarocas. A Knowledge-based Approach to Handling Exceptions in Workflow Systems. *Comput. Support. Cooperative Work.*, 9(3/4):399–412, 2000.

[83] Mark Klein, Chrysanthos Dellarocas, and Abraham Bernstein. Introduction to the Special Issue on Adaptive Workflow Systems. *Comput. Support. Cooperative Work.*, 9(3/4):265–267, 2000.

[84] Justus Klingemann. Controlled Flexibility in Workflow Management. In Benkt Wangler and Lars Bergman, editors, *Advanced Information Systems Engineering, 12th International Conference CAiSE 2000, Stockholm, Sweden, June 5-9, 2000, Proceedings*, volume 1789 of *Lecture Notes in Computer Science*, pages 126–141. Springer, 2000.

[85] Jiri Kolar and Tomás Pitner. Agile BPM in the age of Cloud technologies. *Scalable Comput. Pract. Exp.*, 13(4), 2012.

[86] Kuldeep Kumar and Murali Mohan Narasipuram. Defining Requirements for Business Process Flexibility. In Gil Regev, Pnina Soffer, and Rainer Schmidt, editors, *Proceedings of the CAISE*06 Workshop on Business Process Modelling, Development, and Support BPMDS '06, Luxemburg, June 5-9, 2006*, volume 236 of *CEUR Workshop Proceedings*. CEUR-WS.org, 2006.

[87] Vipin Kumar. Algorithms for Constraint-Satisfaction Problems: A Survey. *AI Mag.*, 13(1):32–44, 1992.

[88] Vera Künzle and Manfred Reichert. PHILharmonicFlows: towards a framework for object-aware process management. *J. Softw. Maintenance Res. Pract.*, 23(4):205–244, 2011.

[89] Craig E. Kuziemsky, Dympna O'Sullivan, Wojtek Michalowski, Szymon Wilk, and Ken Farion. A Constraint Satisfaction Approach to Data-Driven Implementation of Clinical Practice Guidelines. In *AMIA 2008, American Medical Informatics Association Annual Symposium, Washington, DC, USA, November 8-12, 2008*. AMIA, 2008.

[90] David B. Leake and Joseph Kendall-Morwick. Towards Case-Based Support for e-Science Workflow Generation by Mining Provenance. In Klaus-Dieter Althoff, Ralph Bergmann, Mirjam Minor, and Alexandre Hanft, editors, *Advances in Case-Based*

Reasoning, 9th European Conference, ECCBR 2008, Trier, Germany, September 1-4, 2008. Proceedings, volume 5239 of *Lecture Notes in Computer Science*, pages 269–283. Springer, 2008.

[91] Mario Lenz, André Hübner, and Mirjam Kunze. Textual CBR. In Mario Lenz, Brigitte Bartsch-Spörl, Hans-Dieter Burkhard, and Stefan Wess, editors, *Case-Based Reasoning Technology, From Foundations to Applications*, volume 1400 of *Lecture Notes in Computer Science*, pages 115–138. Springer, 1998.

[92] V. Levenshtein. Binary codes capable of correcting deletions, insertions, and reversals. *Soviet physics. Doklady*, 10:707–710, 1965.

[93] Shasha Liu, Manuel Correa, and K Kochut. An Ontology-Aided Process Constraint Modeling Framework for Workflow Systems. In *5th International Conference on Information, Process, and Knowledge Management (EKNOW 2013)*, pages 178–183. Citeseer, 2013.

[94] Ruopeng Lu and Shazia Wasim Sadiq. A Survey of Comparative Business Process Modeling Approaches. In Witold Abramowicz, editor, *Business Information Systems, 10th International Conference, BIS 2007, Poznan, Poland, April 25-27, 2007, Proceedings*, volume 4439 of *Lecture Notes in Computer Science*, pages 82–94. Springer, 2007.

[95] Ruopeng Lu, Shazia Wasim Sadiq, Guido Governatori, and Xiaoping Yang. Defining Adaptation Constraints for Business Process Variants. In Witold Abramowicz, editor, *Business Information Systems, 12th International Conference, BIS 2009, Poznan, Poland, April 27-29, 2009. Proceedings*, volume 21 of *Lecture Notes in Business Information Processing*, pages 145–156. Springer, 2009.

[96] Ruopeng Lu, Shazia Wasim Sadiq, Vineet Padmanabhan, and Guido Governatori. Using a temporal constraint network for business process execution. In Gillian Dobbie and James Bailey, editors, *Database Technologies 2006, Proceedings of the 17th Australasian Database Conference, ADC 2006, Hobart, Tasmania, Australia, January 16-19 2006*, volume 49 of *CRPIT*, pages 157–166. Australian Computer Society, 2006.

[97] Xixi Lu, Dirk Fahland, Frank J. H. M. van den Biggelaar, and Wil M. P. van der Aalst. Detecting Deviating Behaviors Without Models. In Manfred Reichert and Hajo A. Reijers, editors, *Business Process Management Workshops - BPM 2015, 13th International Workshops, Innsbruck, Austria, August 31 - September 3, 2015, Revised Papers*, volume 256 of *Lecture Notes in Business Information Processing*, pages 126–139. Springer, 2015.

[98] Zongwei Luo, Amit P. Sheth, Krys J. Kochut, and John A. Miller. Exception Handling in Workflow Systems. *Appl. Intell.*, 13(2):125–147, 2000.

[99] Eduardo Lupiani, Christian Severin Sauer, and Thomas Roth-Berghofer. Implementation of similarity measures for event sequences in mycbr. In *Proceedings of the 18th UK Workshop on Case-Based Reasoning, Cambridge, UK*, 2013.

[100] Fabrizio Maria Maggi, Marco Montali, Michael Westergaard, and Wil M. P. van der Aalst. Monitoring Business Constraints with Linear Temporal Logic: An Approach Based on Colored Automata. In Stefanie Rinderle-Ma, Farouk Toumani, and Karsten Wolf, editors, *Business Process Management - 9th International Conference, BPM 2011, Clermont-Ferrand, France, August 30 - September 2, 2011. Proceedings*, volume 6896 of *Lecture Notes in Computer Science*, pages 132–147. Springer, 2011.

[101] Lukas Malburg, Ronny Seiger, Ralph Bergmann, and Barbara Weber. Using Physical Factory Simulation Models for Business Process Management Research. In Adela del-Río-Ortega, Henrik Leopold, and Flávia Maria Santoro, editors, *Business Process Management Workshops - BPM 2020 International Workshops, Seville, Spain, September 13-18, 2020, Revised Selected Papers*, volume 397 of *Lecture Notes in Business Information Processing*, pages 95–107. Springer, 2020.

[102] Felix Mannhardt, Massimiliano de Leoni, and Hajo A. Reijers. The Multi-perspective Process Explorer. In Florian Daniel and Stefan Zugal, editors, *Proceedings of the BPM Demo Session 2015 Co-located with the 13th International Conference on Business Process Management (BPM 2015), Innsbruck, Austria,*

September 2, 2015, volume 1418 of *CEUR Workshop Proceedings*, pages 130–134. CEUR-WS.org, 2015.

[103] R. S. Mans, Wil M. P. van der Aalst, Nick Russell, and Piet J. M. Bakker. Flexibility Schemes for Workflow Management Systems. In Danilo Ardagna, Massimo Mecella, and Jian Yang, editors, *Business Process Management Workshops, BPM 2008 International Workshops, Milano, Italy, September 1-4, 2008. Revised Papers*, volume 17 of *Lecture Notes in Business Information Processing*, pages 361–372. Springer, 2008.

[104] Cynthia R. Marling, Mohammed H. Sqalli, Edwina L. Rissland, Héctor Muñoz-Avila, and David W. Aha. Case-Based Reasoning Integrations. *AI Mag.*, 23(1):69–86, 2002.

[105] Andrea Marrella, Massimo Mecella, and Sebastian Sardiña. SmartPM: An Adaptive Process Management System through Situation Calculus, IndiGolog, and Classical Planning. In Chitta Baral, Giuseppe De Giacomo, and Thomas Eiter, editors, *Principles of Knowledge Representation and Reasoning: Proceedings of the Fourteenth International Conference, KR 2014, Vienna, Austria, July 20-24, 2014*. AAAI Press, 2014.

[106] Andrea Marrella, Massimo Mecella, and Sebastian Sardiña. Intelligent Process Adaptation in the SmartPM System. *ACM Trans. Intell. Syst. Technol.*, 8(2):25:1–25:43, 2017.

[107] Ricardo Martinho, Dulce Domingos, and João Varajão. CF4BPMN: A BPMN Extension for Controlled Flexibility in Business Processes. *Procedia Computer Science*, 64:1232–1239, 12 2015.

[108] Rainer Maximini. *Advanced techniques for complex case based reasoning applications*. PhD thesis, University of Trier, 2006.

[109] Asma Mejri, Sonia Ghannouchi, and Ricardo Martinho. Evaluation of Process Modeling Paradigms Enabling Flexibility. *Procedia Computer Science*, 64:1043,Äì1050, 12 2015.

[110] Jan Mendling, Brian T. Pentland, and Jan Recker. Building a complementary agenda for business process management and digital innovation. *Eur. J. Inf. Syst.*, 29(3):208–219, 2020.

[111] Steven Mertens, Frederik Gailly, and Geert Poels. A Generic Framework for Flexible and Data-Aware Business Process Engines. In Henderik A. Proper and Janis Stirna, editors, *Advanced*

Information Systems Engineering Workshops - CAiSE 2019 International Workshops, Rome, Italy, June 3-7, 2019, Proceedings, volume 349 of *Lecture Notes in Business Information Processing*, pages 201–213. Springer, 2019.

[112] Alain Mille. From case-based reasoning to traces-based reasoning. *Annu. Rev. Control.*, 30(2):223–232, 2006.

[113] Mirjam Minor, Ralph Bergmann, and Sebastian Görg. Case-based adaptation of workflows. *Information Systems*, 40:142–152, 2014.

[114] Mirjam Minor, Stefania Montani, and Juan A. Recio-García. Process-oriented case-based reasoning. *Inf. Syst.*, 40:103–105, 2014.

[115] Mirjam Minor, Alexander Tartakovski, and Daniel Schmalen. Agile Workflow Technology and Case-Based Change Reuse for Long-Term Processes. *Int. J. Intell. Inf. Technol.*, 4(1):80–98, 2008.

[116] Steven Minton, Mark D. Johnston, Andrew B. Philips, and Philip Laird. Minimizing Conflicts: A Heuristic Repair Method for Constraint Satisfaction and Scheduling Problems. *Artif. Intell.*, 58(1-3):161–205, 1992.

[117] Stefania Montani. Prototype-based management of business process exception cases. *Appl. Intell.*, 33(3):278–290, 2010.

[118] Hernâni Mourão and Pedro Antunes. A Collaborative Framework for Unexpected Exception Handling. In Hugo Fuks, Stephan G. Lukosch, and Ana Carolina Salgado, editors, *Groupware: Design, Implementation, and Use, 11th International Workshop, CRIWG 2005, Porto de Galinhas, Brazil, September 25-29, 2005, Proceedings*, volume 3706 of *Lecture Notes in Computer Science*, pages 168–183. Springer, 2005.

[119] Abdullah Mueen and Eamonn J. Keogh. Extracting Optimal Performance from Dynamic Time Warping. In Balaji Krishnapuram, Mohak Shah, Alexander J. Smola, Charu C. Aggarwal, Dou Shen, and Rajeev Rastogi, editors, *Proceedings of the 22nd ACM SIGKDD International Conference on Knowledge Discovery and Data Mining, San Francisco, CA, USA, August 13-17, 2016*, pages 2129–2130. ACM, 2016.

[120] Gilbert Müller. *Workflow Modeling Assistance by Case-based Reasoning*. PhD thesis, University of Trier, Germany, 2018.

[121] Gilbert Müller and Ralph Bergmann. Workflow Streams: A Means for Compositional Adaptation in Process-Oriented CBR. In Luc Lamontagne and Enric Plaza, editors, *Case-Based Reasoning Research and Development - 22nd International Conference, ICCBR 2014, Cork, Ireland, September 29, 2014 - October 1, 2014. Proceedings*, volume 8765 of *Lecture Notes in Computer Science*, pages 315–329. Springer, 2014.

[122] Gilbert Müller and Ralph Bergmann. CookingCAKE: A Framework for the Adaptation of Cooking Recipes Represented as Workflows. In Joseph Kendall-Morwick, editor, *Workshop Proceedings from The Twenty-Third International Conference on Case-Based Reasoning (ICCBR 2015), Frankfurt, Germany, September 28-30, 2015*, volume 1520 of *CEUR Workshop Proceedings*, pages 221–232. CEUR-WS.org, 2015.

[123] Gilbert Müller and Ralph Bergmann. Generalization of Workflows in Process-Oriented Case-Based Reasoning. In Ingrid Russell and William Eberle, editors, *Proceedings of the Twenty-Eighth International Florida Artificial Intelligence Research Society Conference, FLAIRS 2015, Hollywood, Florida, USA, May 18-20, 2015*, pages 391–396. AAAI Press, 2015.

[124] Robert Müller, Ulrike Greiner, and Erhard Rahm. $Agent_{Work}$: a workflow system supporting rule-based workflow adaptation. *Data Knowl. Eng.*, 51(2):223–256, 2004.

[125] Saul B. Needleman and Christian D. Wunsch. A general method applicable to the search for similarities in the amino acid sequence of two proteins. *Journal of molecular biology*, 48(3):443–453, 1970.

[126] Jakob Nielsen. *Usability engineering*. Academic Press, 1993.

[127] Selmin Nurcan. A Survey on the Flexibility Requirements Related to Business Processes and Modeling Artifacts. In *41st Hawaii International International Conference on Systems Science (HICSS-41 2008), Proceedings, 7-10 January 2008, Waikoloa, Big Island, HI, USA*, page 378. IEEE Computer Society, 2008.

[128] Hannes Obweger, Martin Suntinger, Josef Schiefer, and Günther R. Raidl. Similarity Searching in Sequences of Complex Events. In Pericles Loucopoulos and Jean-Louis Cavarero, editors, *Proceedings of the Fourth IEEE International Conference on Research Challenges in Information Science, RCIS 2010, Nice, France, May 19-21, 2010*, pages 631–640. IEEE, 2010.

[129] Hubert Österle. *Business Engineering. Prozeß- und Systementwicklung, Band 1: Entwurfstechniken.* Springer-Verlag Berlin Heidelberg, Wiesbaden, 1995.

[130] Hubert Österle, Jörg Becker, Ulrich Frank, Thomas Hess, Dimitris Karagiannis, Helmut Krcmar, Peter Loos, Peter Mertens, Andreas Oberweis, and Elmar J. Sinz. Memorandum on design-oriented information systems research. *EJIS*, 20(1):7–10, 2011.

[131] Nesi Outmazgin and Pnina Soffer. Business Process Workarounds: What Can and Cannot Be Detected by Process Mining. In Selmin Nurcan, Henderik Alex Proper, Pnina Soffer, John Krogstie, Rainer Schmidt, Terry A. Halpin, and Ilia Bider, editors, *Enterprise, Business-Process and Information Systems Modeling - 14th International Conference, BPMDS 2013, 18th International Conference, EMMSAD 2013, Held at CAiSE 2013, Valencia, Spain, June 17-18, 2013. Proceedings*, volume 147 of *Lecture Notes in Business Information Processing*, pages 48–62. Springer, 2013.

[132] Ken Peffers, Marcus A. Rothenberger, Tuure Tuunanen, and Reza Vaezi. Design science research evaluation. In Ken Peffers, Marcus A. Rothenberger, and William L. Kuechler Jr., editors, *Design Science Research in Information Systems. Advances in Theory and Practice - 7th International Conference, DESRIST 2012, Las Vegas, NV, USA, May 14-15, 2012. Proceedings*, volume 7286 of *Lecture Notes in Computer Science*, pages 398–410. Springer, 2012.

[133] Ken Peffers, Tuure Tuunanen, Marcus A. Rothenberger, and Samir Chatterjee. A Design Science Research Methodology for Information Systems Research. *J. Manag. Inf. Syst.*, 24(3):45–77, 2008.

[134] Maja Pešić. *Constraint-Based Workflow Management Systems: Shifting Control to Users*. PhD thesis, Technische Universiteit Eindhoven, 2008.

[135] Maja Pešić, Helen Schonenberg, and Wil M. P. van der Aalst. DECLARE: Full Support for Loosely-Structured Processes. In *11th IEEE International Enterprise Distributed Object Computing Conference (EDOC 2007), 15-19 October 2007, Annapolis, Maryland, USA*, pages 287–300. IEEE Computer Society, 2007.

[136] Maja Pešić, M. H. Schonenberg, Natalia Sidorova, and Wil M. P. van der Aalst. Constraint-Based Workflow Models: Change Made Easy. In Robert Meersman and Zahir Tari, editors, *On the Move to Meaningful Internet Systems 2007: CoopIS, DOA, ODBASE, GADA, and IS, OTM Confederated International Conferences CoopIS, DOA, ODBASE, GADA, and IS 2007, Vilamoura, Portugal, November 25-30, 2007, Proceedings, Part I*, volume 4803 of *Lecture Notes in Computer Science*, pages 77–94. Springer, 2007.

[137] Maja Pešić and Wil M. P. van der Aalst. A Declarative Approach for Flexible Business Processes Management. In Johann Eder and Schahram Dustdar, editors, *Business Process Management Workshops, BPM 2006 International Workshops, BPD, BPI, ENEI, GPWW, DPM, semantics4ws, Vienna, Austria, September 4-7, 2006, Proceedings*, volume 4103 of *Lecture Notes in Computer Science*, pages 169–180. Springer, 2006.

[138] Paul Pichler, Barbara Weber, Stefan Zugal, Jakob Pinggera, Jan Mendling, and Hajo A. Reijers. Imperative versus Declarative Process Modeling Languages: An Empirical Investigation. In Florian Daniel, Kamel Barkaoui, and Schahram Dustdar, editors, *Business Process Management Workshops - BPM 2011 International Workshops, Clermont-Ferrand, France, August 29, 2011, Revised Selected Papers, Part I*, volume 99 of *Lecture Notes in Business Information Processing*, pages 383–394. Springer, 2011.

[139] Charles Prud'homme, Jean-Guillaume Fages, and Xavier Lorca. Choco solver documentation. *TASC, INRIA Rennes, LINA CNRS UMR*, 6241, 2016.

[140] Lisa Purvis and Pearl Pu. Adaptation Using Constraint Satisfaction Techniques. In Manuela M. Veloso and Agnar Aamodt, editors, *Case-Based Reasoning Research and Development, First International Conference, ICCBR-95, Sesimbra, Portugal, October 23-26, 1995, Proceedings*, volume 1010 of *Lecture Notes in Computer Science*, pages 289–300. Springer, 1995.

[141] Gil Regev, Pnina Soffer, and Rainer Schmidt. Taxonomy of Flexibility in Business Processes. In Gil Regev, Pnina Soffer, and Rainer Schmidt, editors, *Proceedings of the CAISE*06 Workshop on Business Process Modelling, Development, and Support BPMDS '06, Luxemburg, June 5-9, 2006*, volume 236 of *CEUR Workshop Proceedings*. CEUR-WS.org, 2006.

[142] Manfred Reichert. *Dynamische Ablaufänderungen in Workflow-Management-Systemen*. PhD thesis, University of Ulm, Germany, 2000.

[143] Manfred Reichert and Peter Dadam. $ADEPT_{flex}$-Supporting Dynamic Changes of Workflows Without Losing Control. *J. Intell. Inf. Syst.*, 10(2):93–129, 1998.

[144] Manfred Reichert, Stefanie Rinderle, and Peter Dadam. ADEPT Workflow Management System. In Wil M. P. van der Aalst, Arthur H. M. ter Hofstede, and Mathias Weske, editors, *Business Process Management, International Conference, BPM 2003, Eindhoven, The Netherlands, June 26-27, 2003, Proceedings*, volume 2678 of *Lecture Notes in Computer Science*, pages 370–379. Springer, 2003.

[145] Manfred Reichert, Stefanie Rinderle, Ulrich Kreher, and Peter Dadam. Adaptive Process Management with ADEPT2. In Karl Aberer, Michael J. Franklin, and Shojiro Nishio, editors, *Proceedings of the 21st International Conference on Data Engineering, ICDE 2005, 5-8 April 2005, Tokyo, Japan*, pages 1113–1114. IEEE Computer Society, 2005.

[146] Manfred Reichert and Barbara Weber. *Enabling Flexibility in Process-Aware Information Systems - Challenges, Methods, Technologies*. Springer, 2012.

[147] Hajo A. Reijers. Workflow Flexibility: The Forlorn Promise. In *15th IEEE International Workshops on Enabling Technologies: Infrastructures for Collaborative Enterprises (WETICE 2006)*,

26-28 June 2006, Manchester, United Kingdom, pages 271–272. IEEE Computer Society, 2006.

[148] Wolfgang Reisig. *Petri Nets: An Introduction*, volume 4 of *EATCS Monographs on Theoretical Computer Science*. Springer, 1985.

[149] Michael M. Richter and Rosina O. Weber. *Case-Based Reasoning - A Textbook*. Springer, 2013.

[150] Cornelia Richter-von Hagen and Wolffried Stucky. *Business-Process- und Workflow-Management - Prozessverbesserung durch Prozess-Management*. Vieweg+Teubner Verlag, Wiesbaden, 2004.

[151] Luiz C. A. Rodrigues and Leandro Magatão. Enhancing Supply Chain Decisions Using Constraint Programming: A Case Study. In Alexander F. Gelbukh and Angel Fernando Kuri Morales, editors, *MICAI 2007: Advances in Artificial Intelligence, 6th Mexican International Conference on Artificial Intelligence, Aguascalientes, Mexico, November 4-10, 2007, Proceedings*, volume 4827 of *Lecture Notes in Computer Science*, pages 1110–1121. Springer, 2007.

[152] Michael Rosemann and Jan Recker. Context-aware Process Design Exploring the Extrinsic Drivers for Process Flexibility. In Gil Regev, Pnina Soffer, and Rainer Schmidt, editors, *Proceedings of the CAISE*06 Workshop on Business Process Modelling, Development, and Support BPMDS '06, Luxemburg, June 5-9, 2006*, volume 236 of *CEUR Workshop Proceedings*. CEUR-WS.org, 2006.

[153] Francesca Rossi, Peter van Beek, and Toby Walsh, editors. *Handbook of Constraint Programming*, volume 2 of *Foundations of Artificial Intelligence*. Elsevier, 2006.

[154] Stuart J. Russell and Peter Norvig. *Artificial intelligence - a modern approach, 2nd Edition*. Prentice Hall series in artificial intelligence. Prentice Hall, 2003.

[155] Stuart J. Russell and Peter Norvig. *Artificial Intelligence - A Modern Approach (3. internat. ed.)*. Pearson Education, 2010.

[156] Marianne Saam, Steffen Viete, and Stefan Schiel. Digitalisierung im Mittelstand: Status Quo, aktuelle Entwicklungen und Herausforderungen, August 2016. `https:`

//www.kfw.de/PDF/Download-Center/Konzernthemen/ Research/PDF-Dokumente-Studien-und-Materialien/ Digitalisierung-im-Mittelstand.pdf, accessed on 05 December 2022.

[157] Stefan Sackmann and Kai Kittel. Flexible Workflows and Compliance: A Solvable Contradiction?! In Jan vom Brocke and Theresa Schmiedel, editors, *BPM - Driving Innovation in a Digital World*, pages 247–258. Springer, 2015.

[158] Shazia W. Sadiq, Wasim Sadiq, and Maria E. Orlowska. Pockets of Flexibility in Workflow Specification. In Hideko S. Kunii, Sushil Jajodia, and Arne Sølvberg, editors, *Conceptual Modeling - ER 2001, 20th International Conference on Conceptual Modeling, Yokohama, Japan, November 27-30, 2001, Proceedings*, volume 2224 of *Lecture Notes in Computer Science*, pages 513–526. Springer, 2001.

[159] Hani Safadi and Samer Faraj. The Role of workarounds during an OpenSource Electronic Medical Record System Implementation. In Rajiv Sabherwal and Mary Sumner, editors, *Proceedings of the International Conference on Information Systems, ICIS 2010, Saint Louis, Missouri, USA, December 12-15, 2010*, page 47. Association for Information Systems, 2010.

[160] Hiroaki Sakoe and Seibi Chiba. Dynamic Programming Algorithm Optimization for Spoken Word Recognition. *IEEE Transactions on Acoustics, Speech, and Signal Processing*, 26(1):43–49, 1978.

[161] Mohamed Yassine Samiri, Mehdi Najib, Abdelaziz El Fazziki, and Jaouad Boukachour. Toward a Self-Adaptive Workflow Management System Through Learning and Prediction Models. *Arabian Journal for Science and Engineering*, 42(2):897–912, 2017.

[162] Erik Schake. Case Retrieval for Workflow Flexibility by Deviation Using Time Series Matching Methods. Bachelor's Thesis, University of Trier, Department of Business Information Systems II, Germany, January 2020.

[163] Erik Schake, Lisa Grumbach, and Ralph Bergmann. A Time-Series Similarity Measure for Case-Based Deviation Management to Support Flexible Workflow Execution. In Ian Watson and

Rosina O. Weber, editors, *Case-Based Reasoning Research and Development - 28th International Conference, ICCBR 2020, Salamanca, Spain, June 8-12, 2020, Proceedings*, volume 12311 of *Lecture Notes in Computer Science*, pages 33–48. Springer, 2020.

[164] August-Wilhelm Scheer. *ARIS–business process modeling*. Springer, Berlin and New York, 3rd ed. edition, 2000.

[165] Daniel Schmalen. *Adaptives Workflow Management - Referenzmodell und Umsetzung*. PhD thesis, Dr. Hut Verlag, 80538 München, 2011.

[166] Helen Schonenberg, Ronny Mans, Nick Russell, Nataliya Mulyar, and Wil M. P. van der Aalst. Process Flexibility: A Survey of Contemporary Approaches. In Jan L. G. Dietz, Antonia Albani, and Joseph Barjis, editors, *Advances in Enterprise Engineering I, 4th International Workshop CIAO! and 4th International Workshop EOMAS, held at CAiSE 2008, Montpellier, France, June 16-17, 2008. Proceedings*, volume 10 of *Lecture Notes in Business Information Processing*, pages 16–30. Springer, 2008.

[167] Helen Schonenberg, Ronny Mans, Nick Russell, Nataliya Mulyar, and Wil M. P. van der Aalst. Towards a Taxonomy of Process Flexibility. In Zohra Bellahsene, Carson Woo, Ela Hunt, Xavier Franch, and Remi Coletta, editors, *Proceedings of the Forum at the CAiSE'08 Conference, Montpellier, France, June 18-20, 2008*, volume 344 of *CEUR Workshop Proceedings*, pages 81–84. CEUR-WS.org, 2008.

[168] Stefan Schönig and Michael Zeising. The DPIL Framework: Tool Support for Agile and Resource-Aware Business Processes. In Florian Daniel and Stefan Zugal, editors, *Proceedings of the BPM Demo Session 2015 Co-located with the 13th International Conference on Business Process Management (BPM 2015), Innsbruck, Austria, September 2, 2015*, volume 1418 of *CEUR Workshop Proceedings*, pages 125–129. CEUR-WS.org, 2015.

[169] David Schumm, Frank Leymann, Zhilei Ma, Thorsten Scheibler, and Steve Strauch. Integrating Compliance into Business Processes. In Matthias Schumann, Lutz M. Kolbe, Michael H. Breitner, and Arne Frerichs, editors, *Multikonferenz Wirtschaftsinfor-*

matik, MKWI 2010, Göttingen, Deutschland, 23.-25.2.2010, Proceedings, pages 2125–2137. Universitätsverlag Göttingen, 2010.

[170] Markus Schwinn. *Ontologie-basierte Informationsextraktion zum Aufbau einer Wissensbasis für dokumentgetriebene Workflows*, volume volume 349 of *Dissertations in Artificial Intelligence*. IOS Press and AKA, Amsterdam and Berlin, 2020.

[171] Sebastian Seer. Unterstützung von flexiblem Workflowmanagement durch Process Mining. Bachelor's Thesis, University of Trier, Department of Business Information Systems II, Germany, October 2018.

[172] Temple F. Smith and Michael S. Waterman. Identification of common molecular subsequences. *Journal of molecular biology*, 147(1):195–197, 1981.

[173] Pnina Soffer. On the Notion of Flexibility in Business Processes. In *Proceedings of the CAiSE'05 Workshops*, pages 35–42, 2005.

[174] Mohammed Sqalli, Lisa Purvis, and Eugene Freuder. Survey of Applications Integrating Constraint Satisfaction and Case-Based Reasoning. In *Proceedings of the 1st International Conference and Exhibition on The Practical Application of Constraint Technologies and Logic Programming, 1999*, April 1999.

[175] Marcus Staender, Aristotelis Hadjakos, and Daniel Schreiber. Adaptive Workflows in Smart Environments: Combining Imperative and Declarative Models. In Anind K. Dey, Hao-Hua Chu, and Gillian R. Hayes, editors, *The 2012 ACM Conference on Ubiquitous Computing, Ubicomp '12, Pittsburgh, PA, USA, September 5-8, 2012*, pages 1171–1174. ACM, 2012.

[176] Armin Stahl and Thomas Roth-Berghofer. Rapid Prototyping of CBR Applications with the Open Source Tool myCBR. In Klaus-Dieter Althoff, Ralph Bergmann, Mirjam Minor, and Alexandre Hanft, editors, *Advances in Case-Based Reasoning, 9th European Conference, ECCBR 2008, Trier, Germany, September 1-4, 2008. Proceedings*, volume 5239 of *Lecture Notes in Computer Science*, pages 615–629. Springer, 2008.

[177] Varintorn Supyuenyong, Nazrul Islam, and Uday R. Kulkarni. Influence of SME characteristics on knowledge management processes: The case study of enterprise resource planning service providers. *J. Enterprise Inf. Management*, 22(1/2):63–80, 2009.

[178] Mohammed Temraz, Eoin M. Kenny, Elodie Ruelle, Laurence Shalloo, Barry Smyth, and Mark T. Keane. Handling Climate Change Using Counterfactuals: Using Counterfactuals in Data Augmentation to Predict Crop Growth in an Uncertain Climate Future. *CoRR*, abs/2104.04008, 2021.

[179] Franco Torquati, Massimo Paltrinieri, and Alberto Momigliano. A Constraint Satisfaction Approach to Operative Management of Aircraft Routing. In *Proceedings of the Third International Conference on Industrial and Engineering Applications of Artificial Intelligence and Expert Systems, IEA/AIE 1990, July 15-18, 1990, The Mills House Hotel, Charleston, SC, USA - Volume 2*, pages 1140–1146. ACM, 1990.

[180] Spyros Tsevas and Dimitris K. Iakovidis. Dynamic time warping fusion for the retrieval of similar patient cases represented by multimodal time-series medical data. *Proceedings of the 10th IEEE International Conference on Information Technology and Applications in Biomedicine*, pages 1–4, 2010.

[181] Wil M. P. van der Aalst. *Process Mining - Discovery, Conformance and Enhancement of Business Processes*. Springer, 2011.

[182] Wil M. P. van der Aalst. Business process management: a comprehensive survey. *ISRN Software Engineering*, pages 1–37, 01 2012.

[183] Wil M. P. van der Aalst and Stefan Jablonski. Dealing with workflow change: Identification of issues and solutions. *Computer Systems: Science and Engineering - CSSE*, 15, 09 2000.

[184] Wil M. P. van der Aalst, Maja Pešić, and Helen Schonenberg. Declarative workflows: Balancing between flexibility and support. *Comput. Sci. Res. Dev.*, 23(2):99–113, 2009.

[185] Wil M. P. van der Aalst and Arthur H. M. ter Hofstede. YAWL: yet another workflow language. *Inf. Syst.*, 30(4):245–275, 2005.

[186] Wil M. P. van der Aalst, Arthur H. M. ter Hofstede, Bartek Kiepuszewski, and Alistair P. Barros. Workflow Patterns. *Distributed Parallel Databases*, 14(1):5–51, 2003.

[187] Wil M. P. van der Aalst and Kees M. van Hee. *Workflow Management: Models, Methods, and Systems*. Cooperative information systems. MIT Press, 2002.

[188] Wil M. P. van der Aalst, Mathias Weske, and Dolf Grünbauer. Case handling: a new paradigm for business process support. *Data Knowl. Eng.*, 53(2):129–162, 2005.

[189] Pim van Leeuwen, Henk Hesselink, and Jos Rohling. Scheduling Aircraft Using Constraint Satisfaction. *Electron. Notes Theor. Comput. Sci.*, 76:252–268, 2002.

[190] Élise Vareilles, Michel Aldanondo, Aurélien Codet de Boisse, Thierry Coudert, Paul Gaborit, and Laurent Geneste. How to take into account general and contextual knowledge for interactive aiding design: Towards the coupling of CSP and CBR approaches. *Eng. Appl. Artif. Intell.*, 25(1):31–47, 2012.

[191] Tatiana Almeida S. C. Vieira, Marco A. Casanova, and Luis Gustavo Ferrão. An Ontology-Driven Architecture for Flexible Workflow Execution. In *Joint Conference 10th Brazilian Symposium on Multimedia and the Web & 2nd Latin American Web Congress, (WebMedia & LA-Web 2004), 12-15 October 2004, Ribeirao Preto-SP, Brazil*, pages 70–77. IEEE Computer Society, 2004.

[192] Tatiana Almeida S. C. Vieira and Marco Antonio Casanova. Flexible Workflow Execution through an Ontology-based Approach. In *Workshop on Ontologies as Software Engineering Artifacts (OOPSLA*, 2008.

[193] Mark von Rosing, Stephen White, Fred Cummins, and Henk de Man. Business Process Model and Notation - BPMN. In Mark von Rosing, Henrik von Scheel, and August-Wilhelm Scheer, editors, *The Complete Business Process Handbook: Body of Knowledge from Process Modeling to BPM, Volume I*, pages 429–453. Morgan Kaufmann/Elsevier, 2015.

[194] Gottfried Vossen and Mathias Weske. The WASA Approach to Workflow Management for Scientific Applications. In Asuman Doğaç, Leonid Kalinichenko, M. Tamer Özsu, and Amit Sheth, editors, *Workflow Management Systems and Interoperability*, pages 145–164. Springer Berlin Heidelberg, Berlin, Heidelberg, 1998.

[195] Thomas Wagner. Agentworkflows for Flexible Workflow Execution. In Lawrence Cabac, Michael Duvigneau, and Daniel Moldt, editors, *Proceedings of the International Workshop on*

Petri Nets and Software Engineering, Hamburg, Germany, June 25-26, 2012, volume 851 of *CEUR Workshop Proceedings*, pages 199–214. CEUR-WS.org, 2012.

[196] Jacques Wainer, Fábio de Lima Bezerra, and Paulo Barthelmess. Tucupi: a flexible workflow system based on overridable constraints. In Hisham Haddad, Andrea Omicini, Roger L. Wainwright, and Lorie M. Liebrock, editors, *Proceedings of the 2004 ACM Symposium on Applied Computing (SAC), Nicosia, Cyprus, March 14-17, 2004*, pages 498–502. ACM, 2004.

[197] James A. Ward. Continuous Process Improvement. *Information Systems Management*, 11(2):74–76, 1994.

[198] Ian Watson. Is CBR a Technology or a Methodology? In Angel P. del Pobil, José Mira, and Moonis Ali, editors, *Tasks and Methods in Applied Artificial Intelligence, 11th International Conference on Industrial and Engineering Applications of Artificial In telligence and Expert Systems, IEA/AIE-98, Castellón, Spain, June 1-4, 1998, Proceedings, Volume II*, volume 1416 of *Lecture Notes in Computer Science*, pages 525–534. Springer, 1998.

[199] Barbara Weber, Manfred Reichert, and Stefanie Rinderle-Ma. Change patterns and change support features - Enhancing flexibility in process-aware information systems. *Data Knowl. Eng.*, 66(3):438–466, 2008.

[200] Barbara Weber and Werner Wild. Towards the Agile Management of Business Processes. In Klaus-Dieter Althoff, Andreas Dengel, Ralph Bergmann, Markus Nick, and Thomas Roth-Berghofer, editors, *WM 2005: Professional Knowledge Management - Experiences and Visions, Contributions to the 3rd Conference Professional Knowledge Management - Experiences and Visions, April 10-13, 2005, Kaiserslautern, Germany*, pages 375–382. DFKI, Kaiserslautern, 2005.

[201] Barbara Weber, Werner Wild, and Ruth Breu. CBRFlow: Enabling Adaptive Workflow Management Through Conversational Case-Based Reasoning. In Peter Funk and Pedro A. González-Calero, editors, *Advances in Case-Based Reasoning, 7th European Conference, ECCBR 2004, Madrid, Spain, August 30 -*

September 2, 2004, Proceedings, volume 3155 of *Lecture Notes in Computer Science*, pages 434–448. Springer, 2004.

[202] Lex Wedemeijer. Transformation of Imperative Workflows to Declarative Business Rules. In Boris Shishkov, editor, *Business Modeling and Software Design - Third International Symposium, BMSD 2013, Noordwijkerhout, The Netherlands, July 8-10, 2013, Revised Selected Papers*, volume 173 of *Lecture Notes in Business Information Processing*, pages 106–127. Springer, 2013.

[203] Mathias Weske. Flexible Modeling and Execution of Workflow Activities. In *Thirty-First Annual Hawaii International Conference on System Sciences, Kohala Coast, Hawaii, USA, January 6-9, 1998*, pages 713–722. IEEE Computer Society, 1998.

[204] Mathias Weske. Formal Foundation and Conceptual Design of Dynamic Adaptations in a Workflow Management System. In *34th Annual Hawaii International Conference on System Sciences (HICSS-34), January 3-6, 2001, Maui, Hawaii, USA*. IEEE Computer Society, 2001.

[205] Mathias Weske. *Business Process Management: Concepts, Languages, Architectures*. Springer, 2007.

[206] Michael Westergaard. Better Algorithms for Analyzing and Enacting Declarative Workflow Languages Using LTL. In Stefanie Rinderle-Ma, Farouk Toumani, and Karsten Wolf, editors, *Business Process Management - 9th International Conference, BPM 2011, Clermont-Ferrand, France, August 30 - September 2, 2011. Proceedings*, volume 6896 of *Lecture Notes in Computer Science*, pages 83–98. Springer, 2011.

[207] Michael Westergaard and Fabrizio Maria Maggi. Declare: A tool suite for declarative workflow modeling and enactment. In Heiko Ludwig and Hajo A. Reijers, editors, *Proceedings of the Demo Track of the Nineth Conference on Business Process Management 2011, Clermont-Ferrand, France, August 31st, 2011*, volume 820 of *CEUR Workshop Proceedings*. CEUR-WS.org, 2011.

[208] Andreas Wombacher and Maarten Rozie. Evaluation of workflow similarity measures in service discovery. In Mareike Schoop, Christian Huemer, Michael Rebstock, and Martin Bichler, editors, *Service Oriented Electronic Commerce: Proceedings zur Konferenz im Rahmen der Multikonferenz Wirtschaftsinformatik,*

20.-22. Februar 2006 in Passau, Deutschland, volume P-80 of LNI, pages 57–71. GI, 2006.

[209] Workflow Management Coalition Standards. The Workflow Reference Model, Version 1.1, 1995.

[210] Workflow Management Coalition Standards. Terminology and Glossary, Version 3.0, 1999.

[211] Raafat Zarka. *Trace-based reasoning for user assistance and recommendations. (Raisonnement à partir de l'expérience tracée pour l'assistance à l'utilisateur et les recommandations)*. PhD thesis, INSA Lyon, Lyon - Villeurbanne, France, 2013.

[212] Raafat Zarka, Amélie Cordier, Elöd Egyed-Zsigmond, Luc Lamontagne, and Alain Mille. Similarity Measures to Compare Episodes in Modeled Traces. In Sarah Jane Delany and Santiago Ontañón, editors, *Case-Based Reasoning Research and Development - 21st International Conference, ICCBR 2013, Saratoga Springs, NY, USA, July 8-11, 2013. Proceedings*, volume 7969 of *Lecture Notes in Computer Science*, pages 358–372. Springer, 2013.

[213] Christian Zeyen and Ralph Bergmann. A*-Based Similarity Assessment of Semantic Graphs. In Ian Watson and Rosina O. Weber, editors, *Case-Based Reasoning Research and Development - 28th International Conference, ICCBR 2020, Salamanca, Spain, June 8-12, 2020, Proceedings*, volume 12311 of *Lecture Notes in Computer Science*, pages 17–32. Springer, 2020.

[214] Christian Zeyen, Lukas Malburg, and Ralph Bergmann. Adaptation of Scientific Workflows by Means of Process-Oriented Case-Based Reasoning. In Kerstin Bach and Cindy Marling, editors, *Case-Based Reasoning Research and Development - 27th International Conference, ICCBR 2019, Otzenhausen, Germany, September 8-12, 2019, Proceedings*, volume 11680 of *Lecture Notes in Computer Science*, pages 388–403. Springer, 2019.

[215] Rui Zhu, Fei Dai, Qazaal Mo, Yong Yu, Leilei Lin, and Tong Li. An Approach to Handling Software Process Deviations. *Lecture Notes on Software Engineering*, 3:238–244, 01 2015.

[216] Michael zur Muehlen and Jan Recker. How Much Language Is Enough? Theoretical and Practical Use of the Business Process Modeling Notation. In Zohra Bellahsene and Michel

Léonard, editors, *Advanced Information Systems Engineering, 20th International Conference, CAiSE 2008, Montpellier, France, June 16-20, 2008, Proceedings*, volume 5074 of *Lecture Notes in Computer Science*, pages 465–479. Springer, 2008.

Index

adaptation, 129
    generative, 166
    null, 164
alignment, 140, 162

block-oriented workflow, 74
    workflow block, 71
build time, 18

case base, 123, 148
case-based reasoning (CBR), 122
computation time, 216
constraint, 84, 87, 95
    adapted, 180
    additional, 98
    control-flow-dependent, 97
    data-flow-dependent, 96
    derived, 176
    instance, 99
    model, 96
    origin, 176
    status, 111
    type, 176
constraint satisfaction problem (CSP), 87, 90
control-flow
    exclusive, 73, 77, 78, 101
    loop, 105
    parallel, 73, 75, 77, 101
    sequential, 72, 75, 100
control-flow sequential, 77

de facto workflow, 20
de jure workflow, 20, 83
decision variable, 87, 91, 97
    extended, 177
deficiency management in construction, 55, 58
deviation, 20, 145
    detection, 111
domain, 87, 93, 97
    extended, 177
dynamic time warping (DTW), 134, 161

exclusive control-flow, 73, 77, 78, 101
execution path, 74

flexibility by deviation, 43
function
    Dec, 100
    $first$, 76
    $last$, 76
    not, 99

gap penalty, 138
generative adaptation, 166

halving distance, 143

indel, 139

loop control-flow, 105

model-consistency, 152, 156

NESTGraph, 130
null adaptation, 164

offset, 259

parallel control-flow, 73, 75, 77, 101
pre-processing, 153, 176
process participant, 19
    experienced, 217
    inexperienced, 217
    non-conforming, 218
process-oriented case-based knowledge engine (ProCAKE), 192
process-oriented case-based reasoning (POCBR), 129

query, 123, 148

retrieve, 124, 149, 150
reuse, 125, 149, 163
run time, 18

scoring matrix, 135, 139, 161
semantic workflow, 130

sequential control-flow, 72, 75, 77, 100
similarity, 127
    node, 160
    score, 163
    task, 160
Smith-Waterman-Algorithm (SWA), 137, 161
solution, 88
    adapted, 259

temporal weighting factor, 162
threshold, 260
transformation function, 100

utility, 218

vector similarity, 142

warp, 136
warping path, 137
work item, 19, 94, 165, 180
workflow, 23
    adaptation, 133
    case, 147
    flexibility, 36
    management system (WfMS), 23
    semantic, 130
    similarity, 132
workflow engine, 26, 88
worklist, 25